DATE DUE

THE CZECHS

STUDIES OF NATIONALITIES
Wayne S. Vucinich, General Editor

The Crimean Tatars
Alan Fisher

The Volga Tatars: A Profile in National Resilience
Azade-Ayşe Rorlich

The Making of the Georgian Nation
Ronald Grigor Suny
(copublished with Indiana University Press)

*The Modern Uzbeks: From the Fourteenth Century to the Present;
A Cultural History*
Edward A. Allworth

Estonia and the Estonians, second edition
Toivo U. Raun

The Azerbaijani Turks: Power and Identity under Russian Rule
Audrey L. Altstadt

The Kazakhs, second edition
Martha Brill Olcott

The Latvians: A Short History
Andrejs Plakans

The Moldovans: Romania, Russia, and the Politics of Culture
Charles King

Slovakia: From Samo to Dzurinda
Peter A. Toma and Dušan Kováč

The Czechs and the Lands of the Bohemian Crown
Hugh LeCaine Agnew

THE CZECHS

and the Lands of the Bohemian Crown

Hugh LeCaine Agnew

HOOVER INSTITUTION PRESS
Stanford University
Stanford, California

www.hoover.org

Hoover Institution Press Publication No. 526
Copyright © 2004 by the Board of Trustees of the
   Leland Stanford Junior University

First printing, 2004
11 10 09 08 07 06 05 04   9 8 7 6 5 4 3 2 1

Manufactured in the United States of America

The paper used in this publication meets the minimum requirements of the American National Standard for Information Sciences—Permanence of Paper for Printed Library Materials, ANSI Z39.48–1992. ⊗

Library of Congress Cataloging-in-Publication Data
Agnew, Hugh LcCaine.
   The Czechs and the lands of the Bohemian crown / by Hugh Agnew.
      p.   cm.— (Studies of nationalities) (Hoover Institution Press publication ; no. 526)
   Includes bibliographical references and index.
   ISBN 0-8179-4491-5 (alk. paper)—
   ISBN 0-8179-4492-3 (pbk.; alk. paper)
   1. Czech Republic—History. I. Title. II. Series. III. Series: Hoover Institution Press publication ; 526.
DB2063.A35 2004
943.71—dc22   2004005044

In memory of
JEANNE STARRETT LECAINE AGNEW
(1917–2000)

Contents

Illustrations

Maps

Tables

Foreword

The Czechs are not one of Europe's unknown nations, but in spite of their central position on the continent, they are hardly among the most familiar European nations. This work will help remedy that situation. Twentieth-century events only brought Czechoslovakia to public attention episodically, if dramatically, from Tomáš G. Masaryk's visit to the United States in 1918 to Václav Havel's apotheosis at the Cathedral of St. John the Divine in New York in 1990. On a grimmer note, the Munich Conference of 1938 paved the way for World War II, and Jan Masaryk's death in 1948 marked a new nadir in the chill of the Cold War in Europe. The Prague Spring of 1968 made Czechoslovakia and its peoples front-page news once more, for a time, and by 1988 coverage of the tottering communist system returned Czechoslovakia to the newspapers and television screens. Now, as the Czech Republic joins the European Union and thousands of American tourists flock to Prague, a reader interested in getting beyond the headlines and tourist destinations to learn more about this people and their land would do well to pick up this book.

The author follows the historical development of the Czechs and their lands from the emergence of a Bohemian duchy under the Slavic

Přemyslid dynasty in the ninth century to the threshold of the European Union in the twenty-first. The volume traces the shifting fortunes of the Czechs and the lands of the Bohemian crown, from periods of power and prestige such as the age of Charles IV in the fourteenth century, to tumultuous episodes like the Hussite Reformation and ensuing wars of the fifteenth century or the Bohemian Rebellion and Thirty Years' War of the seventeenth century. Further chapters cover the Czechs and the lands of the Bohemian crown as part of the Habsburg empire until its collapse at the end of World War I. The second half of the book focuses on twentieth-century Czechoslovakia, from its birth out of the war, through its destruction by Nazi Germany and postwar reconstitution, to its subsequent submergence within the Soviet bloc. The concluding chapters provide one of the first analyses by a historian of the fate of post-communist Czechoslovakia, the "Velvet Divorce" that led to the breakup of the Czechoslovak Federative Republic (ČSFR), and the first decade of the existence of the Czech Republic. The author's close engagement with Czechoslovakia and Czech history for a quarter-century has given him the linguistic tools and the historiographical knowledge to produce a survey that is both scholarly and readable.

A central theme in this work is the connection between history and identity or self-image. The author shows how the way the Czechs interpret their past is closely tied with their present perceptions of and arguments over who they are and where they belong on the map, both literally and figuratively. History is not simply a record of the past; it also matters for how it is interpreted in the present and what "lessons" can (or cannot) be drawn from it in the future. Are the Czechs a small, weak nation, doomed to be dominated by more powerful (usually German) neighbors? Or has their physical smallness been compensated for by intellectual or moral greatness, as possessors of a history that made them the heralds of universal values, be it the Hussite vision of Christianity or Masaryk's ideal of Humanity? Are they an integral part of a European civilization transmitted to them from Latin and Germanic sources, or do they, as the westernmost outlier of the far-flung Slavs, represent a different, younger, better alternative to "Europe"? Variations on these themes of identity and history have been played by many different political forces among the Czechs and their neighbors over the centuries. As they enter the European Union the Czechs will most likely continue to draw from their storehouse of historical images and themes to assert and argue over their proper place in the new Europe.

A broader theme that emerges from this book is the impact of modern nationalism and the idea of the nation-state on a part of Europe ill suited by history, geography, and linguistic variety for the realization of that idea. For much of their history the Czechs have not only formed part of larger political units such as the Habsburg empire, they have also shared their lands with others, be they Latins, Germans, Jews, or, in twentieth-century Czechoslovakia, also Slovaks, Poles, Ukrainians/Ruthenians, and Roma (Gypsies). Yet the course of roughly the last two centuries has seen both the destruction of the larger, multinational political units to which the lands of the Bohemian crown belonged, and the ethnic variety of the Czech lands themselves. The division of the ČSFR into the Czech Republic and Slovakia in one sense completed a process of creating a (relatively) homogeneous nation-state, a process that at its ultimate stage impressed observers with its peacefulness and relative civility. But earlier stages of that process were accompanied by violence and injustice from many sides, in spite of Czechoslovakia's interwar reputation as an "island of democracy" in Central Europe. As a counterpoint to the trend toward creating the homogeneous nation-state, the period since the collapse of the Soviet bloc has seen the Czechs and their post-Soviet neighbors strive to join the institutions of a Europe that seems to have moved back toward a wider, more integrated political ideal, without completely surrendering the form of the nation-state. The Czech experience, and the consequences of the historical development that has brought them to where they are today, will continue to influence their approach to the European Union. They may also serve as instructive case-studies in the interactions between processes of integration and differentiation in contemporary Europe.

The appearance of this book is a welcome event. The author's training and experience have left him with a deep affection for the people and land he studies, without compromising his critical distance as a historian. His work should be accessible to anyone interested in the fascinating history of this nation at the "heart of Europe," and would also serve well as a textbook in courses on Central and Eastern Europe, or on nations and national identity.

Wayne S. Vucinich

Preface

This book arose out of two stimuli. One was the invitation from the editors of the Hoover Institution Press's Studies of Nationalities to prepare a manuscript on the Czechs to submit to their outstanding series for consideration. The other was my frustration, simmering for more than two decades, at the lack of a recent, single-volume general history of the Czechs to use in my own teaching and to recommend to others interested in this people and their country, subjects that are very near and dear to me. Thus I set about attempting to meet both goals, and this book is the result of that effort. It presents an introduction to the major themes and contours of Czech history intended for any interested reader, and if about half the work is devoted to the twentieth century, earlier periods are not entirely ignored. It is a work of synthesis and as such owes a tremendous debt of gratitude to a host of scholars, living and long dead, who have informed my understanding of Czech history beyond my own research. It would be impossible to name them all, but careful readers will find their suspicions confirmed in the notes.

It may seem outdated to produce a history of a people and their land in an age when globalization is an omnipresent reality, and when academic historians are looking for ways to transcend the nation-state as an organizing structure for historical narrative. Nevertheless, even as they enter the European Union, the Czechs and the Czech Republic will not simply disappear. Their past—what they remember, what they choose to forget, and how they choose to remember and forget it—will continue to shape who and what they are. I hope that this book will serve as a starting point for anyone setting out to learn more about that past, with all its lights and shadows. If so, it will repay the debt I owe to R. W. Seton-Watson and S. Harrison Thomson, whose surveys introduced me to Czech history.

Like every other author writing about this region of Europe, I have had to decide what to do about place names and some personal names. In the text, I normally give the present-day Czech name of towns and cities first, followed by the German equivalent at first mention. I assume that most readers opening this book will be more likely to know or find the names in use today, and it seems easier to explain that Liberec was once known as Reichenberg to most of its inhabitants than to call it Reichenberg/Liberec throughout the text. Where an English form has become universally known, I use it instead of a Czech or German form (Prague, not Praha, Vienna, not Wien). Similarly, I write Francis Joseph, not Franz Joseph. In other cases, I choose what seems logical to me, for example František Palacký, but Franz Kafka. Dates following a ruler's name are the dates of his or her reign, not life.

Without financial support to enable research in Europe, writing this book would not have been possible. I began drafting the earliest chapters while on a sabbatical year in Prague in 1994–95, supported by a grant from the International Research and Exchanges Board, with funds provided by the U.S. Department of State (Title VIII) and the National Endowment for the Humanities. The final chapter was completed while on a second sabbatical in 2001–02, funded by the U.S. Department of State under the Fulbright-Hays Faculty Research Abroad program. Additional research travel in intervening years was enabled by generous support from the Institute for European, Russian, and Eurasian Studies and the Elliott School of International Affairs at the George Washington University. I am grateful to all these organizations, none of whom should bear responsibility for any views expressed in this work.

I am also grateful to a number of people who have helped in various ways to see this work to conclusion. The late Jan Havránek, Jitka Malečková, Theodore L. Agnew, Nancy Wingfield, Karen Kadlec, Mills Kelly, and Nancy L. Meyers read and commented on all or part of the manuscript. Other colleagues who assisted me include Markus Cerman, Milan Hlavačka, Lud'a Klusáková, Vladimír Lacina, Jaroslav Pánek, Dana Štefanová, and Luboš Velek. In Prague I am indebted to the Historical Institute of the Czech Academy of Sciences, the staff of the State Central Archives, the Archive of the National Museum, the National Museum Library, the National Library of the Czech Republic, and the ČTK Czech Press Agency. Similar thanks go to their colleagues in Vienna at the House, Court, and State Archive, the Austrian National Archive, and the Austrian National Library, especially the Picture Archive. Researching, writing, and revising were made easier and more rewarding by a remarkable scholar's word-processing program, the Notabene Lingua Workstation. The maps were prepared by Maxwell Ruckdeschel. The friendship and support of the Krasnický family (especially the use of their excellent personal library of Czech history), the Berger family, the Hába family, and the Synek family were, as always, treasured. And for truly Penelopean patience, I am grateful to Wayne S. Vucinich, Patricia Baker, Marshall Blanchard, Ann Wood, and Kathryn Dunn of the Hoover Institution Press.

Hugh LeCaine Agnew

Abbreviations

The abbreviations most widely used in the text refer to political parties or other organizations formed in Czechoslovakia or the Czech Republic. They are taken from the Czech, Slovak, or German originals, not the English translations (thus, KSČ for the Communist Party of Czechoslovakia, not CPCz). Well-known international abbreviations are not included in this list.

ČKD	(Českomoravská-Kolben-Daněk)	Czech-Moravian-Kolben-Daněk enterprise
ČNR	(Česká národní rada)	Czech National Council
ČSAV	(Československá akademie věd)	Czechoslovak Academy of Sciences
ČSD	(Československá sociální demokracie)	Czechoslovak Social Democracy
ČSFR	(Česká a slovenská federativní republika)	Czech and Slovak Federative Republic

ČSL	(Československá strana lidová)	Czechoslovak People's Party
ČSL	(Česká strana lidová)	Czech People's Party
ČSM	(Československý svaz mládeže)	Czechoslovak Youth League
ČSNS	(Československá strana národně socialistická)	Czechoslovak National Socialist Party
ČSSD	(Česká strana socialně-demokratická)	Czech Social Democratic Party
ČSSR	(Československá socialistická republika)	Czechoslovak Socialist Republic
DNP	(Deutsche Nationale Partei)	German National Party
DNSAP	(Deutsche National-sozialistische Arbeiterpartei)	German National Socialist Workers' Party
DS	(Demokratická strana)	Democratic Party
HRM	(Hnutí revoluční mládeže)	Movement of Revolutionary Youth
HSL'S	(Hlinkova slovenská l'udová strana)	Hlinka's Slovak People's Party
HZDS	(Hnutie za demokratické Slovensko)	Movement for a Democratic Slovakia
JZD	(Jednotné zemědělské družstvo)	Unified Agricultural Cooperative
K231	(Klub 231)	Club 231
KAN	(Klub angažovaných nestranníků)	Club of Engaged Nonpartisans
KDH	(Krest'ansko-demokratické hnutie)	Christian-Democratic Movement
KDU	(Křest'anská-demokratická unie)	Christian-Democratic Union
KoB	(Konsolidační banka)	Consolidation Bank

KSČ	(Komunistická strana Československa)	Communist Party of Czechoslovakia
KSČM	(Komunistická strana Čech a Moravy)	Communist Party of Bohemia and Moravia
KSS	(Komunistická strana Slovenska)	Communist Party of Slovakia
NF	(Národní fronta)	National Front
ODA	(Občanská demokratická aliance)	Civic Democratic Alliance
ODS	(Občanská demokratická strana)	Civic Democratic Party
OF	(Občanské forum)	Civic Forum
OH	(Občanské hnutí)	Civic Movement
ROH	(Revoluční odborové hnutí)	Revolutionary Trade-Unions Movement
SDL'	(Strana demokratickej l'avice)	Party of the Democratic Left
SdP	(Sudetendeutsche Partei)	Sudeten German Party
SNR	(Slovenská národní rada)	Slovak National Council
SNS	(Slovenská národná strana)	Slovak National Party
SP	(Strana práce)	Party of Work
SS	(Strana slobody)	Freedom Party
SSM	(Svaz socialistické mládeže)	Union of Socialist Youth
StB	(Státní bezpečnost)	State Security (secret police)
TNP	(Tábor nucené práce)	Forced Labor Camp
ÚDV	(Úřad dokumentace a vyšetřování zločinů komunismu)	Institute for Documentation and Investigation of the Crimes of Communism
ÚNRV	(Ústřední národně revoluční výbor)	Central National Revolutionary Committee

ÚRO	(Ústřední rada odborů)	Central Trade-Unions Council
US	(Unie svobody)	Freedom Union
ÚVOD	(Ústřední výbor odboje domácního)	Central Committee of Home Resistance
VONS	(Vybor na obranu nespravedlivě stihaných)	Committee for the Defense of the Unjustly Persecuted
VPN	(Verejnost proti násil'u)	Public Against Violence

A Guide to Czech Pronunciation

Czech is a Slavic language and uses the Roman alphabet. To represent sounds in their language that the Romans did not have, the Czechs eventually adopted diacritical marks placed above standard Latin letters. The language is entirely phonetic; each letter has only one sound, unlike English. Stress in Czech is always on the first syllable, and even though some diacritical marks placed above vowels look like accents, they do not alter this stress pattern. The following guide aims only to help an English-speaker pronounce the Czech names and other terms in the text approximately correctly, not to satisfy an expert linguist.

VOWELS

Czech (like other European languages such as Italian) does not shade the primary vowel sounds the way English does. The diacritical marks for length do not change stress, though a long vowel is slightly softened compared to its short counterpart.

a, á	"ah" as in father
e, é	"eh" as in bet
i, í	"ih" as in hit if short, closer to "i" in machine if long
o, ó	"oh" as in home
u, ú, ů	"oo" in food
y, ý	as i, í only harder
ě	palatalizes the preceding consonant, pronounced like "ye" in yell.

When vowels are combined they do not become diphthongs; each vowel is sounded equally in succession. Thus -ou- is not "ow" as in "house" but "oh-oo" and so on.

CONSONANTS

Many Czech consonants are pronounced like their English counterparts and are not included here. The ones whose pronunciation differs include the following:

c	"ts" in lets (never the "k" of book)
j	"y" in yell (never the sound of "j" in journey or juice)
č	"ch" as in church
ch	"ch" as in Scottish loch or German Bach
š	"sh" as in show
ž	"s" as in pleasure
ň	palatalized "n" as in tenure
ď, d'	palatalized "d" as in duke (British pronunciation!)
ť, t'	palatalized "t" as in venture
ř	unique to Czech, roughly like English "r" plus the "ž" sound in azure.

R (always pronounced rolled) and L are considered "semivocalic" consonants that can form separate syllables, as in strč, vlk, prst. To the English ear it sounds as though a very short "uh" has been inserted before the r or l.

BEGINNINGS

PART ONE

1 Maps, Epochs, Seers, and Saints

A popular sixteenth-century map-making convention represented Europe as a female figure, with Bohemia, the lands of the Crown of St. Wenceslas, as its heart. This metaphorical location has long appealed to the Czechs and is tailor-made for tourist brochures.[1] Since the heart is the body's center, it reinforces another favorite Czech location on the map of the mind, the center. Milan Kundera, a Czech émigré writer, helped revive the concept of "Central Europe" during the 1980s, but his lament for a lost center resonated with older Czech attitudes about their central position in Europe, rooted in the nineteenth century. This center also represented moderation, opposed to extremes in any direction.[2] Another Czech mental map locates them centrally between the cultural forces of the Germans and Latins (sometimes simply called "Europe") and the world of the Slavs, which could be opposed to Europe if the occasion warranted.[3] As the westernmost Slavic nation, the Czechs have also seen themselves as a bridge centered between the "West" and the "East," a metaphor that saw an unhappy revival after World War II.

The Czechs and their homeland are usually not the center of other people's mental maps. One need not limit oneself to Neville Chamberlain's phrase on the eve of the Munich Conference in 1938, about "faraway lands" and "people of whom we know nothing." William Shakespeare used Bohemia to stand for any far-off, exotic clime, even equipping it with a coastline.[4] In succeeding centuries, as the commercial and then industrial revolutions transformed the European economy, the Austrian Empire and with it the Bohemian crownlands ended up trailing behind and struggling to catch up with the West European powers. Twentieth-century politics also relegated the Czechs to the "Eastern" side of the political divide that shaped the dominant European map for the last two generations. Even since 1989, with thousands of Westerners (including Americans) living in Czechoslovakia and its successor republics, these lands are still hardly in the middle of our mental maps.

SETTING THE STAGE: WHERE ARE THE BOHEMIAN LANDS?

The physical setting for this history is fixed easily enough: the lands of the present-day Czech Republic, which closely correspond to the core of the historical Kingdom of Bohemia (Bohemia proper, Moravia, and part of Silesia) lie between 51° 03′ and 48° 33′ north latitude, and 12° 05′ and 18° 51′ east longitude. The climate is continental and temperate. Physically, the Bohemian lands enjoy natural mountain frontiers: the Krkonoše and Orlické Hory (also known as the Sudeten Mountains) on the northeast bordering Poland, the Šumava mountains blending into the Český Les (Bohemian Forest) along the southern and southwestern frontier with Austria and Germany, and the Krušné Hory on the northwestern border with Germany. The Bohemian-Moravian Plateau marks the border between Bohemia and Moravia; the White Carpathian (Bílé Karpaty) chain separates Moravia from Slovakia in the east. Though lacking Shakespeare's coastline, the Bohemian lands enjoy adequate connections to major European river systems. The Elbe (Labe) flows into the North Sea, the Oder (Odra) into the Baltic, and the Morava (which gives its name to Moravia) into the Danube and thence to the Black Sea. The most significant tributary of the Elbe is the Vltava (Moldau), immortalized in Bedřich Smetana's tone poem "Má vlast" (My Country), which flows from south to north along almost the entire length of Bohemia.

The human inhabitants of these lands have long exploited their natural resources. In prehistoric times copper, tin, and iron ore were mined in the Bohemian lands. Gold was extracted from the sands of the Otava River, and silver from Kutná Hora (Kuttenberg), Jáchymov (Joachims-

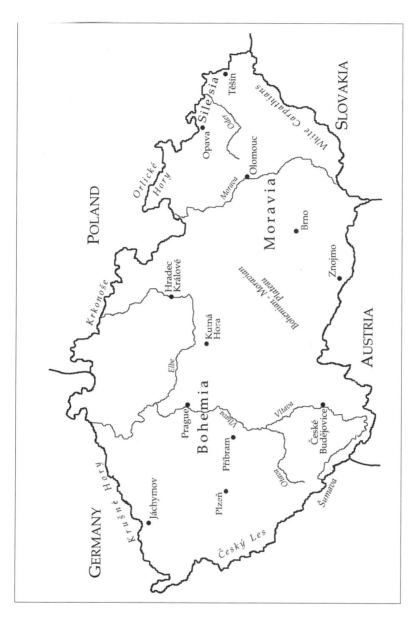

Map 1. The Czech Republic since 1993

thal), and Příbram (Przibram) contributed to the wealth and power of the Bohemian kings, just as Czech uranium (often from the same locations as the medieval silver mines) contributed to the nuclear power of the Soviet Union. Other mineral resources include coal, though high-quality black coal is relatively scarce. Deposits of poorer quality brown coal have been mined extensively, but burning brown coal for power has caused serious environmental damage. Alternative energy sources like hydroelectric and nuclear power remain controversial.[5] High-intensity industrial farming also contributed to environmental degradation through erosion and the buildup of toxic chemical residues from over-use of fertilizers and pesticides.[6] These contemporary ecological problems represent one facet of a relationship between land and people that stretches back over millennia.

In gentler ways, too, centuries of human habitation have shaped the Bohemian lands. Forests (spruce and fir in the higher elevations, with broad-leaved trees such as oak, beech, birch, and linden at lower levels) interspersed with fields characterize the landscape. Human hands felled trees and cleared fields, transforming the woods by removing undergrowth so livestock could graze. The Czech speciality of carp-raising in large ponds, dating back to the Middle Ages, created another typical feature of the countryside. Perhaps there is some affinity between Jakub Krčín of Jelčany, monomaniacal pond builder in the sixteenth century, and the planners of the Lipno, Orlík, and Gabčíkovo-Nagymaros dam projects in the twentieth? At any rate, the relationship between human beings and their land remains significant to Czechs in many ways—from environmental politics to weekend cottages and trips to the woods for mushrooms.

THE CAST OF CHARACTERS: FROM PREHISTORY TO THE SLAVS

What, then, about the people who have inhabited these lands? Recently discovered artifacts have pushed the estimated date for the earliest human presence here to between 1.6 and 1.7 million years ago.[7] Through the long millennia of the Paleolithic, or Old Stone Age, *Homo erectus*, *Homo neandertalensis*, and the anatomically modern *Homo sapiens* left their traces in the Bohemian lands. It is difficult to say whether humans moved into and out of the region with the changing climate during the last Ice Ages, or stayed continuously. When the Ice Ages ended approximately 10,000 years ago, humans had to adapt as the cold, dry steppe habitats, with their herds of large mammals, were replaced by broad-leaf forests and animals similar to today's. The changed hunting conditions encouraged smaller human settlements concentrated along rivers and lakes, where fishing supplemented forest hunting.

Even greater changes in human society came with the introduction of farming and domestic animals—possibly the greatest development in human culture since the use of fire. With the change from hunter-gatherer to agricultural societies, the Neolithic, or New Stone Age, begins. Neolithic settlements in the Balkans pre-date the sixth millennium B.C., in the course of which they spread through the Danubian basin into the Bohemian lands. Scholars argue over whether farming societies arose in Europe independently, through immigrants from the Near East, or through "historical convergences" that spread influences from one people to another. Of the major domesticated plants and animals, only cattle were native to Europe: sheep, goats, wheat, and barley were imports from the Near East.[8]

Farming societies were established in Central Europe by the fifth millennium B.C., and thereafter it appears that human settlement in the Bohemian lands was more or less continuous. Archaeologists usually identify the successive cultures of the Neolithic, Bronze Age (end of the third millennium B.C. to eighth century B.C.), and Iron Age (eighth century B.C. to the present) by some typical feature, often ceramics or burial practices, or by the site where they were first discovered. Without written records it is difficult to say with certainty, but one broadly accepted view holds that most Neolithic Europeans were Indo-European speakers. This probability becomes definite only with the historically documented Celts of the later Iron Age.

When the Celts came into contact with the ancient Mediterranean world, they found their way into the writings of Greek and Roman authors and onto the historical stage. From these references we learn that a Celtic tribe known as the Boii inhabited the region in Roman times, and from them the country derives its common non-Slavic name, Bohemia. The Celts, whose settlements in Bohemia date to the mid-fourth century B.C., were skilled craftsmen, built settled communities, and had a highly developed social organization. The further development of Celtic society in the Bohemian lands, however, ended in the first century

B.C.[9] The most important cause was the arrival of Germanic tribes moving into Bohemia from the north.

The Romans clashed with the Germans beyond their frontier several times during the next centuries, but by the later fourth century Roman power was waning rapidly. At that time the Huns (a nomadic people of Asian origin) attacked the lands of the Ostrogoths near the Black Sea, setting off mass population movements, the "barbarian invasions" linked to the decline of the Roman Empire in the west. During the turmoil of the next century, the Bohemian lands were relegated to the periphery of the Roman world, and historical sources mention them only rarely. The Germanic tribes also disappear from the sources, and instead a new people begin to appear in the region, coming initially from the north and east—the Slavs.

The origins of the Slavs are still much debated. Generally, scholars agree that they expanded in historical times from an area north of the Carpathian Mountains, between the middle reaches of the Dniepr and the upper and middle Oder and Vistula rivers. The Slavs arrived gradually, in small groups, seeping into the spaces left by the departure of the Germans, coexisting with and absorbing remnants of previous communities. By the beginning of the seventh century, Slavic settlements had expanded throughout Central and Eastern Europe and the Balkans, from the mouth of the Elbe and the Baltic coast to the shores of the Black, Adriatic, and Aegean seas.

The Slavs belong to the Indo-European linguistic family, and at the time of their migrations they probably spoke fundamentally the same tongue. Latin and Greek sources refer to them as Sklavenoi, Sclaveni, Sclavi, and so on, but they called themselves, according to the first written records of the ninth century, Slověni. This term is sometimes derived from *slovo* (word, implying the ability to speak intelligibly) while their name for their neighbors to the west was Němci (from *němý*, incapable of speech, mute).[10] Over the course of centuries the Slavic linguistic family differentiated into three branches: the West Slavic (including Czech, Polish, Lusatian Serbian, and dialects of now-extinct Slavs along the Elbe and Baltic coast), South Slavic (Slovene, Croatian, Serbian, Bulgarian, and Macedonian), and East Slavic (Russian, Ukrainian, and Belorussian). The development of separate standard Slavic languages began with the creation of Slavic states during the ninth and tenth centuries.

The early Slavic states formed in a historical setting shaped by the still-existing legacy of the classical world. One source of that legacy, the

Byzantine Empire, preserved an urban, imperial, Christian civilization, ruled by an emperor whose line of succession ran back to Caesar Augustus. In the Romanized provinces of Western Europe the Christian church was well organized, with a hierarchical structure of bishops based on the former Roman cities, owning the supremacy of the bishop of Rome, the pope. The Christian church in the west, however, operated without the powerful political authority represented in Byzantium by the emperor. Even after the papal coronation of Charlemagne, king of the Franks, as emperor in 800, it was the pope who was recognized as the vicar of Christ. From the tenth century onward, the popes balanced between the revived imperial power and other forces, notably the western branch of the Germanic Franks (the future France).[11] As the Slavs moved into Southeastern and Central Europe, including the Bohemian lands, their development would be affected by influences coming from each of these sources.

FROM THE EARLY SLAVS TO THE MORAVIAN STATE

With the arrival of the Slavs in the Bohemian crownlands, the main character of our history steps upon the stage. That at least was how Cosmas of Prague, dean of the cathedral chapter, saw it. Author of a twelfth-century Latin chronicle that makes him the first native historian of Bohemia, Cosmas recounts how the Slavs' tribal leader, Čech, takes them to the summit of mount Říp to look at their new homeland, "that land that I have often promised you, a land subject to no one, filled with game and birds, flowing with sweet milk and honey, and . . . with a pleasant climate."[12] Cosmas's tale of the Czechs taking possession of their promised land reappears in later chronicles, remains until today part of the Czechs' historical imagination, and immediately evokes recognition.[13] Though this story is the stuff of great legends, it has no historical documentation. What we can piece together from fragmentary written sources and archaeological evidence nevertheless gives us a picture of the arrival of the new settlers and their adaptation to their new surroundings. That adaptation—settling beside, displacing, and gradually absorbing remaining groups of non-Slavs—took several centuries.

By the mid-sixth century another group of Asian nomads, the Avars, dominated the Slavs and remnants of Germanic peoples in the Pannonian basin. According to a Frankish chronicle, these Slavs revolted against the Avars in 623 or 624, choosing as their leader a Frankish merchant named Samo. After defeating the Avars, Samo established a personal realm, the earliest state among the Western Slavs, where he ruled for thirty-five years. Samo's empire (which probably included part of the Bohemian lands) dissolved after his death. The Slavs returned to their tribal associations, settling around fortified sites on high ground.[14]

Early sources sometimes use the Latin-derived terms "Bohemia" and "Bohemians" as though they represented a single land and people, but at other times they mention different Slavic tribal names. These tribal groups gradually changed from kinship-based to territorial associations, grouped around a fort and its ruling family. Ninth- and tenth-century sources suggest that Bohemia had three such tribal groupings, including the Czechs in the center, while with the exception of one tribal group in the north, only Moravians are mentioned in Moravia.[15] The free males decided tribal affairs, choosing a leader from among the prominent families. The status and functions of this leader (called in Czech *kníže*, prince or duke) is reflected in the names of some of the early dukes: Svatoslav, Jaroslav (religious ritual), Mojmír, Přemysl (virtues of rulership), Bořivoj, Svatopluk (military prowess). A rudimentary aristocracy of prominent families helped cross tribal boundaries and led to the formation of larger political units.[16]

A powerful and ambitious neighbor, the Germanic kingdom of the Franks, hastened the Slavs' political organization. The Frankish ruler Charlemagne restored the empire in 800, and extended its control through Bavaria, Saxony, and Italy. The Slavic regions beyond also beckoned to Frankish merchants, missionaries, and ambitious noble warriors. From 805 to 806, Charlemagne's armies defeated the Czech tribes and forced them to pay tribute.[17] Following his death in 814, Charlemagne's heirs quarreled, weakening the Frankish state. His grandson, Louis the German, who controlled the eastern portion (Treaty of Verdun, 843), reasserted Carolingian authority by religious expansion. From the bishoprics of Regensburg, Passau, and Salzburg Christian missions set out among the Slavs.

The Slavs in Moravia responded to the Frankish example first.[18] Their duke, Mojmír I, was baptized at Passau in 831, and thereafter the Moravians built stone churches in their fortified settlements, the earliest known example consecrated at Nitra in the 830s by the bishop of Salzburg. In January 845, fourteen "dukes" of the Bohemian Slavs also arrived at Louis's court in Regensburg to accept baptism, but when Louis intervened in Moravia to place Mojmír's nephew Rostislav on the throne, they renounced their politically motivated conversions.[19]

Rostislav had his own interests in Bohemia, where he clashed with the East Franks, highlighting the dangers of Frankish social and religious penetration. In 860, Rostislav asked the pope for Christian missionaries directly from Rome. When his request had no results, Rostislav turned in 863 to the Byzantine Emperor, Michael III, and Patriarch Photius. According to the Slavic *Life of St. Methodius*, the Moravians told the emperor: "We have prospered through God's grace, and many Christian teachers have come to us from among the Italians, Greeks, and Germans, teaching us in various ways. But we Slavs are a simple people, and have none to instruct us in the truth, and explain wisely."[20] The patriarch and emperor selected two Greek brothers from Salonika, Constantine and Methodius, for this task. They knew the Slavic language in daily use around their native city, and translated portions of the liturgy and scriptural texts into it, using a writing system invented by Constantine, the glagolitic script.

During their joint missionary work in Moravia between 863 and 867, Constantine and Methodius educated a number of new priests, using the newly written Slavonic liturgy. Their mission fell foul of the Frankish clergy, however, who complained to the pope. The brothers went to Rome, where Pope Hadrian II supported them, making Constantine a bishop and allowing him to enter a Roman monastery under the name Cyril. After Cyril's unexpected death, Methodius was sent back to Moravia, but the Bavarian clergy imprisoned him. It took Pope John VIII's intervention to get him released, at the price of a ban on using the Slavonic liturgy.[21]

In 870, Rostislav's nephew Svatopluk deposed him. The Bohemian Slavs—including the ruler of the Czech tribe, Bořivoj, the first member of the house of Přemysl mentioned in the documents (872)—supported him against the Franks. Bořivoj accepted Christianity at Svatopluk's court, supposedly from Methodius himself. Svatopluk's attitude to the Byzantine mission was cooler than Rostislav's, however, and when Methodius died in 885, his followers left to take their missionary work to the Bulgarians. Svatopluk's death in 894, and the arrival of new nomads from the east, the Magyars, further weakened his realm. In 903 or 904 the Magyars decisively defeated the Moravians. Its core broken and most of its leaders slain, the Moravian empire fell apart. Protected by its mountains from recurrent Magyar inroads, Bohemia changed from a Moravian periphery to the political center of the western Slavs. The Přemyslids, rulers of the central Bohemian Czech tribe, were the dominant force in this development.

THE EMERGENCE OF THE CZECH STATE

Cosmas's chronicle and other sources preserve the early traditions about the foundation of the Přemyslid dynasty. According to these legends Přemysl was the first duke of the Czechs. Libuše, a prophetess descended from Father Čech, chose him to leave his plow and oxen in the field, wed her, and rule the Czechs from her castle at Vyšehrad. By Bořivoj's time, the core of the Czech territory was probably ruled directly by the duke through a network of such forts. Bořivoj founded Prague by erecting first a church dedicated to the Virgin Mary, and later (perhaps around 885) a new castle on the ridge of Hradčany. Bořivoj's son and successor, Spytihněv I (ca. 894–ca. 915) broke away from Moravian overlordship, paying tribute to the East Frankish king, and placing Bohemia's church under the bishop of Regensburg. The other Czech dukes recognized his supremacy, but maintained a great deal of their own independence.

The turn of the ninth to tenth centuries was turbulent for the Franks too. When the Carolingian dynasty died out, the dukes of the five regional duchies in the old East Frankish kingdom, Bavaria, Saxony, Thuringia, Franconia, and Swabia, contended for the Carolingian succession. The Czechs supported the Bavarians, but in 919 the Saxon Henry I (the Fowler) became king. The implications of that event were not yet clear when the ruling Czech duke, Vratislav I (915–921) died. Vratislav's son, Václav, was still a minor, so his widow, Drahomíra, headed a regency. Rivalry between Drahomíra and Ludmila, Václav's grandmother, ended in 921 with Ludmila's murder. Václav, who began to rule shortly thereafter, transferred her remains to Prague, and supported the clergy whom she had patronized, and who venerated her as a saint.[22]

Václav (921–935) reined in the dependent dukes who had become restive under the regency and used Christianity to strengthen his state. He paid tribute and swore an oath of loyalty to Henry the Fowler in 929, but in return he received relics of St. Vitus for the newly established rotunda of St. Vitus in the Prague castle. Václav and his younger brother Boleslav developed a rivalry that has been interpreted in different ways. Nationalist Czech historians have seen it as a reaction against Václav's supposedly pro-German policies, while the German side (especially during World War II) presented Václav as supporting a realistic policy of Czech submission to a stronger Germany.[23] In the face of the reviving German kingdom under the Saxon Ottonian dynasty, Václav proceeded cautiously; Boleslav later pursued a more energetic policy. The question of Bohemia's relations with the German state (whatever form it took) would remain a constant theme in Czech history.

The conflict between the two brothers culminated on September 28, 935, with Václav's murder by his brother's servants. After Václav's death, Boleslav I (935–972) actively pursued consolidation and a running conflict with Henry the Fowler's son and successor, Otto I. In 950 a strong Saxon army forced him to renew the vassal's oath of fealty, and five years later, Boleslav and the Czechs supported Otto in his great victory over the Magyars near Augsburg. Boleslav also extended Přemyslid control through Moravia and parts of today's Slovakia to Cracow, and farther east, eventually reaching the Bug River.[24]

Boleslav's expansion rested on a more effective system of control.[25] The murdered duke Václav contributed to this consolidation of Přemyslid power. He became—together with his grandmother, Ludmila—one of the Czech patron saints and an emblem of Bohemian statehood.[26] In the struggle to build a firmly organized state, St. Václav (in latinized form, Wenceslas) and St. Ludmila gave charisma to the Přemyslids and Christian legitimacy to the Czech state. The Czechs developed the idea that the country belonged to St. Václav, but in practice the duke as his earthly representative treated it as his possession and its inhabitants as his subjects. He relied upon his armed retainers to support him, fight his battles, and extract contributions and taxes. Traditionally they approved the election of a new duke, a symbolic recognition of their influence, which depended on service to the duke rather than owning land.

The basis of Boleslav's system was the castle or fort, at this time still usually a wood and earth structure, sometimes with an outer wall encased in dry-set stone. Boleslav extended the network of castles and settled officials taken from his retinue in them. From the castles they collected taxes, supplies, and other payments from the local population. The castles with their churches were also centers for the spread of Christianity.[27] Greater stability encouraged trade. Prague hosted foreign merchants, among them Germans, Latins, and Jews. Ibrahim ibn Jakub, a Spanish Jew sent from Cordoba on an embassy to Otto I in 965, wrote that Prague was "built of stone and lime," and emphasized that it was "the largest town [among the Slavs] in terms of trade," exporting slaves, tin, and furs. Bohemia, he wrote, was "the best country of the north."[28]

The Bohemian church was still under the bishop of Regensburg, so Boleslav worked to create his own bishopric in Prague. The pope agreed, and helped establish the Benedictine convent of St. George in the Prague castle, which served as the Přemyslid burial place and a center of St. Ludmila's cult. The emperor approved the Prague bishopric in 973, placing Prague under the archbishop of Mainz: more prestigious, farther away, and less likely to interfere. The first bishop of Prague was a Saxon, but the second, Vojtěch (982) was a native Czech of the Slavník family.[29] The Slavníks were the last ruling tribal dukes in Bohemia, with their own ambitions. Vojtěch urged a vigorous assertion of Christian teaching, and expected secular duties similar to the German clerics. Vojtěch left for Rome in 988, but at the demand of Boleslav II (972–999) he returned in 992, and helped establish the Benedictine monastery of Břevnov in 993. He left Bohemia the next year, and so survived the bloody conquest of the Slavník castle by Boleslav II's retinue and the murder of all Slavníks present in 995.[30]

In Rome, Vojtěch had become close to the young emperor Otto III (crowned in 982). When Vojtěch was martyred in Poland on a mission to the pagan Prussians in 997, Otto sponsored his canonization (999). On a pilgrimage in 1000 to venerate Vojtěch's remains in Gniezno, Otto granted the Polish ruler Bolesław I, the Brave, the royal title.[31] He also established a Polish archbishop in Gniezno. When in the same year Stephen I of Hungary was crowned king, an archbishopric was also established at Esztergom. The Czechs were left with neither king nor archbishop of their own for centuries. Instead, the young Bohemian state experienced a major crisis when Boleslav II died in 999.

2 Dukes and Kings

A country's currency gives it an opportunity to display its symbols, and a measure of its self-image, in this most mundane of public transactions. In the Czech Republic, the twenty-crown note bears a portrait of Přemysl Otakar I, first hereditary king of Bohemia. Achieving the status of hereditary kingdom made Bohemia unique among the territories attached to the Holy Roman Empire and granted it stronger legitimacy and political status. To the Czech Republic, the image of Bohemia's monarch asserted that Czech statehood was not new, but had a historical ancestor in Přemyslid Bohemia. Both then and now the development of Bohemia into a kingdom carried important consequences.

THE BOHEMIAN LANDS
FROM DUCHY TO KINGDOM

The road to the kingly title was not smooth. Bohemia's location between the Holy Roman Empire and the Polish and Hungarian kingdoms influenced its development over the centuries. Czech dukes had to stabilize their political relationship with the German emperor, usually as his vassal, but Bohemia was never integrated into the empire's internal administration. The Czech rulers expanded against their eastern neighbors during times of weakness, but were forced back when the

Polish and Hungarian states recovered their strength. Internally the major questions involved the ducal succession and the relationship between Bohemia and Moravia, which would set the pattern for other lands as the Bohemian state expanded. Conflicts over the succession after Boleslav II's death weakened Bohemia and opened up prospects for its neighbors to meddle, but the situation gradually stabilized in the first decades of the eleventh century.

The Přemyslid Dukes and Their State

Boleslav II's grandson Břetislav I (1035–1055) made the most of the simultaneous weakness of Poland, Hungary, and Germany early in his reign.[1] His efforts to expand into Poland (where he seized the remains of St. Vojtěch in 1039) and Hungary did not last, and though he defeated the German king Henry III at Domažlice (Tauss) in 1040, he had to accept Bohemia as an imperial fief in 1041.[2] But Břetislav stabilized Bohemia within its traditional frontiers, and extended the castles as centers of ducal power into Moravia. Břetislav also established the principle of seniority, which gave overlordship in the entire Přemyslid lands to the eldest member of the family. To his younger sons Břetislav entrusted Moravia, with appanage seats in Olomouc (Olmütz), Brno (Brünn), and later Znojmo (Znaim).[3]

The first Bohemian duke to win the royal title was Vratislav II (1061–1092). Already he had worked to strengthen the duke's position by creating a bishopric in Olomouc in Moravia, thereby limiting the Prague bishop's jurisdiction to Bohemia. He also established a cathedral chapter at Vyšehrad, where he moved his residence. Vratislav took the side of the emperor, Henry IV, in the investiture controversy with Pope Gregory VII, and in 1085 a grateful Henry granted him the title "King of Bohemia and Poland" for his lifetime.[4]

When Vratislav died in 1092, the prominent families beginning to develop into a feudal nobility used the conflicts among his sons to play off rival contestants against each other. The empire also meddled, but the Czechs defeated a German invasion in 1126 at Chlumec, in the foothills of the Krušné Hory. The battle of Chlumec, where the Czechs fought under the emblems of St. Václav and St. Vojtěch, marked a shift in the way the leading Czechs thought about their relationship to the state. No longer were they merely the duke's retainers, they were a nobility defending their land, represented by their patron saints.[5]

Vladislav II (1140–1172) came to the throne as the candidate of this developing nobility, but he deftly used the support of the first Hohenstaufen emperor, Conrad III, to strengthen his position. In the renewed quarrels between the papacy and the Hohenstaufens under Frederick I Barbarossa, Vladislav supported the emperor. As a reward for Czech support, Barbarossa crowned Vladislav King of Bohemia in 1158, again only for his lifetime. When Vladislav abdicated in his son's favor, Barbarossa seized the opportunity to intervene in Bohemia's affairs. Twenty-five years of practically unbroken strife ensued, during which the throne changed hands twelve times, and each time the decisive voice was the emperor's.

During this struggle, Frederick Barbarossa raised Moravia to the status of border county (margraviate) and granted its united territory to one of the ambitious Přemyslid contestants, Konrád Ota of Znojmo, in 1182. In 1187 the Přemyslid bishop of Prague, Jindřich Břetislav, was proclaimed an imperial prince. Both these developments threatened the unity of the Bohemian lands, but they were reversed before the end of the century. An agreement between Vladislav Jindřich (supported by most Czech nobles) and his older brother Přemysl established Přemysl as Czech duke, and Vladislav Jindřich as margrave of Moravia. These decisions ignored the Holy Roman Emperor, affirmed the supremacy of the Czech duke, ensured the unity of the Přemyslid patrimony, and reasserted Moravia's connection to Bohemia, though it remained a margraviate. During Přemysl Otakar I's reign (1197–1230) the Czech lands would begin a century of development, a development building on changes taking place during the turbulent twelfth century.

Economic Development in the Twelfth Century

Internal colonization in the Bohemian lands nearly doubled the area under the plow. Population growth encouraged people to clear the forests near villages or open up new settlements in what had previously been, in the contemporary term, "desert." Dukes encouraged the process in strategic areas, including the borders where colonization from the German side encroached on their territory. Ducal foundations of great monasteries, especially of the Praemonstratensians and the Cistercians, also contributed to colonization.

The nobility, however, was the major force reshaping the countryside. Instability at the beginning and end of the century allowed them to turn offices and associated income (benefices) into hereditary possessions. Nobles supported new settlements around the castles, treating the newly cultivated land as their property, and the peasants on it as their subjects. In this way the ancestors of the leading Czech noble families of the middle ages assembled wide possessions. The nobles also built churches and founded monasteries. All of the monasteries established in Bohemia and Moravia before 1100 were founded by the rulers, but between 1100 and 1205, twenty-seven richly endowed monasteries arose thanks to noble patronage.[6] The castle's importance as a center of trade and craft production increased. Around the larger and more important castles, trading centers grew up that began to resemble towns.

Prague held a unique position. As the duke's residence, it attracted anyone who wanted to be close to the ruler, and they built modest courts, including churches. The clergy of the cathedral chapters at the Prague castle and Vyšehrad required food, luxury and utilitarian goods, and the services of specialized craftsmen. Local peasants and foreign merchants flocked to the markets, and permanent communities of Germans, Latins, and Jews developed.[7] By the end of the twelfth century stone houses surrounded the marketplace in Prague's Old Town, and in 1172 a stone bridge, the oldest in Central Europe after Regensburg's, was built with the support of Vladislav II's wife, Judita.

Duke Konrád Ota II issued a statute in 1189, the first written legal code for the Czechs, which recognized these social and economic changes, including private ownership of land. The political system began to resemble more closely the feudal system common in the west. By the time of Vladislav II, the great noble families had stabilized, and the king was now the feudal liege lord of a nobility that itself represented the land. The cult of St. Václav contributed to this territorialization of originally personal relationships: beginning with Vladislav, the inscription on the ruler's seal suggested that the duke (later king) merely held in his hands and administered the "Pax Sancti Wenceslai" (peace, order, state of St. Václav).

BOHEMIA AS A HEREDITARY KINGDOM

Bohemia's rapid political rise during the next century built upon Přemysl Otakar I's success in regaining the royal title (1198, with papal recognition in 1204) by adroit diplomacy during the Hohen-staufen-Welf conflicts over the imperial crown.[8] Přemysl Otakar I's poli-cies illustrate the Czech kingdom's position as the emperor's power was sapped by the long-running feud with the papacy. The power of the territorial rulers of the Holy Roman Empire increased, and the Czech king might have established an independent kingdom like contemporary Hungary or Poland, or the western dynastic monarchies in France, En-gland, or the Iberian peninsula. Instead, Přemysl chose to retain the Bo-hemian lands' association with the empire.

The terms of that association were codified by the young Hohen-staufen emperor Frederick II in 1212, in the Golden Bull of Sicily.[9] This document reaffirmed the royal title for Přemysl Otakar I and his succes-sors, treating Bohemia as an independent state without severing the ties to the empire that gave it such influence in Central Europe. The royal title, affirming that the king ruled "by the grace of God," added to the monarch's position within Bohemia. As they asserted the principle of primogeniture the kings became less dependent on the nobles for elec-tion.

The Golden Bull of Sicily confirmed the king's right of investiture of the clergy. At this time, the power of lay patrons in Bohemia over the church was still strong. The bishop of Prague, Ondřej, negotiated the Great Privilegium of 1222, which guaranteed church officials in Bohe-mia canonical election and economic and legal immunities. In return the king strengthened royal oversight over church property, doing away with the ducal and castle officials who had previously administered it. The church became a major feudal power, closely linked to the crown, and one of the king's most trustworthy pillars of support.[10]

Přemysl's son Václav (1230–1253) emerged as a talented ruler in his own right, though Přemysl Otakar I's record was difficult to match. Václav I faced challenges equal to his father's. The continuing conflict between the papacy, the Italian towns, the imperial princes, and the Hohenstaufen family defined the political context of Václav's reign. The Czech ruler preserved good relations with Frederick II, the "Stupor Mundi," by his marriage with a Hohenstaufen, Kunhuta. On the other hand, Václav's designs on the Babenberg inheritance were a source of strain. The Babenbergs controlled the duchies of Austria and Styria, the main communication lines between the empire and Italy. The last Baben-berg duke, Frederick II, had no male heirs, and all his neighbors schemed to claim his possessions. Finally, Václav I's second son, Přemysl, was elected duke of Austria in 1250. When the Styrian nobles also accepted Přemysl, the king of Hungary, Béla IV, objected. War with Hungary lasted from 1252 until a peace agreement in 1254 left Přemysl in possession of Austria, while recognizing Béla's claim to Styria. By this time Přemysl was already king of Bohemia.

Colonization in Countryside and Town

Václav I tends to be cast into the shade by his vigorous and long-lived father and his glorious and tragic second son. As king of Bohemia, however, he succeeded in navigating the treacherous waters of the Hohenstaufen feud with the papacy, and positioned Bohemia to benefit from the extinction of the Babenbergs. The Bohemian lands under Přemysl belonged to the most powerful states of Central Europe, in part thanks to developments under Václav I. Internal colonization begun during the twelfth century gathered speed with the arrival of colonists from abroad, mostly Germans. Peasants, burghers, and specialist craftsmen, especially in mining and related trades, settled in the Bohemian lands, accepting land for farming villages or creating towns with charters from noblemen, church institutions, or the king.[11]

Colonization from the west brought with it new legal norms, the *ius teutonicum* (German or emphyteutic law), and German town law. German law was a collection of traditions and practices enshrined in a written agreement spelling out the conditions under which the colonists held their land. Typically, in return for fixed, regular payments in cash and kind, the colonists received the hereditary right to farm the land, limited personal freedom, and some self-government. For both parties German law offered advantages. To the peasant, the clearly defined and fixed obligations provided incentives to adopt more productive farming practices. To the lord it offered cash when established, and a regular and dependable income thereafter. German law spread to older, Slavic communities, especially near the developing towns with their ready markets for agricultural products.

Towns were subject to specific town law, and a large part of the population including free craft workers produced for the market without devoting their time to agriculture. Towns could hold markets, build fortifications, and insist that merchants stop and offer their wares for sale. They also had exclusive rights to establish crafts or inns within a fixed distance from the town. With time, town councils dominated by the patriciate, presided over by the mayor or *purkmistr* (from the German *Bürgermeister*) grew up to represent the town in dealings with its lord. Active in trade, financial, or mining enterprises, the patriciate remained German for many years. The craft workers who formed most of the town population organized themselves in guilds to control training, standards, and access to their crafts. Royal towns were entrusted to the chamberlain or, in the case of mining towns, the master of the mint. When a rich silver lode was discovered at Kutná Hora, the town grew rapidly. German mining experts and workers arrived in great numbers, and in 1300, Václav II established a centralized royal mint there. Imported Italian master minters helped create an entirely new coin, with a standard purity and weight, called the Prague *groš*. This coin would remain the foundation of Bohemia's currency for centuries.

From Přemysl Otakar II to the End of the Přemyslid Dynasty

Under Přemysl Otakar II (1253–1278), Bohemia achieved new heights of influence, made easier by Bohemian silver, and by the long interregnum in the empire after Frederick II's death. The Bohemian lands were united, and the king wielded effective power within them. The Přemyslid kings won the title of imperial cupbearer in 1114, and from the mid-thirteenth century onward, they ranked among the seven electoral princes who chose the emperor.[12] Přemysl extended Czech influence in the Alpine lands, with the strong support of the royal towns (Vienna remained on his side to the bitter end), the archbishop of Salzburg, and other clerics. In 1269, Přemysl succeeded to the Duke of Carinthia's possessions, including also Carniola and the "Wendish marches," peopled by Slavs (today's Slovenia). Přemysl also expanded northward, where Piast Poland was still divided into different principalities. The Bohemian king joined German and Polish knights in crusades against the still pagan Baltic peoples; the city of Königsberg (today Kaliningrad), founded on the Baltic in 1255, was named in his honor.

Thus in a short space of time, the Bohemian king had dramatically expanded his realm (see Map 2, p. 34). Contemporaries admired Přemysl Otakar II, but they also began to fear him. At the imperial election of 1273, the German princes chose the relatively obscure Rudolf of Habsburg. When in 1276 the Alpine nobles rebelled against Přemysl, Rudolf (supported by the other German rulers, the papacy, and Hungary) supported them. It was a revolt by leading Czech nobles, though, that forced Přemysl to capitulate to Rudolf, give up the Alpine territories, and receive Bohemia and Moravia from Rudolf as a fief.

The rapid changes linked to colonization had created conflict between nobles and king. Přemysl consciously used new royal towns and monasteries to reassert royal power against the now territorialized nobles. Royal institutions like the Land Court also undercut the nobles' powers. By the mid-thirteenth century the Land Court was the highest judicial instance in the kingdom. The king also accepted its limitations: he presided as first among equals, along with the officials of the Prague castle and representatives of the great noble families, but it was St. Václav, as reflected in the seal of the court, who acted as the defender of the law.[13]

Přemysl suppressed the noble rising during 1277, and decided to hazard everything on a decisive battle with Rudolf. The second campaign ended in disaster for the Bohemian king on August 26, 1278, at the Moravian Field (Moravské pole, Dürnkrut). As Přemysl saw that his knights were defeated, "still he did not propose to yield to our victorious banner, but defended himself, a colossus in spirit and virtues, with admirable bravery. . . . Here at last this most glorious king, together with the victory, lost his life."[14] Dying as he had lived according to the knightly code, Přemysl Otakar II, "King of Gold and Iron," became an inspiration to contemporary and future writers.

Since the rise of the Habsburgs dates from Rudolf's victory, the German or pro-Habsburg view sees Přemysl as an overweening upstart whose ambitions led to his downfall. Czechs blame the nobles' treachery, which brought to a premature end the chance to build a Czech-dominated greater state out of the German and Slavic eastern marches of the empire.[15] The immediate result of Přemysl's defeat and death was disaster. With the king gone and the heir, Václav, a child, it seemed the realm might fall apart. The widowed queen, Kunhuta, and Přemysl's former client Jindřich, duke of Breslau (Wrocław), received small territories, while Rudolf took Moravia, and Otto of Brandenburg became regent in Bohemia during Václav's minority. Central power weakened, nobles helped themselves to royal property, and the Brandenburgers extracted as much as they could. The impetus to end these "evil years" came from a group of great nobles and the higher clergy, acting politically as a body for the first time. Pressure from this group, and the payment of impressive sums of money, convinced Otto to return Václav

II to Bohemia in 1283. A similar group gained Rudolf's agreement to withdraw from Moravia, and the kingdom slowly recovered.

Václav, married to Guta (Jitka) of Habsburg, shifted his ambitions to the north and northeast, away from direct conflict with his inlaws. He extended feudal overlordship among the Polish dukes of Upper Silesia, took Cracow, and in 1300 was formally crowned King of Poland. He cemented his claim to Poland by a second marriage, to the Piast princess Eliška Rejčka (Richenza). When the Hungarian Árpád dynasty died out in 1301, a group of nobles offered the crown to Václav II, who had his son, also Václav, formally crowned King of Hungary that year. The rapid recovery of Přemyslid fortunes provoked imperial and papal resistance, and Václav withdrew his son from Hungary in 1304 and renounced his claim before his death in 1305. Václav III (1305–1306), however, hoped to retain at least the core of the Czech-Polish dominion. To this end he prepared an expedition to Poland in the summer of 1306.[16] In Olomouc on his way there, however, Václav III was murdered, in circumstances not fully explained to this day. With his untimely end the Přemyslid family, once so numerous, died out in the male line.

CHRISTIANITY AND CULTURE IN PŘEMYSLID BOHEMIA

Accepting Christianity affected the peoples who came into contact with the Christian civilization of Rome and its heirs in many areas, including politics. The most basic political consideration was simple survival: becoming Christian helped prevent extermination. Christianity also contributed to state-building, providing a core of educated, experienced administrators and an organization patterned after the Roman empire. Whether the choice was for Rome or for Constantinople, the new states saw the value of their own church organizations, and native patron saints quickly provided a strong force for cohesion. St. Václav assumed this unifying role among the Czechs. One chronicle tells how, at Chlumec, one of the Czechs holding St. Václav's lance cried out to his companions, "Comrades and brothers, be valiant, for above the point of the holy spear I see St. Václav, who, seated on a white horse and wearing white robes, fights for us; you also behold!"[17] The cult of St. Václav, "eternal duke" of the Czechs, and other patrons remained important in Czech political ideology for centuries.

With Christianity also came writing, and thus literature. Cyril and Methodius's mission had little time to sink deep roots but their legacy did not entirely vanish. The Slavonic rite existed in Bohemia, together with the Latin, through most of the tenth century at least, and with the foundation of the Benedictine monastery of Sázava in 1032 by Procopius a center for the Slavonic liturgy emerged in the eleventh century. The Slavonic liturgical and literary tradition influenced the earliest literary expression in the Czech language, the Czech hymn, "Hospodine, pomiluj ny."[18] Already under Boleslav II the cult of St. Václav produced written texts, the Old Slavonic *Legend of St. Václav* before the middle of the tenth century, and Latin works shortly thereafter. St. Vojtěch, too, quickly became the subject of literary works. The Slavonic tradition was more conservative than the Latin, which opened Czech cultural life to the important influences of Latin Christendom.

The church at first imported Moravian building styles. The most important church in Bohemia, the church of St. Vitus, was constructed as a rotunda in Ottonian style under Václav. In the eleventh and twelfth centuries it was rebuilt as a Romanesque basilica. Twelfth-century Romanesque buildings include St. George's basilica in the Prague castle and Strahov monastery. The Judita bridge in Prague has already been mentioned; not until the second half of the thirteenth century would the stone bridge at Písek rival this achievement. A Romanesque bishop's palace and monasteries graced Olomouc, and in Znojmo the early twelfth-century rotunda of St. Catherine preserves on its walls the Přemyslid vision of Czech statehood, depicting Czech dukes from the mythical Přemysl to the present beside the evangelists and Christ the King.

The church's political role also increased as jurisdictional tensions emerged between religious and secular authorities (the bishops and dukes, abbots of monasteries, and their founders or patrons). Until the middle of the eleventh century the higher church offices were filled by non-Czechs, usually Germans. Czech clerics studied abroad in Germany and France, and on their return entered the church administration or the ruler's service. Thus the first Czech intelligentsia formed, including Cosmas of Prague, whose chronicle transcends the bare recording of local events to give a history of the Bohemian lands as a whole.

When the First Crusade reached Prague in 1096, the crusaders unleashed a pogrom on the Jews, and similar disturbances took place in Brno. Generally, the situation of Jews in the Bohemian lands up until then had been relatively tolerable. From the beginning of the thirteenth century, they were considered unfree *servi camerae regiae*, fiscal subjects directly under the monarch. In return for his protection, they paid various taxes and special contributions. Otherwise, their contacts with Christian society were strictly regulated, and limited mostly to business. Under Přemysl Otakar II, a *Statuta Judaeorum* codified the legal situation of the Jews (its provisions were extended to Jewish communities in Moravia as well as Bohemia), comparing favorably with their situation in neighboring countries. Přemysl Otakar II's statute remained the foundation of Jewish legislation until the eighteenth century.[19]

Gothic style and knightly culture arrived in Bohemia in the thirteenth century. To the traditions of fealty, knightly culture added military training and the art of courtly love. Minnesingers, the German followers of the French troubadour and trouvère, were welcome at the royal court. Nobles built seats with German names, after which they called themselves (the lords of Lemberk, Šternberk, Rožmberk). The old Czech rhyming epic *Alexandreida* (late thirteenth century) reflects their outlook and the military campaigns of Přemysl Otakar II and Václav II.[20]

The royal court was also a center for devotional life (another knightly virtue, in theory at least). Václav I's sister, Anežka (Agnes), took the veil after her engagement collapsed. She devoted the rest of her life to charity and religious devotion, earning beatification and (in 1989) canonization. She brought the Franciscans and the Poor Clares (known for their poverty, fervent devotion, and activity among the people) to Bohemia, and created a Czech order, the Crusaders of the Red Star, also devoted to charitable works. The chorale "Svatý Václave," war hymn of the Czech nobility in the thirteenth century, expresses the intersection of court and cloister.

The Gothic style spread further through royal foundations of monasteries (Zbraslav, established by Václav II), castles, and towns. Anežka's convent and the Old-New Synagogue in Prague are the earliest examples of Gothic in Bohemia. The five-vaulted monastery church at Sedlec, or south Bohemian monastic foundations (Zlatá Koruna/Goldkron, Vyšší Brod/Hohenfurt), represents late thirteenth-century sacred Gothic. The secular side boasts the royal castle at Bezděz (Bösig) in northeast Bohemia, and less-imposing buildings at noble seats. Gothic in Bohemia peaked, however, under the Přemyslids' successors.

With the murder of Václav III in 1306, the ruling family that had dominated the Bohemian lands for more than four centuries died. Though many of the forty Přemyslids who had ruled the Czechs had to struggle against rivals, and many were overthrown, never had the family's right to rule been seriously questioned. It was not immediately apparent how the Bohemian lands would prosper under a foreign dynasty. In fact the next century would see the medieval Bohemian kingdom reach its highest point of power and prestige, only to be plunged once more into crisis and conflict.

GOLDEN AGES AND TIMES OF DARKNESS

PART TWO

3 King Foreigner and *Pater Patriae*

When political legitimacy depended on the right of descent, the extinction of a ruling dynasty spelled trouble. During the four centuries of Přemyslid rule, however, the Czechs created a state with enough territorial and institutional stability to weather these problems. Beginning with the later Přemyslids and continuing under succeeding dynasties, a political system emerged based on estates (lords, knights, towns, and sometimes clergy), giving the Bohemian crownlands their characteristic political structure for the next several centuries. During those centuries, the fluctuating fortunes of the realm would also provide much material for later generations to shape into the historical myth-images of golden ages and times of darkness, of "a nation great in glory and suffering."[1] The first years after Václav III inclined to the latter image.

BOHEMIA UNDER THE LUXEMBURGS: MEDIEVAL HIGH-WATER MARK

After Václav III's death, his sisters Anna and Eliška represented the legitimate Přemyslid line. The Czech nobles preferred Anna's husband, Henry of Carinthia, but Albrecht of Habsburg, King of the

Romans, forced them to accept his son, Rudolf. Rudolf (1306–1307) died the year after his election, whereupon the Bohemian crown went to Henry (1307–1310), but his reliance on the towns and armed support from Carinthia and Meissen made him unpopular. Finally a group of nobles and church leaders approached Henry VII of Luxemburg, King of the Romans since Albrecht's murder in 1308. The Czechs had a friend in the Luxemburg camp, the archbishop of Mainz, who had been Václav II's chancellor. After complex negotiations, Eliška Přemyslovna agreed to marry Henry's son John. In 1310, John's army drove Henry of Carinthia out of Prague, and a year later John was crowned King of Bohemia.

John of Luxemburg: King Foreigner

As Bohemian king, John of Luxemburg (1310–1346) left behind mixed impressions. Coming to the throne as a youth, unable to speak the language, faced with a powerful and self-confident nobility, and married for reasons of state to a proud, passionate, and impetuous queen who saw herself as representing the native dynastic traditions, John never felt at home in the Bohemian crownlands. Instead, he used his position to advance the interests of the house of Luxemburg on the tournament grounds and battlefields of all Europe.[2]

At the start of his reign, John confirmed important political and fiscal rights to the Czech nobility in an inaugural diploma.[3] Nevertheless, the nobles and their new king soon clashed, with the nobility dividing into two competing camps. Eliška entered the rivalries for power, and so did the burghers of Prague, seeking political influence to match their wealth. Into this mare's nest of ambitions John intervened so ineptly that the nobles united against him, and only the intercession of the new Roman king, the Wittelsbach Ludwig of Bavaria, secured a compromise settlement between the king and the nobility at Domažlice in 1318.

Contemporary sources echo the turmoil among the great in the kingdom. The Latin chronicle of Zbraslav abbey supports the crown, while Cosmas's chronicle and the *Alexandreida* emphasize the rights of the native Czech lords and the Czech language against the German-speaking nobles and the town patricians. Another early fourteenth-century Czech source, the *Kronika Boleslavská*, insists that the "true Czechs" (the nobles) represent the whole nation, and that the king should rule in harmony with them. The author expresses such anti-German views that the chronicle influenced Czech national consciousness down to the nineteenth century.[4]

John returned to Luxemburg shortly after the Domažlice agreement. Thereafter, the nobility usually accepted the king's requests for exceptional special taxes, while the king allowed them to administer the kingdom. The result threatened to weaken the king's independent power drastically, a threat increased by John's habit of pawning his own royal domains to the great nobles in return for ready cash. A contemporary chronicler wrote that "during [John's] absence the Czech kingdom enjoys greater peace than during his presence," because he only visited his realm "in order to extract money by force from the whole population of the Czech kingdom, take it away with him, and fruitlessly waste it in foreign countries."[5]

John's "fruitless" diplomatic and military efforts did have some value to the Bohemian crownlands. He added Eger (in Czech, Cheb) to his possessions in 1322, Upper Lusatia from 1319 to 1329, and in 1335, the wealthy town and duchy of Breslau in Silesia. Around it John grouped several other Silesian principalities as vassal territories.[6] John clashed with the Habsburgs and the emperor over control of Tyrol and northern Italy, but before the Luxemburgs withdrew in 1333, his first-born son, Charles, had gained valuable experience there.

Charles was born in 1316 in Prague. Sent in 1323 to the French court, he became familiar with the culture and politics of the Capetian monarchy. There (at the age of seven) he also married Markéta (Blanche) of Valois, sister to the heir to the French throne. Thus ties with France were already long established when the relationship between the Luxemburgs and the Wittelsbach emperor Ludwig worsened during the 1330s. The papacy, too, welcomed the Luxemburgs as an ally in its struggle with Ludwig. Since 1309 the popes had resided at Avignon, working with, or under the thumb of, the king of France. In later years these factors helped bring Charles to the imperial throne.

At the moment, however, the Bohemian lands demanded all his attention. Many of the leading Czech nobles realized that if royal power declined too far, it could threaten the existence of the monarchy and thus their own interests. Leaving Italy at their invitation, Charles returned to the Bohemian lands in 1333. Some months later, his father invested him with the title of Margrave of Moravia, legalizing his presence in the kingdom and his participation in its affairs.[7]

Those affairs were, by Charles's own account, in a near desperate state. "We found that kingdom so devastated," he wrote in his autobiography, "that we could not find even one free castle that had not been pledged with all the other royal estates, so that we had nowhere we could settle, except in burgher's houses like any other burgher." The Prague castle had fallen into ruin, and "the lords had mostly become tyrants and no longer feared the king as they should, since they had earlier divided the kingdom among themselves."[8] Charles succeeded in gaining the support of the great nobles, the leading church dignitaries, and the patriciate of Prague, so that by the early 1340s he had won back most of the usurped royal estates.

Deteriorating relations with Ludwig of Bavaria revived the old connections to France and the papacy, especially after the election of Pope Clement VI, who had been young Charles's tutor and adviser at the French court. The pope supported the heir to the Bohemian throne by approving the elevation of the Prague bishopric to an archbishopric, finally removing its long dependency on German superiors. The pope also paved the way for Charles's election as King of the Romans, by five of the seven electoral princes, in July 1346.

John and Charles immediately set out for France to support the French king against England. There John of Luxemburg perished at Crécy on August 26, 1346. Czech chroniclers praised him in death, quoting England's Edward III, "Never was there anyone like this Bohemian king."[9] His father's death made Charles king twice over, since he was now also king of Bohemia in addition to his contested Roman title. As long as some electoral princes still supported Ludwig, Charles prepared for war, but Ludwig died of a heart attack while bearhunting in 1347. Charles won over the most significant of Ludwig's supporters by marrying his daughter Anna following Blanche of Valois's death. In 1349, Charles was crowned King of the Romans again, this time in the presence of all seven electors.

Charles IV and Bohemia

At his christening, Charles IV (1346–1378) was given the name of the Bohemian patron saint and symbol of Czech statehood, Václav, while at his confirmation he assumed the name of the renewer of empire, Charlemagne. Both these traditions were united in Charles's life, as he united both crowns in his person. He emphasized that on his mother's side he "came from the ancient family of Czech kings," and that he spoke and understood the language "like any other Czech."[10] He also supported St. Václav's cult. He had the splendid chapel of St. Václav built in St. Vitus's cathedral, the seal of his university shows him kneeling at the feet of St. Václav, he had the royal crown, "The Crown of St. Václav," refashioned, he composed a version of the St. Václav legend, and christened his first two sons Václav. Throughout his reign, though, he also left behind memorials to the Carolingian tradition. Outstanding among the foundations dedicated to Charlemagne or bearing his and Charles IV's name is the castle of Karlštejn, built to house the crown jewels, relics, and other treasures of the empire.

Contemporary opponents dubbed Charles IV the "pope's king" for his alliance with the papacy. Czech and German nationalist historians conducted long debates over Charles's nationality. The rhetorical epithet used at his funeral oration, "father of his fatherland" (*pater patriae*), was turned by Maximilian I into the jibe that he was "stepfather to the empire." Later Baroque and nationalist historiography turned this flourish into a literal evaluation, positive (for many Czechs) or negative (for many Germans).[11] A strong foundation of Charles's policy in any case was concern for the dynastic fortunes of the Luxemburgs.[12]

John divided his possessions among his sons, with Charles receiving Bohemia, his brother Jan Jindřich Moravia, and his half-brother Václav (John's son by his second marriage) Luxemburg itself. Technically these lands, along with others added during Charles's reign, belonged to the crown of Bohemia. In a series of documents issued in 1348, Charles stabilized the relationships among the crown's possessions. In addition to Bohemia proper, Moravia, and Luxemburg, the crownlands included the Silesian principalities and Upper and Lower Lusatia. By his second marriage, Charles added parts of the Upper Palatinate, and he was also feudal lord of many castles and towns scattered through the empire. His third marriage brought him the last two independent Silesian principalities. Finally, in 1373, Charles added Brandenburg (with its electoral vote) to the lands of the Bohemian crown.

Bohemia's well-being was central to Charles's concerns, and in spite of dynastic and imperial involvements, he devoted himself to it. His choice of Prague for his residence stimulated a building boom that brought foreign-born masters such as Matthias of Arras and Peter Parler of Gmünd to Prague. These artists worked on the reconstruction of the castle, including St. Vitus's cathedral, in Gothic style. Parler's workshop contributed the church of the Virgin Mary before Týn in Prague's Old Town, and other Gothic churches in Kolín and Kutná Hora. A new stone bridge replaced the Judita bridge, joining Prague's Old Town with the

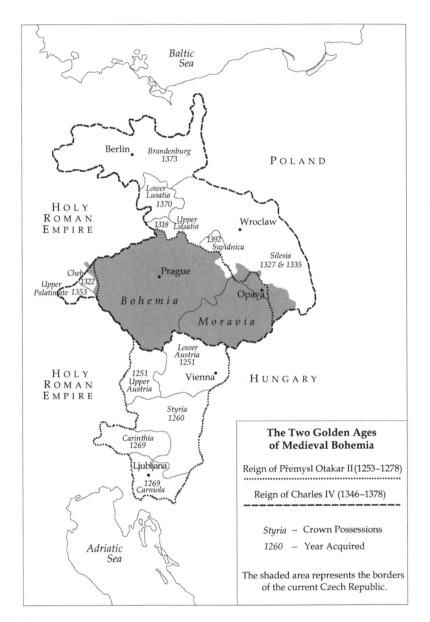

Baltic
Sea

POLAND

Berlin. Brandenburg
1373

HOLY
ROMAN
EMPIRE

Lower
Lusatia
1370

Upper
1318 Lusatia

Wroclaw

1392
Swidnica

Silesia
1327 & 1335

Cheb
Upper 1322
Palatinate 1353

Prague

Bohemia

Opava

Moravia

Lower
Austria
1251

HOLY
ROMAN
EMPIRE

1251
Upper
Austria

Vienna

HUNGARY

Styria
1260

Carinthia
1269

Ljubljana

1269
Carniola

Adriatic
Sea

The Two Golden Ages
of Medieval Bohemia

Reign of Přemysl Otakar II (1253–1278)
···

Reign of Charles IV (1346–1378)
— — — — — — — — — — — —

Styria — Crown Possessions

1260 — Year Acquired

The shaded area represents the borders
of the current Czech Republic.

Map 2

Lesser Quarter beneath the castle. On the Old Town side, Charles erected a splendid tower reminiscent of Roman triumphal arches and displaying in stone his conception of his imperial authority.

Charles IV also founded important cultural institutions, the most outstanding of which was the university that bears his name, established in 1348. Underlying the impact of the Charles University were general developments in schooling, as towns and town culture flourished beside church, court, noble castle, and village. During the thirteenth century many royal towns established schools known as particular schools, which imparted chiefly Latin and the rudiments of the arts. After 1348 responsibility for overseeing these schools was vested in the university, though the monastic or parish schools were controlled by the church.

Charles IV's new university influenced the whole of central Europe. Like other medieval universities, Prague's was international, admitting students from all Christendom. Under its chancellor, the archbishop of Prague, the university was a society of corporations based on territorial principles and known as *nationes*, or "nations." The chief executive officer was the rector, elected by the four nations, while each faculty was headed by a dean. The academic officials, students, and teachers formed a special corporate body with its own privileges, and lived together in colleges. The most famous, the Great College or Charles College, obtained the Karolinum, the oldest surviving building of the university, in 1383. At its height, Prague's university was a fully integrated part of the intellectual world of Western Christendom, developing domestic intellectuals and exposing them to the leading trends of European thought.

The kingdom's stability partly rested on Charles's skill in coping with the Přemyslids' old nemesis, the Czech lords. Charles gave them significant positions in his court, but he used the church as a counterweight to the nobles. The church gave him educated officials to administer his possessions, so Latin was widely used in Charles IV's court, and links existed to the first Italian humanists. German was common, especially for contacts with other parts of the empire. But Czech also made its way into administration and justice, with the first preserved official document in Czech dating to 1370. Charles appointed burghers to the positions of chamberlain or master of the mint. During the 1350s he prepared a body of laws aimed at strengthening the king's powers, known as the *Maiestas Carolina*, but when it threatened to create noble resistance, Charles compromised, withdrawing it in 1355.

Charles IV approached imperial politics with the same realism, compromising with the Wittelsbachs and using the papal curia as a counter-weight to the centrifugal tendencies within the empire. After Clement VI died, his relations with Avignon were never again as close. When in 1355 Charles finally staged his imperial coronation in Rome, a papal representative officiated. Instead of founding a new Roman Empire, as Francesco Petrarca urged, Charles collected money from the Italian imperial cities and returned to the other side of the Alps. There, in 1356, he issued the imperial charter known as the Golden Bull. The Golden Bull established imperial election by majority vote, and confirmed the Bohemian king as the foremost secular elector, with the title of imperial cupbearer. It fixed the number of electors at seven, all imperial princes or bishops, leaving no role for the pope. The Golden Bull also urged the electoral princes to teach their children Italian and Czech as well as German.

Later in life, Charles became increasingly concerned with securing his heirs' position. He had his first surviving son, Václav, crowned King of Bohemia as a two-year-old, and in 1376 added his coronation as King of the Romans. Václav's portion of his father's realm included Bohemia, the Silesian duchies held directly by the king, part of Upper Lusatia, Lower Lusatia, the crown's German possessions, and (in theory) the supreme authority over all the crownlands. Most of Brandenburg went to Sigismund, the second son (born 1368), and Jan, the third son (born 1370), received Upper Lusatia and a piece of Brandenburg. Moravia, divided into three feudal fiefs of the Czech crown, was ruled by Jan Jindřich, younger son of John of Luxemburg, and after his death in 1375, by his sons Jošt and Prokop.

Charles's efforts to secure his inheritance also intersected with the wider problem of the pope's continuing residence at Avignon. One purpose of Charles's second journey to Rome from 1368 to 1369 was to explore moving the papal court back to the eternal city, a goal not achieved until late in the pontificate of Gregory XI, in 1377. The pope's return to Rome did not develop as planned. When Gregory XI died in 1378, his successor, Urban VI, quickly alienated his cardinals. Eventually the majority of the college (overwhelmingly French) withdrew from Rome, declared their election of Urban VI invalid, and chose one of their own number as Clement VII. Clement resettled at Avignon, dividing Western Christendom into rival allegiances. Charles IV supported the Roman papacy of Urban VI, but before he could attempt to heal the schism, he died on November 29, 1378.

Responsibility for the core of Charles IV's dominions thus fell on the shoulders of the seventeen-year-old Václav IV (1378–1419). Václav faced challenges that would have given his father pause, but he did not inherit Charles's political skill and dedication. He abandoned the policy of relying on the church to counterbalance the lords, clashing with the archbishop of Prague. The archbishop's general vicar, Jan of Pomuk, was martyred at the king's command in 1393, to be canonized years later as Saint John of Nepomuk (John Nepomucene). Václav was considered incompetent in the empire, where the religious electors deposed him in 1400 and elected an anti-king.

In Bohemia, too, Václav suffered in the competition among Charles IV's descendants. Twice he was taken prisoner, by the lords in 1394, and by his brother Sigismund in 1402, before a compromise ended the family clashes. Václav resigned his Roman title in 1410 to his cousin Jošt of Moravia, who died in 1411, whereupon it passed to Sigismund. Sigismund, who inherited at least some of his father's political skill, eventually gained recognition as emperor. These quarrels suggest that Bohemian politics was becoming more complex as new groups, including the burghers and the lower nobility, sought a voice in the political life of the kingdom. But the crisis that the Bohemian lands endured under Václav IV involved more than politics.

SOCIAL AND ECONOMIC CHANGE UNDER THE LUXEMBURGS

The remarkable cultural and economic flowering of Bohemia under Charles IV was the culmination of trends begun under the last Přemyslids, especially the wave of colonization and the development of the network of towns and smaller cities. The "Black Death" did not affect the Bohemian crownlands as it did the rest of Europe between 1347 and 1352, but this was because the Bohemian lands lay outside the main European trading routes. This fact affected European trade and the domestic market, with imports of standard consumable items (dried or salted fish, wine, spices, salt, fruits) supplemented by luxury goods for the court, nobility, church prelates, or rich burghers. Bohemian artisan products had no demand abroad, so exports consisted of raw materials, Prague silver coins, or silver ingots.

Relative to its eastern neighbors Bohemia had a well-developed town structure, but powerful patriciates existed only in Prague's Old Town, Plzeň (Pilsen), the silver-mining region with Kutná Hora and Kolín, and Cheb. In Moravia a patriciate also existed in Brno, Jihlava (Iglau, another mining center), and Olomouc. The narrowing of the cultural and political gap between the Bohemian crownlands and Western Europe thus affected a narrow layer, the urban patricians, the noble and royal courts, and the church. The commoners, relatively isolated and still influenced by medieval concepts of space and time, valued stability and the familiar above all.

Crisis caught up with the Bohemian lands at the end of the fourteenth century, beginning with the belated arrival of the plague in 1380. It carried off up to 15 percent of the population, reducing demand and disrupting production. Silver output declined, causing inflation and disrupting trade. Landholders' cash incomes fell, leading them either to ease the peasants' obligations to keep them on the land or to use force to the same end. The plague years and the economic decline were accompanied by internal Luxemburg family conflicts and clashes with the great lords, resulting in a series of petty civil wars. The ruler's prestige and authority declined, to be replaced by the "territorial peace" or *landfrýd*, an agreement to preserve law and order, in which the ruler was one among many parties (even if in first place). Many lesser nobles had few choices except to become the client of a great lord, a soldier of fortune, or a brigand.

Social tension erupted in acts of rage and violence. On April 18, 1389, the Prague ghetto was looted and then burned, and many hundreds were murdered. Perhaps the pogrom of 1389 foreshadowed upheavals to come, but it also expressed the hostility toward Jews spreading in fourteenth-century Europe.[13] These problems also stimulated criticism of society and its powerful institutions. The church drew the most criticism, since it had itself been in crisis for much of the century. The years of the "Babylonian captivity" in Avignon were followed by the schism of 1378, and the attempt to resolve the conflict at the Council of Pisa (1409) ended with three rival popes, each claiming to be the true keeper of the keys of St. Peter. A desire for reform spread in many parts of Europe, both among the university masters and the laity. Social and economic crisis, the decline of important political and religious institutions, and a domestic and international movement for reform culminated in the Bohemian crownlands in the Hussite revolution.

4 Kingdom of Heretics, or, Against All

On July 6, 1415, the Council of Constance paused in its deliberations while sentence was carried out on a condemned heretic, Master Jan Hus of Bohemia. The pyre that ended Hus's life ignited a flame that would spread through the Bohemian crownlands and transform the course of their history, remaining one of the most disputed themes in the Czechs' evaluation of their own past. Was it only one among many medieval heretical or reform movements, or was it something uniquely Czech? Was it primarily a religious protest against an overworldly church, with strong chiliastic overtones, or was it a social revolutionary movement proclaiming freedom of conscience? Was it the Czechs' greatest moment, or one of the darkest pages in their history?[1] Today's Czechs may not venerate the Hussite period the way the nineteenth-century nationalists did, but those nationalist images of the Hussites, expressed in Alois Jirásek's historical novel *Proti všem* (Against All), for example, remain part of the historical consciousness of the present.[2]

THE BOHEMIAN REFORM MOVEMENT

The reform movement in Bohemia developed from stimuli similar to those that resulted in heretical movements in the towns and cities of Europe from the twelfth century onward. Some heretics may have joined the wave of colonists entering Bohemia, especially the Waldensians, followers of a merchant from Lyons named Waldo or Valdes. Charles IV established the inquisition in Prague, and heresy was vigorously pursued.[3] The *devotio moderna* (new devotion), emphasizing the significance of religious experience at the individual, inward level provided another influence. This trend found supporters at the Cistercian monastery of Zbraslav and the newly founded house of Augustinian canons at Roudnice (Raudnitz).

In contrast to this deepening of the individual Christian's religious experience, the church as an institution had become increasingly worldly. Church offices paid the salaries of Charles IV's officials, which led to abuses, neglect of religious duties, and the use of inadequate replacements for genuine pastoral work. In addition, the pope's fiscal demands, already significant during the "Babylonian captivity," were only doubled after the schism of 1378. Simony (the sale of church offices), the sale of indulgences, and constant demands for tithes or special contributions burdened both the ordinary faithful and the church as an institution in the Bohemian crownlands. Though wealthy in terms of land—it owned approximately one-third of all the land in the kingdom—the church sometimes found it hard to meet the demands of the curia.[4]

The Court, the University, and Reform Teaching

Charles IV supported the bishop's invitation to a reforming preacher, the Austrian Augustinian Konrad Waldhauser, to come to Prague in 1363. Waldhauser, who denounced simony and other failings, inspired a Czech reformer, Jan Milíč of Kroměříž, to give up his position in the king's chancellery to devote himself entirely to preaching. Matěj of Janov emphasized the importance of the Bible as the source of true Christian practice. Tomáš Štítný, a lesser noble from southern Moravia, devoted himself to explaining the basic elements of Christian faith in Czech. These reform preachers and writers found eager listeners among the citizens of Prague. In 1391 some of them founded the Bethlehem chapel, devoted to preaching in the vernacular and large enough to hold three thousand listeners. Through the Bethlehem chapel this reform tendency joined with another based at the Prague university.

The university's four nations, the Bohemian, Bavarian, Saxon, and

Polish, were divided by overlapping rivalries. The Bohemian nation's masters were mostly Czechs, while the three other nations were almost all Germans, yet each had one vote in deciding university matters. The nations also quarreled over the nature of general concepts. The "nominalists" (mostly the foreign masters) asserted that general concepts are merely names grouping similar specific phenomena; the "realists" (mostly the Czechs) insisted that general concepts, or "universals," did have genuine reality. Finally, the masters divided over the need for reform. The English Franciscan John Wyclif's works, especially his realism and the criticism of the church he based upon it, acted as a catalyst. The masters of the three foreign nations used their majority in 1403 to have the university condemn forty-five theses taken from Wyclif's texts as errors.[5]

When the university refused (again by a vote of the three foreign nations against the one Czech nation) to support Václav IV's call for a church council at Pisa, the conflict peaked. Václav IV hoped to use the council of Pisa to regain recognition of his claim to the Roman throne, so he issued a decree in 1409 that gave three votes to the domestic, Czech nation and one collective vote to the three foreign nations. The Decree of Kutná Hora transformed the university of Prague into a powerful reform center, but the foreign masters, bachelors, and students departed for other universities (especially the newly founded one in Leipzig) where they denounced their Czech rivals as heretics.

Master Jan Hus

Master Jan Hus, since 1402 preacher at the Bethlehem chapel, emerged as the leader of the Czech reformers. Through the Bethlehem chapel, the university masters' reform program spread among the laity, leading to a running conflict between Hus and the recently appointed archbishop of Prague. The archbishop banned preaching in "private" places (such as the Bethlehem chapel), sided with the Roman pope, Gregory XII, against the king, and burned Wyclif's works at his court. Hus responded by defending Wyclif and attacking book-burning, and appealed to the pope. The archbishop excommunicated Hus, but many of the higher nobility and even the king and queen defended the Bohemian kingdom and the reform party.

Nevertheless, Hus and the reformers parted company with Václav IV in 1412, when the king consented to the sale of indulgences in Prague by representatives of the Council of Pisa's pope, John XXIII. Hus denounced the sale of indulgences as simony. In October 1412 the Pisan pope pronounced a renewed excommunication on Hus, and threatened to place Prague under interdict. An interdict would have meant no religious sacraments for the entire population of Prague, so Hus left the city, appealing to the judgment of Christ.

Already the reform movement had won noble supporters, including several highly placed figures, so Hus found refuge with noble friends in the south and southeast of Bohemia. There he wrote a tract against simony and his treatise *De ecclesia*, and preached his message among the common people. The nobility had asserted a right to defend the common good under both Přemyslids and Luxemburgs, and of course the prospect of taking over church lands attracted them. Many lords also genuinely accepted the precepts of Hus and other preachers as God's word. Lesser nobles also joined the reform movement. In Bohemian towns where the Czech-speaking element competed with the original, often German-speaking patriciate, the Hussite message (with its connection to the Czech vernacular) found ready hearers. In Moravian towns Hussite preaching evoked little echo, though it spread through parts of the countryside. The Hussite movement gained few supporters in the other lands of the Bohemian crown.

The Council of Pisa's failure to end the schism gave impetus to the conciliar movement, which asserted that the pope was not absolute ruler of the church but was subordinate to the whole body represented by the church in council.[6] As secular head of Christendom, Sigismund called for a council to meet at the imperial city of Constance in 1414. Sigismund wanted to resolve the schism, and also to calm the situation in the Bohemian crownlands, to which he was heir. Early in 1414, noblemen in Sigismund's service brought Hus an invitation to attend the council for a public hearing, promising him an imperial safe-conduct pass.

Hus accepted the invitation to attend the Council of Constance knowing the risks, but hoping that a hearing would vindicate him and Bohemia against the charge of heresy. Shortly after his arrival, however, he was imprisoned and examined (safe-conduct or no safe-conduct), and his public hearing resembled a show trial.[7] Stubbornly, Hus refused to recant errors that he had never taught, declaring that to go against his conscience, even at the behest of a church council, would be a mortal sin. An eyewitness account of his death on July 6, 1415, records Hus's final statement: "God is my witness that I have never taught nor preached those things of which I have been falsely accused and which have been ascribed to me through false testimony, but the foremost aim of my preaching and all my other actions and writings has been only to preserve the people from sin. In the true Gospel that I have written, taught, and preached from the words and teachings of the holy doctors, I am willing to die gladly today."[8]

THE HUSSITE REVOLUTION

News of Hus's death provoked a powerful reaction among his friends and supporters in Bohemia. Members of the nobility sent a strongly worded protest letter to the council, sealed by 452 of their number, representing roughly one third of the 90 or so families of lords. Hus's noble supporters found allies among the masters at the Prague university, where Jakoubek of Stříbro (Mies), Hus's friend and student, took a leading role. Jakoubek introduced the requirement of regular, frequent Holy Communion in the forms of both bread and wine. Before his death Hus approved this development. The insistence on communion in both kinds (*sub utraque specie*) made the chalice the Hussite emblem and gave them one of their common designations, Utraquists. When the Council of Constance formally condemned giving the chalice to the laity, the Prague university replied with a decree asserting its orthodoxy in 1417.

The Hussite cause spread even prior to the Council of Constance among the lesser royal towns and also, thanks in part to Hus's sojourn in southern Bohemia, among the peasants in the countryside. Having suffered through the years of plague, economic decline, and moral crisis, many people were ready to act on God's command to reform the secularized church. Hussite noblemen began to staff the parish churches on their land with supporters of the chalice, and some even began to secularize other church properties. Hussite supporters called for the authority of the Bible and the example of the Christian life to be honored in practice. Thus even before the outbreak of the coming revolutionary events, the Hussites included representatives of all political estates and social levels, who generally pursued a common goal.

The Council of Constance ended its deliberations in 1418, having removed all three competing popes and elected their successor, Martin V. Only the scandalous state of affairs in the Bohemian crownlands remained unresolved. Sigismund threatened his brother Václav with a crusade if he did not take decisive action against the Hussites, but the king only gave in partially. He restored all but three of Prague's churches to the Roman priests, and named several opponents of reform to the town council of Prague's New Town. In the countryside, too, the Hussites lost many churches to the Catholics. In an atmosphere of tension and apocalyptic expectation, Hussite priests held services outside, especially on hilltops, to which they gave biblical names (Tábor, Horeb). These services gathered the more radical elements in an expression of popular piety laced with expectation of the Last Judgment. At the summit called Tábor, Hussite radicals from all over Bohemia and Moravia gathered in July 1419.

On July 30, 1419, the electric atmosphere broke into thunder. A radical preacher in Prague's New Town, Jan Želivský, led an attack on the town hall, the mob threw the anti-Hussite town councillors out the window (the first Defenestration of Prague), and Hussites replaced them. The king accepted this change, but the events so affected him that on August 16, 1419, he died, according to the chronicler, "roaring like a lion."[9] With the attack on the New Town Hall and the king's death, the Hussite movement entered a revolutionary phase.

In Defense of the True Faith

For the next seventeen years, until the agreement between the Hussites and the Council of Basel, the Hussites in the Bohemian lands were formally at war with the rest of Western Christendom.[10] The anti-Hussite crusades were supported by the papal curia, Sigismund, and the conciliar movement. Internal conflicts, not only with those towns and nobles who remained loyal to Rome and Sigismund, but among the various Hussite tendencies, also marked this period. It was not long before several distinct groupings emerged among Hus's followers. The moderates included almost all the great Hussite noblemen, a part of the lower nobility, and some patricians of Prague's Old Town. This tendency considered Hus's prerevolutionary teachings sufficient, and when it became clear that the rest of Europe would not heed them, sought an agreement to allow an autonomous, Hussite church within the Roman Catholic communion.

Prague (except for the university masters and moderates among the Old Town burghers) occupied a place somewhere between the moderates and the radicals. As capital city it enjoyed a certain prestige that it could hope to translate into influence. Continual quarreling between Old Town and New Town weakened its position, however, with the New Town burghers tending to more radical views, while Old Town generally followed Jakoubek of Stříbro and Jan Rokycana.

Hussite radicals, strong in certain towns and in the countryside, never formed a single stream, but shared a common aim of reorganizing life as quickly and thoroughly as possible to conform with the law of God. Already at the beginning of the revolution, three general branches of radicals emerged. In eastern Bohemia, they went by the name of Orebites, from the name they gave their place of assembly. Their religious teaching resembled Prague's, but politically they were less willing to compromise. Another powerful radical force was the Táborites, so called from the fortified camp they had built on a hilltop named after the biblical Mount Tábor. Originally, Tábor was founded as a community of brothers and sisters, where most property would be held in common, as the earliest Christians in the Bible did. Within a year of its establishment, however, Tábor was collecting contributions from the surrounding villages, and during the next year the most radical sectarians were forced to leave. Eventually Tábor developed into a military and artisan center, leading a group of southern and southwestern Bohemian cities in a powerful military league. Tábor alone created its own religious organization, electing Mikuláš of Pelhřimov (known as Biskupec) as elder. A final radical center in the northern Bohemian towns of Žatec (Saatz) and Louny (Laun) usually cooperated with the Táborites.

The fundamental Hussite program, accepted by all as a minimum, was worked out during meetings in May 1420 in Prague. Summarized into the four Articles of Prague, this program demanded: (1) complete freedom to preach the word of God (that is, as the Hussites understood it), (2) the granting of communion in both kinds to clergy and laity, (3) the renunciation of worldly property and secular power by the church, and (4) the punishment of mortal sins and other transgressions by the secular authority. The first three articles expressed the basic criticisms of the reform movement; the fourth was added at the insistence of the Táborites and other radicals.

With Václav's death in 1419, Sigismund, Charles IV's second surviving son, claimed the Czech throne. The moderate Old Town burghers and some Hussite lords opened negotiations with him in December 1419, but Sigismund refused to discuss anything before his coronation.

Meanwhile, most of the Moravian nobility swore their oath of loyalty to him as margrave. At the imperial diet in Breslau in March 1420 Sigismund also published the papal proclamation of a crusade against the Hussite heretics. The noble lords in Bohemia responded by denying Sigismund's claim to the throne, but a leading Hussite nobleman, Čeněk of Vartenberk, opened the gates of the Prague castle to Sigismund's soldiers in May 1420. Prague's Hussite-dominated towns appealed to the Táborite and Orebite radicals for assistance, and they responded by sending forces to the aid of the capital. Sigismund besieged the city, but could not dislodge the Hussites from the height of Vítkov (now Žižkov), overlooking Prague from the east. Táborite forces commanded by Jan Žižka of Trocnov turned back all attacks with the help of reinforcements from Prague. Žižka, a lesser nobleman from Southern Bohemia, nearly sixty and blind in one eye from years as a soldier-of-fortune, quickly became the most feared Hussite military leader.

The failure to close the blockade around Prague meant the collapse of the first Hussite crusade. Sigismund hurriedly had himself crowned in St. Vitus's cathedral, but shortly thereafter the crusading armies began to disperse. The citizens of Prague's two towns formed an alliance, created an elected joint council, and proceeded with far-reaching secularization of church property. Similar seizures of church estates were carried out in the Hussite countryside, and even in the Catholic areas church property ended up in secular hands, since Sigismund used it as collateral to gain desperately needed funds for his military operations.

The Hussite armies, fighting in the conviction that they were defending God's truth as well as their homeland, turned back successive crusades launched against them from the Empire. In 1421 an imperial army invaded Bohemia and besieged Žatec, but withdrew when reinforcements under the would-be king Sigismund failed to arrive. Sigismund's army occupied Kutná Hora, but the united Hussite armies under Žižka (now blind in both eyes) forced it to withdraw and defeated it utterly near Německý Brod (Deutsch Brod, today Havlíčkův Brod) in January 1422. After Žižka's death at Přibyslav in Moravia on October 11, 1424, his followers (now calling themselves Orphans) cooperated with Táborite forces to crush a Saxon invasion at Ustí nad Labem (Aussig) in June 1426.

By 1427, a Hussite bloc of Táborites, Orphans, and Praguers dominated the main lines of Czech politics. In each camp, the leading figure was a priest. Prokop Holý (the Bald), also known as Prokop the Great, led the Táborites, while the Orphans' leader was another Prokop, called Malý (the Small) or Prokůpek. Jan Rokycana was the most influential figure in the Prague league, though he did not take a direct military role. Prokop Holý argued strongly that after years of defending their homeland, the Hussites should go on the offensive. First they had to meet another crusading army that besieged Stříbro (Mies) in western Bohemia, but ran away before offering resistance to a united Hussite army. By August 1427, the Hussites were ready to take the struggle to their opponents' territory. Already the connections to Moravia had facilitated Hussite invasions into northern Hungary (today's Slovakia). Other campaigns into Silesia, Upper and Lower Lusatia, and Austria were followed in December 1429 by a combined invasion through Meissen into Franconia by no fewer than five Hussite columns.

Although the Hussite armies carried out propaganda, economic considerations also drove this tactical change. By the later 1420s, the two main radical Hussite leagues, the Táborites and the Orphans, had established permanent field armies. The Bohemian economy could not supply such a large community (as many as 12,000 men), so the field armies had to live from the countryside or booty. Even before the emergence of the field armies, Hussite tactics had proved remarkably successful. In addition to the tricks of the brigand's trade, familiar to many Hussite captains, the major Hussite methods of warfare were creative adaptations to circumstances (such as the famous war wagons), mostly credited to Žižka. He guarded the movements of his infantry forces with columns of war wagons, which could form into wagon forts if threatened by the enemy. The Hussites also rapidly adopted the gunpowder weapons that were beginning to enter European military arsenals via the Turks.

Catholic Europe proclaimed yet one more anti-Hussite crusade in 1431. Two armies invaded the kingdom. The one coming from the west met up with the Hussites at Domažlice on August 14, 1431, and there the crusaders took to headlong flight supposedly just from hearing the strains of the Hussite war hymn, *Ktož sú boží bojovníci* (All ye warriors of God). So complete was their rout that Cardinal Cesarini, who organized the crusade for the pope, abandoned all his baggage, including his cardinal's hat and the pope's proclamation of the crusade.

Repeated crusading invasions usually created a united Hussite front, but otherwise the various parties frequently quarreled among each other, especially after a major victory removed the need for unity. A Hussite diet in June 1421 proclaimed the four articles of Prague a fundamental law of the land, and declared Sigismund's coronation in Prague invalid. The diet also elected a commission made up of five great lords, seven members of the lesser nobility, and eight burghers of the Hussite towns to administer the kingdom. No agreement could be reached about the vacant throne. Some radical Táborites suggested the Hussites dispense with a king altogether. Žižka and the mainstream of the radicals joined with Prague and the eastern Bohemian Hussites in favoring a member of the Polish-Lithuanian Jagiellonian dynasty. Jakoubek of Stříbro alone dared to suggest selecting a worthy Hussite nobleman, arguing that only such a ruler could guarantee the Hussite achievements.

In Prague the defeat of the second crusade led to open conflict between conservative Utraquist burghers from Old Town and New Town radicals. Jan Želivský and his followers took over the city government and united the two towns under a dictatorship supported by the radicals. By February 1422 Želivský had lost the support of the other Hussite leagues, and the conservatives in Prague struck back. They invited him to the Old Town city hall, arrested him, and in March had him executed. Until 1427, the conservative Prague burghers in alliance with the Utraquist nobility once more controlled the capital. The attempt to settle the succession failed, however, when the Polish-Lithuanian prince Sigismund Korybut, after a brief and turbulent period of residence in Bohemia, was summoned back to Poland in 1423.

Internal strife in Tábor forced Žižka to leave at the end of 1422 and establish himself in eastern Bohemia. Most towns of eastern Bohemia and local Hussite noblemen supported Žižka. His main pillar of strength, however, remained the field army, which had developed into a permanent organization with its own administration. Žižka's new brotherhood defeated a coalition of moderate Hussites, the conservatives in Prague, and members of the Catholic nobility at Malešov in June 1424, and seemed set to advance on Prague. Negotiations led by Jan Rokycana convinced Žižka to refrain, and instead both sides agreed on the military expedition to help the Hussites in Moravia on which Žižka met his death.

After the victory at Ústí in 1426, once more internal tensions flared up, this time within Prague. Korybut (who had returned to head the Prague-led league of Hussite towns) provoked suspicion among the Hussite burghers by his rapprochement with the Catholic side. An uprising of both Prague towns in 1427 forced many of the less radical masters to leave the university and held Korybut hostage in the countryside.

Eventually he was released, but never returned to Prague, finding scope for his ambitions in Silesia until called back into the family struggles of the Jagiellonians in Poland-Lithuania, where he died in 1435.

Toward a Compromise

The victory at Domažlice and the convocation of an ecumenical council at Basel in the same year helped finally to bring about talks between the Hussites and the Catholic church. The conciliar movement had established a requirement that church councils meet regularly, but Martin V and his successors did not accept the doctrine of papal subordination to the church in council. The council for its part sought a major issue—such as a reconciliation with the Hussites—to enhance its prestige and position against the pope. Cardinal Cesarini, who knew the futility of using force, chaired the council's sessions. Sigismund, still hoping to occupy the Czech throne before his death, also strongly supported the overture to the Hussites, which was extended in October 1431. A Bohemian diet in February 1432 accepted the invitation and from January to April 1433 a delegation led by Prokop Holý debated with the council in Basel. They did not overcome their differences, but agreed to continue negotiating in Prague.

To force greater flexibility on the Catholic side, a force of Táborites and Orphans laid siege to Plzeň in the summer of 1433. Amid increasingly open disputes among the military leaders (Prokop Holý was dismissed, but his replacements proved less competent), the radical armies suffered a disastrous defeat on an expedition into Bavaria for supplies. The Utraquist and Catholic nobility, together with Prague under Jan Rokycana, now formed an alliance of convenience and gained control of the whole city. In response the radicals lifted the siege of Plzeň, restored Prokop Holý to his place at the head of the Táborite armies, and turned back to secure their rear. On May 30, 1434, the two sides met in battle at Lipany. The result was an overwhelming defeat for the radical brotherhoods, the death of Prokop Holý, and the end of the field armies. Subject, like so much connected with the Hussite movement, to conflicting interpretations, the battle of Lipany certainly marked the end of the revolutionary phase of Hussitism.[11]

The Hussites in the land diet now represented the moderate strains of Utraquism, and since the diet was the negotiating partner for the would-be king and the council, their significance increased. Jan Rokycana's election as archbishop of Prague in 1435 solidified their position. The theologians at Basel were loath to accept the Articles of Prague, but the aging Sigismund wanted general recognition as king before his death. Finally, in 1436 a compromise known as the *Compactata* or Compacts of Basel was reached. It guaranteed communion in both kinds to the Hussite laity in Bohemia and Moravia (not the other Bohemian crown-lands), while accepting the Utraquist communion as part of the one, apostolic, Catholic church. The council accepted the remaining three articles only in a watered-down form or still resisted them. In spite of these qualifications, however, the *Compactata* were the first recognition of a separate confessional group within Western Christendom.

The changes in property relations wrought during the Hussite wars could not be undone. Too many nobles, both Hussite and Catholic, had seized church estates, and the royal domain had also suffered greatly. Overall the church in Bohemia lost four-fifths of its property, though in Moravia its position was rather better. Some towns, especially Prague's Old Town and Louny, increased their landholdings, and Sigismund made Tábor a royal free town with moderate estates in the surrounding area. The greatest beneficiaries, however, were the nobles. Even many of the lesser nobility emerged from the conflicts enriched, which increased their weight at the diets. In contrast the clergy as an estate disappeared altogether. The resulting shifts in political power meant that the traditional counterweights to the nobles, the church and the king, were much weaker, while the towns (in which the Czech-speaking element had largely replaced the German) had increased in influence and to some extent in wealth. Although the common interests of those who benefited from the Hussite revolution prevented a wholesale restoration of the prewar situation, religious differences continued to divide every social level.

BOHEMIA
UNDER THE HUSSITE KING,
JIŘÍ OF PODĚBRADY

On August 14, 1436, Sigismund of Luxemburg was festively proclaimed King of Bohemia and the lands of the Crown of St. Václav on the square at Jihlava in southern Moravia.[12] The remnants of radical resistance were overcome by the agreement with Tábor and the capture and execution of the last great radical captain, Jan Roháč of Dubá (September 1437). The Land Court once more began regular sessions, but clashes between Sigismund and Jan Rokycana, the Utraquist archbishop of Prague, ended with the latter seeking the safety of his eastern Bohemian estates. Increasing conflict with the Hussite nobles and burghers convinced Sigismund (also concerned with the political situation in his Hungarian realm) to leave for Hungary. Whether his departure was the prelude to renewed conflict with the Hussites remains unknown, since Sigismund died at Znojmo in Moravia on December 9, 1437.

The succession question exposed the cleavages within the Bohemian political classes. Sigismund's son-in-law and sometime Margrave of Moravia, Albrecht of Habsburg (reigned as Bohemian king, 1437–1439), was the traditional choice. The eastern Bohemian Hussites, supported by Tábor and Rokycana's representatives, urged the estates to choose the Polish prince Kazimir. Military conflict between the Habsburg and Polish supporters ended when Albrecht died in October 1439, leaving behind him a pregnant wife. For the next decade the kingdom was maintained by each district's *landfrýd*. Jiří of Poděbrady's eastern Bohemian *landfrýd* supported strict adherence to the *Compactata* as a fundamental law of the land. Fearing that the Prague Utraquists were too accommodating to the Catholics, Jiří's forces seized the town in a coup in September 1448 and established Rokycana's followers in control. In 1452, Jiří of Poděbrady was elected governor of the land with the support even of many Catholic lords.

As land governor, Jiří subdued Tábor, dissolving the separate Táborite church organization. This move united all the Hussite streams in one group with Jan Rokycana as its spiritual head. The Catholic league of Strakonice (Strakonitz) and the Plzeň *landfrýd* also accepted Jiří's authority. When Albrecht's son Ladislav (called Posthumous since he was born after his father's death) formally assumed rule in 1453 over the Kingdom of Bohemia, Austria, and Hungary, Jiří became Bohemian regent for the thirteen-year-old king.

During Ladislav Posthumous's minority, Jiří partly rebuilt the king's own domains and maintained law and order on the trade routes. When Ladislav died in 1457, shortly before his age of majority, the Czech estates gave up Charles IV's succession arrangements and on March 2, 1458, elected Jiří of Poděbrady king. "All true Czechs rejoiced therefrom," wrote a chronicler, "many shed tears of joy, that their dear Lord God had finally liberated them from the power of the German kings, who always bore ill will to the Czechs, especially those who held to the Holy Writ [the Hussites]."[13] Jakoubek of Stříbro's advice, that to preserve the Hussite achievements the Czechs would have to elect a Hussite king, was finally followed.

The nobles' election of a member of their own order to the vacant throne was a previously unheard of step, though the Hungarian lords had shortly before elected Mátyás Korvin (Matthias Corvinus) king. Jiří of Poděbrady was not only an upstart, he was a "Czech heretic" whose family had close personal ties with Hus and Žižka. In addition, his election was at first accepted only by Bohemia; the other lands of the Crown of St. Václav refused to acknowledge him. Adroit diplomacy and marriage contracts between his daughters and neighboring potentates (including Korvin) gained Jiří both domestic and international acceptance.

This promising start quickly ran into difficulties in Rome. The popes had never formally accepted the Council of Basel's decision regarding the Hussites, and when a Czech embassy went to Rome in 1462 to urge Pius II to accept the *Compactata*, he declared them invalid, and the Czech Hussites heretics. When the pope excommunicated Jiří and declared him deposed in 1466, Jiří's son-in-law Mátyás Korvin placed himself at the head of a renewed anti-Hussite crusade. In 1468 he overran much of Moravia. Fortunes of war fluctuated, but politically Mátyás Korvin scored a great coup when some Moravian Catholic lords elected him king at Olomouc in May 1469. Both Lusatias and Silesia quickly recognized his claim to the Crown of St. Václav, in effect limiting Jiří's authority only to the Utraquist regions of Bohemia proper. Now in the kingdom of two religions there were two kings. War continued off and on until March 1471, when Jiří of Poděbrady died.

Before his death, Jiří urged the estates to offer the crown to a Jagiellonian prince. The diet at Kutná Hora in 1471 duly elected Vladislav (Władysław) king of Bohemia. Immediately Vladislav II (1471–1516) had to fight Mátyás Korvin for his new crown. When it became clear that neither side could win a decisive victory, a negotiated agreement in 1479 accepted that Vladislav would rule in Bohemia, while Mátyás would continue to rule in Moravia and the other lands of the Crown of St. Václav, and both would call themselves King of Bohemia.

Although the agreement of 1479 stabilized the position of Bohemia, at the price of loosening the ties between the crownlands, the reintegration of the Catholic lords into the land's institutions was not easy. In an effort to gain papal recognition, Vladislav tried to replace the Hussite town councils, provoking an uprising of all three Prague towns in September 1483, in the course of which Vladislav's councillors were murdered and replaced by new ones loyal to the chalice. Support from other royal towns and leading figures of the Utraquist nobility ensured that the king (who did not risk reentering Prague for a year) accepted these dramatic changes.

The Prague uprising of 1483 demonstrated that a resolution to the problem of coexistence of Catholic and Utraquist by force was impossible. Thus it led directly to the conclusion, at a land diet at Kutná Hora in March 1485, of a formal agreement establishing religious toleration between the two confessions. The religious peace of Kutná Hora accepted the *Compactata* as a fundamental law of the land, ending the period of the Hussite revolution and resulting wars. The moderate, Utraquist version of Hussitism was established as the majority confession, but both Catholic and Utraquist were recognized as subjects of the monarch and members of the body politic. The succeeding years showed that the coalition supporting Prague in 1483 was to be the last of the great religious leagues that crossed social and political boundaries.

The majority of the kingdom's inhabitants (approximately 70 percent) followed the Utraquist church, headed by the elected bishop Jan Rokycana, with a seat at the church of the Virgin Mary before Týn, on Old Town Square. St. Vitus's cathedral remained in Catholic hands, but the Catholic church in Bohemia suffered great losses. Monasteries were destroyed, the bishopric of Litomyšl disappeared, and the archbishop's throne in Prague remained empty until 1561. The Catholic church was headed by an administrator in the Prague castle. During the quarrels between Jiří of Poděbrady and the papacy, the administrator moved to Plzeň. A dissident Hussite trend known as the Unity of Brethren (*Unitas Fratrum, Jednota bratrská*) was left out of the peace of Kutná Hora. Rooted in the teachings of Petr Chelčický, the Brethren arose out of dissatisfaction with developments after Lipany. Brethren rejected worldly wealth and power while advocating passive resistance to authority and voluntary poverty.[14] Though intermittently persecuted, they found protectors among some Bohemian noblemen because they were industrious and peaceful subjects. In Moravia, the situation was somewhat different, thanks to the survival of the bishopric of Olomouc and most of the monasteries, while the other lands of the Crown of St. Václav remained entirely Catholic until the Lutheran reformation.

The years of stabilization under Jiří of Poděbrady saw a cultural quickening. The first printing press in the Bohemian crownlands was set up in Catholic Plzeň in 1468. Its usefulness as a polemical weapon was quickly recognized, and presses spread to Brno, Prague, Olomouc, Vimperk, and Kutná Hora. By the 1460s humanist thought once more began to enter intellectual circles in the Czech lands, more quickly among the Catholics than the Hussites. The Jagiellonian court began a major reconstruction of the Prague castle. Vladislav II took up residence there in 1485, leaving the royal court in Prague's Old Town. Even before his move, the Old Town burghers had erected the late Gothic tower known as the Powder Tower (Prašná Brana) nearby, the work of the self-taught Matěj Rejsek. Rejsek's skills were in high demand, both in Prague and in other places such as Kutná Hora, where he worked on the completion of St. Barbara's church and built the decorated town fountain.

Most secular architecture still reflected Gothic features, as can be seen in some of the castle reconstructions Benedikt Ried undertook for leading nobles. Early signs of the Renaissance include the windows Ried incorporated into his masterpiece, the late-Gothic Vladislav Hall of the Prague castle, and features of its Louis wing. Towns, too, increased their building activities with the return of more settled times and a slow economic recovery. In church architecture the Gothic remained dominant through the late fifteenth and the sixteenth century. In other areas of architecture and arts, Gothic was already giving way to Renaissance influences, just as religious issues began to give way after the religious peace of Kutná Hora in 1485 to political and social conflicts between the two estates that the revolution had most strengthened, the lords (both great nobles and gentry) and the towns. Under a new dynasty, the Renaissance would arrive in full force, yet religious issues and their political consequences would also remain vitally important to the culture of the Bohemian crownlands.

5 Recovery and Renaissance

The ongoing jousting for influence in the Bohemian crownlands took place in a dramatically altered world. The rise of the Turkish threat in the Mediterranean stimulated navigators from Portugal and Spain, followed quickly by the English, French, and Dutch, to embark on the high seas in search of alternate routes to the riches of the East. The "Voyages of Discovery" shifted the political and economic center of gravity in Europe to the former European periphery through the conquest of overseas empires and the subsequent commercial revolution. The widening of the physical horizon had its counterpart in the theoretical understanding of the heavens and the beginnings of the scientific revolution. These changes echoed in cultural life, where the Renaissance superseded the late Gothic, and Italian humanism found ready imitators throughout Europe. In the Bohemian crownlands these new trends provided fruitful stimulus to local cultural developments, resulting in a synthesis in which they took on locally specific forms.

THE BOHEMIAN KINGDOM IN THE HANDS OF THE ESTATES (1485–1620)

Changes on the European stage also affected the Bohemian crownlands and the Czechs. The looming Turkish threat directly contributed to the eclipse of the Bohemian-Hungarian Jagiellonians by the Habsburgs. While the rise of Muscovy distracted the Polish-Lithuanian Jagiellonians, the Habsburgs united the crowns of St. Stephen and St. Václav, once a bone of contention among Přemyslids, Luxemburgs, Mátyás Korvin, and Jagiellonians. Thus it was the Habsburgs who faced the Reformation at the head of the Catholic side. The Protestant Reformation struck rich soil in the Bohemian lands, breaking the isolation of the Czech Utraquists. Lutheranism spread rapidly among them and their German-speaking countrymen, while Calvinism influenced the Unity of Brethren. Since the Habsburg king of Bohemia was also Holy Roman Emperor after 1556 and thus secular leader of universal, Catholic Christendom, conflicts between crown and the overwhelmingly Protestant estates in Bohemia over political power intersected with, and reinforced, religious divisions.

Society and Economy in the Estates Monarchy

The estates were fundamental to the structure of society, still theoretically based on the medieval doctrine of the threefold people, lords, clergy, and others. Each estate within this order was fixed and supposedly immutable, though contemporaries complained that pride drove some to seek to rise above their station.[1] There were several marginalized groups who had no settled place in the order, including vagabonds and beggars, the poorest town-dwellers, wage-laborers, and those considered infidels, such as Jews.[2] In the narrower sense, the estates were those whose ownership of land gave them political rights. In this sense the Estates were a political community, and each Bohemian crownland had its own Estates. By the end of the Hussite revolution there were three Estates represented in the Bohemian diet: the lords, the knights, and the free towns.[3] In Moravia and Lower Lusatia the church retained its position in the diet. Upper Lusatia's diet had only two Estates, the lords and the towns; in Silesia there were dietines for some of the individual principalities, and a general diet of the princes.[4]

These Estates competed among themselves and with the crown. When Vladislav II assumed the throne, as the Old Czech Annals noted, "the new king was still young, had no money, no idea how to wage war, and the royal estates and castles were firmly in the hands of the Czech lords who were his supporters."[5] Royal authority in the Bohemian kingdom weakened further after 1490, when Vladislav also became king of

Hungary and moved to Buda. Thereafter, he returned to Prague on two occasions, and then only briefly. The king's absence meant that the affairs of the kingdom were left in the hands of the Estates.

The most important political institution of the Estates monarchy was the Land Diet. The diet approved the ruler's requests for taxes, but it could also legislate, grant citizenship, permit local military forces to be used abroad, and generally seek the common good. The diet's decisions were written into the Land Registers, which made them law. By the late fifteenth century, they appeared in print. The land diet of Bohemia considered itself first among the lands of the Bohemian crown, claiming the right to elect the king. There were local dietines for some frontier areas and the fourteen circuits into which the kingdom was divided. The dietines elected the knightly representatives to the land diet and dealt with circuit affairs. The king could summon a general diet of all five crownlands to meet in Prague. General diets met for royal coronations or to consider pressing matters of defense, religion, or security; eleven times between 1530 and 1595 they were summoned to provide men or money to meet the Turkish threat. Ferdinand I tried to convoke a meeting of the Estates of the Bohemian kingdom, the Austrian duchies, and Hungary, but the Bohemian and Hungarian Estates refused to leave their own lands.[6]

The Land Court was the highest legal instance in the land. An exclusively noble tribunal, it had no representation for the towns. The king presided over the court if he were present, and the supreme burggrave in his absence. Its officers included the land judge, the supreme notary, who kept its records, and the supreme chamberlain, who maintained the land registers. These and other holders of land offices amounted to a "government." Many officials had originally been direct servants of the ruler, but now swore allegiance both to the king and the Estates community. The supreme burggrave of the Prague castle, who represented the king in his absence, was the most important of them. The supreme chancellor gave his consent to the publication of the more important royal decrees, and commanded a chancellery that extended to all five lands of the Crown of St. Václav. The chamberlain administered the royal estates including the royal towns. Other officials included the burggraves of Karlštejn and Hradec Králové. The knightly Estate provided the land notary, the burggrave of Hradec Králové, and sometimes the chamberlain (who otherwise could be a burgher of Prague Old Town); all the other offices were filled by the great lords. These officers made up the royal council, granting a relatively small group of powerful lords and knights a preponderant influence in the affairs of the kingdom. This structure remained in place until after 1620.[7]

Without a strong royal power, conflict within the Estates surfaced easily, especially after the religious peace of Kutná Hora. In earlier decades an alliance between the Utraquist lesser nobles and the towns usually countered the largely Catholic greater lords, but shortly after 1485 a realignment took place setting the towns against the nobility (both the lords and the knights). These conflicts arose not only out of the lords' long-established attitude that they had a special right to decide the kingdom's affairs, but also from economic motives.

The tumultuous century from 1380 to 1483 had a dramatic impact on the lords' incomes.[8] Cash payments from subject peasants and towns declined owing to population loss and inflation, and the lords had to search for other sources of income. Efforts to prevent peasants from leaving their lands culminated in a diet decision of 1487 strictly limiting their rights to move without the lords' permission. Landlords also increasingly used subject labor, or *robota*, on their own manorial land. The best way out of their problems, many noblemen found, was through their own economic activity. They supported the crafts and products of their subject towns and established their own enterprises, especially fishponds and breweries (a lucrative source of income). These activities directly violated the rights of royal free towns, already affected by the limitations on migration from the countryside, and the burghers refused to accept them unchallenged.

At the beginning of the sixteenth century a new legal document, the Vladislav Land Ordinance, strengthened the lords and knights against both the crown and the towns.[9] The towns protested against limits on their judicial independence, participation in the diet, and traditional rights to market, brewing, and other privileges, but the king supported the lords. By 1513, armed conflict between towns and lords threatened, but before it came to blows, Vladislav II died. In the St. Václav's Treaty (1517), all three Estates, "as people of one language and from one kingdom," reached a compromise.[10] The lords accepted traditional town rights in judicial matters, but the towns had to give up their exclusive medieval economic privileges.

Vladislav's son and successor, the young king Louis (Ludvík, 1516–1526), resided in Buda, and intervened directly in the Bohemian crownlands with only limited success, failing to curb the great lords' powers or to cope with the impact of the Lutheran Reformation. These problems, which would surely have dominated much of his reign, remained unresolved when an Ottoman invasion of Hungary called the twenty-year-old king to the defense of his realm. On August 29, 1526, the Hungarian army (with some Bohemian allies) was destroyed near Mohács, and Louis drowned during the retreat.[11]

Vladislav II and Maximilian I, the Habsburg emperor, had arranged marriages in 1515 between Louis and Mary, Maximilian's granddaughter, and between the emperor's grandson, Ferdinand, and Louis's sister Anna. When Ferdinand claimed the throne, the Bohemian Estates refused to recognize his hereditary right to the crown, but after some hesitation—and his promises to accept their conditions—they elected him king on October 23, 1526. The other lands of the Crown of St. Václav, stung by the Bohemian Estates' refusal to let them take part in the decision, accepted Ferdinand as king by right of succession through his Jagiellonian wife, Anna.

The Estates Monarchy under the First Habsburgs

The election of Ferdinand I (1526–1564) to the Bohemian throne had significant consequences for the Bohemian crownlands and all of central Europe.[12] After the great Hungarian nobles offered him the crown of St. Stephen, Ferdinand ruled (in theory) over a widespread realm centered in the Austrian, Czech, and Hungarian lands. The Turkish conquest of a large part of Hungary (the Turkish army besieged Vienna in 1529), and their support of a native rival to his claim, limited Ferdinand's control of Hungary. The Habsburg king ruled in so-called Royal Hungary, basically today's Slovakia, western Croatia, and a strip of territory bordering his Austrian possessions. The royal capital moved to Pressburg (Pozsony, Prešpurk, today's Bratislava). The struggle to regain all of Hungary increased the significance of the Bohemian crownlands as a source of men and money, but the association with the Habsburgs also involved them in other European conflicts affecting the family's interests.

Thanks to the Protestant Reformation, "heresy" no longer isolated the crownlands, and as reformed teachings spread, links developed to other Protestant areas. Under the stimulus of Lutheranism, the Utraquist church developed two tendencies, the Old Utraquists, who were content with the *Compactata* and prepared to draw closer to the Catholics, and

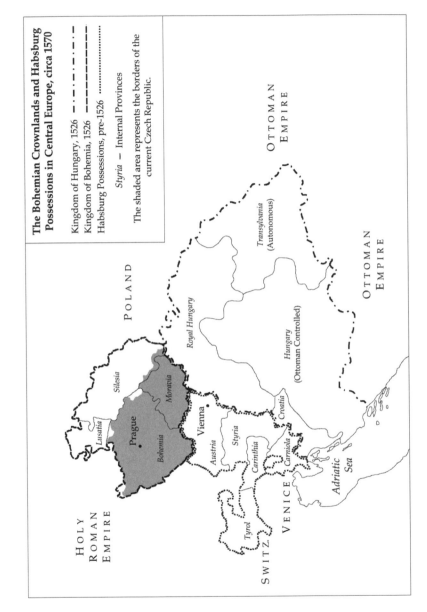

The Bohemian Crownlands and Habsburg
Possessions in Central Europe, circa 1570

Kingdom of Hungary, 1526 — ·· — ·· — ··
Kingdom of Bohemia, 1526 ————
Habsburg Possessions, pre-1526 ·········

Styria — Internal Provinces

The shaded area represents the borders of the
current Czech Republic.

HOLY
ROMAN
EMPIRE

POLAND

Silesia

Lusatia

Prague

Bohemia

Moravia

Royal Hungary

Vienna

Austria

Styria

Carinthia

Tyrol

SWITZ.

VENICE

Carniola

Croatia

Adriatic
Sea

Transylvania
(Autonomous)

Hungary
(Ottoman Controlled)

OTTOMAN
EMPIRE

OTTOMAN
EMPIRE

Map 3

the Neo-Utraquists, who were ready to establish a separate church organization. The Unity of Brethren represented a third current of Bohemian reformed religion. After 1490, when they dropped the requirement of voluntary poverty, the Brethren gained adherents among the well-to-do burghers and nobles. From the middle of the sixteenth century, they established contacts with the Calvinists in Germany and France. Thus both Lutheranism and Calvinism influenced and supplemented the domestic legacy of the Hussite revolution.[13]

In this situation, the Estates' efforts to defend their position against the king, and the religious tensions already existing in the Bohemian crownlands (now strengthened by the Protestant Reformation) intersected. In Ferdinand I, however, the Estates faced a gifted and determined politician, adept at using the cleavages within his realm to his own advantage. In addition, unlike the Jagiellonians, Ferdinand's family ruled over a vast and wealthy realm. Ferdinand's share included the Austrian lands as well as the crowns of Bohemia and Hungary, and in 1556 he became Holy Roman Emperor. In his lands he strengthened royal power in French and Burgundian style, and worked to restore Catholicism.

Ferdinand banned meetings of the dietines or the free towns without royal permission, and he separated the administration of Prague's towns. He seized for the crown the mines at Jáchymov (Joachimsthal) in 1528, where since the early sixteenth century the Counts Šlik had been mining silver and minting their own coins. In 1530, Ferdinand dismissed the greatest magnate of the Jagiellonian era, Zdeněk Lev of Rožmitál, signaling his determination to strengthen the crown's authority. To do so, he created offices directly under the monarch in Vienna, including the Privy Council, the Court Council, the Court Chancellery, and a central financial office, the Court Chamber. The court chamber in Vienna directed the Bohemian one in Prague and the Silesian one in Breslau. The growing royal administration offered positions to ambitious Bohemian nobles, and a pro-Habsburg faction developed within the Estates, including the lords of Hradec, the Popels of Lobkowicz, and the Berkas of Dubá.

The Estates sought to check Ferdinand's assertiveness. When war broke out in the empire between the Lutheran princes of the Schmalkaldic League and Charles V in 1546, the Estates opposition in Bohemia used the opportunity to undo Ferdinand's moves against their traditional powers. When Ferdinand summoned the kingdom's military levies to help his brother, the Estates prevaricated, but stopped short of armed resistance, especially after Moravia and Silesia refused to join. Charles V's success in Germany on April 24, 1547, left them without allies and their opposition collapsed.[14] Ferdinand punished only the most radical noblemen (especially the Brethren) by confiscating their estates or imprisoning them, instead concentrating on the royal towns. Two knights and two burghers were executed in Hradčany (Castle Town) Square in 1547. Ferdinand levied heavy fines against the towns, removed their privileges, disarmed them, and placed them under royal officials. He also removed their legal autonomy, erecting a court of appeal at the Prague castle that was superior to the town courts. After 1547 the nobles were the only real power in the Estates.

In religious affairs Ferdinand supported Catholicism, in keeping with his family tradition and his position as Holy Roman Emperor. He insisted on the preservation of the outmoded *Compactata*, refusing any changes in the religious situation as it was in 1485. In 1535 he prevented an attempt to grant legal status to the Brethren, and between 1539 and 1543 refused to allow a separate, Lutheran-style church structure for the Utraquists.[15] Noble power was enough to force Ferdinand to move indirectly against Protestantism in the crownlands.[16] In 1556, Ferdinand invited the Society of Jesus to Bohemia and gave them the Clementinum in Prague's Old Town. From this base the Jesuits worked, through preaching and education (in which they achieved remarkable levels), to win over especially the children of the nobles and the wealthy burghers for the renewed Catholic faith. In 1561, Ferdinand restored the Prague archbishopric, thereby creating a firm base for a renewed Catholic church administration. A year later, he asserted royal control over appointments to the Utraquist consistory, removing the native Hussite church from Estates control. In 1564, Ferdinand gained papal confirmation of communion in both kinds, but this satisfied only the Old Utraquists.

When Charles V abdicated in 1556, Ferdinand succeeded to the imperial title. His other possessions he divided among his sons, making the eldest, Maximilian, his successor in the Bohemian kingdom and Hungary. In 1564, when Ferdinand died, Maximilian also became emperor. Maximilian II (as Bohemian king Maximilian I, 1564–1576) lacked the political determination of his father, and was religiously indifferent, if not personally inclined toward Lutheranism. During his reign the Neo-Utraquists, Lutherans, and Brethren drew closer together, eventually accepting a common statement of faith at the diet in 1575. Based largely on the Lutheran Augsburg confession, this Bohemian Confession nevertheless represented a minimum common position for all the non-Catholic Estates. Maximilian traded verbal, not written, approval of the Confession for the Estates' agreement to accept his son Rudolf as king.[17]

Thus, when Maximilian died in 1576, Rudolf II (1576–1611) became Bohemian king. Rudolf was an intelligent, artistically sensitive person, Spanish-educated but not a bigoted Catholic.[18] He was also sickly and mentally unbalanced. When he moved his court from Vienna to Prague in 1583, he inaugurated one of the most fascinating periods in the history of the Bohemian crownlands. During his reign Prague became a cultural center, where thanks to his patronage a host of artists, scientists—including the astronomers Tycho de Brahe and Johannes Kepler—and charlatans gathered around his court.

CROWN, ESTATES, AND CULTURE IN BOHEMIA IN THE RENAISSANCE ERA

Cultural life in Bohemia under Rudolf II developed on foundations laid in previous decades, as the new movements of Humanism and the Renaissance made their way into the Bohemian crownlands.[19] Education occupied an important place in this culture, driven by urban development and economic change.[20] The ability to read, write, and do sums gained importance in trade and production, and a mastery of foreign languages became increasingly necessary with the linking of the lands of the crown of St. Václav to the other Habsburg possessions. German was the primary second language of the Czech lords and knights, reinforced by the Habsburg monarch, the Lutheran reformation, and renewed German colonization in the borderlands. Italian and Spanish were also popular among Catholics and nobles close to the court. Particular schools remained the basic type of educational institution, though the Greek term *gymnasium* was increasingly used for schools teaching the humanities. Gymnasia in the Bohemian crownlands followed their founders' religious orientation, so most of the town schools were non-Catholic. The Utraquist university of Prague maintained oversight of the majority of particular schools, but after the mid-sixteenth century the reputation of Brethren's gymnasia rose.

Jesuit gymnasia, established at Prague's Clementinum in 1556, in Olomouc in 1566, in Brno in 1578, and in subject towns belonging to great Catholic families such as the Rožmberks of southern Bohemia earned the order a high reputation. The Jesuits also expanded the Clementinum and their college in Olomouc (1573) to the university level.[21] In comparison, the Prague university still suffered from its fifteenth-century isolation and the Utraquist masters' opposition to humanist influences. Rudolph II's court proved more attractive than the university environment. There the Danish astronomer Tycho de Brahe worked and died (his tomb is in the Týn church on Old Town Square), and his pupil and successor, Johannes Kepler, developed two of his planetary laws of motion.[22] Other figures at Rudolph's court included astrologers and alchemists, whose services were also sought by great magnates such as Vilém of Rožmberk.[23]

Those who could afford it studied abroad, and during the sixteenth century many scions of Czech noble families, but also many burghers, studied or traveled in other parts of Europe. The Czechs' horizons also widened toward the Balkans and Near East, whence the Turkish threat originated and whither their taxes flowed and their soldiers marched. Some among them traveled there as diplomats in royal service, others as individuals interested in the Muslim lands or in the ancient sites of the Holy Land. Several such travelers wrote accounts of their adventures, the most famous of which, for its literary quality as well as its picaresque story, is the *Příhody* (Adventures) of Václav Vratislav of Mitrovice.

Renaissance architecture arrived in the late fifteenth century, and though Gothic showed remarkable tenacity in sacred building, secular structures increasingly imitated the new styles. Italian influences had to be adapted, not least to the transalpine climate. The result was a localized Czech version of Renaissance, in which domestic artisans learned from and absorbed the immigrant masters, usually Italians, who were brought into their midst by royal and noble patrons. Noblemen abandoned their Gothic castles in uncomfortable and inaccessible locations, now rendered obsolete by advancing military technology. Instead they devoted resources to reconstructing or creating new, more comfortable seats in Renaissance style. The royal court continued the rebuilding of the Prague castle complex, with the summer palace for Ferdinand I's wife, Anna (the Belvedere, built between 1536 and 1563). In the cities and towns, where the narrow Gothic lots did not allow for major structural changes in the houses, the impact of Renaissance features can be seen in the fluid façades, often decorated with *sgraffito*, designs scraped into layers of plaster to create geometric and other effects.

Eventually, under the influence of later sixteenth-century models from Saxony and the Low Countries as well as Italy, the love of decoration outweighed function in the style known as Mannerism, foreshadowing the later Baroque. Mannerism flourished at Rudolph II's court, where the monarch amassed a treasure trove of works by artists of the first order.[24] In retrospect the appearance of Mannerism in the Bohemian crownlands seems to express the tensions of a society riven by political and religious strife, in a world whose very physical contours were changing. Those accumulated tensions would eventually erupt into open rebellion.

THE COMING OF
THE BOHEMIAN REBELLION

At the end of the sixteenth century, the situation in the Bohemian crownlands changed dramatically in favor of the Catholic side.[25] Between 1598 and 1603, supporters of post-Tridentine Catholicism held the highest offices in both Bohemia and Moravia, threatening renewed actions against non-Catholics.[26] To defend themselves, the Estates opposition used a quarrel between Rudolf and his brother Matthias over Protestant rights in Hungary to extract the Letter of Majesty from Rudolf on July 9, 1609. This document affirmed the Bohemian Confession of 1575, extending the right to religious freedom to nobles, burghers, and subject peasantry. A month later a similar Letter of Majesty was granted to the Silesian Estates, fully legalizing Lutheranism.[27] Rudolf's Letter of Majesty was a document without parallel anywhere else in Europe. Not only did it guarantee religious liberty to free subjects, it extended freedom of conscience to the subject peasantry.[28] It was also a step that Rudolf took only under extreme pressure, and hoped to undo as soon as possible. In 1611, with the help of an army sent by his cousin Leopold, bishop of Passau, Rudolf attempted to crush his opposition and defeat his detested brother at the same time. The Passau army pillaged through southern Bohemia on its way to Prague, where it devastated the Lesser Quarter, provoking resistance not only from the Estates opposition but also from Archduke Matthias. Rudolf resigned the throne to his brother, who also became emperor on Rudolf's death in 1611.

Matthias (1611–1619) once more united the lands of the Bohemian crown and the other Habsburg possessions in central Europe under one rule, but he continued in the centralizing and pro-Catholic policies of his predecessors. After 1612, he moved back to Vienna, ruling the Bohemian crownlands through personally appointed lieutenants. The "Spanish party," the pro-Catholic faction of the Estates, demonstrated its recovering strength at the land diet of 1615, which granted Matthias his tax demands for a period of five years.[29] A more burning question was the succession. Neither Matthias nor his brothers had legitimate heirs, so the next king would come from either the Spanish Habsburgs, or the junior, Styrian branch. By a secret agreement of 1617, the Spanish Habsburgs renounced their claim, so the family decided that the succession would pass to Ferdinand of Styria. Because Ferdinand had relentlessly driven the Protestants out of Styria, his selection did not augur well for the non-Catholics in the Bohemian crownlands. Nevertheless, in spite of some lords' strong opposition, the land diet in 1617 accepted Ferdinand as Matthias's successor, after gaining his promise to recognize the Letter of Majesty of 1609.

Emboldened by the writing on the wall, the Spanish party provocatively destroyed Protestant churches on estates belonging to the Benedictines and the archbishop of Prague. When the non-Catholic Estates met in March 1618 to protest to Matthias, he rejected the protest and strictly forbade any further meetings. The opposition defiantly gathered at the Prague Carolinum on May 21, 1618, and the next day the radicals met in secret to plan a decisive action. On May 23, 1618, a delegation of the disaffected Estates entered the office of the king's representatives in the Prague castle, and after an improvised trial, threw the two royal lieutenants, Vilém Slavata of Chlum and Václav Bořita of Martinice, out of the window. The Defenestration of Prague of 1618 symbolized a decisive break between the Estates and the Habsburg king.[30]

The Estates elected a government of thirty directors, ten from each estate, and hired an army of their own. At a general diet in Prague in July 1619, they established a confederation of the Estates of Bohemia, Moravia, Upper and Lower Lusatia, and Silesia, incorporating the Letter of Majesty in the constitution. The diet deposed Ferdinand, and elected a prominent Calvinist ruler, Frederick of the Palatinate, king (1619–

1620). Frederick's wife was the daughter of the English king James I, and the Estates hoped in vain that Britain would support them.

Without significant allies (Britain, France, the Netherlands, and even the league of Protestant princes in Germany remained neutral), the Bohemian Estates were also weakened by internal divisions. The towns regained the status they had had before 1547, but the lords limited their participation in administration while ensuring that they bore the brunt of the financial burdens. The subject peasantry suffered from the mercenary armies of both sides, and showed no great enthusiasm for the struggle. The Bohemian rebellion remained an uprising of the privileged and powerful Estates, not a movement that united all social classes, as the Hussite revolution had done.

Twice during 1619 the Estates' army attempted to take Vienna and failed. In 1620 the situation took a sharp turn in Ferdinand's favor. His imperial troops, supported by a Bavarian army, invaded Bohemia from the south, while the elector of Saxony threatened it from the north (the Saxon ruler, though Lutheran, had designs on the Lusatias and Silesia). The Estates' armies had to fall back toward Prague. On an elevated site outside the city called White Mountain (Bilá Hora) the tired, poorly organized, and ill-paid soldiers of the Estates faced a slightly larger force loyal to Ferdinand. In a two-hour battle on November 8, 1620, they suffered a catastrophic defeat. Shortly after news of the disaster reached Prague, Frederick and his court fled the city, never to return. The rebellion of the Estates was over. The Thirty Years' War had just begun.[31]

6 Rebellion and Catastrophe

The Thirty Years' War was the last great religious war in Europe, and the first Europe-wide conflict of balance-of-power politics. Beginning with the Bohemian rebellion in 1618, the war grew into a confrontation between the German Protestant princes and the Holy Roman Emperor, and finally became a contest between France and the Habsburgs' two dynastic monarchies, involving practically all other powers. The war may be divided into four phases: the Bohemian-Palatinate War (1618–23), the Danish War (1625–29), the Swedish War (1630–35), and the Franco-Swedish War (1635–48). When the war finally ended with the Peace of Westphalia in 1648, the treaties set the groundwork for the system of international relations still in effect today. The outcome of the war integrated the Bohemian crownlands more fully with the other Habsburg possessions in a family empire that aspired to maintain its position as one of the powers in the international state system. This aspiration involved recurrent conflicts, on one side with the Turks, and on the other with Louis XIV's France.

VAE VICTIS!:
THE BOHEMIAN CROWNLANDS
IN THE THIRTY YEARS' WAR

After the Battle of the White Mountain and Frederick's flight from Prague (his brief reign earned him the epithet "The Winter King"), the last garrisons loyal to the Estates in southern and western Bohemia surrendered in May 1622. Even before these victories Ferdinand II began to settle accounts with his Bohemian opponents. On June 21, 1621, twenty-seven leaders of the Estates' rebellion were ceremonially (and in some cases exceedingly cruelly) executed in Prague's Old Town Square.[1] Ferdinand issued edicts confiscating the properties of a host of others, and many who had fled were sentenced to death in absentia. The Prague university was handed to the Jesuits, who also organized schools and missions to spread Catholicism in the countryside. In 1624 all Protestant clergy were banished, and three years later all non-Catholic burghers and nobles had to follow.

As the war continued and Denmark under King Christian IV entered the fray, the role of one of Ferdinand's military commanders, Albrecht of Wallenstein (Valdštejn), increased. Wallenstein parlayed conversion from the Brethren to Catholicism into a rapid rise to power and wealth. Granted the duchy of Frýdlant (Friedland) in northern Bohemia in 1624, Wallenstein also collected over fifty confiscated estates. Using this economic base, he raised an army of 70,000 in 1625, became generalissimo of the imperial forces, and won a great victory at Dessau in 1626. In 1628, Wallenstein received the duchy of Mecklenberg, and in May 1629, the Danes signed a treaty at Lübeck, ending the second phase of the Thirty Years' War.

Ferdinand's next move was the Edict of Restitution of March 29, 1629. All property seized from the Catholic church since before the Peace of Augsburg (1555) was to be returned. The Edict of Restitution provoked a revival of anti-Habsburg efforts among the Protestants, and even Catholic rulers in the empire had reservations. An imperial diet at Regensburg in 1630 shelved the edict, and recalled Wallenstein from his position.

In Bohemia in 1627 and Moravia the following year, Ferdinand issued the Renewed Land Ordinance, which superseded all previous constitutional laws. The ordinance proclaimed all the lands of the Bohemian crown hereditary dynastic possessions of the House of Habsburg, and stripped the Estates of their legislative, judicial, and executive authority. Catholicism was the sole legal religion—Ferdinand destroyed Rudolph's Letter of Majesty with his own hands—and the clergy regained its position as the first estate. German enjoyed equal rights in public life with Czech. Unlike the Edict of Restitution, the Renewed Land Ordinance remained in effect.[2]

In the summer of 1630 the war entered its third phase, when the Swedish king Gustavus II Adolphus entered the conflict. Brandenburg and Saxony soon joined the Swedes, who as Lutherans proclaimed themselves the protectors of Protestant rights. In September 1631, following a Swedish victory, the Saxons invaded Bohemia and occupied Prague. Many Czech exiles returned with the Saxons, but only for a time. Ferdinand reinstated Wallenstein, who pushed the Saxon army out of Bohemia. In November 1632, Wallenstein fought the Swedes to a standstill at Lützen, where Gustavus Adolphus was killed.

While negotiating with the Saxons, Wallenstein also secretly began discussions with French and Swedish diplomats and representatives of the Czech exiles. Throughout his career, Wallenstein displayed great ambition, and it may be he was playing for the Bohemian crown itself. His hesitation to declare himself openly, however, led all parties to suspect him. In January 1634, the emperor dismissed him again, most of his subordinates abandoned him, and on February 25, 1634, Wallenstein was assassinated by imperial officers at the fortress of Cheb.

That same year, a major Imperial victory over the Swedes and German Protestants at Nördlingen led to a separate peace with the German Protestants at Prague (1635). The Edict of Restitution was rescinded, the princely armies were placed under imperial command, and Saxony was confirmed in its possession of Upper and Lower Lusatia, former possessions of the Crown of St. Václav. The Swedes temporarily lost their allies, but the apparent stabilization reawakened French efforts to undermine the Habsburgs. Urged on by Cardinal Richelieu, the French concluded an alliance with Sweden and the Netherlands and declared war on Habsburg Spain.

In this final, Swedish-French phase of the war, the Swedes invaded Bohemia between 1639 and 1642, but this time the arrival of Protestant forces did not arouse enthusiasm. Swedish forces also operated in Moravia in 1643, when the hopes of taking Vienna once more surfaced as the

Transylvanian prince joined the anti-Habsburg cause. In 1645, Ferdinand's son and successor, Ferdinand III (1637–1657), suffered a crushing defeat. A separate peace with Transylvania rescued the Habsburgs, and the Swedes withdrew their field army from Moravia. In 1648 they returned to lay siege to Prague, but this time the population actively resisted them. A voluntary legion with the university students in the vanguard held the stone bridge after the Swedes had taken Hradčany and the Lesser Quarter. Their resistance became another symbol (one with Catholic and pro-Habsburg overtones), and a Marian column was erected on Old Town Square in memory of their victory (destroyed in 1918). The Swedes, burdened with booty from Rudolph II's art collections in the Prague castle, had to withdraw.

That same year finally produced the Peace of Westphalia, which confirmed a new balance of power. France and Sweden emerged with territorial gains and new status as dominant powers; the Holy Roman Empire and Spain declined correspondingly. The United Provinces of the Netherlands were recognized as an independent state, and Switzerland's ties with the empire were ended. The Peace of Westphalia strengthened the territorial princes against the emperor, but the Habsburg ruler's position within his Central European possessions was also strengthened.

In religious matters, the Peace of Westphalia followed the principle *cuius regio, eius religio* (whose the rule, his the religion) as in the Treaty of Augsburg in 1555. The base year was 1634, which ended the Czech exiles' hopes of returning to their country. The ruler determined the legal religion, free citizens of other faiths had to convert or leave, while the subject peasantry had no choice. In the Bohemian crownlands the Peace of Westphalia presaged the triumph of the Counter-Reformation. Lutherans retained religious rights in Silesia, thanks to Saxon pressure.

Religious conviction (or fanaticism) was not the only reason Ferdinand II and Ferdinand III insisted on restoring Catholicism. Contemporary opinion saw religious divisions as a source of political instability, a view confirmed by the Estates' rebellion. Thus for both political and religious reasons many nobles and burghers had to choose exile. Up to one quarter of the free population—exact figures are impossible to arrive at—fled their native land. In their new homes, in the neighboring Protestant states, in Upper Hungary (Slovakia), or in Poland, they assimilated into their surroundings. Many peasants also fled the country, motivated equally strongly by the desire to escape the desperate economic conditions at home.

ECONOMIC AND SOCIAL
IMPACT OF THE
THIRTY YEARS' WAR

The Thirty Years' War left lasting traces on the economy, society, politics, and culture of the Bohemian crownlands.[3] The population dropped drastically: an estimated 1,700,000 people lived in Bohemia before 1618, in the mid-seventeenth century there were only around 950,000. In Moravia out of approximately 900,000 there were only 600,000 people left. Overall losses are estimated at one-third of the population. Cadastral surveys from 1682 suggest that in that year over 20 percent of the peasant land still lay fallow. Agricultural output did not recover to prewar levels until the end of the seventeenth century.[4]

The victorious Habsburg rulers rewarded their supporters with the estates of nobles who had emigrated or been proscribed. Thus the original old Czech and German noble families were joined, and often overshadowed by, newcomers from all the Catholic regions of Europe. The internal structure of the noble estate also shifted significantly. The clergy regained its status as the first estate, while of the more than 1,000 knightly families in the Bohemian Estates before the Battle of the White Mountain, by the end of the seventeenth century there were only 238.[5] The lower nobility played a major role in neighboring Poland and Hungary in preserving the political privileges of the traditional estates, and their disappearance in the Bohemian crownlands correspondingly weakened the Bohemian Estates.

Their liberties curtailed already after 1547, the royal free towns also saw their participation in the Estates restricted to a symbolic level. In the Bohemian diet, only six towns had representation after 1627, a number that by 1709 had been reduced to the three towns of Prague. In Moravia all seven royal towns were still represented, though until 1711 they had to stand during diet sessions as a mark of subordination. In both Bohemia and Moravia the towns had a single collective vote, whereas members of the prelates' or nobles' estates each had a vote. Under these conditions, what political power remained to the Estates was controlled by the upper nobility.[6]

Habsburg victory over the Bohemian rebellion changed forever the balance between crown and Estates. In all branches of public affairs, royal power dominated. Yet, in the absence of a professional, salaried bureaucracy, the Habsburg kings still had to rely on the nobility to staff the administration. In a reversal of the fifteenth-century process, the major offices in the Bohemian kingdom were now appointed by the king and swore allegiance to him. Though officials within the crownlands still had to hold citizenship, it was the king who now granted it.[7]

The existence of the Bohemian Court Chancellery maintained the memory of the unity and autonomy of the lands of the Crown of St. Václav, but it was an instrument of centralized royal control, transferred to Vienna in 1624. The main financial organ, the Bohemian Chamber, functioned directly under the Viennese Court Chamber rather than through the Bohemian Court Chancellery. The Viennese chamber also maintained direct relations with similar offices in Moravia and Silesia. The Bohemian Court Chancellery could now hear appeals from the old Estates-dominated judicial organ, the Land Court.

Still, although they had lost their religious freedom and their political power had declined, the nobles maintained their social and economic position. Well into the eighteenth century, the local lords remained the main contact between the subject peasantry and the crown. These subjects, making up probably 90 percent of the population, lived on land belonging to nobles or church institutions, and these landed properties made up the fundamental administrative units of the country. The lord or his administrator was responsible for the application of royal decrees and regulations, for collecting state taxes and military recruits, and for dispensing justice among his subjects in civil and criminal cases.

The so-called "second serfdom" in the Bohemian crownlands differed from lands farther east (Poland, eastern Prussia, Russia). Though some landlords did concentrate on large-scale production for export, the extensive cultivation of grain for the market was not so firmly established. Side-by-side with such estates existed farms worked by peasants producing for the local market, and often competing effectively with the lord's estates. Noble producers thus preferred to concentrate in areas such as logging, fish-farming, or export-oriented crops. In addition, the landlords still enjoyed monopolies of various kinds, especially in brewing and distilling, so peasants provided consumers for the lord's products during a time of collapsing markets.[8]

Nobles depended more and more on *robota* labor. Generally, peasants had to provide labor, including draft animals, for three days a week. At harvest, this requirement could go up to six days a week, with days

off only on Sundays or church holidays. The economic depression following the Thirty Years' War led the landlords to rely more on their
subjects' labor, but the peasants had no incentive to work well for the
lord. Evidence suggests that productivity on dominical land was from
eight to ten times lower than on rustical land, where the peasant worked
for himself. Low productivity led landlords to increase their demands
for *robota*, while at the same time the state raised taxes, almost exclusively levied on rustical land. The landlords' self-interest partly limited
peasant exploitation, since they represented both the lord's labor and
his consumers. Nevertheless, their life was hard, and resentments led to
open rebellion.[9]

During the Thirty Years' War, peasant disturbances were usually
reactions to re-Catholicization. Economic grievances, however, touched
off the greatest peasant rebellion of the century in 1680.[10] The imperial
court moved to Prague to escape the plague in Vienna, but there the
peasants flooded it with petitions against the *robota*. When Leopold I
(1657–1705) reaffirmed the lords' rights, the peasants seized whatever
weapons they could find and gathered to march on Prague. The rebellion
was crushed by the army and its leaders executed or sentenced to hard
labor, but it forced the emperor to intervene in landlord-peasant relations. In a patent issued in June 1680, Leopold confirmed the traditional
three-day labor requirement, higher during harvest time, but demanded
that the lords not mistreat their peasants. Similar *robota* patents were
enacted under Charles VI, in 1713, 1717, and 1738. The state also
began to intervene in landlords' judicial powers. Royal patents of 1717
established a hierarchy of appeals, beginning with the circuit captain
and ending with the Bohemian chancellery. Peasant resistance to the
robota remained a constant factor throughout the eighteenth and into
the nineteenth century.

The Chod rebellion in western Bohemia from 1692 to 1695 reflected
these continuing social tensions. In return for special privileges, the
Chods were charged with patrolling the kingdom's western boundaries.
By the mid-seventeenth century their privileges had eroded, and their
new lords demanded *robota* for large-scale economic enterprises. The
Chods, appealing to traditional liberties, refused and sent delegations to
Vienna to plead their case. They were crushed by force, and their leader,
Jan Sladký Kozina, executed at Plzeň in 1695. Nineteenth-century au-
thors created a powerful myth-image of the Czech Chods resisting social
and national exploitation by their German lords. In its causes and form,

the Chod rebellion in fact typifies contemporary peasant resistance: against rising economic pressure, especially demands for *robota*, the peasants appealed to traditional privileges and rights, trusting in the just ruler, who would correct the abuses of the unjust landlord. The existing social and economic system was not questioned, the national motive was absent, and the peasants demanded only justice.[11]

CULTURE IN THE
AGE OF THE BAROQUE

The years between the Battle of the White Mountain and reforms of Maria Theresa and Joseph II were long known in Czech nationalist historiography as the "time of darkness." In this depiction the White Mountain signaled both the loss of Bohemian independence and the destruction of Czech culture.[12] Even today the White Mountain and its consequences remain an important issue in Czech historiography and national consciousness, though the nationalist picture of cultural destruction has gradually been modified. Nevertheless, the White Mountain represents at least a partial caesura in the cultural history of the Bohemian crownlands.[13]

When the victorious Habsburg authorities executed the ringleaders of the "odious rebellion," many of them were significant cultural figures. Many other leading intellectuals went into exile. The loss of the emigrants was certainly a heavy blow, especially in literary disciplines. On the other hand, the reintegration of the Bohemian crownlands into Catholic Europe brought more direct exposure to other artistic styles and approaches. If initially these impulses were alien, they were eventually absorbed and transformed, giving rise to the Czech version of the next dominant cultural style, the Baroque. The greatest Czech exile was the last bishop of the Unity of Brethren, Jan Amos Komenský. Comenius, as he was known abroad, published in many fields, especially pedagogy, where he enjoyed an international reputation. He also published significant works in Czech, including a moving lament expressing his despair after the Peace of Westphalia sealed the fate of the exiles.[14]

Émigré works had little direct influence in the Bohemian crownlands, where the Jesuits controlled censorship and the Catholic faith was reestablished.[15] Both secular and religious authorities concentrated on missionary work, reorganizing the Catholic church administration, and developing Catholic-controlled schooling at all levels. The state issued laws and administrative decrees, and set up a Reformation Commission, backed by military force, in each circuit. The practical work, however, fell to the church. Two new bishoprics were created, Litoměřice (Leitmeritz) in 1655 and Hradec Králové in 1664. Parish priests kept a register of confessants, which after 1656 was sent to the governor's chancellery. Only in the isolated frontier regions such as the foothills of the Krušné Hory and around Aš (Asch), and in the mountains of Moravia and eastern Bohemia, did secret non-Catholics remain (mostly German-speaking Lutherans in the former areas and Czech-speaking Brethren in the latter). By approximately 1680 the first wave of Catholicization was complete, but the government still feared secret Protestantism, issuing renewed patents against heresy in 1717.

Teaching and other work among the people was vital to winning the Czechs back to the Catholic fold. The Jesuits returned immediately after White Mountain, and the established orders (Benedictines, Praemonstratensians, and Cistercians) were joined during the seventeenth century by others such as Piarists, Irish Franciscans, and Black Benedictines. The merger of the university with the Clementinum (definitively in 1654) formed the Charles-Ferdinand university. Other orders ran their own gymnasia, notably the older Benedictines and the newer Piarists. Basic education was provided in town and village schools, where the local parish priest was usually the teacher.[16]

Church rituals punctuated everyday life: sacraments (baptism, confirmation, marriage, extreme unction) accompanied the stages of individual life, and regular confession was enforced by the authorities. Church holidays (there were many) and other occasions meant festive celebrations, processions, and services in churches decorated with statues and highly ornate altars, to the accompaniment of music, incense, and ritual. Processions and solemn pilgrimages to shrines, usually connected to the Virgin Mary, also formed part of popular religious life. The cult of the Virgin Mary was particularly popular in the Catholic reformation, and she was joined after 1729 by a newly canonized Czech saint, John Nepomucene, whose veneration spread during the eighteenth century, even overseas.[17] Returning the Bohemian crownlands to the Catholic church was thus a more complicated matter than the phrase "forcible conversion" suggests. Post-Tridentine Catholicism was also appealing in its buildings, monuments, and rituals.

The newly introduced Baroque style, with its movement, contrast, and tension, expressed well the religious fervor of the reformed Catholic church. In the Bohemian crownlands Baroque arrived abruptly, introduced by Italian or German-Austrian masters such as Carlo Lurago, Francesco Carrati, and Johann Bernhard Fischer von Erlach, but it reached its highest achievements in the works of local architects, notably Christoph Dientzenhofer and his son, Kilian Ignaz. Their masterpiece, the Jesuit church of St. Nicholas in Prague's Lesser Quarter, remains one of the most striking Baroque monuments in the Bohemian crownlands.

If Baroque art, architecture, and music reached world standards, the intellectual censorship stifled literature. In addition, equality between Czech and German meant that the use of German spread among the upper and middle classes. Without an educated public for Czech-language works, literature in Czech was oriented to the masses. The church recognized that Czech was essential to its activity among the people, and its writers produced many polemical and devotional works. Baroque preaching, religious theater, and verse reached respectable levels. Nevertheless, in comparison with the vernacular literature in contemporary France and England, the Bohemian crownlands remained far behind, even further than during the Renaissance.

From such aspects of cultural development after 1620 the nationalists drew their image of a cultural "time of darkness." There was a social price, too. Josef Pekař, otherwise not hostile to Baroque culture, contrasted the poverty of the peasantry with the glories of Baroque architecture in Prague and the countryside: "here the new Czechia rejoices, triumphs, and thanks heaven in joyfully agitated situation, the new Czechia of a few thousands, or rather hundreds of people, whose power and glory rests on the ruins of hundreds of thousands."[18] Some contemporaries, Czech-born servants of the church, raised in the Jesuit order, still expressed a clear sense of Czech patriotism and defended Czech culture. The Jesuit Bohuslav Balbín collected monuments of Czech learning through which he contributed to later developments in Czech historical studies. He also composed a lament on the Czech language, published posthumously in 1775. This work had a tremendous impact on the first generation of the Czech national renascence.[19]

THE HABSBURG MONARCHY
IN THE BALANCE OF POWER

The myth-image of a political "time of darkness" in Bohemia after the Thirty Years' War is also one-sided. Nevertheless, the Bohemian crownlands declined in significance relative to other Habsburg concerns, and their fate was increasingly decided in Vienna. Bohemian and Moravian aristocrats made successful careers serving the emperor, but the concrete distinctness of the Bohemian crownlands (since 1635 without the two Lusatias) eroded. The gradual Habsburg reconquest of Hungary and the years of conflict with France focused royal attention on the eastern and western frontiers. The Bohemian crownlands increasingly figured as a source of money and recruits for these wars, whose outcome altered both the European balance of power and the internal dynamics of politics within the Habsburg possessions.

The Turks had generally refrained from entering directly into the Thirty Years' War, but conflict with the Habsburgs broke out anew in 1663. As Habsburg military successes raised the prospect of a reconquest of Hungary, Leopold faced conspiratorial resistance from some great Hungarian aristocrats. The second Turkish siege of Vienna failed in 1683, marking the beginning of the end of Turkish control in Hungary. Conflict continued for many years, but the Habsburgs gradually advanced. From these campaigns against the Turks the French prince Eugene of Savoy emerged as one of Austria's finest military leaders. Under his command the liberation of Hungary was finally completed (Treaty of Karlowitz, 1699), the Banat of Temesvár conquered, and for a time even parts of Serbia (including Belgrade) and western Wallachia occupied (Treaty of Passarowitz, 1718).

The Habsburgs' frequent involvement in wars with France culminated after 1700, when the Spanish Habsburg line finally died out. Leopold I claimed the throne for his second son Charles, and the ensuing War of the Spanish Succession continued through the reign of Leopold's elder son, Joseph I (1705–1711). With his death the international situation changed, since Joseph's successor was his brother, Charles VI (1711–1740). Europe's fear of a French-dominated Spain was now replaced by the threat of a reunited Habsburg dominion.

The Bohemian nobles did not mount serious resistance to the government's demands for contributions and recruits for the wars. Nevertheless, during Joseph I's reign there were some changes in how the central authorities approached the Estates, including the creation in 1710 of a commission to revise the Renewed Land Ordinance for Bohemia. In addition, members of the old Czech nobility such as Václav Vratislav of Mitrovice (ambassador to London and chancellor) and Václav Norbert Kinský held high imperial offices. After Charles came to the throne, however, the Bohemian aristocrats in Vienna were eclipsed by the Spanish advisers with whom he had surrounded himself as pretender to the Spanish crown.

Shortly after Charles VI's accession to the imperial title, Britain opened peace negotiations with France. The resulting treaties of Utrecht (1713) and Rastatt (1714) ended the War of the Spanish Succession and confirmed the Habsburg loss of Spain. The war had demonstrated dramatically the fate that might overtake powerful empires faced with a crisis of succession. Increasingly Charles VI devoted his attention and efforts, domestically and internationally, to ensuring a unified order of succession for his realms.

When Charles announced his plans in 1713, his goal was to ensure that his descendants, not Joseph's, succeeded him. The male line was granted precedence, but the female line was also included, if all male descendants died out.[20] Charles presented the new order of succession, the Pragmatic Sanction, to the Estates of his realm for approval. The Austrian, Bohemian, Moravian, and Silesian Estates accepted it in 1720, the Croatian in 1721, and the Hungarian and Transylvanian Estates in 1722–23. Lombardy and the Austrian Netherlands followed in 1724 and 1725. Gaining the Estates' formal acceptance guaranteed (at least in theory) the cooperation of the politically privileged bodies. In the process his dominions—including the lands of the Crown of St. Václav—revived memories of their separate historical and political existence. For the Bohemian crownlands the procedure also helped further modify some of the harshest provisions of Ferdinand II's Renewed Land Ordinance, which had in any case already established the right of female succession.[21]

Charles was also determined to gain international acceptance of the Pragmatic Sanction, and he subordinated his foreign policies to that aim. Between 1726 and 1732, Spain, Britain, Prussia, the Netherlands, and Denmark formally agreed to recognize the Pragmatic Sanction. Getting France's support cost Charles VI Lorraine and most of the Habsburg Italian possessions, in the War of the Polish Succession (1733–35). Russia's agreement was bought at the price of Austrian support in another war with the Turks (1737–39), this time without Eugene of Savoy, who died in 1736. All Charles's Balkan gains were lost by the Treaty of Belgrade (1739), but Habsburg control of Hungary and Transylvania was not threatened.

The true value of Charles VI's diplomatic agreements would be revealed when he died and his daughter succeeded him. Maria Theresa, in the meantime, gained a consort in Francis Stephen of Lorraine, dispossessed by the War of the Polish Succession but compensated with the hand of Charles's heir in 1736. This diplomatic alliance turned into a true love match, and ended the threat of Habsburg extinction through its admirable fruitfulness. But the political survival of the house of Habsburg-Lorraine was to be sorely tested in the storm that erupted—in spite of the Pragmatic Sanction—when Emperor Charles VI died in 1740.[22]

UNDER THE DOUBLE EAGLE

PART THREE

7 Reform, Revolution, and Reaction

The accession of Charles VI's daughter, Maria Theresa—the first woman to reign over the Czechs since the legendary Libuše—marked another watershed in the development of the Bohemian crownlands and the Habsburg monarchy. The power of the Bohemian Estates had been broken after the White Mountain, but the institutions of the Estates monarchy had continued to exist, even if in attenuated form. With the loss of Spain in 1714, the center of gravity of the Habsburg realm shifted to Central Europe. But it was under Maria Theresa (1740–1780) that concerted and continuous efforts began to forge a unified, centralized, bureaucratically administered realm at least out of the non-Hungarian possessions of the monarch.[1] For the remainder of the monarchy's existence the Bohemian crownlands would be treated more or less as one province among many.[2] At the outset, however, it seemed more likely that the monarchy itself would melt down altogether in the crucible of war into which Frederick II of Prussia plunged it a scant two months after Charles VI's death.

THE BOHEMIAN CROWNLANDS IN THE WARS OF THE EIGHTEENTH CENTURY (1740–1790)

In December 1740, Prussia invaded Silesia, a Bohemian crownland since John of Luxemburg, defeated the Austrian armies, and occupied most of the province. Frederick's victory spawned a coalition of Charles Albert of Bavaria, Frederick Augustus III of Saxony and Poland, and Philip V of Spain, supported by his French nephew, Louis XV, each of whom had designs on the Habsburg inheritance. By the end of 1741, a combined French and Bavarian army had occupied Prague. On December 7, 1741, Charles Albert had himself proclaimed King of Bohemia and a part of the Bohemian Estates swore the oath of fealty. A few months later he was elected Holy Roman Emperor as Charles VII.[3]

Maria Theresa regrouped, winning the support of the Hungarian lords, but in June 1742 she had to surrender most of Silesia in a separate peace with Frederick at Breslau. After driving the French and Bavarians out of Bohemia, Maria Theresa had herself crowned in St. Vitus's Cathedral in May 1743. Though she treated the seriously embarrassed Bohemian Estates with leniency, she never thereafter looked at the Bohemian lords as sympathetically as she did at the Hungarians.[4] Maria Theresa was well aware, though, of what Bohemia meant to Austria's position as a power. She devoted scarce resources to forcing the Prussians out of northeastern Bohemia in 1744, but a series of defeats in 1745 led to the treaty of Dresden. Charles Albert's unexpected death that year, and his heir's renunciation of Bavarian claims, enabled Francis Stephen's election as Holy Roman Emperor. After three more years of conflict the peace of Aix-la-Chapelle (Aachen) ended the War of the Austrian Succession in 1748.[5]

None of the protagonists expected the treaty to be more than a temporary truce. Maria Theresa, advised by the Silesian nobleman Friedrich Wilhelm Haugwitz, began to centralize her administration so as to prepare the Habsburg monarchy for another war with Prussia. Meanwhile, Frederick had also been preparing for war. In 1756, Prussia concluded the Convention of Westminster with Great Britain. In response, Maria Theresa, aided by state chancellor Wenzel Anton Kaunitz, member of an old Moravian noble family, allied with Russia and France. This realignment of the European alliances set the stage for another conflict over Silesia.

The Seven Years' War began with a Prussian attack on Saxony. The following year the Prussians overran most of northern Bohemia and besieged Prague. A decisive Austrian victory over Frederick in June 1757 ended the siege and forced a Prussian withdrawal, and a renewed invasion of Moravia was defeated in 1758. In 1759, a new Habsburg-French-Russian coalition inflicted one defeat after another on Frederick, but French overseas losses at British hands weakened their support for Austria, and Russian Empress Elizabeth's death and the accession of Peter III—mentally unstable, and an admirer of Frederick the Great—led Russia to withdraw from the coalition in 1762. Maria Theresa had to recognize Prussia's annexation of Silesia as final in 1763, in the treaties of Paris and Hubertusburg.

Grabbing Silesia set Prussia well on the road to becoming a European power. For Austria, losing the populous and economically significant province was a hard blow, yet the outcome of the Seven Years' War reaffirmed the Habsburg monarchy's status in Europe. The loss of Silesia reduced the lands of the Crown of St. Václav to the dimensions of the Přemyslid kingdom. Bohemia, Moravia, and the Silesian duchies of Opava (Troppau), Těšín (Teschen), and Krnov (Jägerndorf) now formed the Bohemian crownlands until the collapse of the monarchy, the western part of Czechoslovakia after 1918, and the Czech Republic today. The loss of heavily German Silesia changed the linguistic balance in the Bohemian crownlands, confirming their Czech-speaking majority, and possibly providing more favorable conditions for the future revival of the Czech language and culture.

The Habsburg dynasty reestablished its claim to the imperial title in 1764, when Maria Theresa's son Joseph II was elected to succeed his father as Holy Roman Emperor, which he did in 1765. Joseph II (co-regent from 1765, as sole ruler, 1780–1790) pursued an active foreign policy. A permanent Austro-French alliance did not develop even though Maria Theresa's youngest daughter, Marie Antoinette, married the future Louis XVI. Austria instead cooperated with Russia and Prussia in the partition of Poland in 1772–73. The Habsburg share of southern Poland was organized into the "Kingdom of Galicia and Lodomeria." Joseph II also took Bukovina from the Ottoman Empire in 1774. These territorial changes did not affect the Bohemian crownlands directly, but they were not insignificant either. Relatively undeveloped Galicia and Bukovina represented a potential market for the Bohemian crownlands' manufactures. The monarchy's expansion eastward absorbed lands that were not part of the German Holy Roman Empire. Strengthening the Slavic element added another complicating factor to the monarchy's future. A more immediate, and negative, impact was a new war with the Turks in 1787. Joseph contracted fever at the front and died in 1790, leaving his realms discontented by the combined impact of the wartime difficulties and his ambitious reform program.[6] By that time, however, Europe's attention was already riveted to events in France.

ENLIGHTENMENT AND ABSOLUTISM

During the eighteenth century the idea spread that reform was possible and desirable, bringing with it a serious challenge to the twin authorities of religion and tradition. The Enlightenment subjected problems to critical scrutiny, and proposed remedies based on the application of human reason through scientific method. Enlightenment ideas spread eastward as rulers attempted to compete with such powerful states as France and Great Britain. In this struggle, rulers like Frederick the Great of Prussia, Catherine II of Russia, and Maria Theresa and Joseph II of Austria undertook reforms that have been called "enlightened absolutism." These monarchs did not strive to realize an Enlightenment Utopia, but the Enlightenment provided the critical and theoretical work from which they and their advisers sought to adopt and adapt whatever would help in achieving their goal: to increase the power and security of their states.

Reform Efforts under Maria Theresa

The practical goal of power and security dominated Maria Theresa's early efforts at administrative reform.[7] Realizing that the surviving noble-dominated institutions in her realm prevented the monarchy from tapping needed finances and manpower, Maria Theresa concentrated on taxation and administrative reforms. A key success came in 1748 when through Haugwitz's efforts the Bohemian Estates (with their counterparts in the other non-Hungarian lands) accepted the decennial recess, approving taxes for ten years. Maria Theresa thus gained the financial resources to settle the state debt, establish a state bureaucracy, and equip an army of more than 100,000 men. Reforms also placed tax and military matters in the hands of newly created royal offices, after 1763 called *gubernia*. The previously existing Estates offices became only personal distinctions of their holders. Between 1748 and 1751 a salaried circuit captain, resident in the district town, replaced the former system of two Estates captains, one lord and one knight.

In 1749 a major change in central administration abolished the Bohemian and Austrian court chancelleries, replacing them with two institutions common for both the Bohemian crownlands and the Austrian provinces. Administration and financial matters were linked in the United Bohemian and Austrian Court Chancellery; judicial matters were placed under the Supreme Court. These reforms increased the ties binding the Bohemian crownlands directly to Vienna, while loosening further their mutual connections. The central administration in Vienna did not include Hungary, however: already under Maria Theresa the basic outlines of the dualistic system later established in the Compromise of 1867 emerged.[8]

Maria Theresa's practical goals—and the monarchy's difficult financial situation—also forced her to consider the economy. As a consequence of the Seven Years' War the state debt grew from around 100 million gulden a year at the end of Charles VI's reign to almost 300 million in 1764. By 1780, in spite of improvements in the budget balance, it had risen to 376 million gulden.[9] Leading Austrian cameralists believed that the state needed to promote trade through developing domestic productivity. Thus in addition to customs and currency reforms, Maria Theresa's government improved the communications infrastructure, stimulated manufacturing (in which Francis Stephen was very active on his Bohemian estates), and removed or limited the traditional guild restrictions on the development of artisan production.[10]

The loss of Silesia increased the significance of the remaining Bohemian crownlands in craft and manufacturing production. Textiles led the way, and Bohemian linen, wool, and to some extent cotton manufacturing expanded during the second half of the eighteenth century.[11] This development concentrated where water power was plentiful, mostly in northeastern Bohemia and Moravia and the remnant of Silesia. Mills processed hand-spun and woven cloth, so individual artisans produced most Bohemian textiles up to the end of the century, helping to account for the dominance of textiles in manufacturing employment.[12] An industrial exhibition was part of the festivities surrounding Leopold II's coronation as king of Bohemia in 1791.

Though manufacturing developed, the Bohemian economy remained overwhelmingly agricultural. Reliance upon *robota* labor limited the lords' ability to innovate or increase production, while the peasants were hampered by the relative scarcity of cash and land (in the 1780s better than two-fifths of all the agricultural land was dominical). The hated *robota* limited the effect of changes such as adopting crop rotation, introducing new industrial plants, different food crops, and fodder crops to allow stall-feeding of livestock. These gradual changes were in part driven by the rising population, which increased over the eighteenth century from between 1.6 to 1.8 million for Bohemia proper to 2,580,000 (4,150,000 for all the Bohemian crownlands).[13]

Maria Theresa supported some attempts at state intervention in the landlord-peasant relationship.[14] By 1748 a new survey of the rustical land was completed, and reissued in revised form in 1756. The state's financial needs placed a heavy burden on the peasantry, with taxation demanding up to 42 percent of their gross production. Only increasing agricultural productivity and a rising population, so the prevailing mercantilist and populationist logic ran, could possibly improve this picture. Following the revised cadastral survey, the state tried to improve the legal situation of the peasant, and especially to intervene if the landlord grossly mistreated his subjects or illegally transferred their land to his demesne (thereby removing it from taxation).

In 1771 Bohemia suffered its last great famine, during which as many as half a million people, approximately 12 percent of the total population, died. Emperor Joseph II personally investigated conditions in Bohemia during 1771–72, and returned to Vienna horrified by what he had learned. In 1771, a new *robota* patent was issued for Silesia, and an urbarial commission in Bohemia began work on distributing the state's demands more equitably between subjects and landlords. The lords' delaying tactics were interrupted in 1775 by the greatest peasant rebellion in the Bohemian crownlands in the eighteenth century.

Early in 1775, the Bohemian peasantry responded to rumors that the lords were purposely keeping secret a "golden patent"—freeing them from *robota*—with a spreading wave of strikes and forced reduction of *robota* demands. On March 20, 1775, a large band of peasants set off from near Trutnov (Trautenau) in northeastern Bohemia toward Prague, while other bands of insurgents headed into the interior, or along the mountain foothills seeking support. Although the peasant columns were dispersed in a series of skirmishes with the army between March 24 and 28, recurrent local disturbances continued through the summer.[15] Several hundred rebels were arrested, but the government declared an amnesty after a few exemplary executions.

The uprising removed the lords' resistance, and the government quickly finished and promulgated a new *robota* patent for the Bohemian crownlands, on August 13 in Bohemia and September 7 in Moravia. Maria Theresa's patent of 1775 provided only a partial solution: it fixed *robota* obligations based on the peasants' tax assessment and established a system of eleven grades of *robota* workers with different obligations, but to the peasant it did not go nearly far enough. Neither did the concept of "Raabization," Hofrat Franz Anton von Raab's plan to divide dominical land among the peasants, in return for cash payments in place of their *robota* obligation. Raabization was carried out on the crown's former Jesuit estates in 1773, and later on other crown and town lands in Bohemia. Maria Theresa never made Raabization compulsory, however, and few noble landlords were willing to imitate it.

Maria Theresa's government, advised by Johann Andreas Felbiger, introduced important reforms of elementary education. The General School Ordinance of 1774 created three basic types of schools: the trivial schools, one-year elementary schools with compulsory attendance teaching reading, writing, and arithmetic—the "trivium" of the traditional seven arts—in every parish seat; the main schools in every district town, which added history, geometry, drawing, further German language, and some vocational training; and the model, "normal" school in the capital of each crownland, providing the terminal education for middle-class youth as well as training a body of teachers for the rest of the system. In Bohemia the director of Maria Theresa's school policies was Ferdinand Kindermann, who had already introduced education reforms in southern Bohemia. Kindermann's greatest experiment was the industrial school, where vocational education predominated over academic subjects.

After the dissolution of the Jesuits in 1773 other teaching orders, notably the Piarists, took over their schools. At the universities the state established the content of lectures and textbooks, and appointed the heads of faculties, choosing supporters of Enlightenment ideals in education. Maria Theresa established several new specialized professional institutions, including the Theresianum in Vienna, set up in 1749 as a training school for higher administrators, the military academy in Wiener Neustadt (1752), the Oriental Academy in Vienna (1754), and the Commercial Academy (1770). These schools were not, however, dedicated to learning for its own sake, but to preparing professionally trained servants of the state.

Maria Theresa wanted to preserve and extend state control over church administration, though she left the church's internal organization alone. Mercantilist thought emphasized preserving bullion reserves, so state oversight over church finances had to be extended. Populationist concern for the birthrate and productive employment of the population frowned on the diversion of workers into monasteries and religious orders. Thus, the government forbade the acquisition of new landholdings by the church without state approval, limited the number of religious holidays, and restricted recruitment to monastic orders.

Nevertheless, Maria Theresa remained a devout, not to say bigoted, daughter of the church. While many of her fellow monarchs in Catholic Europe abolished the Jesuit order, she supported it until the pope himself suppressed the Jesuits. Several times during her reign she renewed measures against non-Catholics (especially patents from 1748, 1754, and 1764). Using the excuse of their supposed disloyalty during the Franco-Bavarian occupation of Prague in 1741–42, Maria Theresa ordered the expulsion of Prague's 20,000 Jews in 1745. Even though the Prague magistrates and the Bohemian Estates protested, Maria Theresa not only stuck by her decree but widened it to include all the Jews in Bohemia and the major towns of Moravia. Only after two years of sabotage of her orders by local authorities and protests from various quarters did Maria Theresa relent, and even then she imposed heavy "voluntary" payments on the Jews in return.[16] By the end of her reign, Maria Theresa was in frequent conflict with some of her most significant advisers on the question of religious toleration.

Joseph II and Enlightened Absolutism

Maria Theresa's death on November 29, 1780, changed the tempo and the general atmosphere surrounding reform. Joseph II's approach was characterized by centralism and rationalism, and by a deep and fundamental utilitarianism. It was also definitely a transformation from above. If the emperor was the "first servant of the state" under Joseph, power ultimately rested in the first servant's hands. The Josephinist tradition in Austria remained visible long after his death in a belief in a centralized, well-administered state with a common German culture. Later attempts to make Joseph II either a nineteenth-century anticlerical liberal or a German nationalist were mistaken. What is unmistakable, however, is that Joseph II left a deep and indelible imprint on his possessions, including the Bohemian crownlands.[17]

In religious matters, Joseph promulgated on October 13, 1781, a patent granting toleration to Lutherans and Calvinists, as well as regulating the status of Orthodox Christians. Czech non-Catholics (some 50,000 registered) could not follow the faith of the Brethren or the Czech Confession of 1575; they had to opt for either the Augsburg or the Helvetian confessions. Joseph also reduced the restrictions on the Jews, opening trades to them, allowing them to live outside the ghetto, and removing the demand that they wear distinctive clothing. Joseph's aim was not only economic advantage but also the equality of all subjects. The Josephine state viewed its people as citizens whose conscience was not the state's concern as long as they behaved properly and contributed to the public welfare.

Joseph strengthened the state's role in church administration through a commission at court for spiritual affairs. The state established general seminaries, one in each crownland, to educate the clergy. Joseph also abolished all monasteries that did not fulfill social charitable functions. In the Bohemian crownlands more than one third of the monasteries were dissolved, including several with ancient traditions (St. George's Benedictine convent in the Prague castle, the Benedictine monastery at Břevnov, the Cistercian foundation at Zbraslav, and many more). Their property went into a religious fund that was used to nearly double the number of parishes, whose boundaries were rationalized. The priests also had to keep more accurate records. Joseph dissolved a number of churches and chapels, whose buildings were converted to secular uses, and reduced the number of church holidays, feasts, and pilgrimages.

Joseph II continued his mother's administrative policies, maintaining the United Chancellery in Vienna. He also took more direct steps to remove the Estates' participation in the administration. In 1783 the land committees were abolished, and their remaining functions transferred to the state. Henceforth the Estates had only the right to elect two deputies from a list of six government nominees to sit in the *gubernia*. The land courts were also integrated into the state justice system. Joseph II even began to appoint state bureaucrats to the traditional land offices instead of members of the noble estates. As though to symbolize his vision of a unified, centralized empire, Joseph II refused to be crowned king of Bohemia.

Joseph II challenged the noble interests most directly in his reforms of the landlord-peasant relationship. His patent of November 1, 1781, abolished serfdom in the empire and substituted for it a state of "moderate subjection." From now on, all peasants, dominical and rustical alike, had the right to marry without their lord's permission, to move where they liked under certain limited restrictions, and to send their children to learn a trade or study. The economic obligations of the peasant to the landlord, however, were not removed. *Robota*, payments in kind, and cash rents were still regulated according to the Theresian patent of 1775.

Joseph II proposed to transform this situation in his most far-reaching reform. New cadastral surveys between 1785 and 1789 prepared the way for a reapportionment of the tax burden, to make the lords bear a larger share. The peasant was to retain 70 percent of the gross output of his holding for his own consumption and local, school, and church payments. Of the remaining 30 percent, the state was to receive 13 percent, leaving 17 percent for cash payments to the landlord in lieu of *robota* labor and other obligations. These reforms ran into stiff resistance from the lords, and uncomprehending opposition from the peasants. In the military and economic crisis toward the end of his reign, the threat of outright rebellion forced Joseph to rescind most of his reforms, except for the edict of toleration, the abolition of serfdom, and the monastic legislation. The emperor's brother Leopold succeeded him in 1790.

REVOLUTION, THE FRENCH WARS, AND REACTION (1790–1815)

Leopold II (1790–1792) had shown an interest in enlightened reform as Grand Duke of Tuscany, but his major task now was to contain the upheaval threatening his realm. To do so required tactical retreats in domestic policies. Tragically, Leopold died after only two years, leaving open the question whether his initial retreat would have been followed by somewhat more tactfully pursued reforms. Certainly his son Francis II (1792–1835) did not further the changes Joseph began. Incapable of perceiving the French Revolution as an expression of social and political pressures that could have been treated by astute reforms, Francis saw it as mere anarchy and terror unleashed by conspiratorial elements. After his accession, a reactionary mood dominated in Austria.

Leopold II: Compromise with Resistance

As a first step, Leopold convoked the diets of all his possessions in 1790, and invited them to submit their complaints and requests to him.[18] None of the Estates of the Bohemian crownlands challenged the existence of the United Bohemian-Austrian Chancellery, though they called for a return to Estates government within each land. In addition, the Silesian Estates requested administrative separation from Moravia. The Estates of Bohemia called for the land offices to be filled in consultation with the Estates, and for the Viennese official responsible for Bohemian affairs to be a noble with Bohemian citizenship. Interestingly, the language in which the Estates phrased their requests reflected Enlightenment political thought, presenting them as the representatives of the nation, with whom the ruler concluded a social contract.

Leopold limited his concessions to the Estates. Instead of concluding a new contract with the "nation" he reverted to the situation of 1764. He also filled several long-empty traditional offices, agreed to renew the land committees for Bohemia and Moravia, give them control of the domestic fund, and consult the Estates diet in all customary matters. In a brilliant symbolic move, Leopold staged a festive coronation as king of Bohemia on September 6, 1791, having earlier ceremonially transferred the crown from Vienna back to Prague. The coronation, coming nearly half a century after Maria Theresa's, was accompanied by public celebrations, including several that reflected increasing interest in the Czech language.[19] Prospects for further reform, however, ended with Leopold's premature death on March 2, 1792. The challenge of revolutionary and Napoleonic France dominated government policy thereafter.

In foreign affairs, Leopold laid the foundation for meeting this challenge by achieving a rapprochement with Prussia and ending the war with Turkey. In August 1791, he met the Prussian king Frederick Wil-

Coronation of Leopold II in Prague's St. Vitus's Cathedral, part of his successful policy of pacifying the Estates of his possessions. (Courtesy of the State Central Archive of the Czech Republic, Prague)

liam II at Pillnitz in Saxony, where they issued a declaration warning the French assembly of the concern of the European powers. The Declaration of Pillnitz was followed on February 7, 1792, by a treaty of alliance between the Habsburg monarchy and Prussia. Shortly afterward, Leopold II died. Under Francis, Habsburg policy became more openly antirevolutionary, until on April 20, 1792, the French Constituent Assembly declared war on "the king of Bohemia and Hungary" (Francis did not become Holy Roman Emperor until July 1792).

Francis and the French Wars

The conflict that began with the First Coalition War lasted until 1815. Under Francis, the Habsburg monarchy took part in the first three anti-French coalitions, in 1792–97, 1799–1801, and again in 1805. The Bohemian crownlands were not a direct theater of conflict in the First Coalition War, which failed to prevent the execution of Louis XIV, reduced to "Citizen Capet," on January 21, 1793. Austria's armies fought the French with limited success, as their Prussian ally concluded a second partition of Poland with Russia, leaving the Habsburg monarchy entirely without compensation. The Polish reaction, a national uprising under Tadeusz Kościuszko, was crushed in the third partition in 1795. The Habsburgs received additional territory, but they had to accept Prussia's desertion of the coalition. While Habsburg armies retreated along the Rhine, a rising star in the French military firmament, Napoleon Bonaparte, defeated them in Italy. The Treaty of Campo Formio (1797) ended the First Coalition War.

Russia and Britain immediately drew Austria into the Second Coalition, and during the winter of 1798–99, Russian armies crossed the Bohemian crownlands on their way to northern Italy. War began with a French declaration on May 19, 1799, but after initial successes the Russian armies abruptly withdrew (crossing Bohemia again in the winter of 1799–1800). The Russian armies in the Bohemian crownlands provoked interest, especially among the Czechs, who recognized the Russians as fellow Slavs. Without allies, however, the Austrians were crushed in Italy and forced to sign the treaty of Lunéville on February 9, 1801.

Napoleon's coronation as Emperor of the French in May 1804 symbolized on the one hand the definitive close of the revolutionary phase of the French wars. On the other hand, it spelled the end of the ancient Holy Roman Empire, whose title had been in Habsburg hands since the fifteenth century. If it disappeared, Francis would be merely King of Hungary and Bohemia, while the upstart Corsican took precedence. He therefore assumed the title of Emperor of Austria (as Francis I) on August 11, 1804. The proclamation explicitly assured his possessions of the undisturbed continuity of all their titles, dignities, and constitutional privileges, but it further weakened the status of the Bohemian crownlands and strengthened centralism.

Within a year the new Emperor of Austria was at war again with the Emperor of the French. In the Third Coalition War, Napoleon occupied Vienna in November 1805, and then defeated the combined Russian and Austrian armies near the village of Slavkov (Austerlitz) outside Brno, on December 2, 1805. The Treaty of Pressburg on December 26, 1805, forced Austria to accept French hegemony in Italy and along the Rhine. Francis I formally resigned the title of Holy Roman Emperor on August 6, 1806. That autumn Napoleon crushed Prussia so thoroughly that it disappeared as a European power, and by the Treaty of Tilsit of 1807 he aligned a reluctant Russia with his European system, proclaimed in Berlin in December 1806. This Continental System created a European economic union that completely excluded Great Britain, while subordinating the economies of Napoleon's European allies to France.

When an anti-French guerrilla insurgency broke out in Spain in 1809, the Austrian government decided (with British encouragement) to renew hostilities. This time, influenced by German refugees in Bohemia, the state attempted to stir up German national feeling and appeal to the traditional provincial identities of its subjects, including the Hussite military traditions in the Bohemian crownlands. After some initial successes, the Austrians were decisively defeated at Wagram. The peace treaty of Schönbrunn (October 14, 1809) confirmed Austria's subordination to France, and the new chief of Austria's diplomacy, Count (later Prince) Klemens Wenzel Metternich, negotiated a marriage alliance with Napoleon, who divorced his first wife and married Francis's daughter, Marie Louise.

The opportunity to break away from French domination came with Napoleon's ill-fated invasion of Russia in 1812. Austrian forces accompanied their French ally, but avoided conflict with the Russians. When Napoleon's expedition ended in disaster, Austria concluded a truce with the Russians and after some hesitation joined with Great Britain, Russia, and Prussia against the French in the "Battle of the Nations" at Leipzig on October 16–19, 1813. The coalition armies entered Paris as Napoleon abdicated in April 1814, and from September 14, 1814, to June 19, 1815, they met in Vienna to forge a peace. Their guiding principles were to restore Europe's political conditions before 1792 (if possible), to restore the powers of "legitimate" ruling dynasties (in particular the Bourbons in France), and to preserve this restored order from the threat of renewed revolution. In spite of disagreements, the four powers were united enough to respond to Napoleon's escape from Elba and his return to France. Napoleon's "Hundred Days" shook Europe, but the last hurrah ended in one of the fiercest battles of the wars near the Belgian village of Waterloo, on June 18, 1815.

Meanwhile, the Congress of Vienna's final agreements, signed on June 8 and 9, 1815, confirmed that Austria would regain its lost territory, and added Lombardy and Venetia in Italy in return for Austria's surrender of the Belgian provinces to the new Kingdom of the Netherlands. Austria also received back its share of the first Polish partition. With the exception of Cracow, supposedly a free city under four-power guarantee, the rest went to the newly created Kingdom of Poland attached to the Russian crown. Rather than attempt to revive the Holy Roman Empire, the Congress of Vienna replaced it with a German Confederation, linking thirty-five sovereign territories (far fewer than the old empire) with four self-governing cities. The presidency of this confederation was vested in the Austrian Empire. Prussia and Austria eventually agreed that Bohemia, Moravia, and both Austrian and Prussian Silesia would enter the confederation.

Francis I's government after the Congress of Vienna retained features that it had assumed during the struggle with France. The freer cultural atmosphere connected with the Enlightenment was long a thing of the past. Censorship regulations were strengthened after 1789, and Leopold II further developed Joseph's police system, using informers and provocateurs to undermine aristocratic opposition. A supposed Jacobin conspiracy uncovered in 1794 seems to have had its origins in such tactics against Hungarian opposition.[20] Although the public generally reacted negatively to the revolution, the authorities in the Bohemian crownlands carefully followed the opinions of the population and severely limited what could be published. The resulting stultification of cultural life continued beyond Francis's reign. Although these conditions stamped some specific features on the emerging modern Czech nation and national culture, they did not halt the process, which had its origins in the preceding decades.

BEGINNINGS OF THE CZECH NATIONAL RENASCENCE

In Czech historiography, the emergence of the modern Czech nation and national culture is called the Czech national renascence, usually describing the development of Czech language and literature up to the revolution of 1848.[21] Such a renewal is not unique to the Czechs: the Czech national renascence is one of many similar movements in Europe, and shares common features with them.[22] Nor did the movement emerge out of nowhere, though contemporaries did speak of their national "rebirth" or even "resurrection." The immediate origins of the renascence lie in the economic, demographic, cultural, and political changes in the Habsburg monarchy during the second half of the eighteenth century, in particular the impact of the Enlightenment and the reform program of enlightened absolutism.

Enlightenment concepts of the theater influenced Count Franz Anton Nostitz-Rieneck to establish a theater in Prague specifically for the performance of serious works by German playwrights, as well as Italian operas. The new theater, a true gem of classicist architecture, was built from 1781 to 1783 directly beside the oldest part of the university, still symbolizing the Jesuit education against which the Enlightenment set itself. If theater was to enlighten the people, some attention would have to be paid to the people who did not speak German. The center of Czech-language theater in this period was the Patriotic Theater, which was established in 1786 in a temporary wooden structure on the Horse Market (today's Wenceslas Square) in Prague's New Town. Czech translators and authors such as Karel Hynek Thám and Prokop Šedivý provided the Czech-reading public with statements of the Enlightenment understanding of the didactic role of the stage, which persisted long into the next century.

The size of the reading public and distribution of reading material in the Bohemian crownlands also grew. Books were published in Latin, German, and Czech, though the production of Czech reading material lagged far behind in both genres and quality. Many publishing houses became centers of literary life, and associations formed around them. The most significant such circle for the Czech-speaking public was the *Česká expedice* (Czech Expedition), created by the journalist Václav Matěj Kramerius to publish Czech-language material.

In 1781, Joseph II liberalized censorship, unleashing a veritable explosion of publication, but with the outbreak of the French Revolution the trend reversed. In the Bohemian crownlands the government was particularly worried about newspapers, both German and Czech, though the Czech-language press received special attention. In 1798 a court decree made it illegal to place uncensored newspapers in coffeehouses or pubs. In spite of the cooler atmosphere, the circulation of the main newspapers published in Prague in Czech and German continued to rise through the last decades of the eighteenth century.[23]

The development of a reading culture also expressed itself in the organization of learned societies, including short-lived private examples in the Bohemian crownlands (the Olomouc Societas Incognitorum, 1747, Prague's Learned Club, 1772). A private Society for the Development of Mathematics, Patriotic History, and Natural History in Bohemia formed in Prague around 1772, and issued six volumes of its proceedings between 1775 and 1784. Finally it transformed itself into the Bohemian Society of Sciences, eventually adding the adjective "Royal."[24]

In the Masonic lodge noble and non-noble could associate as social equals. The first Masonic lodges in Prague were established around 1742 with the help of French officers then occupying the Bohemian capital. As a result, under Maria Theresa the masons suffered from official suspicion, yet by the 1770s there were already three lodges in Prague, pursuing charitable and intellectual activities. Government concerns about the Freemasons increased under Francis to such levels that in 1794 the Masonic lodges in Prague and Brno voluntarily suspended their activities. Former masons still participated in unofficial circles, and many of the people implicated in the "Jacobin conspiracy" of 1794 were or had been Freemasons.[25]

Aristocrats' involvement in intellectual and cultural life and their support of non-noble scholars linked cultural developments in Bohemia to the aristocratic resistance to government reforms. For these nobles, the word "nation" still referred to the social corporation granted political rights, the nobility. Belonging to this corporation did not depend on language. The Enlightenment also saw patriotism as loyalty to the land where one lived, held property, and undertook what activities one chose. Thus the term "territorial patriotism" is commonly used to describe noble attitudes in the Bohemian crownlands. The aristocracy—even descendants of families that arrived after the White Mountain—naturally turned to traditions of the separate existence of the Bohemian crown-lands to defend their prerogatives. They patronized Czech history and saw the Czech language as a symbol of the separate traditions of the Czech kingdom, if not a means of communication. The Czech national renascence drew on these elements of reaction to the reforms of Maria Theresa and Joseph II, but the reforms also stimulated it.[26]

The acceptance of critical principles by most historians in the Royal Bohemian Society of Sciences—Josef Dobrovský was the most rigorous of them—ensured the dominance of the new trends. The specific aspects of Czech history they studied reinforced the historical separateness and unique traditions of Bohemia, which pleased the nobility. Count Franz Joseph Kinský's comment that "if the mother tongue of a Frenchman is French and of a German, German, then the mother tongue of a Czech must be Czech," reflected the symbolic value of the Czech language.[27] Patriots challenged the nobility to prove their love of their homeland through supporting Czech.[28] At the same time, philologists were shaping modern literary Czech. Leopold II approved the creation of a chair of Czech language and literature at the Prague university in 1791. Literary history drew on historical and philological interests to demonstrate that Czech had once been a language of high culture. Czech works from the later fifteenth and sixteenth centuries, published in new editions, pro-vided models for the patriots attempting to write in Czech. They helped reinforce the classicist approach to Czech and the myth of a previous "golden age." Some patriots also experimented with journalism, drama, and poetry, laying the groundwork for nineteenth-century Czech culture and its characteristic "linguocentrism."[29]

Other patriots concentrated on the common people. Enlightened re-forms tried to improve the social, economic, and cultural condition of the countryside. Many writers and publicists involved in these tasks also tried to heighten the Czech consciousness of the people and improve the Czech language in everyday use.[30] By involving the common people, they began redefining the meaning of nation. Because language determined who belonged to the nation, and because the upper classes refused to adopt the Czech language, the importance of those who actually did speak Czech increased. Eventually the concept of nation would include all Czech speakers. Even though the school system assumed that pupils would learn German, enlightened absolutism led to a greater use and awareness of Czech. And in its efforts to rally popular support against the French, the government used Czech history, even the Hussite tradition—at least in its military aspects—to drum up support for the land militia. In these and other ways, through newspapers, market broadsheets, plays, odes, and festivals, some of the traditions that would be adapted to Czech nationalism were revived and spread among the broader masses.

This early phase of the national renascence also reflected a Czech awareness of the wider Slavic world. Yet Slavism was almost always subordinate to specifically Czech aims. The Napoleonic wars exposed many Czechs directly to the Russians, and interest in this Slavic ally among intellectuals and the urban classes was common, but Russophilism was limited to some younger intellectuals. This younger generation came to the fore as the French wars drew to a close. Under conditions of Francis's police absolutism, these younger patriots would push the national renascence into a new phase, in which active patriotic agitation replaced scholarly investigation of the language, customs, and history of the nation.

8   The "Springtime of Nations"

"One must not dream of reformation while agitated by passion," wrote Metternich to Russia's Tsar Alexander I in 1820; "wisdom directs that at such moments we should limit ourselves to maintaining."[1] Thus Metternich encapsulated the principles of Francis I, the emperor he served until forced from office by the Revolution of 1848. Maintaining the stability of the order created at Vienna in 1815 became the main objective of Austrian policy. The era of the Enlightenment had come to an end in Europe, to be replaced by Romanticism. As though reflecting the failure of the "Age of Reason," Romanticism rejected Enlightenment rationality, setting in its place feeling, intuition, the heart. Romanticism turned away from classical antiquity and celebrated the Gothic of the middle ages. In addition, the Romantics hailed the common people, who preserved the traditions of the nation and a link back to an "unspoiled" past. This Romantic historicism became a feature of Europe's nationalist movements (including the Czech one).

Biedermeier, the style of the Austrian *Vormärz* or Pre-March era, added specifically central European features to the dominant Romantic style. Instead of finding an outlet in the creative genius of the great individual, or a retreat to the Gothic of the middle ages, Biedermeier sought refuge in a small-scale, comfortable, useful, middle-class world of intimate family life, of resignation to the established order, of enjoyment of nature in the idyllic, pastoral context of well-cultivated countryside, and of love of the homeland.[2] Biedermeier corresponded well to the conditions prevailing in the Austrian empire up to the 1848 Revolution.

RESTORATION AND
PRE-MARCH (1815–1848)

The international system established at the Congress of Vienna was symbolized by the Holy Alliance of 1815, proposed by the Tsar and dedicated to conservative, Christian principles. The Quadruple Alliance linking Great Britain with Austria, Russia, Prussia, and after 1818 France represented a more practical force. In spite of mutual wariness among Austria, Prussia, and Russia, and continuing British suspicion of France, this consortium of European powers preserved the restoration order through 1830. In that year revolution overthrew Charles X in France, spread to the Belgian provinces of the Netherlands, and in November erupted in rebellion in Russian Poland. The Polish insurrection, finally crushed in 1831, prevented Russia's Nicholas I from intervening elsewhere, while Austria's shaky finances kept it passive, except in Italy. Metternich had to accept a new dynasty in France and the independent Belgian kingdom.

Within the German Confederation, Austria faced renewed German nationalism after 1830. The customs union created in 1834 on Prussia's initiative limited its influence. Francis I and Nicholas reaffirmed Russian-Austrian cooperation, on the other hand, at a meeting in Mnichovo Hradiště (Münchengrätz) in 1833, where Nicholas promised to support Francis's heir, Ferdinand. Russia and Austria also jointly crushed the Polish uprising in Cracow in 1846, during which Galicia was swept by a peasant *jacquerie*. Cracow was annexed to Austrian Galicia.

The internal administration of the Austrian Empire and the Bohemian crownlands after 1815 also reflected the ideal of maintaining stability and combating revolution. What Francis I's policies still shared with Joseph's or Leopold's was the goal of a centralized, bureaucratic realm with German as the state language. Enlightenment, however, was replaced with an all-pervasive political police. Police directorates in both Prague and Brno operated almost entirely independently of the land *gubernia*, reporting directly to Count Joseph Sedlnitzky's Supreme Court Police and Censorship Office in Vienna.

When Francis I died in 1835, he was succeeded—as he had himself insisted—by his eldest son, Ferdinand (1835–1848). Though he was the legitimate heir, Ferdinand was physically and mentally incompetent to shoulder the burdens of state. While Ferdinand ruled in name, a reorganized state conference functioned as a regency council. Archduke Ludwig chaired it, and Metternich and Count Franz Anton Kolowrat-Liebsteinsky advised on foreign and domestic matters, respectively. Kolowrat belonged to one of Bohemia's great aristocratic families, and though he supported the central government, he was sympathetic to noble claims to political and cultural privileges. Metternich and Kolowrat were also bitter rivals, so the state conference was usually paralyzed and simply avoided decisions.

In the Bohemian crownlands the highest level of the state administration was still the Bohemian and Moravian-Silesian *gubernia*, in Prague and Brno, respectively. After 1815 the police directorates overshadowed the *gubernia* in censorship and publication (except for Czech-language books, which were the responsibility of the *gubernia*). They also supervised all public activity, observed foreigners, state officials, and politically suspect individuals, and in the process collected information from a wide range of informers and spies, much of it less than reliable.

The chief officer of each *gubernium* was its president. Until the 1848 revolution, the Bohemian *gubernium* president was usually also the highest burggrave, now only a ceremonial distinction. Kolowrat held this office from 1809 to 1825, when he was succeeded by Count Karl Chotek from 1826 until 1843. In matters where Vienna was not directly concerned they each had some leeway. They improved the state and local roads, and supported roadworks and public parks in Prague. Kolowrat helped found the Patriotic Museum in Bohemia (the future Czech National Museum) in 1818; Chotek supported the Union for the Encouragement of Industry in Bohemia (1833) and organized industrial exhibitions.[3] Anton Friedrich Mitrowsky, governor in Brno from 1815 to 1827, pursued similar aims, though the Moravian museum created in 1817 developed much more slowly than the Bohemian one owing to financial difficulties.

The land diets still existed and usually met regularly, but their political influence was reduced practically to nothing. Though Ferdinand's formal coronation (as Czech king Ferdinand V) took place in Prague in 1836, even this event passed without extraordinary excitement.[4] The land committees of the Estates, however, supported scientific and historical research. The Bohemian Estates appointed a young scholar from Moravia, František Palacký, as their official historian in 1838, a year after Antonín Boček received a similar appointment to the Moravian Estates. The gubernial and Estates archives in each land were also professionally organized under the land committee's authority.

Toward the end of the 1830s the Bohemian Estates began to voice political discontent and cautiously demand change.[5] The example of Hungary, where the diet had developed a program of national reform and raised audacious demands for more political power, stimulated the aristocratic leaders, Counts Friedrich Deym and Leo and Joseph Matthias Thun. In 1841, the opposition in the Estates attacked Count Chotek for mismanaging the domestic fund. Chotek resigned in 1843. That same year the Estates organized a lecture series by their historian, Palacký, on the development of the Estates constitution since 1620. The Estates adopted a formal statement of their rights on February 18, 1847. In May they presented it to the government in Vienna, which rejected it, so at their August 1847 session the Estates refused to sanction the taxes. The government simply collected them anyway, yet aspects of the nobility's program—its criticism of absolutism, its stress on Bohemia's separate legal and constitutional traditions, and the use of parliamentary forms and tactics—influenced other social levels. The real challenge to absolutism in the Austrian empire, however, would come from national movements based on other social groups, in a society that had been undergoing major economic and social change.

INDUSTRIALIZATION AND THE BOHEMIAN CROWNLANDS

The Napoleonic wars created hardship but also stimulated forces of economic change.[6] Supplying the army strained the domestic economy, and the long conflict stimulated inflation. Napoleon's Continental System hampered activities aimed at export or dependent on imported materials like cotton. At the same time domestic agriculture, craft, and manufacturing efforts that had previously struggled with British competition developed more rapidly. In 1811, the state declared bankruptcy. Creditors and those on fixed incomes suffered, and the state bankruptcy also had negative long-term effects on public confidence in the state's financial strength and its paper money. On the other hand, many agricultural producers and traders profited from the bankruptcy, and the war years also made fortunes for military suppliers and speculators.

The Bohemian crownlands' population increased from 4.8 million in 1815 to 6.7 million in 1847. Even the great cholera epidemic of 1831–32 (when more than 50,000 people died) and smaller outbreaks in 1836–37 and 1843 caused only temporary fluctuations. Rising population and wartime demands stimulated agriculture. Low agricultural costs and high prices lasted into the 1820s, but thereafter prices fell while costs remained constant. Producers moved toward specialized crops or sheep raising on the great landed estates. By the early 1840s there were 2.5 million sheep in the Bohemian crownlands, and the industrial demand for wool actually slowed other developments in modernizing agriculture. Nevertheless, a recovery began again from the end of the 1830s. New seed strains, crop rotation, better agricultural techniques, and the introduction of artificial fertilizers increased the yield of most grain crops. The potato finished conquering the Bohemian crownlands, and among the peasants it became a crucial part of the diet.

The stimulus given to cotton spinning and weaving by the continental blockade encouraged the expansion of manufactories and the construction of machine-equipped shops around Brno, Liberec (Reichenberg), and Prague. By the 1820s cotton spinning was largely mechanized, initially using water power, but later steam. Machine printing of cotton prevailed by 1848, but hand weaving was still the norm, with skilled labor cheap thanks to the tradition of linen weaving. By 1841 the production of cotton had reached roughly the same level as linen. Wool production, concentrated around Brno (the "Austrian Manchester") and Liberec, approximately equaled the production of cotton and linen combined.

Other agricultural industries also developed during the postwar decades. Following its postwar collapse, the sugar beet industry began to expand in the 1830s with the introduction of new machinery and techniques. Gradually sugar production concentrated in mechanized factories, increasing overall output. The small, scattered breweries belonging to tradesmen or landowners (1,475 of them in 1841) gave way to joint companies with better equipment. The famous Plzeň brewery was founded in 1842 by a group of burghers, and with the adoption of the bottom-fermentation method created an entirely new type of beer named after the town. By the 1840s flour milling, too, was transformed by the introduction of steam-driven mills. While the traditional manufacturing industries concentrated in the German-inhabited border regions, the agricultural industries developed in the Czech-speaking agricultural heartland.

The introduction of machines, especially steam engines, created demand for domestic machine-building industries, usually developed with foreign, often British, specialists. The machine-building industry and the beginning of railroad construction increased demand for iron and coal, essential raw materials for both enterprises. The first blast furnace using coke was built in 1836, but much iron production still came from small workshops using charcoal. Ostrava's development as a center for heavy industries began during these decades.

Transportation still made use of rivers, but both private and state capital was invested in roads and railways. In 1832 a horse-drawn railway was opened between České Budějovice and Linz in Upper Austria, and by 1839 the northern route from Vienna to Galicia, intended for steam locomotives, had reached Brno. The first steam train pulled into Prague in 1845. Morse's telegraph linked Vienna and Brno in 1846, and lines were extended from there via Olomouc to Prague in 1847, but it was reserved for official use only until 1850.

From impoverished masters and craftsmen, from hand spinners and weavers increasingly competing with machines, came the first wave of an industrial working class. The most significant workers' protest in the first half of the century took place in June and July 1844. The workers in one of Prague's cotton-printing factories, protesting against low wages, destroyed the printing machinery and attacked Jewish shops and merchants. Similar disturbances took place near Liberec and among the railroad construction workers in Prague's Karlín suburb. The authorities crushed the disturbances with the army and police, and created an investigating commission at the *gubernium* to keep watch on workers' organizations.[7] The modern middle classes also began to emerge from various elements. State officials were joined by others who worked in various professions that were not guild trades, landowning, or military service. These teachers, doctors, lawyers, private tutors, and others formed the nascent intelligentsia from which many of the active patriots of the Czech national renascence came.

The fundamental social axis of the Bohemian crownlands during the first half of the nineteenth century, however, remained that between landowners and subject peasants. After Joseph II's urbarial reforms were revoked the peasant enjoyed the freedoms established by the serfdom patent of 1781, but he was still under the landlord's jurisdiction, even if the state increasingly intervened. Worst of all, he was still obliged to perform the *robota*. The last great peasant uprising against *robota* occurred in Moravia in 1821. By the 1840s the problem of agrarian reform was recognized even among landlords, and discussed in pamphlets and newspapers, both smuggled from abroad and printed under Austrian censorship.

CULTURE AND NATIONALISM TO 1848

The government's concern for order and stability determined cultural conditions in the Austrian empire before 1848. Francis neither wanted public support, nor welcomed it when it arose. Wartime efforts to generate an Austrian patriotism based on anything other than loyalty and obedience to the ruler withered.[8] Nevertheless, Francis's dislike of change prevented him from thoroughly purging the state bureaucracy, so at least some officials (who with the army formed the main bearers of a general, all-Austrian concept of the state) continued the influence of Josephinism. One expression of this lingering influence of Joseph II was the general civil code promulgated in 1811 but begun under Joseph II. Covering property, inheritance, ownership, and other aspects of private law, the code introduced equality before the law in these areas, but not political rights and civic freedoms.

Pre-March Culture in the Bohemian Crownlands

Francis maintained state oversight of the church, but the position of the Catholic church strengthened during and after the Napoleonic wars. When the pope restored the Jesuit order in 1814, it also reentered the Habsburg monarchy. The civil code of 1811 included provisions of canon law, such as prohibiting Catholic divorce. Church influence in primary and intermediate education was strengthened, and the universities (including Prague and Olomouc) fell behind their counterparts in the German Confederation. Like the state bureaucracy, however, the church still included parish priests and members of the hierarchy who had been influenced by the Catholic enlightenment. Nevertheless, the authorities moved against suspicious views, as in the dismissal of Bernard Bolzano as professor at the Prague university.

In its schools Francis's state taught students to be industrious and obedient subjects. Teachers had to follow prescribed textbooks, and pedagogical methods stagnated. Nevertheless, after 1815 compulsory school attendance at least in the primary grades reached most communities in the Bohemian crownlands. The schools continued to spread the German language. Czech was the language of instruction in trivial schools in Czech-speaking areas, but even there teachers had to include German instruction. The main schools in the towns and especially the Prague normal school also emphasized German. Mastering German was a prerequisite for further study, especially at the highest level. Czech was still recognized as necessary for parish priests in Czech-speaking areas, and was part of the curriculum in pastoral theology at the Prague university. In 1816 a decree extended the teaching of Czech in the gymnasia, but it gradually lapsed in the face of official inertia and indifference.

The Bohemian aristocracy remained important to the cultural life of the Bohemian crownlands. The Patriotic Museum was only one of many institutions to which the nobility contributed. The nobility were significant patrons of other cultural activities, including building—notably with the renovation of noble residences in the Empire style of the first decades of the nineteenth century. In the 1840s Romantic historicist styles predominated, such as in the reconstructed Schwarzenberg chateau at Hluboká, in English neo-Gothic. The state also influenced construction activity through centrally directed building offices in each land capital. Trained construction engineers and architects set out to build administrative, judicial, military, and postal buildings throughout the monarchy. The Empire style, synthesizing Classical features and modern needs, best suited these state-sponsored structures. Empire also influenced railway tunnels and viaducts, the chain bridge over the Vltava in Prague (1841), and the six new gates carved into Prague's fortifications to accommodate the arrival of railroads.

Increasing urban populations also stimulated building. Usually cities expanded outward, though Prague still had room within Charles IV's city boundaries. Public projects included strengthening the Vltava's banks in Prague, parks and gardens, and buildings with social, medical, or charitable functions. Squares and streets were paved, sewers were introduced (in Prague already from 1816), and street lighting was improved (in Prague the first gas lamps were installed in 1847). The land offices developed the health spas and mineral baths at Teplice (Teplitz), Karlovy Vary (Karlsbad), Mariánské Lázně (Marienbad), and Františkovy Lázně (Franzensbad). Urban building also reflected Romantic neo-historical styles, the foremost example of which was the neo-Gothic new wing of the Prague Old Town Hall (1846–48).

The Bohemian aristocracy rarely engaged actively in the national renascence. Nevertheless, many noblemen continued to sympathize with and support Czech cultural efforts during the politically more active 1840s. On questions of linguistic nationalism, the nobility attempted to stay outside either the German or the Czech camp. J. M. Thun wrote in 1846 that as far as his own nationality was concerned, "I am neither a Czech nor a German, but only a Bohemian," and that he supported the Czech literary strivings "since I consider it my knightly duty to take the side of the weaker party."[9] Bernard Bolzano expressed a nonaristocratic version of this Bohemian identity in his university lectures, linking enlightened concepts of patriotism with practical Christian respect for others. He argued for a united political nation with two branches, Czech and German, linked by common civic equality, education, and active love of neighbor.[10] His influence was limited to his former students at the university, and following his dismissal in 1820 Bolzano's pleas for mutual acceptance increasingly fell on deaf ears.

A New Phase of the National Renascence

During the final years of the Napoleonic wars, the upsurge of German nationalism had its counterpart especially among younger patriots in the Bohemian crownlands. Their attitudes were already influenced by early Romanticism, turning their interest in the language, history, and customs of the Czechs from an antiquarian curiosity or scholarly study into a committed activity aimed at expressing and strengthening Czech national consciousness. Though the Czech movement did not yet have a mass base, it had entered a phase of national agitation by a larger group of patriots with a much wider territorial and social base.

The Czech-speaking population in the lands of the crown of St. Václav was approximately 60 percent in Bohemia, something over 70 percent in Moravia, and only about 20 percent in Austrian Silesia. In spite of the smaller proportion of Czech speakers than in Moravia, the Czech renascence in Bohemia progressed more rapidly and enjoyed wider social foundations. Prague was the administrative, economic, and cultural center, giving it a unique place. Though it would be decades before Prague's appearance or city government became Czech, already in the first decades of the nineteenth century, strengthened by its historical associations with Czech statehood and its role as seat of Czech political and cultural institutions, it was the center of the Czech national movement. In contrast, Prague was only one of several provincial centers for the Bohemian Germans.

The Czech movement in Moravia had no dominant center, though Brno and Olomouc competed for the honor.[11] From Moravia, Vienna was much more directly accessible than Prague. Not only did Moravia's dialects differ from Bohemia's, but also the province's typically stronger Catholicism made some Moravians suspicious of Bohemian influence. In addition, the Estates emphasized Moravia's independent position under the crown of St. Václav. Thus Moravianism was the predominant orientation among intellectuals—not anti-Czech, but not yet reflecting the Czech national consciousness developing in Bohemia. Efforts to establish a Moravian literary language eventually failed.[12] In Silesia the situation was further complicated by the presence of Polish-speakers (approximately 35 percent) as well as Germans (45 percent). There the non-Germans identified territorially with Silesia, moving toward Polish or Czech identities.

In Bohemia, larger and medium-sized towns were centers of patriotic activity.[13] In small towns and villages, most active patriots were parish priests. Although the majority of Czech-speakers were peasants, peasant engagement in the national movement began only shortly before 1848. Where the countryside was involved, it was where market relations already existed between agricultural regions and the capital, other local centers, or the industrially developed eastern and northeastern regions. In those areas identifiable groups of patriots (subscribers to the journal of the museum, or contributors to the cultural foundation Matice česká) were active in most towns with more than 1,000 inhabitants. Elsewhere in the north and in the west and southwest, such activity was common only where administrative offices and gymnasia were located; southern and southeastern Bohemia were even less active.

Many Catholic parish priests, especially in Czech-speaking areas, were active patriots, although their role declined as others threatened or stimulated by social and economic change became more involved. The Czech-speaking artisans and shopkeepers in towns, faced with competition from enterprises owned by German-speakers, participated along-side manorial officials who could only speak Czech. The most active enthusiasts were those for whom a larger public role for the Czech language opened up prospects for advancement. Public school teachers (there were about five thousand by the 1840s) and Czech university students joined in the agitation demanding greater public status for Czech in the Bohemian crownlands.

Josef Jungmann dominated the beginning of this new phase of the renascence. In a series of articles between 1806 and 1813 Jungmann expressed a new understanding of "nation" based on language. The true patriot would use Czech for all his intellectual and cultural endeavors. Jungmann accepted that this meant "losing" most of the nobility, but he was not concerned: "The people is still Czech; as for the lords, let them speak French or Babylonian. . . . Every language is, in its own home, a peasants' language, and since the peasant is the foremost inhabitant of the land, he could with justice demand: '. . . speak so I can understand you!' "[14] Jungmann's earliest works were translations of world literature, but his greatest achievement was a Czech-German dictionary (5 volumes, 1834–39) that helped prepare Czech for the role the national movement now assigned it. As a teacher at the gymnasia in Litoměřice and later in Prague, Jungmann influenced a wide circle of other patriots.

Russia's role in defeating Napoleon stimulated the vague notion that all Slavs belonged in one family that—as such German Romantics as Johann Gottfried von Herder predicted—was destined for greatness. A Slovak Protestant, Jan Kollár, who had imbibed German Romanticism at the university in Jena, expressed the Romantic idealization of the Slavs most vividly. Kollár's *Slávy dcera* (The Daughter of Sláva, 1824), celebrated the peace-loving, democratic Slavs and denounced the warlike Germans. František Ladislav Čelakovský wrote verses inspired by Russian and Serbian, as well as Czech folk songs. Another Protestant Slovak, Pavel Josef Šafařík, presented a scholarly picture of the culture and life of the ancient Slavs in his *Slovanské starožitnosti* (Slavic Antiquities, 1836–37), marked by typical Romantic enthusiasm.

The Protestant Slovak milieu worked strongly on František Palacký. Palacký studied at the Evangelical lyceum in Prešpurk, where he became acquainted with Šafařík. In 1823 he came to Prague; with Dobrovský's recommendation he gained a position as Sternberg family archivist, and in 1827 he became historian of the Estates. That year Palacký also became editor of the Patriotic Museum's new journal, published as a monthly in German and a quarterly in Czech.[15] The German-language version foundered, but Palacký's Czech journal survived and became an important link between Prague and the countryside. With Jungmann and J. S. Presl, Palacký founded the Committee for the Scientific Development of the Czech Language and Literature at the museum, from which the literary foundation Matice česká emerged in 1831. Unlike the museum, which long reflected Bohemian territorial patriotism, the Matice česká quickly became an important Czech national organization, raising funds for the publication of Czech works. The Matice also provided a final arbiter in questions about the Czech language.

Palacký's lifework was the history he began at the end of 1832. Its first volume was published in German in 1836. Two years later, Palacký began working on the Czech version, whose first volume appeared in March 1848. Palacký's history provided a key element of Czech national ideology, its image of its own past. He wrote that "the main content and fundamental course of all Czech and Moravian history is . . . conflict with Germandom, or the acceptance or rejection of German ways and customs by the Czechs."[16] Palacký accepted the Romantic idealization of the ancient Slavs and Czechs, which he contrasted to the feudal social order and military organization of the Germans.

As the Czechs turned to their early medieval past, where the distance was too great or the mists of time too thick to see clearly, they forged their own historical monuments. The most famous examples are the *Rukopis královédvorský* (Dvůr Králové/Königinhof manuscript) and the *Rukopis zelenohorský* (Zelená Hora/Grünberg manuscript, collectively referred to as RKZ), supposedly discovered in 1817 and 1818, respectively. These manuscripts contained fragments of epic and lyric verse, even older than the German *Niebelungenlied*. To the enthusiastic patriots, the RKZ confirmed the quality of the Czech language as well as the democratic social order among the earliest Czechs. Czech society— except for Dobrovský, at some cost to his standing among the patriots— accepted them as genuine. Palacký based his interpretation of the early Czechs in his history on the RKZ, which were also greeted with interest abroad. The RKZ are now regarded as fakes, but they remain a remarkable literary achievement (usually ascribed to Václav Hanka, librarian at the museum, and his friend Václav Linda), and generations of Czech artists and patriots drew from their themes and characters.[17]

In literature, poetry took pride of place over prose, but large-scale dramatic or epic works were scarce. Václav Kliment Klicpera and Josef

Kajetán Tyl contributed prose stories and dramas, often taking their themes from the great moments of Czech history. Both Klicpera and Tyl also drew themes from contemporary life, Klicpera most brightly in his farces, but Tyl also in stories reflecting contemporary social reality. Tyl is best remembered, however, for the patriotic lyric, "Kde domov můj?" (Where is my home? 1843). Set to music by František Škroup, it became the Czech national anthem.[18]

The Polish insurrection and liberal revolutions of 1830 excited the younger patriots, while Jungmann's generation still held fast to its Russophilism and dislike of social upheaval.[19] Secret groups attempted to help Polish refugees escape into exile (František August Brauner participated in such actions), or tried to maintain contact with the Polish émigré organizations after the uprising was crushed. After 1837, František Ladislav Rieger emerged as a leader among the university students in Prague who were active in the national movement.

Karel Hynek Mácha reflected some of the new currents in his work. From typical patriotic beginnings, Mácha found an individual poetic voice, which sounds especially clearly in his greatest achievement, the lyric epic *Máj* (May, 1836). In his own lifetime, Mácha was criticized for placing his subjective art above the national struggle. Mácha's pessimistic nihilism and romantic rejection of everyday reality may have annoyed his contemporaries, but *Máj* was the starting point for modern Czech poetry and remains popular among Czechs up to the present.

Through the 1840s political controls restricted Czech journalism and the press. Čelakovský was fired as editor of the official *Pražské noviny* when he criticized a speech by the Tsar on the Polish question, but he made the newspaper's literary supplement, *Česká včela* (Czech Bee), an influential literary voice. Other cultural journals included *Čechoslav*, and especially *Květy* (Blossoms), edited by Tyl. As venues for serious literature in Czech emerged, Palacký noted in the museum's journal in 1837 that the survival of Czech was assured. Now Czechs faced a different task, to "strive . . . for the palm of genuine scientific, aesthetic, and industrial enlightenment."[20] Under pre-March conditions such strivings would be primarily cultural, but increasingly the Czech movement discussed political questions.

Bohemia's Germans followed a different path starting from a favorable position. German had been the language of administration, education, and culture in Bohemia since the eighteenth century. Industrialization, which began in the German-populated frontier regions, concentrated capital in German hands. This situation affected German identity, because it made it seem self-evident.[21] Austrian Germans, like those in the confederation, had both regional and all-German identities; they were both "Austrian" and "German." But in addition to that, they could also be Bohemian, Moravian, or Silesian. Since Czech history and culture were part of this provincial identity, many Bohemian German liberals looked with sympathy on the Czech past and Czech cultural strivings. Moritz Hartmann and Alfred Meissner celebrated the Hussite heroes or the legendary Libuše in their verses.

German liberals also assumed that Czechs and Germans would work together for liberal goals. Yet to them, the Bohemian crownlands were German and would belong to a liberal, national Germany. By the mid-1840s, such questions were debated by Czech and German writers in liberal newspapers smuggled into Austria, like the Augsburg *Allgemeine Zeitung* and the Leipzig *Grenzboten*. The German writers, however, concentrated on transforming Austrian police absolutism into a constitutional system with civic freedoms, not on linguistic or nationality questions. Writers with a Czech or Bohemian outlook, in contrast, assumed the liberal ideals, and concentrated on language, education, or constitutional issues.[22]

The Union for the Promotion of Industry provided another public venue for Czech patriotic activity. After changes in its bylaws in 1843, many bourgeois Germans and Czechs joined. The Czechs concentrated on the section for industrial education, where future leaders such as Brauner and Alois Pravoslav Trojan gained experience in debate. The Czechs started a campaign to create a Czech industrial school. It was taken up in the *Pražské noviny*, now edited by the young Karel Havlíček, but the government finally banned the project in 1847. The Czechs established the Civic Club (Měšt'anská beseda) in 1845. From its inauguration in 1840 the annual Czech ball, at which only Czech was spoken, marked the social assertiveness of the Czech middle classes, and similar functions burgeoned. Less formal groups gathered at favorite pubs; from one such group the Czech radical association, "Repeal," developed. Repeal took its name from the Irish nationalist movement publicized (in a thinly veiled reference to Austria) by Havlíček's *Pražské noviny*. Key figures included Karel Sabina and Emanuel Arnold, who were radical activists in 1848.

In spite of the censorship, the official *Pražské noviny* became a Czech liberal voice, seconding Palacký's call for more practical, constructive Czech activity. Havlíček (who had spent two years in Russia as a private tutor) rejected the concept of Slavic reciprocity, saying that he had returned from Russia "a *Czech*, a simple, unyielding Czech, even with a certain secret bitterness against the name Slav, which seemed to me, having become acquainted adequately with Russia and Poland, to have a whiff of irony about it."[23] He insisted that "Slav" was only a geographic and ethnographic term, and that the Czechs should cooperate with other Slavs only where their interests dictated it, especially with other Austrian Slavs.

By 1848, then, the Czechs had developed social, cultural, and political self-consciousness to a degree hard to imagine at the beginning of the century. They had differentiated their goals both from the nobility's Bohemianism and the liberalism of the German Bohemians. They had critically examined Slavism, and decided that their aims could best be reached by cooperation with other Austrian Slavs. They called for recognition as a separate, equal nation within Austria, and for equality between Czech and German in the Bohemian crownlands. They had also articulated their refusal to become part of a united, liberal Germany. As Havlíček put it in 1846: "We are Czech by nationality . . . but politically we form together with other nations the Austrian Empire. About a German Empire we know nothing and wish to hear nothing."[24]

THE REVOLUTION OF 1848

The gathering crisis in European society and politics finally erupted starting in January 1848. A detailed account of the revolutions of 1848 does not belong here, but enough must be said to provide the wider context for understanding developments in the Bohemian crownlands.[25] In France, the establishment of a republic in March was followed by clashes with the radicals of Paris in June, and in December, the French elected Napoleon's nephew, Louis Napoleon Bonaparte, president. In 1852 Louis Napoleon carried out a coup d'état and established the Second Empire, taking the title of Napoleon III. In Italy, after hopes that Pope Pius IX would commit himself to Italian unification were disappointed, the king of Piedmont-Sardinia, Charles Albert of Savoy, headed a movement for national unity. He supported revolution against Austria in Lombardy and Venetia, only to be crushed by Field Marshal Joseph Radetzky in July 1848. An attempt to renew the conflict in 1849 was decisively defeated in March and the king abdicated in favor of his son, Victor Emmanuel II, who sued for peace. Austrian, French, Spanish, and Neapolitan forces liquidated the revolution in the Roman and Venetian republics.

In the German Confederation, liberals created a preliminary parliament on March 31, 1848. It set up elections to a constituent assembly, convened on May 18, to decide where "Germany" was. The *kleindeutsch* (Small German) solution preferred uniting the German Confederation without Austria. The *grossdeutsch* (Great German) solution insisted on including the Austrian lands with Bohemia, Moravia, and Silesia but not Hungary. Neither solution was acceptable to the Habsburg dynasty. When finally the *kleindeutsch* solution won out at the beginning of 1849, the parliament offered the German crown to the Prussian king. Frederick Wilhelm declined, curtly refusing a crown "from the gutter," and Prussia's army crushed the last radicals in Saxony, the Palatinate, and Baden. The Frankfurt Parliament collapsed.

German and Italian events had a great impact on developments in the Bohemian crownlands, as did the interplay between Vienna, Hungary, and Bohemia.[26] The radicals from Czech Repeal announced a mass meeting on March 11, 1848. Czech and German liberals preempted the radical organizers and took over the resulting St. Václav Committee, which drafted a petition to the emperor. The petition demanded liberal political freedoms, abolition of *robota*, and religious liberty, but also reflected the Czech program. It called for all citizens to be represented in the Bohemian land diet, a common diet for the Bohemian crownlands with an administration in Prague, and equality of Czech with German in schools and offices.

On March 19 a delegation took the petition to Vienna, but when they arrived they found a transformed situation. Between March 13 and 15, mass demonstrations in Vienna led to Metternich's resignation and the promise of a constitution. Meanwhile the Hungarian diet had adopted measures that created a separate, liberal Kingdom of Hungary. The original Bohemian demands now seemed excessively moderate, and when the delegation returned on March 27, there was general disappointment. A new petition, adopted on March 29, called for a modern elected government for the united Bohemian crownlands, with a separate ministry in Prague.

On April 2 a delegation took the new petition to Vienna. Negotiations with the government led to the Rescript of April 8, 1848, accepting almost all the Czech demands. Unification of the Bohemian crownlands was reserved for "the next Reichstag," but the text promised a central administration for Bohemia proper, expanded the diet, and recognized the legal equality of Czech and German in public life. Count Rudolf Stadion resigned as *gubernium* president and Leo Thun replaced him. Just before his resignation, Stadion created a Governmental Commission in the hopes of forcing the St. Václav Committee to disband, but instead the two merged into a new, liberal-dominated National Committee.

Prague in March was filled with an atmosphere of national cooperation.[27] On March 21 over fifty Czech and German intellectuals issued a declaration supporting national equality, signed by the leading Czech writers and such German Bohemians as Karl Egon Ebert, Ignatz Kuranda, Hartmann, and Meissner. This atmosphere did not last very long. Ludwig von Löhner formed the Union of Germans from Bohemia, Moravia, and Silesia for the Preservation of their Nationality to agitate against the petition in early April, calling for German as the language of Bohemia's institutions, and for Bohemian union with Germany.[28]

German unification was the strongest force dividing Germans from Czechs, whose political demands began with "the separation of the Czech Crown, that is Bohemia, Moravia, and Silesia, from the German *Bund*."[29] When the Frankfurt liberals invited Palacký (as an Austrian) to join them, he published his reply in Prague's Czech and German newspapers. He refused because "I am not a German, at least I do not feel myself to be one. I am a Czech of Slavic stock." Historical ties between the Bohemian rulers and the Holy Roman Empire never constituted a union of the German with the Czech nation, which had a right to its own existence. The Czechs' future would best be guaranteed within a reformed Austria, resting on equal rights for all its nations. Otherwise the small nations of Central Europe would fall prey to Russian hegemony. "If Austria had not existed already for centuries," he concluded, "it would be necessary in the interest of Europe, nay of humanity itself, to create it as quickly as possible."[30]

Most German Bohemians supported German unification, and they withdrew from the National Committee and formed the Constitutional Union. A propaganda battle ensued over whether Bohemia should vote in the elections to the Frankfurt Parliament. Only districts with large German majorities voted regularly; in purely Czech districts no voting took place at all.[31] Thus the Austrian delegation to Frankfurt was overwhelmingly German liberal, though their instructions stated: "The sovereignty and integrity of Austria cannot and must not be sacrificed by adherence to Germany."[32]

After Frankfurt came the promised Austrian parliament. The Vienna government tried to draft the constitution itself, provoking protest demonstrations on May 15. On May 16 the government accepted that a Reichstag elected on a popular, direct franchise would write the constitution. As a direct result, Ferdinand fled Vienna on May 17 for Innsbruck. In Innsbruck, Ferdinand was removed from the Viennese crowds, and also his own responsible government. On the other hand, any party who traveled to Innsbruck could deal with the crown directly.

Events in Vienna exposed differences within the Czech camp. Palacký and the leading middle-class liberals supported Leo Thun; the radical students and artisans favored the Viennese. Thun summoned the diet for July 7, and named a provisional Government Council, sending Rieger and Count Albert Nostitz to Innsbruck to request imperial approval. The emperor dissolved the council because of the Vienna government's opposition, but approved the Bohemian diet elections. The Czech liberals wanted early elections to reform Bohemia's administration before the Reichstag convened. Some German towns either refused to hold elections, or demanded that they be postponed. The press, especially Havlíček's new *Národní noviny* (National News), stressed the significance of the elections. Regular voting was not possible in all districts, but 284 delegates were elected (178 Czechs, the rest Germans) representing most of the rural districts and (except for Prague and some German towns) the urban centers. Most Czech delegates were peasants, since the diet was to deal with *robota* abolition and land reform, but leading liberals including Palacký, Rieger, Šafařík, and Brauner were also elected.[33]

The Bohemian diet's fate in 1848 became entangled with the Prague Slav Congress, itself a riposte to the Frankfurt Parliament. The idea of a Slav gathering emerged during the spring, a committee was formed in April, and invitations were published in May.[34] When the congress opened at the beginning of June, it prepared a manifesto to the peoples of Europe, an address to the Austrian emperor, and specific recommendations to be sent to the governments. The manifesto condemned the oppression of the Slavs, called for a European congress of free peoples, and closed with the French slogan of liberty, equality, and fraternity—for nations, not for individual citizens. The address to the emperor was

„Hab' ich im vorigen Jahr dieses Liedel geblasen auf Fagott und hate nicht gefallen, na, vielleicht machte jetzt bessere Wirkung, wann nimmte man Bombardon."

An Austrian-German caricature of František Palacký from 1849. Driving an apparently reluctant Bohemian lion in front of him, Palacký plays a tune entitled "We Aren't Coming" on the tuba. (Bildarchiv, Österreichische Nationalbibliothek) more cautious, calling for autonomy for the Austrian Slavs. Before the Slav Congress could get down to crafting practical proposals, however, it dissolved itself during the crisis that erupted on the Monday after Pentecost, June 12, 1848.[35]

Prince Alfred Windischgrätz, the military commander of Bohemia, helped provoke the crisis.[36] In the atmosphere created by the diet elections and the Slav Congress, friction between the army and Prague's population was predictable. On June 12, after a special "Mass of Brotherhood" in Wenceslas Square, students and others clashed with the army. The radical head of the Prague student legion, Josef Václav Frič, seized the lead as people hastily erected barricades. Following plans laid in advance, Windischgrätz withdrew and positioned his artillery overlooking the city. After a day of intermittent shelling, Prague surrendered on June 17. Martial law was imposed, the army rounded up radical leaders, and the revolution in Bohemia ended.

Most Austrian Germans hailed Windischgrätz's actions as a defeat for Czech pan-Slavism, oblivious of the possible threat to the liberal government in Vienna.[37] In spite of Thun's repeated efforts to get Vienna's permission, the Bohemian diet never met. Instead, attention focused on the elections for the imperial Reichstag, held on the basis of nearly universal manhood suffrage in the Bohemian crownlands, the Austrian provinces, and Galicia. The Reichstag convened in Vienna on July 22, 1848.

The peasant question and the constitution dominated the Reichstag.[38] Remembering the Galician *jacquerie* of 1846, a group of Bohemian nobles had petitioned the emperor in March to abolish *robota*, and an imperial decree on March 28 promised its abolition by March 31, 1849.[39] Bohemian peasants submitted petitions to the National Committee in Prague demanding the abolition of *robota*. The Reichstag took up the issue four days after it opened. On September 7, 1848, it abolished the peasants' subject status and the distinction between rustical and dominical land. It also abolished without compensation all dues and services based on the peasant's personal subjection, and those owed to the lord as landlord with "moderate compensation." One-third of the total was deducted as the equivalent of taxes and other expenses the lord no longer bore; the state paid one-half of the remainder and the peasants the other, spread out over twenty years.

The abolition of their subject status and *robota* pacified the peasantry, allowing the Reichstag to turn to the constitution. Constitutional issues divided it deeply, especially Austria's relationship to Hungary and Frankfurt. The German Left welcomed the Magyar liberals' preference for the *grossdeutsch* resolution of the German question; the Czechs and most other Slavs opposed the Magyars' refusal to grant equal status to the non-Magyars. As the liberal government in Vienna attempted to maintain its authority both in Frankfurt and in Hungary, the Czechs increasingly turned to the dynasty as their surest support. As a result they were easily tarred with the brush of counter-revolution.

The court returned to Vienna in August, partly at the constitutional Reichstag's request, but partly in response to the changing balance of power. Windischgrätz's conquest of Prague had begun a counter-revolution, and Radetzky's victories freed the army for other uses. Besides Windischgrätz, policymakers included his brother-in-law Prince Felix Schwarzenberg, the Croat Ban (Governor) Josip Jelačić, and the Archduchess Sophie, whose husband and son were next in line for the throne. When Jelačić invaded Hungary on September 11, war between Hungary's "Lawful Revolution" and the Habsburgs began.[40] The Hungarians requested a hearing in the Reichstag, but a Czech-led majority refused to admit them. On October 6 an Austrian regiment refused to board its trains in Vienna to reinforce Jelačic, and soon the city was in an uproar. The next day Ferdinand and his court fled to Olomouc, while the army crushed the Viennese rising.

The emperor summoned the Reichstag to the Moravian town of Kroměříž (Kremsier), on November 22, 1848, where it debated the draft Austrian constitution. Rieger distinguished himself with a ringing speech on the sovereignty of the people.[41] In the constitutional committee, Palacký argued for a federation of national crownlands; in one draft, he even accepted separation of the German regions of the Bohemian crownlands, while claiming the Slovak territories of Hungary for the Czech crownland. The final version reflected a compromise between the federalist and centralist conceptions of the state.[42]

The Kremsier Reichstag and its constitutional draft were doomed because the court was now committed to a counter-revolution. On November 27, Schwarzenberg became prime minister of a new government with Stadion as minister of the interior and Alexander Bach (a revolutionary shifting to a conservative position) as justice minister. In preparation for a military showdown with Hungary, Ferdinand abdicated on December 2, 1848, in favor of his nephew, Francis Joseph (1848–1916). In the name of the new emperor, Windischgrätz renewed the campaign against Hungary, occupying Buda on January 5, 1849. Once committed to a military conquest of Hungary, the government and the new emperor turned on the remaining revolutionary institution, the parliament. On March 7, 1849, the assembly was dissolved, and its meeting place sealed by Austrian troops. On the same day, a new constitution, drafted by Stadion, was issued by imperial decree or "octroi." To complete the counter-revolution the octroyed constitution was suspended on New Year's eve, 1851, inaugurating a renewed period of absolutism.

9 *Viribus Unitis*

Francis Joseph adopted as his personal motto the slogan "Viribus unitis" (with united strength). Instead of a constitutional union, however, the emperor offered his people unity "from above," without giving them a direct say in their government. Thus the dissolution of the Imperial Reichstag marks one possible end of the Habsburg Revolution of 1848. It consolidated counter-revolution in the western part of the empire, and created a basis from which it could be extended to Italy, Germany, and Hungary. The dissolution of the Kremsier Reichstag also meant that the Czech policy of cooperating with the dynasty had failed. As they returned to Prague, the Czech delegates published a self-defense, blaming the government for their failure. While a few youthful radicals dreamed of conspiratorial resistance, and Karel Havlíček carried on a rearguard action for press freedom and liberalism, most of the leading figures of the Czech movement of 1848 sought refuge in academic or personal pursuits.

A DECADE OF NEOABSOLUTISM (1849–1859)

Counter-revolution in Austria ultimately depended on the strength of the army. The Russian intervention hastened the Hungarians' defeat, but some historians argue that Hungary could not have held out once Austria was secure elsewhere.[1] Francis Joseph and his advisers did not take long to jettison even the appearance of constitutional rule, but if the counter-revolutionary success depended on Austria's military strength, and that in turn on the financial health of the monarchy, what would happen when each faltered? That question arose more than once in the succeeding decades, as the emperor groped toward a political and constitutional system that would preserve his realm, and its status as a Great Power, intact.

Mopping Up

Radetzky's Italian victories left Austria in possession of Lombardy and Venetia. In Germany, the Prussian king's rejection of the *klein-deutsch* crown returned the German problem to its previous status.[2] But in Hungary, Habsburg arms suffered a series of reverses, prompting the Hungarian Parliament to declare Hungary independent and depose the House of Habsburg in April 1849. The declaration convinced Schwarzenberg and the emperor to accept Nicholas I's urgent offers of Russian military assistance. The Hungarian armies surrendered to the Russians at Világos on August 13, 1849, while Kossuth fled into exile.[3]

The Reichstag's dissolution deepened fissures between the Czech radicals and the liberals. Their hopes ended and influence undermined, they mostly withdrew from active public life. Palacký devoted himself to his history, Rieger traveled abroad, others became conservatives. Some radicals established contacts with Mikhail Bakunin, uninvited guest at the Slav Congress, who was in Saxony. With radicals in Germany and the German students in Prague, they plotted uprisings in Prague, Dresden, and other cities. They were betrayed to the police and arrested on May 9 and 10, 1849. Martial law was again proclaimed in Prague, where it lasted until 1853. With the participants sentenced to lengthy prison terms, the May Conspiracy marked the end of the radical democrats for the moment.[4]

Havlíček remained the most persistent thorn in the government's side. His *Národní noviny* was officially suspended in January 1850, but he moved to Kutná Hora to produce a political weekly, *Slovan* (The Slav). Havlíček was acquitted twice on press charges, but he chose to suspend *Slovan* in August 1851, in advance of its banning. Arrested in December 1851, he was deported to Brixen in Tyrol, returning to Bohemia only in 1855, to die of tuberculosis in Prague on July 29, 1856. His funeral brought together many of the Czech figures of 1848 in one of the first manifestations of the Czech movement under neoabsolutism. Havlíček, the "martyr of Brixen," became a symbol claimed by many Czech political forces.[5]

The "Bach Era"

The Sylvester Patent of December 31, 1851, preserved civic equality, peasant emancipation, and freedom for recognized religions, but anything else reflecting the revolution was removed. The new system is often identified with Alexander Bach, the ex-revolutionary who became Minister of the Interior in 1849, but in addition to Schwarzenberg, Francis Joseph must not be overlooked. All ministers were responsible to him, and powerful institutions (police, army, foreign affairs) were conducted either directly by him or by ministers who reported to him, not to Bach. It was Francis Joseph's decision that Austria should revert to absolutism.

The essence of neoabsolutism was the state bureaucracy: supranational, centralized, in theory incorruptible, and controlled from Vienna. Through it all the Habsburg possessions were for once in their history knit into a single unit with a uniform administration. The internal language was German, a rule made official in the Bohemian crownlands in 1852. This German character was not yet consciously aimed at Germanizing the monarchy's citizens. The state placed itself above, and refused to grant recognition to, any national feelings. The basic administrative unit was the district headed by a captain, and divided into smaller judicial districts. In Bohemia and Moravia the next level of state administration was the circuit, much larger than before 1848, which supervised the districts and reported to the Ministry of the Interior in Vienna. The *gubernium* was dissolved, much of its power transferred to the circuits, and a governor's office, headed by an appointed governor, replaced it. The land diets were never summoned.

Neoabsolutism rested on several pillars besides the bureaucracy: the army (larger than before 1848), the police (uniformed and secret), and a newly organized rural gendarmerie. The Catholic church, another pillar, regained much of its independence in the Concordat of 1855. The Concordat strengthened Catholic oversight over culture, especially education, and gave ecclesiastical courts competence in marriage questions.

In spite of its negative reputation in nationalist eyes, neoabsolutism had some positive achievements. The administration functioned more efficiently and honestly, not least because Bach improved pay and working conditions. Aspects of the administrative reorganization survived well into the twentieth century. The regime supported freedom of trade and enterprise and unified the customs structure, with liberalized access to the German customs union. It set up Chambers of Commerce and Industry in the economically significant towns in 1850. The state also developed communications such as railways, the telegraph (made available to the public from 1850), and postal service (the first Austrian postage stamps date from 1850). Much of the later economic development of the monarchy rested on these foundations.

The neoabsolutist regime also completed peasant emancipation. Peasants familiar with the market and with enough land adapted quickly and did quite well, but peasants with little or no land still had to work for the lord. The cash economy with its need for credit increasingly affected their lives. Some landowners did well with compensation, investing in new industries or improving their land, but smaller landowners who had been dependent on *robota* labor found that the compensation did not make up for having to hire labor at market rates. One consequence of emancipation was an increase in the proportion of land held in large estates.

The educational reforms of Count Leo Thun, who joined the government in 1849, also had many positive effects.[6] The philosophical faculty became a full-fledged university faculty, and eight-year gymnasia now prepared students for university study. Thun established a model Czech gymnasium in Prague. A Czech technical secondary school was also established in Prague, but it had to accept German as an alternate language of instruction in 1854. During 1853 and 1854, German language of instruction was reintroduced into the other middle-level schools in the Bohemian crownlands. At the primary level the vernacular was still the initial language of instruction, but the proportion of "mixed" schools increased.

The Crimean War in 1854 upset the stable international environment on which neoabsolutism depended. Russia's Tsar Nicholas I expected Austrian support in gratitude for Russian help in 1849, but Francis Joseph pursued an independent course: an Austrian ultimatum forced Russia out of Moldavia and Wallachia, which the Austrians occupied in August 1854. At the peace negotiations in Paris (March 1856), Austria was isolated. Instead it was Piedmont who cashed in on its support for the allies, winning Napoleon III's backing for another round with Austria. This Italian war ended in Austrian defeat in 1859, and though it only lost Lombardy, the unification of Italy under Piedmont continued. Equally significant were the internal consequences of yet another military and financial debacle.

THE ROAD TO THE *AUSGLEICH* (1860–1867)

The disastrous outcome and financial strains of the Italian campaign of 1859 forced Francis Joseph toward hesitant reform of the neoabsolutist system. In March 1860, the emperor summoned a special "Reinforced" version of his advisory Reichsrat to discuss necessary financial matters. The Reinforced Reichsrat quickly moved on to discuss alternatives to neoabsolutism. The majority, still mostly titled aristocrats, preferred a federal system based on the historic provinces. Most of the middle-class members urged a centralized, constitutional system. In the absence of the Czech liberal politicians, the most significant voice representing Bohemia belonged to Count Jindřich (Heinrich) Jaroslav Clam-Martinic. He favored the federal line taken in the Imperial Diploma of October 20, 1860.

October Diploma and February Patent

The October Diploma sketched out a system with a central Reichsrat and land diets in each of the historic provinces. It foreshadowed the future dualism by providing that the Reichsrat could meet with only the non-Hungarian lands present. The re-creation of the land diets was a welcome step in the direction of federalism, but the leading Czech politicians criticized the October Diploma because it failed to recognize Bohemia's special historic state right and because they were not consulted.

On February 26, 1861, the new minister of state, Anton von Schmerling, issued a patent reinterpreting the October Diploma in a centralist sense.[7] The Reichsrat was now bicameral. The House of Lords included church dignitaries, hereditary members, and life members appointed by the emperor. The House of Deputies had 343 delegates, chosen by the land diets. The February Patent also allowed for a "narrower" Reichsrat to meet without the Hungarians, but now all matters not assigned to the land diets were reserved to this narrower Reichsrat. The diets' competence was limited to agriculture, social welfare, public works, and the land budgets, and to applying Reichsrat legislation in education, religion, and communal administration.

Members of the land diets were elected by four colleges or *curiae*: the great landowners, the chambers of commerce and industry, the towns, and the rural communes. Property qualifications determined the right to vote: ownership of entailed or registered landed estates in the first curia, property other than land in the second, and payment of at least ten gulden in direct taxation in the town and rural curiae. In the rural curia, voters selected electors who chose the delegates. The seats in the land diets were divided among the four curiae to favor the wealthy and urban elements, and hence, in the context of the Bohemian crownlands, the Germans.[8]

A general loosening of political conditions accompanied the October Diploma. Leading Czech liberals established a new political newspaper, *Národní listy* (National Paper), edited by the young lawyer Julius Grégr. In its first issue, on January 1, 1861, Rieger led off with an article in which he set out the Czech national program. He called for national equality, wide-ranging self-government, and fundamental civic rights.[9] The Czech leadership sought a rapprochement with the traditional nobility on the ground of Bohemia's traditional state right, sealed at a meeting in January between Rieger and Clam-Martinic. This alliance with the historic nobility represented a step back from the assertion of the natural right to self-determination expressed in 1848, but it would remain characteristic of Czech politics for more than thirty years.[10]

The alliance with the nobility convinced the Czech liberals—now led in the Reichsrat by Rieger, since the emperor had appointed Palacký to the upper house—to enter the Reichsrat in May 1861 instead of boycotting it altogether. At the Reichsrat the twenty Bohemian Czech deputies were joined by four Czechs from Moravia, led by Alois Pražák. Pražák had known the Bohemian Czech liberals since 1848, and he led the Moravian Czechs to associate with Bohemia in a common national movement.[11] The Czechs failed to create a federalist coalition in the Reichsrat, however, and in 1863 the Bohemians withdrew, joined by the Moravians in 1864.

Czech abstention from the central parliament was inspired by the Hungarian example. Led by the veteran of 1848, Ferenc Deák, the Hungarians had maintained since 1861 that the April Laws of 1848 were their only valid constitution, and they denied the authority of an empire-wide legislature. Hungary's refusal to enter the Reichsrat, to pay taxes, or in any way to recognize the regime finally forced the government to admit defeat. Francis Joseph dismissed Schmerling in July 1865, and appointed a new ministry led by Count Richard Belcredi, which "suspended" the February Patent and instituted measures that leaned toward federalism. Among them was the recognition of Czech as an official language for contacts with the public in the courts and administrative offices in Bohemia and Moravia.

Königgrätz and Compromise

The following year, however, the chance that Belcredi's government might commit Austria to greater provincial autonomy and federalism was thwarted by war between Austria and Prussia. Austrian armies fought the Italians in Venetia and the Prussians in Bohemia. Victorious in Italy, the Austrians suffered a catastrophic defeat in Bohemia on July 3, 1866, near Hradec Králové (Königgrätz). Bismarck sought no annexations; he simply wanted Austria out of his way to German unity under Prussian hegemony. In the end, Austria had to accept exclusion from Germany and pay Prussia an indemnity, while ceding Venetia to Napoleon III, who gave it to Italy.[12]

Once again, as in 1859, a foreign disaster made a resolution of the monarchy's internal problems imperative, and the court returned to discussions with Deák and Gyula Andrássy. The result, the compromise (*Ausgleich*) of 1867, established the dualist system that lasted until the collapse of the monarchy in 1918. Hungary was granted its old constitution, and its diet met and accepted a common military, common foreign affairs, and common finances. These institutions, and the monarch's person, were the only links between Hungary and the rest of the Habsburg empire. On June 8, 1867, Francis Joseph was crowned king of Hungary in Buda. The necessary constitutional changes for the rest of the empire were embodied in five fundamental laws adopted by the Reichsrat on December 21, 1867.

The Habsburg Monarchy now consisted of the Kingdom of Hungary, and another part whose only official name was "the Kingdoms and Lands represented in the Reichsrat," commonly called "Cisleithania," since the frontier between Lower Austria and Hungary was the river Leitha. The ruler, as Emperor of Austria and King of Hungary, joined these two halves of Austria-Hungary, which shared common ministries of foreign affairs, the army, and finance. Delegations, committees of sixty members of each parliament, met annually to approve the budget for common affairs. Otherwise, each half of the monarchy had its separate parliament and government, headed by a minister president. The agreements between the two halves of the monarchy on tariffs, trade, and the state budget were to be renegotiated every ten years.

The December Constitution of 1867 established the political structure of Cisleithania. The bicameral Reichsrat was retained with legislative initiative. Ministers could be impeached if they violated the constitution, but the government was not responsible to parliament. The lower house was elected from the land diets according to the curial system. When the Reichsrat was not in session, § 14 allowed the government to legislate by decree, although retroactive parliamentary approval was necessary. The constitution specified fundamental rights, including "an inalienable right to the maintenance and cultivation of its nationality and language" for all peoples of the monarchy. That equality included education, which was to be organized so that "each of those peoples receives the necessary facilities for education in its own language without being compelled to learn a second language."[13] Justice was separated from the administration and judicial independence affirmed. Legislation also freed the educational system from the Catholic church and introduced compulsory attendance through the first eight years. Altogether, the December Constitution created a basically liberal framework for the political, social, and economic development of the Bohemian crownlands until the end of the monarchy. Nevertheless, the Czech response to the *Ausgleich* was overwhelmingly negative.

The Czechs from October to December

Czech society and the national movement had matured significantly by 1860, yet Czech influence in the diet and Reichsrat was not enough to achieve their goals there. Instead, the new institutions of self-administration gave Czech activists a fruitful field. Legislation in 1863 and 1864 returned municipal autonomy to the towns and villages. Municipal committees, elected by three curiae based on tax payments, chose the mayor and town councils. At the district level in Bohemia, the self-governing body was the district representation, established in 1864. It was also elected by four curiae, and it selected an executive committee headed by a mayor. The land committee of the diet directly supervised the municipal governments in Moravia and Silesia, and the district representations in Bohemia. These bodies were responsible for roads and communications, social welfare, financial support for public schools, and security of person and property. They operated independently of the state bureaucracy in a "two-track" system. In the 1861 municipal elections the Czechs gained control of most towns in the interior of the country. The Czech candidate, František Pštross, also won in Prague, and Czechs controlled the city government from then on. Czechs used their control of public expenditure in these bodies to support the political efforts and social and cultural development of the Czech nation.

Such public activities included the publication of Rieger's monumental encyclopedia, *Riegrův slovník naučný* (1860–74), which took as its motto, "Work and knowledge are our salvation." Rieger also worked hard to resuscitate the National Theater committee. He helped set up the Provisional Theater in 1864, which presented at least one performance a day in Czech. The 1860s saw the first operas of Bedřich Smetana, who after becoming the Provisional Theater's conductor in 1866 performed them under his own baton. Looser press laws led to the foundation of many new journals and newspapers, though the government still frequently applied administrative restrictions on the popular press. *Národní listy* long maintained the dominant position it established in 1861.[14]

Legalizing the right of association enabled the foundation of several organizations that further developed Czech culture and national confidence.[15] The patriotic gymnastic organization Sokol (Falcon), established in 1862 by Miroslav Tyrš and Jindřich Fügner, led the way. The Czech Sokol cultivated the physical and moral health of the nation through gymnastics and other patriotic activities. Josef Mánes designed Sokol uniforms and banners in a folk style, and other Slavic peoples rapidly established similar groups. The choral union Hlahol (1861) pursued national goals through organizing singing clubs, and the Umělecká beseda (Artists' Club), founded in 1863, brought together artists from all genres. Women became involved, not only in singing societies or as Sokol supporters, but in their own associations. In 1865, the American Club of Czech Women, founded by the sisters Karolina Světlá and Sofie Podlipská, supported by Vojtěch Náprstek, created an institution to advocate more opportunities for women.

Two tendencies emerged within the National Party: the Old Czechs, led by Palacký and Rieger, and the Young Czechs, including former 1848 revolutionaries like Alois Pravoslav Trojan and Karel Sladkovský. *Národní listy* eventually became the mouthpiece of the Young Czechs, who were divided from the Old Czechs more by political rivalries than by a generation gap. Julius Grégr's older brother Eduard played a leading role among the younger generation of Young Czechs. Whatever the differences between the two groups, they were united in their support for Bohemia's state right and their dislike of the looming dualist compromise.

František Palacký warned against dualism in the Old Czech paper, *Národ* (The Nation) in 1865. Only federalism could accomplish Austria's mission: to preserve and protect the small nations under its rule. Both centralism and dualism worked against the fundamental purpose of Austrian history. Dualism would result in continuous conflict, of unforeseeable proportions, with unpredictable consequences. "We Slavs," Palacký concluded, "will look on at that with genuine pain, but without fear. We existed before Austria, and we will still exist after her."[16]

FROM PASSIVE RESISTANCE TO ACTIVE POLITICS (1867–1891)

When it came, the *Ausgleich* seemed a poor recompense for Czech loyalty in 1848 and 1866. Czech tactics in response continued to copy the Hungarian example in two respects. First, the Czech deputies announced a boycott of the diets and Reichsrat until Bohemia's state right was recognized. Second, they looked for foreign sympathy and support, as the Magyars had found in Berlin. A delegation of Austrian Slavs, mainly Czechs led by Palacký, Rieger, and Julius Grégr, demonstratively set out to attend an ethnographic exhibition in St. Petersburg and Moscow in May 1867. They were received by Tsar Alexander II, but without concrete results, except to reinforce the Czech reputation for uncritical Russophilism. In 1869, Rieger submitted a memorandum to Napoleon III, arguing that it was in French interests to support the Slavs in Austria, but this effort did not bear fruit, either.

A Compromise for the Czechs?

Czechs also expressed opposition to the *Ausgleich* on a mass scale. Large crowds demonstrated at occasions like the return of the Crown of

The Old Czech leaders František Palacký and his son-in-law František Ladislav Rieger. (Bildarchiv, Österreichische Nationalbibliothek)

St. Václav from Vienna to Prague in 1867, and the laying of the future National Theater's cornerstone in 1868. More overtly, political mass public meetings began in May 1868 with a gathering of nearly 40,000 Czechs on the summit of Říp. These gatherings, called *tábory* in an echo of Hussite memories, spread throughout Bohemia, choosing meeting places significant in the nationalist view of Czech history (Vítkov, Blaník, Říp). The demonstrators approved petitions reaffirming Bohemia's state right and demanding reforms, including universal manhood suffrage.[17] Further *tábory* responded to the declaration of a Czech boycott of the land diet on August 22, 1868. The Czechs asserted only a personal link between the Bohemian crownlands and the other Habsburg possessions, denied the validity of legislation by the Reichsrat in Vienna for Bohemia, and argued that only the Bohemian land diet could decide financial questions.[18] The Moravian Czech deputies issued a similar, though more moderate, declaration.

Government measures against the *tábory* had only limited success. The opposition press was muzzled, and a state of emergency declared in Prague on October 11, 1868, but this only weakened the movement. Foreign policy was more influential in the emperor's decision to attempt a Czech compromise. After 1866, the Habsburg Monarchy could not openly prepare a war of revenge against Prussia, but it did seek—through abortive contacts with Napoleon III and even the Italians—to create a favorable diplomatic situation. War with Prussia could not be ruled out, and the Bohemian crownlands were the easiest point of attack should it come. The rapid collapse of the Second French Empire in 1870 and the proclamation of the German Reich in 1871 made these fears even more pressing. They also made the German patriotism of the Austrian Germans less valuable to the dynasty, which could seek a Slavic counterweight to a German-Austrian yearning toward the Reich.

The emperor thus sought agreement with the Czechs and conservative nobles, first under the Galician Polish magnate Count Alfred Potocki, and then under Count Karl Sigmund Hohenwart. Negotiations between Rieger, Pražák, Clam-Martinic, and Hohenwart's Minister of Commerce, Albert Schäffle, produced a compromise with the Czechs in a series of Fundamental Articles.[19] The Czechs accepted the *Ausgleich*, but in other respects Bohemia enjoyed a separate status, not quite as independent as Hungary. Though the land diet "voluntarily" surrendered part of its competence to an organ joining all the Cisleithanian lands, otherwise its powers were greatly increased, and a land government was created under a reinstated Bohemian Court Chancellor. In an official rescript of September 12, 1871, Francis Joseph referred to the past glories of the Czech crown and repeated his willingness to confirm them in his coronation oath.[20]

Serious problems emerged when Moravia and Silesia refused to accept a common government with Bohemia. The German deputies withdrew from the Bohemian diet and staged their own mass protests. Faced with opposition from his foreign minister and Andrássy as head of the Hungarian government, Francis Joseph decided at a ministerial council meeting on October 20, 1871, to withdraw the articles as they stood. The Czechs in the diet refused any amendments, and Hohenwart resigned. He was replaced by Adolf Auersperg, supported by the German liberals, the foundation of Auersperg's governments until 1879.[21]

To Boycott, or Not?

The collapse of the Czech compromise was a bitter disappointment. Czech leaders, especially Palacký and Rieger, argued that the Czechs should renew their boycott of the land diet and Reichsrat. The diet elections in 1872, marked by shady dealings that secured the Germans a safe majority, strengthened their arguments. The decision to return to passive politics in 1873, however, accelerated the separation of Old Czechs and Young Czechs. The boycott robbed the Czechs of the tribune of the diet and Reichsrat, and any chance to influence public affairs. Both Old and Young Czechs remained active in self-administration institutions, but the Young Czechs argued that this base was not enough. The Moravian Czechs reentered their diet in 1873, and in 1874 they took up their seats in the imperial Reichsrat. Seven Young Czech deputies to the Bohemian land diet followed their example on September 15, 1874. On December 27, 1874, the Young Czechs founded a separate National Liberal Party.

Rieger's calculation that new foreign upheavals would force Francis Joseph to return to a Bohemian compromise proved false. The rapprochement between Austria and Germany after the failure of the Fundamental Articles led to the first Three Emperors' League, linking Austria-Hungary with Germany and Russia. Czech leaders hoped that the rebellion in the Ottoman provinces of Bosnia and Hercegovina in 1875 would cause a Balkan crisis in which Russia could help their cause. When Turkey and Russia went to war in 1877–78, the Old Czechs organized demonstrations of support, and asked Russia's ambassador in Vienna to intervene on the Czechs' behalf. The Congress of Berlin in 1878, however, led to the collapse of the Three Emperors' League. The Congress also charged Austria-Hungary with occupying and administering Bosnia and Hercegovina, ostensibly on behalf of the Sultan.

Two other consequences of this Balkan crisis set the parameters for Czech politics in subsequent years: the Dual Alliance of 1879 with Germany confirmed Austria's pro-German foreign policy, and German liberal resistance to the occupation of Bosnia and Hercegovina caused Francis Joseph to drop them and make his boyhood friend, Count Eduard Taafe, minister-president. Taafe's appointment coincided with the Old Czechs' decision, against Rieger's opposition, to abandon passive politics and enter the land diet in September 1878. Contacts between Taafe, the Bohemian conservative nobles, and both Czech parties led to a Czech return to the Reichsrat on September 18, 1879. There the Czechs joined the Galician landowners and the Party of the German Right (conservative and clerical) under Hohenwart, in a pro-government majority known as the "Iron Ring of the Right." Taafe proved an agile politician who lasted in office until 1893, longer than any other minister-president under dualism.[22]

Taafe once described his policies as aimed at "keeping all the nationalities of the Monarchy in a condition of even and well-modulated discontent."[23] The Czechs began every parliamentary session with a formal reservation of Czech state right, but they supported the government in return for piecemeal concessions. They won three major concessions: a new ordinance on language use in the bureaucracy, the division of the university in Prague into separate Czech and German institutions, and an electoral reform lowering the tax qualification in the town and rural curiae to five gulden, a step that gave the vote to many more Czechs than Germans. When similar reforms to the Bohemian diet in 1885 created a permanent Czech majority, the Bohemian Germans began a boycott of their own in 1887.

The language decrees, issued by Minister of Justice Stremayr in 1880, established Czech as an external service language anywhere in Bohemia and Moravia, enjoining officials to reply to cases in the language in which they originated. The internal service language, used within offices and for correspondence between them, remained German. The division of the Charles-Ferdinand University in Prague, carried out in 1881–82, capped a Czech-language school system now extending

In der politischen Schmiede.
(Gez. von **Klič**.)

Clam-Martiniç: Hau' zu, Rieger, denn man muß das Eisen schmieden, so lang es warm ist.
Rieger: Čert a peklo, der da ist doch aber weder warm noch kalt, und waßme überhaupt nit, ob schlagme was heraus aus ihm.

"In the Political Smithy," a Viennese caricature from 1879. Count Heinrich Clam-Martinitz (for the conservative nobility) and Rieger (for the Czechs) hammer away at Count Taafe, forging the "Iron Ring of the Right." (Bildarchiv, Österreichische Nationalbibliothek) through all levels of education. The Czech university attracted talented and ambitious younger academics, including the historian Jaroslav Goll, the philologist Jan Gebauer, and Tomáš Garrigue Masaryk, who had qualified at Vienna in philosophy and sociology.

The Czech Club in the Reichsrat split during the 1880s, and in 1887 a group of Young Czech deputies led by Eduard Grégr and Josef Herold went into opposition. They took four out of five Reichsrat by-elections, and in 1889 took 39 seats in the Bohemian land diet, against 58 Old Czech seats. The Old Czechs, sensing the end of their dominance, accepted Taafe's invitation to negotiate with the German liberals. Both sides, threatened by radicals, hoped that by a compromise they could win votes, while Taafe wanted the Germans to reenter the Bohemian diet. The Young Czechs were not invited to the discussions in Vienna in January 1890, which agreed on a series of points (*punktace*) that divided the judicial districts and circuits, chambers of commerce and industry, and school boards according to national criteria, in effect splitting Bohemia into German and Czech zones. In the German region the internal and external service languages would be German, but in the Czech zone only the external language would be Czech. The German politicians and press celebrated the *punktace* as a great victory, but Czech public opinion, influenced by *Národní listy*, was overwhelmingly opposed. Rieger insisted that the *punktace* did the Czechs no harm, and in many respects were to their advantage, but to no avail.[24] The turmoil over the *punktace* effectively destroyed the Old Czech party. In the Reichsrat elections in 1891, the Young Czechs won a resounding victory (37 seats to two for the Old Czechs), and became the leading force in Czech national politics.

INDUSTRIALIZATION AND SOCIETY IN THE BOHEMIAN CROWNLANDS

Deepening social and economic changes accompanied the political turmoil. The industrial sector developed further, and agriculture, though it remained important, was itself increasingly affected by industrialization and its accompanying scientific and technical advances. The social structure of the Bohemian crownlands still reflected the survival of the aristocracy and the peasantry, but the middle classes now enjoyed political and cultural predominance, while the growing significance of the working classes could no longer be ignored. These changes also affected relations between Czechs and Germans in the Bohemian crownlands.

Industrialization Deepens

Industry in the Bohemian crownlands continued to grow after 1848 until the Viennese financial market's collapse of 1873.[25] Recovery began by around 1880, however, and continued (with renewed interruptions during a depression from 1901 to 1903) until 1914. By 1880 Bohemia and Moravia-Silesia accounted for approximately two-thirds of Cisleithania's industrial production. Railway construction and the demands of the light industrial and agricultural sectors of the economy stimulated heavy industry. Coal had by now almost entirely replaced charcoal as the main fuel in iron production, greatly stimulating the mining industries. After the depression of 1873, the development of the iron and steel industries in the Czech lands continued as technology allowed local high-phosphorous iron ores to be used effectively. Between 1876 and 1896, the Bohemian crownlands saw their share of Cisleithanian iron production rise from 35 to 61 percent.[26] Iron and steel were the mainstays of the machine industries that grew up in and around Prague, with other enterprises in Plzeň and, after 1872, the suburbs of Brno. The domestic market required steam engines, railway equipment, machines for the food-processing industries (especially brewing, milling, sugar refining, and distilling), agricultural machines and implements, and mining. The old industrial workhorse, the steam engine, was being replaced by the lighter and more efficient electric and internal combustion engines.

The chemical industry in the Bohemian crownlands produced alkalis and artificial fertilizers, whose use illustrates the integration of agriculture into an industrialized economy. Demand for food rose as the population grew (from 7 to 10 million inhabitants during the second half of the century) and a smaller proportion of the population worked in agriculture. Agricultural prosperity continued from the 1840s until the crisis of 1873. After 1878, competition from imported cereals caused a shift to potatoes, barley (less sensitive to depression and foreign competition because of its role in the brewing industry), and hops, and in the vicinity of the larger urban centers, vegetables. Intensive methods were usually introduced on successful large estates, though richer peasants, and even some smallholders, also adopted new practices.

The social structure mirrored these changing patterns of production.[27] Great aristocrats still maintained a presence in administration (at least at its highest levels), the army, and the diplomatic corps. The curial voting system protected their political influence, and they generally survived the economic buffets of these decades as well. A few great Bohemian landowning families like the Lobkowiczes, the Schwarzenbergs, the Colloredo-Mansfelds, and the Liechtensteins owned the largest estates in the monarchy outside of Hungary.[28] Middle-class entrepreneurs and professionals provided leaders for German and Czech political parties, and overshadowed the old aristocracy economically. Emil Škoda provides a classic example. Škoda, solidly middle class, became chief engineer in the machine plant owned by Count Wallenstein in Plzeň in 1866, and within three years had purchased it. During the next nineteen years he took a small workshop employing 33 workers and turned it into a major concern with 4,000 workers and 200 administrative employees. The middle class also predominated at least numerically in two of the chief pillars of the monarchy, the bureaucracy and the army.[29]

Factory production forced many of the small bourgeoisie to become industrial workers or emigrate. Similar forces affected the countryside, where peasant holdings fragmented after the liberals allowed the subdividing of landholdings in 1868. Many smallholders or landless peasants sought an outlet in colonization in Russia or in emigration overseas, while others found an escape from the overcrowded countryside in the factories of the growing towns. The proportion of the economically active population in agricultural sectors shrank from 54.9 percent in 1869 to 43.1 in 1890, while the industrial sector grew from 29.3 percent to 37 percent.[30]

The Bohemian crownlands played a leading role in the overall economy of the Habsburg monarchy in the second half of the nineteenth century. Recent research has suggested that this economic development, though it fell short of the classical "takeoff" of West European industrialization, produced sustained economic expansion and industrial growth. The result of these developments was intense political conflict. Seeds of the collapse of the monarchy, then, lay not in its failure to modernize its economy, but in the failure of its political institutions to cope with the consequences of its modern economic development.[31]

Social Change, Political Pressures

Access to capital was crucial to the development of an industrial middle class that would support Czech or German liberal political parties.[32] The Bohemian crownlands remained largely dependent on Vienna and Germany for capital until 1869, when the authorities finally approved the first Czech commercial bank, the Tradesmen's Bank for Bohemia and Moravia (Živnobanka). It weathered the financial collapse of 1873, and even after competitors emerged, the Živnobanka still led the way in investing in Czech agro-industrial enterprises, and also in exporting capital to other regions of the empire and beyond, often concentrating on Slavic areas.

Cooperative self-help associations among the workers began when the Prague-based Oul (Beehive), was founded in 1868.[33] At its height, Oul had a membership of 3,000 and a capital base of 60,000 gulden. In 1871 there were 279 similar organizations in Bohemia and 46 in Moravia. Self-help ideas were also popular among the middle classes, whose savings and loan associations helped found commercial banks. Consumers' and producers' cooperatives spread in the countryside also. In the 1880s and 1890s credit unions and other rural cooperatives stimulated the Young Czech supporter Alfons Šťastný to form a regional organization to pressure the party to deal with agrarian issues. With Young Czech help he organized the Provincial Peasants' Union for the Kingdom of Bohemia in 1889. That same year, he began to publish the *Selské noviny* (Peasants' News), which he continued until 1912.

Old and Young Czechs stood at the cradle of the workers' movement, but in general the workers tended to go their own way. When the first Austrian socialist party was organized in 1874, there were ten Czechs among the seventy-four working-class leaders gathered there.[34] The transfer of the party's headquarters from Vienna to Liberec in 1877, and the recognition of *Dělnické listy* (Workers' News) as an official organ beside the Viennese *Gleichheit* (Equality) reflected the significance of the Bohemian crownlands to the socialist movement. Josef Boleslav Pecka and several associates established the Czech wing of Austrian Social-Democracy in 1878.[35]

Taafe responded with a combination of repression and conservative social legislation. In the early 1880s, he declared a state of emergency in Vienna and used an 1886 "anarchist law" to break up the workers' organizations. However, between 1885 and 1887 Taafe also limited the workday, established a compulsory day of rest on Sunday, and forbade the employment of children under twelve. Factory inspectors and accident and sickness insurance were introduced, and a workers' curia for Reichsrat elections was at least considered.[36] The Viennese physician

Viktor Adler and others reorganized the socialist party in 1889, a year after the Czech section reestablished itself in Brno.[37] The new party helped found the Second International in 1889, and in the 1890 May Day demonstration, the Austrian Social Democrats announced their return. In Prague 30,000 marched for an eight-hour day and universal suffrage.[38]

Masaryk developed a critical approach to both Old and Young Czechs that he called Realism. In 1886, he created a furor when his journal *Athenaeum* published an article by Gebauer questioning the authenticity of the Zelenohorský and Královédvorský manuscripts. He subjected them to the analysis Dobrovský had suggested when they were discovered, and concluded that they were forgeries. Since the RKZ were a nationalist holy of holies, opinion was overwhelmingly against Gebauer and Masaryk. The scandal gave the realists and their ideas publicity. With Josef Kaizl and the young journalist Jan Herben, Masaryk established the journal *Čas* (Time) in 1887. Other collaborators included Karel Kramář, who helped Kaizl and Masaryk establish a separate Czech Realist party in 1889.[39]

Czech culture by the 1880s did not need the RKZ to prove its worth, for it was truly on a European level. The National Theater in Prague, completed to the designs of Josef Zítek in 1881, nearly destroyed by fire the same year, and rebuilt by 1883, symbolized that development and provided an appropriate culmination of the national theater movement. The inscription over the proscenium, "Národ Sobě," or "The Nation to Itself," emphasized the contributions from ordinary people that helped to finance its construction. Zítek's colleague Josef Schulz worked on its restoration after the fire, and designed the new museum building, also in neo-Renaissance style, built from 1885 to 1890 at the upper end of Wenceslas Square.[40] During the 1870s the almanac *Ruch* and the journal *Lumír* expressed differing attitudes to literature's role in Czech society. *Ruch* (its first issue came out in 1868) maintained the traditional view of literature serving the nation. *Lumír* looked to world literature, attempting to introduce influences from other literatures into Czech, but it was one of the *lumírovci*, Jaroslav Vrchlický, who wrote: "We have only two weapons: the book and the school."[41]

The metaphor of school and book as "weapons" reflected increasing national polarization. Until mid-century at least, most people did not base their primary identity on language, which reflected social, not "ethnic" differences. With the rise of Czech-speaking middle classes, how-

Dr. Thomas Masaryk

Universitätsprofessor

A caricature of Tomáš Masaryk during his years as professor at Prague's Czech university. (Bildarchiv, Österreichische Nationalbibliothek)

ever, the German-speaking elements defined themselves as a "German" community to defend their economic predominance. The proportion of the German population did not change dramatically (37 percent in Bohemia, 29 percent in Moravia). The influx of Czech-speaking workers into industrially developing regions did lead to local Czech minorities in certain formerly German towns, but overall the location of the language frontier did not change either. What did change was the perception of the situation on both sides.

Czech and German nationalists each felt like a threatened minority, the Czechs in Cisleithania, the Germans in Bohemia. While the Czechs profited from concessions on local issues, the Germans advocated preserving the German character of the state, and their "national cultural property" within Bohemia.[42] Organizations on both sides sprang up to "defend" the national position, especially on the linguistic frontier. Nevertheless, such antagonism is not the whole story. Many tradesmen in mixed communities used both languages and served all customers, in spite of the slogan "Svůj k svému" (Each to his own).[43] At the personal level, friendships and even intermarriage remained perfectly normal. These personal relations still often reflected social level and not ethnic identity, and each society was still marked by clear social cleavages. As the century drew to a close, politics increasingly reflected this diversity of social interests, and both Czech and German multi-party systems developed. But even these parties were not immune to nationalism, not even the Social Democrats who preached that the workers of the world should unite. The nationalist rhetoric and antagonisms developed during the era of dualism would continue to resound through the end of the Austro-Hungarian monarchy and beyond.

10 Fin-de-Siècle and Empire's End

The Young Czechs dominated the political scene from the elections of 1891 until 1906, but they faced more competition from other Czech parties than the National Party had. Multi-party politics did not lessen the influence of nationalism, since the parties competed with each other over who truly represented the national interest. The radical nationalist parties tried to control the national discourse to define the parameters of politics, and in response, the Young Czechs increased their own appeals to nationalism.[1] A similar process affected the Bohemian Germans, leading to obstruction in the land diet and Reichsrat, and spilling over into street violence. Before 1914, the struggle among the national movements in Cisleithania, however bitter, remained a struggle over relative position *within* the Austrian state, not *against* Austria.[2] The stresses and strains of four years of war eroded this situation, until in 1918 the Habsburg monarchy collapsed, to be succeeded by a new and supposedly more just order in Central Europe, whose legitimacy rested on the ideologies of nationalism so disruptive to the old one.

POSITIVE POLITICS, OPPOSITION, OR OBSTRUCTION? (1891–1914)

After 1891 the Young Czechs struggled to hold together their victorious electoral coalition of Old Czech defectors, Masaryk's Realists, and vocal elements of the petty bourgeoisie, radical students, and working-class youth. As the party debated how to move beyond rejection of the *punktace*, influential figures such as former Realists Kaizl and Kramář called for a more moderate, gradualist approach, which they called a politics of stages or positive politics.

The Young Czechs and the Challenges of Success

The first to part company with the Young Czechs was the Progressive Movement, which had originated among Czech university students in 1887.[3] After 1891, the Progressives joined the Social Democrats to agitate for universal suffrage in street demonstrations that took on an anti-dynastic tone by the summer of 1893.[4] After protesters repeatedly clashed with police and the army, the governor, Count Franz Thun-Hohenstein, declared martial law in Prague and arrested many Progressives. The ensuing mass trial of a supposed secret conspiracy, "Omladina" (Youth), resulted in sixty-eight prison sentences ranging from several months to eight years.[5]

During the Omladina trials the Young Czechs protested in the Reichsrat but accomplished little else. At a party conference in Nymburk in November 1894 the Young Czechs distanced the party from the demonstrations, calling for a determined and constructive opposition to the Vienna government. They also declared the Moravian People's Party, established in 1891–92 by Adolf Stránský, and its newspaper *Lidové noviny*, a special Moravian Young Czech organization. Masaryk resigned both his diet and Reichsrat mandates after the imposition of martial law in Prague in 1893, and at Nymburk he left the party leadership.[6] Masaryk criticized Young Czech policies in a series of works, especially *Česká otázka* (The Czech Question, 1895). Masaryk set forth his own views on the meaning of Czech history and the Czech question, while attacking the Young Czechs from an independent position. Kaizl responded for the Young Czechs in his *České myšlenky* (Czech Thought, 1895), expressing reservations about Masaryk's wider philosophical and historical views and strongly defending the party's practical policies.[7]

The Young Czechs' program was more than a version of the Old Czech policies they had once derided as "picking up the crumbs under the table." The Young Czechs called for professional, experienced, qualified politicians, capable of formulating practical policies. In a lengthy Reichsrat speech in December 1895, Kaizl rejected the all-or-nothing attitude of the radicals. The Czech goal of Bohemia's state right, he said, would be won "by stages," each tending in the same general direction. The first two stages were franchise reform and further revision of the language statutes.[8]

Franchise reform brought down Taafe's government in November 1893, ending the longest tenure by a minister-president in the history of dualist Austria. His immediate successor, Prince Alfred Windischgrätz, had no better luck. In October 1895 Count Kazimierz Badeni, a former Galician governor considered a political strongman, took over the office. Badeni eased some press restrictions, lifted the state of emergency in Prague, and amnestied the eleven Omladina prisoners still serving their sentences. With resulting Young Czech support, he forced his electoral reform through the Reichsrat. The system retained the four curiae (lowering the tax hurdle for the two lower ones to four gulden), but added a fifth, in which all males older than twenty-four (even those who had a vote in one of the other four) could vote.[9]

New Reichsrat elections in March 1897 gave the Young Czechs all but two mandates in the Czech Club, but the successes of the relatively new Christian Socialist Party and the Social Democrats warned of coming challenges. The Young Czechs continued the tradition of reasserting Bohemia's state right in the opening session. In response, the five Czech Social Democrats rose with an Anti–State Right Declaration, protesting against "the excavation of threadbare historical privileges and documents" and demanding "modern institutions for ourselves and all nationalities of Austria." The socialists called for the abolition of political inequalities based on birth or means, and denounced the Young Czech program as the "fantastic, state-rights, erroneous path."[10] This attack on state right touched off a nationalistic anti-socialist campaign, and paved the way for the formation of the Czech National Socialist Party a year later.

The major agenda item at the Reichsrat was the upcoming decennial agreement with Hungary. The Young Czechs' price for supporting Badeni was revision of the language ordinances. In April 1897 Badeni issued new regulations for Bohemia and Moravia that extended the use of Czech in public contacts to three further ministries, and provided that cases would be handled internally in the originating language. Employees would have to be bilingual by July 1, 1901. German was still the language of internal business, and of communication with Vienna, but otherwise Badeni's decrees gave Czech equality with German on the entire territory of Bohemia and Moravia. The Young Czechs ended their opposition.

In buying Czech support through language concessions, Badeni sowed the wind: he reaped the whirlwind. German obstruction prevented the Reichsrat from functioning for the remainder of the session, while during the summer recess, demonstrations throughout Cisleithania (especially in the German towns of Bohemia) demanded the preservation of Cisleithania's German character by repealing the ordinance. From imperial Germany the Pan-German League denounced Badeni's decrees as undermining the Austro-German alliance of 1879. The famous German historian Theodor Mommsen wrote to the Vienna *Neue freie Presse* on October 31, 1897, calling the Czechs "apostles of barbarism" who would swamp German cultural achievements in "the abyss of their *Unkultur*." The German response, he noted, had to be tough, because "the Czech skull is impervious to reason, but it is susceptible to blows."[11]

Such toughness was the order of the day when the Reichsrat reconvened in September. Mass street demonstrations in Vienna were echoed in the Reichsrat, where the Pan-Germans Georg von Schönerer and Karl Hermann Wolf led ever more violent obstruction. The crisis peaked on November 26, when Kramář, acting speaker of the Reichsrat, called the police to eject eight German obstructionist delegates. After another day of unabated obstruction in parliament and fresh street riots in Vienna, Badeni resigned, to German celebrations. Czech resentment, rumors of anti-Czech violence, and a march by Prague's German students in honor of the obstructionists set off a violent Czech response. On November 29, groups of Czechs attacked German demonstrations, beat students, trampled imperial banners, stoned the houses of German politicians, and vandalized German and German-Jewish shops in Prague. On December 2, the Bohemian governor proclaimed a state of emergency. The police and army restored order with fixed bayonets, but the violence of 1897 made the prospect of any future compromise remote.

New Political Parties Emerge

In 1897 former Progressives established a separate Radical Progressive Party.[12] Early in 1899, some of their associates who still supported state-right tactics, such as Alois Rašín and Karel Baxa, counsel for the defense in the Omladina trial, founded the State Rights Radical Party. The State Rights Radicals and the Radical Progressives remained parties of professionals and intellectuals. Like them, the Czech People's Party, founded in 1900 by Masaryk and several associates, remained numerically small but intellectually influential. When Alois Hajn brought a splinter group of the Radical Progressives over to Masaryk's party in 1906 it renamed itself the Czech Progressive Party, but it was commonly called the Realist party.

In April 1898 a meeting of Czech workers and tradesmen established the Czech National Socialist Party under another former progressive, Václav Klofáč. The National Socialists agitated against Germans and two Czech parties: the Young Czechs for being insufficiently democratic and radical, and the Social Democrats for betraying the nation.[13] The Czech Social Democrats, operating as the Austrian party's autonomous Czech section, competed with the National Socialists for Czech working-class votes. The Social Democrats also suffered from national tensions, reacting hesitantly to violence between Czech and German workers during 1897. At a party congress in Brno in 1899, therefore, the Austria-wide party adopted a nationality program that urged the democratization of Austria-Hungary in self-governing districts on national criteria, in place of historical political units.[14] Cooperation between Czech and Austrian-German socialists continued on this basis until a definitive separation in 1911.

Of these parties, only the Social Democrats and the National Socialists offered serious competition to the Young Czechs. Certainly the Old Czechs were completely cast into the shade: aside from the House of Lords their representation was negligible in the Reichsrat after 1891, and in the Bohemian land diet after 1895. In the Moravian diet elections of 1896, however, the Old Czechs still clung to thirteen mandates, and they remained influential in the organs of local self-administration and in various cultural, scientific, and economic institutions.

The Agrarian party (emerging between 1899 and 1905) also challenged the Young Czechs. The franchise reforms of 1882 and 1897 encouraged a group of former Old and Young Czech agrarian leaders to establish a Czech Agrarian Party in 1899, which absorbed Šťastný's Peasant Union, and merged with regional organizations in 1905. In May 1905 the Czech Agrarian Party joined with its Moravian and Silesian counterparts to create an Agrarian party for all the Bohemian crownlands. Under the slogan "The Countryside is One Family," the Agrarian Party claimed to represent all country-dwellers against socialist threats to property, and the Catholic parties' clericalism. Already before 1914 Antonín Švehla was emerging as a future leader.

Political Catholicism developed during the 1890s in Bohemia in reaction to the staunchly anti-clerical Young Czechs. Two distinct trends emerged, one representing a national Czech version of traditional clericalism, and the other, stimulated by Pope Leo XIII's encyclical *Rerum novarum*, calling for social justice for the "little people" whose interests the Young Czechs ignored. A Christian Social party emerged out of various organizations in 1899. Led by the Moravian theologian Jan Šrámek it became a strong advocate of socially conscious Catholic activism. The Christian Social Party was strong in Moravia, but weaker in Bohemia, where it competed with Agrarians and Social Democrats for the same voters. The Czech Christian socialists had difficulty cooperating with German clericals, in spite of similar world-views.

Among the German liberals a division between "old" and "young" also emerged. Eduard Herbst and Ernst von Plener, both Bohemian Germans, held various strands together in the United German Left until the 1880s. A group of dissidents adopted a critical program at Linz in 1882. One of them, Schönerer, mixed nationalism with virulent anti-Semitism in his Pan-German Party, creating a corrosive movement that undermined Austrian liberalism.[15] A German-Austrian Christian Socialist movement also weakened liberalism after 1890. Karl Lueger, its major figure, also used anti-Semitism as a weapon against liberalism.[16] At the height of the Badeni disturbances almost all German parties formed a common German Front, and in 1899 they agreed on a minimum program.

Czech Politics into the Twentieth Century

The Czech Agrarians and the Czech and German radical nationalists cut slightly into the strength of the established parties in the 1901 Reichsrat elections. Under a competent government headed by a permanent civil servant, Ernst von Koerber, the Young Czechs pursued an opportunistic policy. Two Young Czechs successively served as ministers for Czech affairs in Koerber's cabinets, but the party adopted nonviolent obstruction in the Reichsrat to gain more concessions on language. After Kaizl's death in 1901 Kramář continued this version of "positive politics." It achieved some practical results, such as government support for flood control along Bohemia's rivers, the urban renewal of Prague, an art gallery in Prague, and a Czech pedagogical school in Silesia. The Young Czechs failed to establish a second Czech university in Brno, and Koerber could not get agreement on language issues in 1900 and 1903. Koerber, called by one historian "perhaps the most able Minister President in Austrian history," achieved what he did by relying on the administrative bureaucracy and making use of § 14 of the constitution of 1867.[17]

Czechs and Germans eventually reached an agreement in Moravia. The Moravian Pact, approved by the emperor on November 27, 1905, added a fourth, universal suffrage curia to the diet franchise, similar to the Reichsrat reforms of 1896. Under the Moravian Pact, however, the lower three curiae were divided along national lines, with Czechs and Germans allotted a fixed number of seats. Voters declared themselves either Czech or German and were recorded in national registries. Each national group then elected only its allotted members, avoiding nationality as an electoral issue. Language regulations applied to the autonomous administrative bodies and school boards effectively divided administration in Moravia on national lines.

This agreement has sometimes been cited as evidence that Austria-Hungary's nationality problems were not insurmountable. Nevertheless, the Moravian Pact had serious flaws. It preserved the undemocratic electoral system that greatly overrepresented the aristocracies of birth and wealth, and slightly overrepresented the German element. By forcing voters to choose Czech or German identities, it sharpened divisions and placed national identity above all other interests. The specific situation of Moravia (a higher proportion of Czechs in the total population but a lower intensity of national strife) contributed to the success of compromise there, and its repeated failure in Bohemia. In the final analysis, piecemeal compromise could probably never have resolved national conflicts, which were now the prism through which all issues were viewed, while a thoroughgoing restructuring of the empire would endanger its continued existence.[18]

Further franchise reform might loosen the logjam in Cisleithanian parliamentary life. The government threatened to extend the franchise in Hungary in 1902 in a quarrel over military recruits, but the idea also reinvigorated the Cisleithanian struggle.[19] The Russian Revolution of 1905 added further impetus to demonstrations in Bohemia culminating in a massive protest in Prague on November 5, 1905. A general strike that brought out 300,000 Viennese workers and nearly 100,000 in Prague reinforced Francis Joseph's order to the government to introduce legislation, finally passed in the Reichsrat on January 26, 1907.[20] A new chamber consisting of 516 members elected under general, equal, direct, and secret ballot by all males over twenty-four years of age replaced the old House of Delegates. The Bohemian crownlands received 194 seats—130 for Bohemia, 49 for Moravia, and 15 for Silesia—of which 108 were in Czech-majority districts.[21] The land diets retained their undemocratic franchise, however, while without ministerial responsibility to the Reichsrat, the parliament did not genuinely govern Cisleithania.

Some had hoped that giving the vote to peasants and workers would dampen the nationalist quarrels that kept parliament from functioning smoothly, but the two elections under the new franchise, in 1907 and 1911, though they showed changing support for Czech and German parties in the Bohemian crownlands, did not produce that result (see Table 1). The Czech parties usually held together on national questions, with the Young Czechs, the Agrarians, and Catholic parties formally coordinating their policies. The Czechs also cooperated with other nonsocialist Slav parties, notably with the South Slavs. Trading support for concessions produced little progress on either of the major Czech goals, the creation of the Czech university for Moravia and the further Czechization of the bureaucracy in the Bohemian crownlands. By 1913 the Czech parties were once more in opposition, the Agrarians and the National Socialists even reviving obstruction. Finally, in March 1914, the Reichsrat was adjourned, and when World War I began in the summer it had not yet been reconvened. It would not gather again until the penultimate year of the war. Elections to the Bohemian diet in 1908 confirmed Czech dominance, and the Bohemian Germans began permanent

TABLE 1

ELECTION RESULTS FOR CZECH AND
GERMAN PARTIES, 1907 AND 1911

	Popular vote %, 1907	Mandates, 1907	Popular vote %, 1911	Mandates, 1911
Czech parties				
Social Democrats	38.1	24	35.3	26
Agrarians	19.65	28	24.0	38
Young Czechs	11.1	18	9.1	18
Catholic parties	17.3	17	19.7	7
National Socialists	7.15	9	7.0	16
Other parties	6.7	11	4.9	3
German parties				
Social Democrats	38.25	21	37.7	10
Agrarians	16.55	19	16.9	22
Progressives	10.05	14	8.6	12
People's Party	9.1	13	5.5	9
German radicals	11.25	12	14.05	22
Christian Socialists	10.3	1	9.3	1
Other parties	4.5	3	7.95	7

SOURCE: Otto Urban, *České a slovenské dějiny do roku 1918,* 2d ed. (Prague: Aleš Skřivan ml., 2000), pp. 240–41.

obstruction in the diet. The continued paralysis of the Bohemian diet led
the government to promulgate the St. Anne's Patents (July 26, 1913).
They dissolved the diet until elections at a more "convenient" time, and
replaced the land committee with an appointed administrative commission.

SOCIETY AND CULTURE
IN THE FIN-DE-SIÈCLE

By the turn of the century, Czechs and Germans stood on
effectively the same social and cultural level, and the Bohemian crownlands were one of the most socially and economically developed regions
of Austria-Hungary. Economic development underpinned the increasingly pluralistic political life of the crownlands. One barometer of this
connection between economic and social change and politics is the fact
that the Bohemian crownlands, together with Upper and Lower Austria

and the coal and iron regions of Styria and Carinthia, gave the Social Democrats their most significant electoral base, while they also had the strongest radical nationalist parties.

Economic and Demographic Development

The ongoing spread of the industrial economy meant that the agricultural share of the population in the Bohemian crownlands declined from nearly 55 percent in 1869 to just over 52 percent in 1900 and only 42.5 percent by 1910, while the industrial share (including small workshops as well as factories) rose from slightly more than 29 percent in 1869 to well over 33 percent in 1900 and 38.4 percent by 1910. Most factories were still small (only 2 percent of them employed more than twenty workers), but the large factories employed nearly half of all industrial workers. Overall, the Bohemian crownlands had by some measures surpassed France and were gaining on Germany, though they still lagged far behind Great Britain.[22]

Infrastructure in the Bohemian crownlands kept pace with the growth of the industrial and agroindustrial sectors of the economy. The railroad network was completed and supplemented by local and connecting lines, and new forms of urban and suburban transportation grew along with the cities and metropolitan areas. Electric lighting spread rapidly, until by 1914 the Bohemian crownlands hummed to the activity of 290 generating plants, supplying about 1,500 communities with 3.8 million inhabitants, roughly equivalent to one-third of the land area. The telephone had joined the telegraph, with the first local exchanges in Prague in 1882, followed rapidly by Brno, Liberec, and Plzeň. By 1914 there were around 200 telephone exchanges in the Bohemian crownlands, with 35,000 subscribers. Transportation reflected the dawn of the automobile era: by 1911 there were over 2,000 automobiles and nearly 4,000 motorcycles registered in the Bohemian crownlands, and the first official traffic regulations were issued in 1905.[23]

In spite of growing emigration, the population increased from 8.7 million to 10.1 million between 1890 and 1910 (nearly half a million inhabitants had emigrated). Lower Austria, especially Vienna, attracted most emigrants, though overseas destinations including the United States accepted a rising share. Bohemian and Moravian cities absorbed almost all the population increase. Typical small towns of up to 10,000 people showed lively growth, but the greatest expansion took place in the large urban centers. Prague by 1910 had already more than 600,000 in its metropolitan area; Brno had grown to over 200,000. Other large urban centers included Ostrava with 167,000 and Plzeň with 109,000 inhabitants.[24]

The balance between Czechs and Germans remained stable, with Bohemia just over 60 percent Czech, Moravia over 70 percent Czech, and Silesia only 24 percent. The location of the language frontier still did not shift greatly overall, but this stability did not dampen the mutual Czech and German nationalist propaganda conflict that had emerged in the 1880s.[25] Dramatic local changes took place in some sensitive spots, such as Prague, where by 1900 the city was overwhelmingly Czech with a German minority of little more than 7 percent. Some industrial areas near the linguistic frontier also saw major changes, such as Most and Duchcov (Dux), where a Czech minority of less than 10 percent in 1880 had grown to over one-quarter by World War I. In Moravia, Uherské Hradiště, where Czechs leaped from less than half to more than 80 percent of the population, and Kroměříž, where the Czech proportion went from three-quarters to 90 percent, were the most dramatic cases. Jihlava, Mikulov (Nikolsburg), Šumperk (Schönberg), and Znojmo preserved their ancient German character and greater than fourth-fifths German majorities; the two largest Moravian cities, Brno and Olomouc, were still two-thirds German in 1900. In Moravská Ostrava (Mährisch Ostrau), in fact, Czechs actually declined from 76 percent of the population in 1880 to slightly more than 50 percent in 1910. Opava in Silesia remained more than 90 percent German.[26]

Cultural Trends

Turn-of-the-century nationalist tensions arose in part out of feelings of being threatened by uncontrollable change, especially among German-speakers. The completion of the process of social development and differentiation among the Czech-speaking population that began in earlier decades reinforced these feelings. At every social level there were now self-consciously and even assertively Czech elements, who half a century earlier would have naturally assimilated to German culture. The further expansion of education in the Bohemian crownlands since the mid-nineteenth century played a vital role in this development of Czech society.[27]

Elementary schools, and the proportion of Czech schools among the total, had steadily increased throughout the second half of the century though they still did not quite reach the proportion of the Czech population. Statistics on literacy rates confirm their significance: in 1900 the percentage of illiterates over six years old was 4.26 among the Czechs and 6.83 among the Germans.[28] Czech classical and practical gymnasia and other technical secondary schools built on these achievements, and their growth was one of the successes of practical politics. By 1912 the proportion of Czech secondary schools corresponded to the proportion of Czechs in the total population. The Czech university in Prague capped this system after 1882. The Czech university was a unique and central part of Czech culture, while in contrast, the German university in Prague was one of nearly forty such institutions in German-speaking Europe. The Czech university was twice its sister institution's size in 1909, and rivaled it in reputation.

The development of education, the rise of Czech nationalism, and growing Czech-German tension affected the Jews in the Bohemian crownlands. Since German liberalism carried the torch of Jewish emancipation and civic equality, until the later nineteenth century most of the Jewish commercial and intellectual strata supported German liberalism and assimilated into German culture, without entirely losing Jewish identity. As demagogues like Schönerer made political anti-Semitism a powerful weapon against liberalism, the Jews' identification with German liberalism bound them to a declining force. At the same time both Old and Young Czech national liberals equated Jews with Germans, while the Czech radicals, especially the National Socialists under Klofáč, reached for the same anti-Semitic weapons used by Schönerer. Czech clericals expressed a more conservative and traditional anti-Semitism.

The trial in September 1899 of a Jewish youth, Leopold Hilsner, for the ritual murder of a Czech girl brought these hostilities into the open. The nationalist and clerical press unleashed a virulent anti-Jewish tirade not only against the unfortunate defendant but against anyone who spoke up for him. Masaryk set himself against this stream, publishing a brochure demanding a revision of the original guilty verdict. The social democratic, student, and realist press lined up behind Masaryk, but he was bitterly attacked in the rest of the Czech press and at the university. The supreme court overturned the verdict, but a retrial still found Hilsner guilty, though Francis Joseph commuted his death sentence to life imprisonment. For Masaryk, this case (like the manuscripts affair in the 1880s) was an unpopular cause that he took up on principle, arguing that the national movement had a moral and ethical dimension as well as a practical and political one.[29]

The tensions in the coexistence of Germans, Jews, and Czechs in the Bohemian lands at the turn of the century, especially in Prague, created a cultural milieu that produced many significant writers. Among those whose works helped define the idea of "Central European literature" for the twentieth century, pride of place must go to Franz Kafka. His close friend Max Brod, talented in his own right, also deserves credit for saving Kafka's work for us. Gustav Meyrink, Egon Erwin Kisch, Rainer Maria Rilke, and Franz Werfel also contributed to shaping and recording Prague's cultural scene.[30] Since these writers, dramatists, critics, poets, and scholars wrote in German, their names were widely known in Europe, and they belonged to the German and German-Jewish cultural world of Prague and Vienna. Their Czech contemporaries produced works of a similar literary standard, though less well known abroad. By the 1890s, Czech literary life was no longer organized around the rivalries between the *lumírovci* and *ruchovci*. In 1895, a loose association of younger writers and critics published a manifesto announcing the arrival of Czech modernism.[31] The Czech Modernists denounced the artistic and political attitudes of their day and called for complete liberty, including liberty in artistic expression. Their insistence on the individuality of artistic vision was reflected in the lack of a single, dominant literary trend during a period in which older styles of romanticism and realism coexisted with neoromanticism, symbolism, naturalism, expressionism, and decadence.

Many writers engaged in social and political issues, while others expressed their rejection of bourgeois philistinism in the lively cabarets and bars of Prague's "Bohemian" underworld. Probably the best-known denizen of Prague's "Bohemia" is Jaroslav Hašek, whose fame, if not fortune, was sealed by the postwar publication of the *Adventures of the Good Soldier Švejk*. Among prose writers the genuine heavyweights, at least in popularity, were the historical novelists, especially Alois Jirásek, whose monumental works expressed his generation's historical consciousness. Jirásek's friend Mikoláš Aleš brought his characters to life vividly. Aleš found scope for his talents, generally unrecognized by formal artistic circles, in murals and mosaics decorating new public buildings in such places as Písek, Plzeň, and Prague.

These buildings were part of a prodigious boom in construction accompanying the growth of cities and the maturation of middle-class society. Entirely new city quarters sprang up, and town councils undertook extensive reconstructions of historical town centers, including Prague's major urban renewal between 1893 and 1908. Modern cities demanded new public works, not only the theaters, museums, schools, and galleries of cultural life, but the railway stations, administrative buildings, and even water towers and sewage systems of the everyday. New apartment blocks established better living conditions, not only for the middle classes but even for at least parts of the working class. Historicist styles predominated, with Czechs favoring neo-Renaissance (the National Theater and National Museum), although classicism (Prague's German theater, today the State Opera) and neo-Gothic were also popular. The ambitious program to finish St. Vitus's cathedral in Prague, ultimately completed only in 1929, was not the only neo-Gothic project on church or other buildings. By the turn of the century Art Nouveau or Secessionist style predominated, exemplified by such structures as the main railway station in Prague and the Municipal House erected next to the Powder Tower on the edge of Prague's Old Town.

Those who cared to could follow debates about art in a wide range of serious and intellectually demanding journals. An outstanding achievement both of Czech publishing and Czech intellectual life was the encyclopedia published by Jan Otto, *Ottův slovník naučný* (28 volumes, 1888–1909).[32] Newspapers spread at all levels. Typically, daily newspapers were linked with a political party, and journalists competing for circulation often expressed themselves much more radically than parliamentary deputies. Beside the nonofficial Young Czech *Národní listy*, Herben's *Čas* and the Social Democratic Party's *Právo lidu* (The People's Right) also upheld high standards. The National Socialist newspaper *České slovo* (Czech Word) provided many a fiery editorial on political, social, and cultural issues. Of course many people limited their reading to calendars, entertaining supplements, lurid pulp fiction, romantic novels available in installments at low cost, and other forms of mass writing.

The Jubilee Exhibition of 1891 perhaps catches the atmosphere at the close of the nineteenth century most vividly.[33] Honoring the centenary of the exhibition that accompanied Leopold II's coronation in 1791, it reflected the confidence in technological progress and the pride in productivity and development typical of the successful Czech businessmen and industrialists who were involved in organizing it. When agitation over the *punktace* led the German-Bohemians to withdraw os-

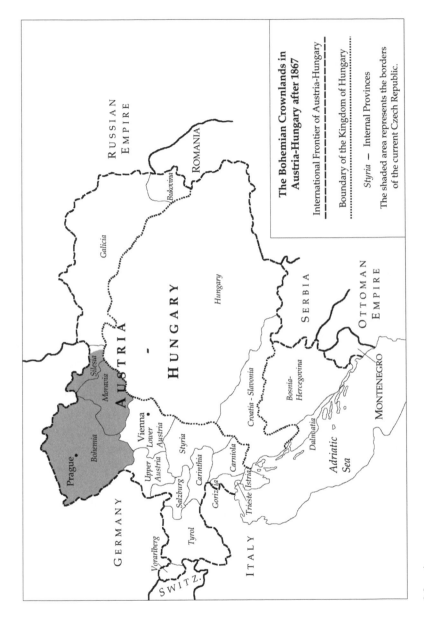

The Bohemian Crownlands in Austria-Hungary after 1867

International Frontier of Austria-Hungary

Boundary of the Kingdom of Hungary

Styria – Internal Provinces

The shaded area represents the borders of the current Czech Republic.

Map 4

tentatiously from participating, the Czechs went ahead and organized the exhibition anyway, turning it into a Czech national manifestation. It proved to be a tremendous success, demonstrating in public the achievements of the Czech nation and giving weight to its claims for political, cultural, and economic recognition.

WORLD WAR I (1914–1918)

On July 29, 1914, subscribers to *Národní listy* could read with varied emotions Francis Joseph's declaration that though "it was my most fervent wish that I could consecrate to the works of peace the years that may still be granted to me by God's grace, . . . the machinations of an opponent filled with hatred have forced me, in order to defend the honor of my state, to protect the esteem and power it enjoys, and to secure its possessions, to take up the sword after long years of peace."[34] After years of mounting tension, Austria-Hungary had declared war on Serbia. That declaration set in motion forces that soon had every major power in Europe involved in a war that would bring down in ruins the monarchy whose honor it had been started to protect.

The Czechs and Austro-Hungarian Foreign Policy

The Habsburg monarchy's road to Sarajevo followed basic signposts that were established by the wars against Italy in 1859 and Prussia in 1866. Thereafter it had little choice but to concentrate its interests, and stake its reputation as a Great Power, on the Balkans. Here it came into conflict with Russia, unfortunately for Austria-Hungary a genuine power, whatever its weaknesses. Since the 1870s, Austria-Hungary pursued three basic methods of dealing with Russia: cooperating in a genuine entente, limiting Russia's freedom of maneuver by linking potential Russian clients to itself, or deterring Russia with the support of another major European power.[35]

Austria-Hungary had defended its interests through the first method for most of the nineteenth century, most recently (1897–1908) by a direct understanding with Russia. The annexation crisis over Bosnia in 1908 ended this entente, and the second method faltered after the Serbian change of dynasty in 1903. Hungary resisted lowering agricultural tariffs for potential clients, while Russia sponsored a league of Balkan states. That left the method of finding another power to support the Habsburg position, but by now the list of possible supporters was perilously short. France feared Germany, welcomed entente with Russia, and accepted its influence in the Balkans. Britain was also concerned over Germany, and had just resolved its colonial rivalries with Russia in 1907. Italy, an Austrian ally since 1882, had its own aims on Ottoman territory in North Africa and Albania. Only Germany remained as a potential Great Power supporter. Yet German support was not a foregone conclusion, nor an unmixed blessing. Since the 1890s Germany had asserted its interests without taking account of Austria-Hungary's position. Austria-Hungary was the weaker power, who offered advantages only if Germany needed support. That was the case in 1908 and again in 1914, but Germany threatened to be such a dominant partner that Austria-Hungary would cease to exist as an independent Great Power, win or lose.

The Czechs remained frustrated that, in spite of their political, social, and economic progress since the 1860s, they had no influence on Austria-Hungary's foreign policy. Of course, parliament did not control foreign policy, as the fall of the German liberals after 1879 showed. The delegations, however, did debate the funding for the ministry of foreign affairs, and there Kramář, Masaryk, and later Klofáč, expressed a Czech view of Austria-Hungary's foreign policy. The major Czech parties realized that Austria could not ignore Germany, but they argued that over-reliance on Germany was against Austria-Hungary's interests and a threat to its non-German peoples, and pleaded for closer ties with France and Russia.

Masaryk emerged as a leading supporter of the South Slavs when, in a Reichsrat speech in May 1909, he criticized the Zagreb treason trial.[36] In the related libel suit by Serb and Croat politicians in December 1909, Masaryk demonstrated that key documents in the case were forgeries emanating directly from the Foreign Ministry. This embarrassment and Masaryk's continued criticism of the monarchy's Balkan policy increased Czech sympathy for the South Slavs.[37] Masaryk had already forged personal links with leading Serb and Croat intellectuals at the Czech university in Prague, where he became a full professor in 1897.[38] Similar ties linked Masaryk with Slovak students. Several of them established a journal, *Hlas* (The Voice), where they advocated cooperation with the Czechs. The 1895 Ethnographic Exhibition in Prague included displays devoted to the Slovaks, and stimulated the creation of the Czechoslovak Union in 1896. It sent books to Slovakia, supported Slovak students in Prague, and encouraged Czech investment there. It also published a collection of readings (1911) and a revue, *Naše Sloven-sko* (Our Slovakia, 1907–10). The frontier between Cisleithania and Hungary still limited Czech and Slovak cooperation, but these connections provided some foundation on which cooperation during World War I could build.[39]

Kramář supported Neo-Slavism, which flourished between 1908 and 1913, and reflected his views in its fundamentally pro-Russian outlook.[40] Two Slav congresses, modeled on the meeting of 1848, were held in Prague in 1908 and in Sofia in 1910. The aim of the Neo-Slav movement was a new foreign policy agreement with Russia similar to the defunct Three Emperors' League. In the atmosphere of Balkan competition after the Bosnian annexation of 1908, this goal proved totally unrealistic. The Balkan Wars of 1912–13 touched off a sympathetic reaction among many Czechs, who cheered as the Balkan Slavs drove the Turks out of Europe, and looked with hostility at Austria-Hungary's efforts to limit Serbia's gains.

Thus by the time the heir-apparent, Archduke Francis Ferdinand, went to Bosnia in June 1914, Czech attitudes to Austria-Hungary's foreign policy were at odds with its direction. Neither the future emperor's personality nor his probable policies generated Czech enthusiasm. He was a notorious clerical and ardent militarist; he was married (against the emperor's wishes) to a Bohemian countess with Slavic ancestry, but his political views were centralist and sympathetic to the Germans; he toyed with constitutional reform, but Trialism—the idea of replacing dualism with a three-way structure including a South Slav unit—offered the Czechs nothing, and was clearly intended to break the Magyar position in Hungary, not benefit the Slavs.[41] Nevertheless, the assassination of the Archduke and his wife in Sarajevo on June 28, 1914, was a great shock.

During the four weeks between the assassination and the Austro-Hungarian declaration of war, the clouds apparently receded, only to gather rapidly again with the presentation of an ultimatum to Serbia. A complete account of the origins of World War I here would be superfluous, but certain features bear repeating. Austria-Hungary sought a war with Serbia, believing that they must settle accounts sooner or later. It sought and received Germany's support, in spite of the knowledge of Russia's commitment to Serbia, and of the likelihood that both France and Great Britain would be drawn into the conflict. The war had myriad causes, and "war guilt" can be spread widely, but in the final analysis World War I began when and where Austria-Hungary chose. Most people who lived through it looked back on the war as a watershed separating one era from another. At the time, nearly everyone had only vague or erroneous ideas of what modern war would be like. The next four years would provide a cruel enlightenment.

The First Years of War, 1914–1916

The war began in an upsurge of patriotic fervor that was cooled only by the first baptism of fire. In Austria-Hungary the Croats, Germans, and Magyars evinced the same kinds of war excitement as did the French, British, and Germans. Among Austria-Hungary's Serbs, Ruthenes, and Czechs, however, the situation was different.[42] Czech soldiers reported to their units, but neither they nor the Czech public exhibited exceptional enthusiasm. The sullen bewilderment of many was captured by a verse reportedly carried on a banner by some Czech soldiers on their way to the front: "Červený šátečku, kolem se toč, pudeme na Rusa, nevíme proč" (Red-colored handkerchief, wave through the sky, we fight the Russians, though we don't know why).[43]

The immediate situation provided little in the way of a convincing "why." German propaganda about the struggle with Slavdom would hardly whip up Czech enthusiasm. The Reichsrat had been prorogued in March and was simply left in adjournment. The government ruled through the bureaucracy, and in areas near the front direct military administration took over. Klofáč, the most outspoken antimilitarist Czech politician, was arrested in September 1914, and political newspapers were suspended or censored. Czech political parties were reduced to silence or to consulting among themselves about what to do.

Russia's offensive in August 1914 stirred up some Czech pro-Russian sympathies as it pushed into Galicia. In mid-September the Russian Supreme Command issued a manifesto to the peoples of Austria-Hungary with vague promises of freedom and justice. Copies or imitations with more concrete promises of Czech independence circulated among the people. The Czech front-line soldiers showed signs of wavering loyalty, especially early in the war. After scattered cases of Czech desertion, the 28th Prague Infantry Regiment surrendered almost to a man in the Carpathians on April 3, 1915. The 36th Mladá Boleslav

Infantry Regiment followed its example a month later, and both regiments were dissolved as a sign of their "disgrace."[44]

The Russian steamroller, however, faltered and the Galician front stabilized. A counteroffensive by the Central Powers in May 1915 accompanied a further tightening of domestic controls. The governor of Bohemia, Thun, had been forced to retire in March because the General Staff considered him too pro-Czech. In May, Kramář and Rašín were arrested along with the head of the Prague Sokol, Josef Scheiner. The Sokol was disbanded in November 1915. Other sources of trouble such as the long-planned anniversary of Hus's martyrdom in 1915 were quashed. The names of the executed leaders of the Bohemian Estates were removed from Prague's Old Town Hall, textbooks were rewritten, books removed from the libraries, even pictures on postcards, playing cards, and matchboxes were censored.[45] Tried between December 1915 and July 1916, Kramář and Rašín were convicted of treason and sentenced to death, though they were not executed for the time being.

Austria-Hungary showed more serious signs of economic trouble sooner than the Western powers or even its German ally. Fixed prices failed to stop inflation, and the authorities introduced food rationing by the spring of 1915. The coupon rationing system was extended to include most articles of consumption, but supply problems meant that often there was simply no food in the shops. Mobilization disrupted the agricultural labor force, and the harvests of 1915 and 1916 were much worse than in 1914. On top of that, the Hungarian government, burdened with supplying the army, released to Cisleithania only what it could spare, and that at high prices. Though there were muted protests as early as April 1915, the people generally suffered and grumbled, but did not yet take action.

By 1915 the Czech political parties began to shake themselves out of their lethargy. Their policy of "activism" worked within Austria-Hungary for specific Czech interests in the traditions of the nineteenth century. It also countered the wartime assertion of a "German" character for Cisleithania. On November 19, 1916, the Czech members of the last prewar Reichsrat created the Czech Union, and most Czech political parties formed a National Committee. Thus when Francis Joseph died two days later, the Czech political parties had agreed on a common approach and established common organs.

Several Czech political figures chose to go into exile, where they organized a movement aimed at destroying Austria-Hungary. Though not the first, Masaryk proved by far the most significant. Masaryk went abroad during the winter of 1914–15 to try to influence Entente policy toward Austria-Hungary while maintaining contact with the Czech lands through a secret group of collaborators known as the *Maffie*. In Geneva on July 6, 1915 (the anniversary of Hus's martyrdom), he called for the destruction of Austria-Hungary and the creation of an independent Czech state. Masaryk tried to build support for his movement among Czech and Slovak emigrants, but distance and rivalries divided them, especially the Russian communities and those in France, Great Britain, and the United States.

A pro-Russian orientation initially flourished, though Masaryk opposed a Russian-ruled Bohemian state. In turn, the Tsarist authorities looked on him with suspicion.[46] In Russia, formal permission to organize Czech military units (the Czech *Družina*) came at the beginning of August 1914, but they were kept small and used mostly for intelligence. Czech and Slovak émigré organizations in Russia united in a formal umbrella organization only in March 1915. With Kramář and Rašín under arrest, no other prominent Russophile politician was likely to go abroad, and after his Geneva speech Masaryk began to gain recognition as a Czech spokesman.

In September 1915, Edvard Beneš joined Masaryk in Paris, where Milan Rastislav Štefánik, a Slovak serving in the French air force, added his contacts with French leaders to the cause. Together they coordinated the various strands of the Czech and Slovak movement abroad. One success came in Cleveland on October 22, 1915, when American Czech and Slovak groups adopted a declaration promising to cooperate. On November 14 Masaryk announced the creation of a Czech Committee Abroad. In February 1916 it became the Czechoslovak National Council, with Masaryk as chairman, Josef Dürich and Štefánik vice-chairmen, and Beneš in charge of its secretariat in Paris.[47] In the summer of 1916 trouble arose in Russia, where Dürich had gone to coordinate activity. Instead, in January 1917 Dürich became chairman of a Russophile and pro-Tsarist Czechoslovak National Council in Russia. When the Russian monarchy collapsed a few weeks later, however, he lost all influence.

Francis Joseph's death in November 1916 brought his grandnephew Charles to the throne. Charles and his newly appointed Foreign Minister, Count Ottokar Czernin, promised to seek peace, but they had to coordinate their efforts with their allies. American president Woodrow Wilson intervened on December 20, asking all warring powers to state their aims. A formal Entente response dated January 10, 1917, specifically listed "the liberation of the Italians, Slavs, Romanians, and Czechoslovaks" from foreign rule as one of the Entente's war aims.[48] In response, Czernin orchestrated declarations of loyalty from Austria-Hungary's political parties. On January 31, 1917, the Czech Union insisted that "the Czech nation sees its future and the conditions for its development now, as always in the past and in the future, only under the Habsburg scepter."[49] This declaration was a setback to the Czechoslovak National Council's claim to represent its fellow countrymen at home. Within the next few months, however, two events fundamentally altered the situation: the Russian Revolution and the U.S. entry into the war.

The Final Phase of the War and the Collapse of Austria-Hungary, 1917–1918

The fall of the Tsar and the creation of a provisional government in Petrograd dismayed Kramář and Rašín (who heard the news while still in prison), but encouraged Masaryk. He could now go to Russia, where he arrived in May, as the first provisional government was crumbling. Masaryk's objective was to establish an independent Czechoslovak army in Russia. The Tsarist regime had finally expanded the Czech *Družina* to battalion size by recruiting prisoners of war. After the Czechoslovak units distinguished themselves during the battle at Zborov on July 2, 1917, the Russian high command and Kerensky's government recognized Masaryk's Czechoslovak National Council as the political authority over the Czechoslovak army units in Russia. In August 1917, Beneš won permission to establish a legion in France, followed in December by recognition of Czechoslovak political authority over the troops. The Italians began using Czech and Slovak prisoners of war in labor battalions in December 1917, but efforts to create independent military units there bore fruit only in April 1918.

The Russian revolution increased Austrian fears, as the grumbling of the previous year changed into open protests about the worsening food supply situation.[50] The Austrian government under Count Heinrich Clam-Martinic convened the Reichsrat (based on the 1911 elections) for May 30, 1917. On May 17 a group of 222 writers and scholars published a manifesto calling on the deputies resuming their Reichsrat seats "to champion Czech rights and Czech demands most decisively and most selflessly, for now the Czech fate will be decided for entire centuries!" If they could not, they should resign.[51] At the Reichsrat's opening session, František Staněk read out a declaration on behalf of the Czech Union denouncing dualism and demanding, based on the right to national self-determination, "the joining together of all branches of the Czechoslovak nation in a democratic Czech state, including also the Slovak branch of the Czechoslovak nation, living in a coherent unit with the historic Czech homeland." Though not an open rejection of the common state, the call for union with the Slovaks—included thanks to Vávro Šrobár, a Hlasist who was in Prague to consult with the Czech Union—implied the end of Dualism and the breakup of the monarchy.[52]

Kramář, Rašín, and Klofáč were released under an amnesty in July 1917, speeding up a Czech political reorganization. The Social Democrats replaced the "activist" Šmeral with Gustav Habrman in September 1917. When they could not agree on a merger with the Social Democrats, Klofáč reorganized the national socialists as the Czechoslovak Socialist Party on April 1, 1918. The agrarians changed policies but kept Švehla, while the Catholic parties held the activist line until summer. Kramář and Rašín reassumed leadership of the Young Czechs, and on February 9, 1918, merged with other right-of-center groups into the Czech State Right Democracy. At the beginning of March the Old Czechs joined the new party.

Both exiled and domestic politicians realized that the Entente powers and the United States still hoped for a separate peace with Austria-Hungary. From the time of Charles's initial peace feelers in March 1917 until his definitive failure in April 1918, the Entente powers would not commit themselves to Masaryk or his Yugoslav colleagues. Wilson delayed declaring war on Austria-Hungary until December 7, 1917, and even in his famous Fourteen Points speech of January 8, 1918, only called for "autonomy" for the peoples of the monarchy. British Prime Minister David Lloyd George also reassured Austria-Hungary in January that its destruction was not one of the British war aims. The Sixtus Affair finally brought this hesitation to an end. When Czernin made a slighting public reference on April 2, 1918, to French offers of a separate peace, the French premier Georges Clemenceau published a letter from Charles to his brother-in-law, Prince Sixtus of Bourbon-Parma, in which he promised to support France's "just claims" in Alsace-Lorraine. Charles denounced the letter as a forgery, but Czernin resigned on

April 14, and on May 12 the Habsburg emperor and his generals made a humiliating pilgrimage to German headquarters, to reaffirm their loyalty in terms that left them effectively under German control.[53]

The Bolshevik revolution in November added to the complications facing all sides. The Bolsheviks immediately issued a decree on peace, and offered to negotiate with other nations on the basis of "no annexations, no indemnities." Instead, after an armistice on December 5, 1917, the negotiations at Brest-Litovsk clearly constituted an old-fashioned dictated peace. The Treaty of Brest-Litovsk, signed on March 3, 1918, enabled Germany to concentrate forces in the West for what it hoped would be a decisive offensive. The prospect kept Austria-Hungary's leaders from risking the serious concessions required for a separate peace from the Allies, until the Sixtus Affair made it impossible to extricate themselves from their ally's embrace.

In April 1918 Italy held a "Congress of Oppressed Nationalities" in Rome. There, representatives of the Czechs and Slovaks, together with the South Slavs, raised demands for self-determination. Under the impact of the Sixtus Affair and the Treaty of Brest-Litovsk, the United States shifted its position. Secretary of State Robert Lansing expressed on May 29, 1918, the U.S. government's "earnest sympathy" with the Czechoslovak and Yugoslav desire for freedom. The British, French, and Italian prime ministers associated themselves with his declaration on June 3. By then Masaryk was in the United States, where he scored a diplomatic success when he and the American Czech and Slovak organizations signed an agreement at Pittsburgh on May 30, promising to work for a common state with federal institutions and a separate Slovak diet.[54]

The Czechoslovak Legion in Russia constituted a disciplined, well-armed, pro-Entente force of tens of thousands.[55] Hopes of reconstituting an Eastern Front died hard, and strategists worried that war matériel sent to Russia might fall into German hands, raising the strategic value of the Czechoslovak movement. Masaryk insisted that the Legion should stay out of Russia's internal quarrels, and negotiated to get it to the Western Front, where it could fight the Central Powers. During evacuation on the Trans-Siberian railroad to Vladivostok, friction with local authorities led to conflict. Beginning with an incident at Cheliabinsk on May 14, 1918, the Czechoslovak forces quickly occupied the entire Trans-Siberian railway, precipitating a new stage in the Russian civil war and encouraging an Allied intervention. The Czechoslovak "Anabasis" in Siberia also caught the public imagination in the Entente. On June 30, 1918, the French government recognized the Czechoslovak National Council as an authorized representative of the Czechoslovak people, and the British did the same on August 3. The United States in its note of September 3 recognized the Czechoslovak National Council as "a *de facto* belligerent government," entitled to "direct the military and political affairs of the Czecho-Slovaks."[56]

On January 6, 1918, Czech Reichsrat and diet deputies issued a declaration demanding independence for the nation "in its own state, sovereign, with complete rights, democratic, socially just, and built on the equality of all its citizens within the frontiers of its historic lands and seat and that of its Slovak branch."[57] The "Epiphany Declaration" was the strongest domestic statement of support for Masaryk's policies yet. Jirásek's "National Oath" read aloud to a meeting at Prague's Municipal House on April 13, 1918, also supported the exiles. On July 13 the National Committee, which had been dormant since March, was reconstituted. All Czech parties participated in proportion to their vote in the 1911 elections, with Kramář as chairman, Švehla and Klofáč vice-chairmen, and František Soukup secretary. On September 6 the two socialist parties created a Socialist Council to coordinate the Left.

By the late summer of 1918, the Central Powers could no longer fight. Both Germany and Austria-Hungary addressed separate notes to Wilson on October 4 requesting an armistice on the basis of the Fourteen Points. On October 16, Emperor Charles published a manifesto federalizing the Austrian half of the monarchy. Masaryk responded with a declaration of Czechoslovak independence, dated in Paris on October 18, 1918, but handed to the Allied governments on October 17. The Americans' reply to the Austrian note on October 18 stated that only the Czechoslovak and Yugoslav movements could decide what Austrian actions were a satisfactory foundation for negotiations.

On October 21, 1918, the German-Austrians, basing themselves on the manifesto of October 16, formally withdrew from the Reichsrat and constituted themselves the provisional national assembly of independent German-Austria. On October 24, the Italians began their last offensive and Austrian resistance collapsed. Meanwhile, the domestic Czech leaders sent a delegation to Geneva, where on October 28, unaware of events in Prague, they held talks with Beneš.

On October 27 the Austrian authorities accepted Wilson's conditions, and asked for an armistice. The news reached Prague by

10:00 A.M. on October 28. The interim leaders of the National Committee, Rašín, Jiří Stříbrný, Soukup, and Švehla, organized a meeting for that evening in the Municipal House. Fortuitously, Šrobár had just returned to Prague, so when the National Committee issued its first law, stating that "the independent Czechoslovak state has come into being," a Slovak was present. Independently of events in Prague, on October 30 a meeting of Slovak leaders in Turčiansky Svätý Martin created a Slovak National Council and asserted their right to self-determination as a branch of the "Czechoslovak nation."[58]

While the negotiators in Geneva were approving the exiles' actions abroad and creating a government, in Prague the local Austro-Hungarian military command was surrendering authority to the National Committee. On October 31 the Geneva talks agreed on a democratic Czechoslovak republic with Masaryk as president, Kramář as prime minister,

Crowds flood Prague's Wenceslas Square on October 28, 1918. (ČTK photo)

Beneš as foreign minister, and Štefánik as minister of war. The delegation returned to Prague on November 5, two days after the Austrians signed an armistice. On November 11 Emperor Charles announced his withdrawal from the affairs of his people, and the next day German-Austria was declared a republic and announced its annexation to Germany. On November 13 the National Committee adopted a provisional constitution creating a Revolutionary National Council, which elected Masaryk president and invested Kramář's new government on November 14. The four centuries of association between the Czech lands and the House of Habsburg were formally at an end.

THE CENTURY OF "ISMS"

PART FOUR

11 An Island of Democracy?

The new state that "came into being" on October 28, 1918, brought with it many legacies from Austria-Hungary, not all negative. The Czechs registered impressive cultural, economic, and political achievements while part of the Habsburg monarchy. They gained valuable experience in representative, multiparty politics, local self-government, and bureaucratic administration. On the other hand, their political parties had more experience in parliamentary obstruction than in responsible government; the self-governing bodies exchanged Vienna-based for Prague-based centralism; and the bureaucracy, though basically honest, was slow moving and patronizing.[1] Other aspects of Czechoslovakia's inheritance were equally mixed. Slovakia and Subcarpathian Ruthenia added new tensions to the existing Czech-German rivalry. Czechoslovakia inherited the lion's share of Austro-Hungarian industry, but that made the loss of the monarchy's internal market all the more severe. The Austrian and Hungarian parts of the country reflected different levels of economic development. Finally, Austria-Hungary's collapse raised security issues for those who had been submerged, but also protected, within the larger state. Coping with this historical inheritance demanded time. Masaryk remarked in the early 1930s: "Thirty more years of peaceful, rational, efficient progress and the country will be secure."[2] Instead, Czechoslovakia's time ran out before the end of its second decade.

SHAPING A NEW STATE

"Where is my homeland?" asks the song that now became part of the official Czechoslovak national anthem. Working out an internationally recognized answer to that question headed the provisional government's agenda after October 1918. The new state also required political institutions and a constitutional structure. Resolving the territorial issues depended on the decisions of the Paris Peace Conference from January 1919 to June 1920, though the Czechoslovaks also shaped their frontiers by their own actions. Writing a constitution fell to the Revolutionary National Assembly between November 14, 1918, and February 29, 1920.

Drawing Czechoslovakia's Frontiers

Czech political tactics for decades had stressed Bohemia's historic state right. To ensure that it controlled the territory and to maintain its claim to Bohemia's historic frontiers the National Council decided, after failed negotiations with German Bohemian leaders, to occupy four "Austrian" provinces created in German-inhabited districts between October and December 1918 by the Bohemian and Moravian Germans.[3] Lacking mutual communications and dependent economically on the Czech interior, these regions could only survive if Austria's call for union to Germany were accepted in Paris.[4] The occupation succeeded in spite of local skirmishes, and all Austria could do was appeal to self-determination and await the peace conference's decision.[5]

Count Mihály Károlyi's liberal Hungarian republic used historical rights arguments against Czechoslovakia's claim to Slovakia (Upper Hungary), so at Paris Beneš added strategic, geographic, and economic considerations.[6] The Czechoslovak National Council appointed a commission to administer Slovakia, and Czechoslovak troops began to occupy the territory in November 1918 but withdrew in the face of Hungarian counterattacks. Meanwhile, Masaryk had returned to Prague on December 20 with the Czechoslovak Italian legion under Italian command. New forces moved east against a freshly proclaimed "independent" Slovak state in Košice. On December 30 they occupied Košice while other Czechoslovak troops occupied Prešpurk, soon to be renamed Bratislava, between January 1 and 2, 1919.[7] The situation changed again on March 21, 1919, when Béla Kun established a Hungarian Soviet republic.[8] The newly reorganized Hungarian Red Army attacked in Slovakia on May 1, 1919, and rapidly overran two-thirds of Slovak territory. On June 16, a Slovak Soviet Republic was proclaimed in Prešov, but the peace conference had already established the frontier with Hungary, and an Allied ultimatum forced Kun's army to withdraw. The Czechoslovaks occupied all of Slovakia after the Slovak Soviet Republic collapsed on July 7, 1919.[9]

The peace conference gave Czechoslovakia another formerly Hungarian region, Subcarpathian Ruthenia.[10] This heterogeneous territory strategically divided Bolshevik Russia from Hungary and provided Czechoslovakia with a frontier with Romania. In November 1918, a Ruthenian congress in Scranton, Pennsylvania, endorsed a proposal for autonomy within Czechoslovakia, confirmed by a plebiscite held in December by the emigrant organizations and church parishes. In Ruthenia itself the major political movements put aside their rivalries long enough to call for union with Czechoslovakia in May 1919. During the war with Soviet Hungary, Ruthenia was occupied by the Romanian army, and when it withdrew in August 1919 Czechoslovak troops under a French general replaced it.[11]

A frontier controversy over the duchy of Těšín, one of the three remnants of Austrian Silesia, embroiled Czechoslovakia with Poland. Těšín contained crucial coal fields and one of the few railway connections between the Bohemian crownlands and Slovakia. In January 1919, against Masaryk's misgivings, Czechoslovakia occupied the territory it claimed. The Poles withdrew but appealed to the peace conference. On February 1, the Council of Ten imposed a temporary demarcation line. Finally, on July 28, 1920, the Council of Ambassadors arbitrated the dispute, leaving Czechoslovakia the coal basin and the railway line. Neither side was satisfied, and the division of Těšín symbolized continuing discord between the two new states.

International recognition of Czechoslovakia's frontiers came at the Paris Peace Conference.[12] The council's Commission of Czechoslovak Affairs upheld Beneš's claims for Bohemia's historic frontiers, a southern border for Slovakia justified on economic and strategic grounds, and the addition of Ruthenia. In early April, the Commission's recommendations were approved. The Treaty of Versailles with Germany (June 28, 1919) added a salient of German Silesia with a majority Czech-speaking population, Hlučinsko (Hultschin). The Treaty of Saint-Germain with

Austria (September 10, 1919) added two minor rectifications in Czech favor. Czechoslovakia also signed the Minorities Treaty, which established League of Nations protections for the ethnic minorities, and a treaty settling its financial obligations to the allies.

The Treaty of Trianon with Hungary was not signed until June 4, 1920, after the fall of Kun's regime and the installation of a right-wing government under Regent Admiral Miklós Horthy. Hungary ceded Slovakia, including the plains north of the Danube (with a sizable Magyar population) and Ruthenia.[13] With the signing of the Treaty of Trianon and the resolution of the Těšín controversy, the physical shape of the new Czechoslovak state was settled. In almost every case the settlement confirmed a situation that the Czechoslovaks had influenced—with the acquiescence of the Western powers—by their own actions.

The Czechoslovak Constitution of 1920

The Revolutionary National Assembly created internal institutions within these frontiers.[14] The assembly was created by enlarging the National Committee on November 13, 1918, using the 1911 election results among the Czech parties, and adding forty (later fifty-four) coopted Slovak representatives, largely selected by Šrobár. This step ensured that some Slovak voices would be heard, but no minority representatives participated in drafting the constitution. The Germans refused to recognize the National Assembly, hoping to vote for the Austrian Republic's parliament in 1919. On March 4, the day the Austrian assembly convened, nervous Czech gendarmes fired on demonstrating German protesters in several places, killing a total of fifty-two people and wounding dozens, notably at Kadaň (Kaaden) and Šternberk (Sternberg).

The assembly's legitimacy was in fact revolutionary—from a revolution in the name of the Czech and Slovak (or Czechoslovak) nations, with all that implied for Germans, Hungarians, or other minorities. This assembly had to work out a new constitution to replace the provisional charter adopted on November 13. The permanent constitution, submitted in February 1920, asserted that Czechoslovakia was the work of the "Czechoslovak nation," a nation-state for the Czechs and Slovaks. The constitution established a republic with a president elected by a bicameral parliament with a 300-seat lower house and a senate of 150. Seats in parliament were divided by proportional representation using fixed party lists and universal (male and female), equal, direct, and secret suf-

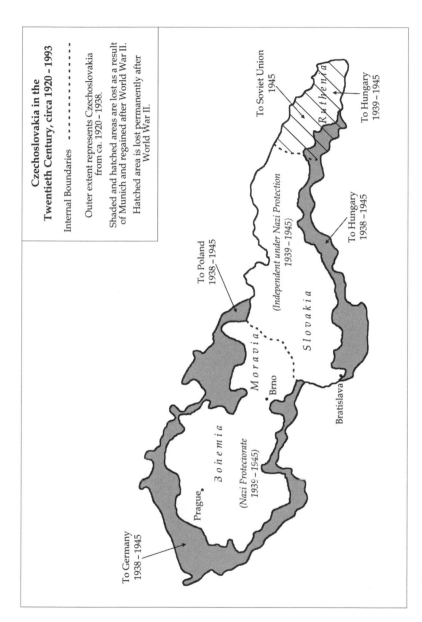

**Czechoslovakia in the
Twentieth Century, circa 1920 – 1993**

Internal Boundaries - - - - - - - -

Outer extent represents Czechoslovakia
from ca. 1920 – 1938.

Shaded and hatched areas are lost as a result
of Munich and regained after World War II.

Hatched area is lost permanently after
World War II.

To Germany
1938 – 1945

Prague

B o h e m i a

*(Nazi Protectorate
1939 – 1945)*

To Poland
1938 – 1945

M o r a v i a

Brno

*(Independent under Nazi Protection
1939 – 1945)*

S l o v a k i a

To Hungary
1938 – 1945

Bratislava

To Hungary
1939 – 1945

R u t h e n i a

To Soviet Union
1945

Map 5

frage. The constitution confirmed basic civil and political rights for all citizens equally, and the provisions for minority protection followed the international obligations accepted when the Treaty of Saint-Germain was signed.[15]

Five basic laws submitted together with the draft defined "Czechoslovak" as the official state language, effectively making Czech and Slovak equal. Minorities were guaranteed freedom to use their language in daily life and schools, and in official contacts with the state where they made up 20 percent of the local population. Slovak autonomy was not included in the constitution, and the Slovak populists accepted the law on state administration only with reservations. It established self-governing prefectures to harmonize the Hungarian and Austrian systems, but the system was not applied in Bohemia and Moravia because at least two of the new prefectures would have German majorities. On February 29, 1920, the National Assembly unanimously adopted the new constitution.

DEVELOPMENT OF CZECHOSLOVAK POLITICS

Proportional representation ensured that Czechoslovakia would be governed by multi-party coalitions. Most political parties in interwar Czechoslovakia had a pedigree that stretched back to the Habsburg monarchy, though some new parties emerged between the wars. There were never fewer than fourteen parties in parliament, and many more failed to win enough votes to gain a seat. Major parties were organized on social or ideological bases, though in Slovakia personalities also played a strong role, as did nationality everywhere. The proliferation of parties did not mean, however, that Czechoslovak politics was totally fragmented. The fundamental division was between parties that accepted and those that rejected the republic, with a group in the middle whose attitude was neither unconditional acceptance nor rejection. Nearly all the Czech and Slovak parties supported the state, and thus in spite of the large numbers of parties and the frequent cabinet reshuffles, interwar politics had an underlying stability.

Political Forces in Interwar Czechoslovakia

The Agrarian Party, still led by Švehla, was the backbone of that stability, participating in every coalition government between the wars.[16]

In 1922 the Slovak agrarians under Šrobár and Milan Hodža merged with it. The Czechoslovak Social Democratic Party emerged from the war with the strongest voter support, but the split with the radical left wing caused a temporary decline. The Czechoslovak (National) Socialist Party, still led by Klofáč, normally strongly supported Masaryk and Beneš (the latter joined it in 1923). The right of center included the People's Party, formed in 1919 when various Catholic-oriented movements merged and led from 1922 by the veteran priest Jan Šrámek. Kramář's National Democratic Party, heir to the Young Czechs, shared the center-right with the populists. Kramář's interwar authority rested on the aura of martyrdom he and Rašín earned for their wartime death sentences, and he served as the first Czechoslovak prime minister, but that marked the National Democrats' high-water mark.[17] The centrist Tradesmen's Party also supported the state.

Slovak voters could choose between parties with a Czechoslovak (centralist) orientation, or the Slovak populists. The centralists merged or cooperated with their Czech counterparts, but (with the exception of the communists) no party established a countrywide base. The Slovak populists, like the Czech People's Party, had a Catholic orientation and were led by a priest, Andrej Hlinka. Hlinka's career began under Hungary, first within the Hungarian clerical movement, and then in a separate Slovak People's party, named Hlinka's Slovak People's Party (HSL'S) in his honor in 1925.

The German parties in Czechoslovakia also had roots in Austria-Hungary. The strongest German party immediately after the war was the German Social-Democratic Workers' Party, followed by the German Christian-Social People's Party, and the German Agrarian League. The German National Socialist Workers' Party (DNSAP) and the German National Party (DNP) represented radical right-wing nationalism. In the mid–1920s the mainstream parties moved toward "activism," working within the state for German interests. The German Agrarians led the way, followed by the Christian Socialists and later joined by the German Social Democrats.

The other national minorities had their own parties, forced by the threshold for entering parliament to contest elections in a bloc or electoral coalition. The Communist Party of Czechoslovakia (KSČ) had a peculiar position: it was never outlawed and functioned legally, but for much of the period had to deny the legitimacy of the Czechoslovak state. It was the only Czechoslovak party to represent all the minorities. The establishment of a truly "Bolshevik" leadership had to wait until 1929, when Klement Gottwald aligned the party with Moscow.[18]

President Masaryk represented another important political force. Instead of remaining "above the clouds," Masaryk used his personal political and moral stature to try to shape Czechoslovakia's policies.[19] From his office an informal group of politicians and intellectuals influenced public issues, especially foreign affairs. Known as the Castle, this group had the support of the Social Democrats and National Socialists, the Sokol, and the legion veterans' organizations. Kramář, who disputed Masaryk's view of the exiles' role in achieving independence, was its leading critic. Other right-wing elements later attacked the Castle for cosmopolitan, unpatriotic, or even pro-German policies. The German negativist parties and the communists joined the anti-Castle chorus.[20] The Castle derived its significance from Masaryk's personal position: revered as the President-Liberator, his influence exceeded his formal constitutional prerogatives. The public's regard for Masaryk resembled the semi-affectionate respect once accorded the aging Francis Joseph. As one scholar notes, "Masaryk's countrymen were accustomed to an emperor, and he exploited their monarchical tendencies in an effort to establish the new republic on firm foundations of authority."[21]

Postwar Stabilization

After October 28, 1918, the National Committee rapidly gained control of essential services and law and order, decreed that existing Austro-Hungarian laws would remain in effect, and kept most administrative and police officials in their places. The creation of the Revolutionary National Assembly and Kramář's government clarified and stabilized authority. Kramář's "all-national" coalition dealt with food shortages, inflation and the black market, and the need to revive economic life and the transportation system. After Kramář left for Paris and the peace conference, Švehla, minister of the interior, headed the government in his absence.

In the first municipal elections in Bohemia and Moravia in June 1919 (because of the turmoil in Slovakia and Ruthenia there were no elections there), the Social Democrats won nearly 30 percent of the vote, the Agrarians had more than 21 percent, the National Socialists–Progressive bloc took almost 16 percent, and even the Populists did better than Kramář's National Democrats. In July the All-National coalition resigned, and was replaced by a coalition of Socialists, Agrarians, and National Socialists led by the Socialist Vlastimil Tusar. The "Red-Green" Coalition carried out full elections in May 1920. These elections confirmed the socialists' popularity and the coalition continued to govern. Internal turmoil in the Social Democratic Party forced Tusar's second government to resign on September 14, 1920, and the next day Masaryk appointed a nonparty government of experts.

Since the cabinet was nonparty, the five largest Czechoslovak parties established an unofficial coordinating committee to steer its program through parliament. Quickly dubbed the "Pětka" (*pět*, five), this committee became a stable, if unconstitutional and unforeseen, element of the Czechoslovak political scene. Švehla and the agrarians became the core of the system. The Pětka's decisions were binding on its members in parliament and in the government. The Pětka (enlarged according to the participants in further coalitions to as many as eight) provided much needed stability during the frequent cabinet changes of the interwar years.[22]

Kramář's and Tusar's governments weathered the initial storm of postwar stabilization.[23] Rašín's currency reforms of February 1919 ended the threat of hyperinflation, caused by the old Austro-Hungarian crown (still being printed freely in Vienna and Budapest). Czechoslovak banknotes were overprinted to separate them from the other successor states' currency, and 50 percent of cash holdings and savings were held as a forced loan to the state. Another measure, the nostrification law (December 1919), decreed that foreign companies in Czechoslovakia had to have their directorates on Czechoslovak territory. Nostrification increased the ownership share of Czech capital and Czech financial institutions in enterprises in Czechoslovakia.

Three major land reform laws between April 1919 and April 1920 also transformed property relations in Czechoslovakia. The state gained the right to confiscate agricultural properties larger than 150 hectares or any other estates larger than 250 hectares. Such estates, many of them in the hands of German or Hungarian nobles, or the church, made up practically 22 percent of the agricultural land in the country, while over two-thirds of all landowners farmed only 7 percent of the agricultural land. The Agrarian Party, which controlled the State Land Office created in June 1919, used the reform to strengthen its position. The Land Office could keep "residual estates" intact on economic grounds, and Agrarian party supporters benefited. Expropriated landowners were compensated by the state. Throughout the 1920s, land reform affected about 28 percent of all land, more than half of it agricultural. The state kept most of the remaining 1.7 million hectares, largely forest. Middle-sized Czech and Slovak farmers benefited the most. Hungarians and Germans claimed that the reform was aimed at them, though German farmers also received some land, contributing to the activist trend in the German agrarian party. Most of the land distributed to landless peasants or smallholders quickly changed hands again, further strengthening the middle elements.[24]

Land reform addressed one pressing social issue, but the economic difficulty and political radicalization caused by the war led to demonstrations, protests, and strikes throughout 1919. In response, the government enacted the eight-hour day, unemployment support, sickness and accident insurance, and even a law authorizing the establishment of workers' councils in factories. Though politicians debated widespread "socialization" (nationalization) of heavy industries like coal and steel, the socialists failed to push the idea through.

Tensions between the radical left and the moderate leadership of the Czechoslovak Social Democratic Party culminated in 1920. Before the September party congress, a radical meeting in Prague on September 5 called on the party to accept Lenin's twenty-one conditions and join the Comintern. The moderate-controlled executive committee postponed the congress until December, and demanded that delegates reject the Comintern in writing. The defiant radicals held the congress as planned, claiming that two-thirds of the delegates attended, and elected a new executive committee under Bohumír Šmeral. They took over the party's headquarters, the People's House, and began issuing their own party newspaper, *Rudé právo* (Red Right). The moderates took the dispute to the courts, who decided in their favor, and the police forced the radicals out of the People's House on December 9.[25]

A general strike called in protest for December 10 lacked mass support, though there were factory seizures and protests in industrial centers. Coming after the summer's tension and the outbreak of nationalist rioting in Prague and the German-Czech borderlands in the autumn, the strike raised fears of revolution.[26] The government responded with vigorous police action, and the strike collapsed by December 15. The failure of the general strike hastened the split in the Social Democratic Party. Already in January 1920 radicals in Slovakia and Subcarpathian Ruthenia had organized Communist parties, and the German Social

Democrats expelled their radicals early in 1921. In May 1921 the Czech radicals formally established the Czech Communist Party, and after criticism from the Comintern, all the communist sections joined together into the Communist Party of Czechoslovakia at a congress in October 1921.[27]

Slovak autonomy emerged as the major demand of the Slovak People's Party during the first years of the new republic. In the summer of 1919, Hlinka learned of the Pittsburgh Agreement and in August secretly traveled to Paris to submit a memorandum to the peace conference demanding Slovak autonomy. Denounced by the other Slovaks in Prague and suspected of treason, Hlinka was arrested on his return and interned in Moravia. Tusar's government was forced to admit that Hlinka had only violated the passport regulations, and after the new constitution was adopted, he was released without charges. The whole affair only damaged the government in Slovakia while solidifying Hlinka's reputation as a courageous spokesman for his people.[28]

Politics in the Twenties

The nonparty cabinet remained in power until September 1921, while the parties tried to agree on a new government. Švehla finally established a renewed All-National coalition in October 1922. With the Social Democrats weakened, the agrarians were now the strongest party, and Švehla headed every Czechoslovak cabinet until 1929. The coalition's base in the Pětka and acceptance by the German parties (then moving toward activism) helped as it struggled with renewed economic turmoil. Between 1921 and 1923, Czechoslovakia was hit by a general European postwar economic depression. Industrial production stagnated and unemployment rose. Many enterprises located in Slovakia could not survive the increased competition, adding an ethnic element to a social problem. At the height of the depression in 1922, unemployment rose to 440,000 workers, or about 22 percent of the labor force.[29] The government responded with deflationary policies, especially under Švehla's first cabinet, in which Rašín served as minister of finance. Rašín insisted on a strong currency as a matter of prestige, in spite of its effects on the balance of trade. Made the scapegoat for economic difficulties by the left-wing press, Rašín was shot by a mentally disturbed youth on January 5, 1923, and died a month later.[30]

With the return of European prosperity in 1924, the tensions within the coalition became harder to contain. The agrarians pushed for flexible tariff legislation to protect the farmers, while the Social Democrats feared that high food prices would hurt the working class and called for social legislation to win back its support. After tough negotiations, the coalition accepted the Social Insurance Law, which linked old age, sickness, and health insurance into a single system. When the agrarians attempted to pass their protective tariff, the socialists opposed it, but in June 1925 the agrarians pushed it through anyway. The controversy over making July 6 (the anniversary of Hus's martyrdom) a state holiday also strained the coalition by offending the populists. When President Masaryk and most of the cabinet attended the 1925 celebrations, the papal nuncio demonstratively left Prague. The government retaliated by breaking off diplomatic relations with the Vatican, offending Czech and Slovak Catholics. With the populists convinced that the public mood favored them, new elections were scheduled for November 1925.

The 1925 parliamentary elections confirmed the decline of the socialists, the strength of the agrarians, and the gains of the populists. Emboldened by the outcome, the Czechoslovak agrarians (supported by their German counterparts) demanded fixed agricultural tariffs, and the Czech People's Party proposed government salaries for the clergy. The socialists rejected both proposals, and on March 18, 1926, Švehla, pleading ill health, resigned. President Masaryk appointed a second nonparty ministry, which remained in office until October 1926. Meanwhile, efforts to form a stable political coalition continued, led by Hodža while Švehla recuperated.

With the great compromiser Švehla ill, the Pětka's discipline temporarily relaxed and political conflicts emerged with greater clarity. Even Masaryk was not spared: some National Democrats and right-wing Agrarians accused him of undermining parliamentary government through nonparty cabinets. Beneš came in for attack, both on his own account and as a stand-in for Masaryk, whose popularity deterred some politicians from naming him directly. The anti-Castle faction in Beneš's own Czechoslovak Socialist Party, led by Stříbrný, sought to unseat him in June. Beneš left the party instead, while Klofáč organized the pro-Castle wing to expel Stříbrný at the party congress in September, when the party officially resumed the title Czechoslovak *National* Socialist Party. Beneš reentered the party, and Stříbrný began his slow drift toward the extreme right, continuing to attack the Castle, Masaryk, and Beneš on the way.

Švehla returned to politics in September 1926, and crafted a center-right coalition, including the two German middle-class parties, the agrarians, the Czech populists, and the tradesmen's party. The Czecho-slovak and German socialists went into loyal opposition. This "Gentle-men's Coalition" remained in power until 1929. Among its accomplish-ments was Masaryk's reelection in May 1927. Fixed agricultural tariffs were enacted in 1926, as were the clergy salaries, a decision that ensured Czech populist support, and could be used to woo the Slovaks. The modus vivendi with the Vatican in 1928 was also popular with Czech and Slovak Catholics. It settled the quarrel over the Jan Hus holiday, redrew diocesan boundaries to match Slovakia's frontier, and freed Slo-vak bishops from the jurisdiction of the archbishop of Esztergom in Hungary.[31]

In 1928 the prefectures were replaced by a provincial system, in

A moment of relaxation at President Tomáš G. Masaryk's retreat in Topol'čianky, Slovakia, autumn 1926. From left to right: Masaryk, Edvard Beneš, František Chvalkovský, Karel Čapek, and Antonin Švehla. (ČTK photo)

which Bohemia, Moravia-Silesia, Slovakia, and Ruthenia each had an assembly presided over by a provincial president. The assemblies' powers were limited, and the provincial president and one-third of the assembly's members were government appointees. Nevertheless, the new system created an assembly of sorts for Slovakia, and helped bring the HSL'S into the "Gentlemen's Coalition" at the end of 1927. Merging Silesia and Moravia again avoided creating an administrative unit controlled by Germans, but did not help the German activist parties among their constituents.

The HSL'S membership in the coalition became an issue after New Year's Day, 1928, when Vojtech Tuka, editor of the party organ, *Slovák*, published an article asserting that the Martin agreement of 1918 had a secret clause limiting it to ten years. After that, a legal vacuum would exist and Slovakia could renegotiate its relationship to the state. HSL'S opponents (including Slovak centralists) demanded that Tuka's parliamentary immunity be lifted so that he could be tried for treason. The government reacted slowly, since the HSL'S was a coalition partner, but after provincial elections in December 1928 suggested the populists were losing support, Tuka was arrested in January 1929. His trial began in May and lasted until October 5, 1929 (just before early parliamentary elections). He was found guilty of espionage and treason and sentenced to fifteen years in prison.[32]

Hlinka supported Tuka steadfastly throughout the affair, even expelling old associates who accepted Tuka's guilt. After the verdict he took the HSL'S out of the coalition. The results of the election, however, suggested that in the short term the Tuka affair had cost the populists. Otherwise, the 1929 election reflected continuing agrarian strength, the recovery of the social democrats, a strong showing by the national socialists, and a decline of the Czech populists and nationalists. A new right-center-left government, the "Broad Coalition," including the socialists (Czechoslovak and German) and the Czech populists as well as the agrarians, but without the Slovak populists or the German Christian Socialists, assumed office in December 1929.

Beneš served as foreign minister without interruption throughout the 1920s. He was Masaryk's personal choice, but though a close associate and protégé, Beneš was unlike him in character and personality. He had risen through education, effort, and relentless self-discipline, training himself to apply his intellect and reason to problems, not his feelings. He considered foreign policy a science to be pursued in a rational, scientific way, and was sure that he could recognize historical trends and adjust his country's policies accordingly.[33] Czechoslovakia was a committed status quo state, opposed to any revision of the Treaty of Versailles.[34] When hopes of a permanent Franco-British agreement faded, Beneš signed a treaty of alliance with France in 1924 (revised and strengthened in 1925). Beneš was also a strong supporter of the League of Nations and of collective security. He excelled on the stage of Geneva, serving six times as chairman of the League Council and once of the Assembly. In anchoring Czechoslovakia's foreign policy in democracy, collective security, and the post-Versailles status quo, Beneš followed a very Czech pattern of linking national interests with universal values.

Beneš pursued what were initially called "correct" relations with Weimar Germany.[35] Czechoslovakia also sought good-neighborly relations with Austria, though it opposed Austrian Anschluss with Germany. Beneš treated Italy with caution insofar as it clashed with France in international affairs. He did not share the anti-communism of the National Democrats, but their opposition to closer ties with Moscow prevented Czechoslovakia from going beyond the commercial agreement signed in 1922 until the international situation changed dramatically in the 1930s.[36] Relations with Poland were difficult, because Beneš considered Poland likely to cause conflict with either Russia or Germany, if not both. Poland was also a French ally (February 1921), but Beneš did not pursue an alliance. Apart from anything else, Warsaw was on good terms with Budapest, and toward Hungary Beneš remained reserved to the point of hostility.

Hungary was the catalyst for Beneš's major foreign policy success of the 1920s, the Little Entente. Born out of the efforts of Charles of Habsburg to claim the Hungarian throne in 1921, it linked Czechoslovakia, Yugoslavia, and Romania in a defensive alliance. All three were part of the French alliance system in the East, solidified during the 1920s by treaties signed between France and Czechoslovakia (1924–25), Romania (1926), and Yugoslavia (1927).[37] France's allies did not form an integrated security system capable of defending the region against an outside great power. The Little Entente's primary aim was to check the threat of Hungarian revisionism, and on that the three members could agree. In other respects their interests were not easily harmonized. Romania sought good relations with Poland, while fearing the USSR; Yugoslavia saw Italy as a strategic threat, but also sought agreements with it; and neither partner shared Czechoslovakia's concerns about Germany.[38]

International developments also contributed to the Little Entente's difficulties, as France's German policy shifted from confrontation to seeking accommodation. The Locarno Treaties, signed in October 1925, symbolized that shift. They guaranteed the German frontiers with France and Belgium, while pointedly ignoring the eastern frontiers. Germany and France signed arbitration treaties with Poland and Czechoslovakia, but these treaties were not part of the multilateral international agreement. Following Locarno, Germany entered the League of Nations in 1926, raising hopes that it could be brought into the system of collective security. "Friendly relations" replaced "correct relations" in Czechoslovakia's German policy.

WORLD ECONOMIC CRISIS AND GROWING EXTERNAL THREAT

The Great Depression hit Czechoslovakia with full force in 1930, and it took years for the country to recover. By the time it did, the depression's impact on Europe and the rest of the world had changed the international situation beyond recognition, contributing to an increasing internal threat to the state from its national minorities, especially the Germans. No country escaped the effects of the Great Depression, but the specific shape it took in Czechoslovakia depended on structural and regional characteristics of the Czechoslovak economy, many of them inherited from the Habsburg monarchy.

The Czechoslovak Economy and the Great Depression

Comprising only some 21 percent of Austro-Hungarian territory, Czechoslovakia inherited between 60 and 70 percent of its industrial capacity, mostly concentrated in Bohemia and Moravia-Silesia. The end of the Austro-Hungarian customs union hurt industries dependent on the old internal market, while protectionism and the autarkic policies followed throughout postwar Central Europe affected international trade. Capacity in sugar production, glassmaking, and textiles far exceeded domestic demand, so Czechoslovakia had to reorient its trade to West European and world markets. Especially after Germany's economy stabilized in 1924, Czechoslovakia faced stiff competition. Her reliance on France in foreign policy paid no economic dividends, while the domestic policies of the Little Entente members prevented them from developing effective and complementary economic ties among themselves.[39]

Thus the world economic crisis had a dramatic economic, social, and political impact on Czechoslovakia. International markets for sugar declined drastically by 1928, and other agricultural prices fell during 1929. By 1930, the Great Depression had begun to affect industry as well. Light consumer industries, overwhelmingly concentrated in the German-inhabited border regions, were affected first and most heavily, adding a political and national dimension to the economic crisis. By 1933 overall production in industry had sunk by at least 40 percent compared with 1929, and levels of foreign trade had declined by one third. Unemployment, which had reached a postwar low in 1929, increased rapidly. At its height in 1933, official unemployment figures were over 900,000; estimates of the actual number go as high as 1,300,000.[40] Proportionally, the crisis hit Slovakia and Subcarpathian Ruthenia most harshly.

The agrarian-led governments of the Broad Coalition responded slowly to the challenge. Following orthodox economic policies, the government tried to keep the exchange rate stable and wage and price levels adjusted to avoid inflation. In June 1933 parliament accepted a special powers law, extended until 1937, that allowed the government to decree economic policy. It introduced a state grain monopoly in 1934, stabilizing prices and thus protecting middle and well-to do farmers. Livestock producers and consumers, on the other hand, faced higher prices for feed, meat, and grain products. Other measures to help credit and investment postponed the execution of farm bankruptcies and attempted to lower interest rates and stimulate exports. Over conservative resistance, the crown was devalued by some 16.66 percent. Compared with devaluations of 30 to 40 percent already carried out in the sterling trade area, this drop was too small to affect Czechoslovakia's exports. Increases in domestic investment, especially armaments after 1935–36, were more significant in pulling production out of the slump.[41]

The Depression and Czechoslovak Politics

The terrible economic conditions increased social and political tension within Czechoslovakia. Jobless workers joined protest marches, demonstrations, and mass strikes, while intellectuals and cultural figures supported them. Frequently the authorities responded with force. Between 1930 and 1933, 29 people were killed and 101 injured in clashes between protesters and the police or gendarmerie.[42] Both on the right and the left, political extremism benefited from the willingness of suffering people to listen to social demagoguery. Political polarization and increasing radicalism hit the government parties too, especially the agrarians. The tension between their right wing, led by Beran, who was elected party chairman in 1935, and the pro-Castle faction threatened at times to splinter the party itself. Hodža's position improved, since his Slovak agrarians usually held the balance between right and left.

Slovak populist demands for autonomy intensified during the depression, reflecting the economic hardship, and also a generational change within the HSL'S. Party members active before 1918, some expelled during the Tuka affair and others retiring, were replaced by younger men to whom Hlinka gave a fair degree of freedom. Karol Sidor, pro-Polish and something of a hothead, succeeded Tuka as editor of *Slovák*. Jozef Tiso became the chief political planner, and an even younger group, called Nástupists after their journal, *Nástup* (Step Forward), waited in the wings.[43] In Slovakia autonomy began to attract support among Slovak Protestants. In a meeting at Zvolen in 1932, Hlinka and Martin Razus, leader of the mainly Lutheran National Party, agreed to cooperate. In December 1932, Hlinka expressed an ominous shift in his attitude toward the state, when he swore to protect his nation even "at the cost of the republic."[44]

While minister of education, Ivan Dérer, a consistent if tactless Slovak centralist, promoted a Slovak language reform that brought it closer to Czech. These actions led to a revolt within the Slovak cultural foundation Matica slovenská, and in May 1932 HSL'S supporters took over the Matica. Official commemorations of the 1,100th anniversary of the consecration of Pribina's church at Nitra, originally planned as a religious ceremony, became a political contest, which Hlinka turned into an antigovernment demonstration. Centralists argued that autonomy would not work because Slovakia could not pay its own way, citing the gap between disbursements in Slovakia and tax receipts. Autonomists countered that most firms doing business in Slovakia had their main offices in Prague and paid taxes there, and that industry in Slovakia suffered from transportation costs and a lack of government support.

The Germans also claimed they were discriminated against for ethnic reasons.[45] The Great Depression created higher unemployment in the German regions than in the Czech interior, and German radicals blamed the government. Though social support payments from the Ministry of Social Welfare, directed by the German Social-Democrat Ludwig Czech, were also proportionally higher in German regions, they did nothing to change German attitudes. Membership more than doubled in the DNSAP. Finally, the government cracked down in the 1932 trial of seven leaders of the DNSAP youth organization. Hitler's rise to power in Germany increased the political tension between Prague and the German radical parties, who finally dissolved themselves in September 1933.[46] The banner bearer for German radical nationalism now became Konrad Henlein's newly founded Sudeten German Homeland Front. Henlein's movement, transformed into the Sudeten German Party (SdP) shortly before the 1935 elections, took over many members of the banned DNSAP and the NDP, and with them their Nazi ideas.

The Great Depression also cast its pall over Czechoslovakia's foreign policy. As the Little Entente's economic problems worsened, the need for markets for agricultural products opened up the Yugoslav and Romanian economies to German penetration. Czechoslovak-German relations were ruffled by proposals for an Austro-German customs union in 1931, which Prague saw as a step toward the forbidden Anschluss. The failure of the disarmament conference (at which Beneš was secretary-general, 1932–34), Germany's departure from the League, the collapse of the Tardieu plan for economic recovery in Central Europe, and the signing of the Rome Protocols, linking fascist Italy with Austria and Hungary, were ominous storm signals.[47]

Both Beneš and Masaryk believed that the Soviet Union should be brought into the European international system, and these setbacks reinforced the idea. After the Polish-German nonaggression treaty of 1934, French Foreign Minister Louis Barthou came forward with the idea of an Eastern pact, which Beneš enthusiastically supported. The Soviet Union also put aside its suspicions of the West, and entered the League of Nations in 1934. Soviet foreign policy stressed collective security, which suited Beneš's longstanding beliefs. His hopes of a collective treaty, however, died along with Barthou, an unintended victim of the assassination of King Alexander of Yugoslavia in Marseilles in 1934. In 1935, spurred on by the Saar plebiscite and German rearmament, the discussions between Paris, Prague, and Moscow ended in bilateral Franco-Soviet and Czechoslovak-Soviet treaties of mutual assistance.

The treaty between Czechoslovakia and the Soviet Union, preceded by formal diplomatic recognition in 1934 and signed on May 16, 1935, linked the Soviet commitment to France's fulfillment of her 1925 treaty with Czechoslovakia. This was as close as Beneš could get to his preferred tripartite treaty, and it helped Czechoslovakia avoid tying itself solely to the Soviet Union. Nevertheless, the treaty quickly became a target of Nazi propaganda, as well as of right-wing attacks at home.[48]

Against this backdrop of increasing tension, Masaryk suffered a stroke shortly before his presidential term expired. He decided to seek reelection only because he was unsure that parliament would accept Beneš as his successor. Over Communist opposition, Masaryk was elected for the fourth time on May 24, 1934. The last interwar parliamentary elections took place the next year. Besides the SdP, a new National Union formed by merging Kramář's National Democrats with Stříbrný's National League and another right-wing organization, the National Front. The Slovak populists joined in an Autonomist Bloc with the Silesian Polish Party and a small Ruthenian Agrarian Party, while the Hungarian parties also formed an electoral alliance. The Communist Party adapted to the Czechoslovak-Soviet treaty and the Comintern's new "Popular Front" policy by dropping its hostility to the state and becoming centralist.

The election results showed all the government parties slipping slightly. The Czech right-wing National Union did no better than its member organizations had done in 1929, though the fascists won 6 seats. The Communists retained roughly the same level of support, but now from Czechs and Slovaks, not minorities. The Autonomist bloc in Slovakia gained 30 percent of the vote and 22 seats, of which the HSL's kept 19, allowing its associates one each. The genuine electoral bombshell was that Henlein's SdP eclipsed its activist opponents, winning over 15 percent of the total vote, and gaining 44 seats, only one fewer than the Czechoslovak agrarians. The German socialists lost half their seats, the German Christian socialists more than half, and the German agrarians fully two-thirds. The SdP won two-thirds of the German vote.

The coalition parties readmitted the Tradesmen's Party, but otherwise, neither policy nor personnel changed until Masaryk appointed Hodža prime minister on November 5, and then on November 21 announced his own resignation, pleading advancing age (he was eighty-five) and ill health. He again called for Beneš to succeed him. Though

the right-wing parties put up an opposing candidate, eventually the support of Hodža's Slovak agrarians and the HSL'S swung the tide in favor
of Beneš. He was duly elected Czechoslovakia's second president on December 18, 1935.[49]

The Last Years of the Republic

Beneš's presidency before Munich was overshadowed by the sense
that Czechoslovakia was in peril, internally from Henlein's SdP and ex-
ternally from Nazi Germany.[50] Beneš continued to influence Czechoslovakia's foreign policy when his own candidate, the historian Kamil
Krofta, replaced Hodža as foreign minister in February 1936. Attempts
to deal with the national minorities were largely led by Hodža, a Slovak,
who could negotiate with German politicians free of Czech emotional
baggage. At the beginning of July 1936 these talks bore fruit when the
German Christian Socialists reentered the government, taking a ministry
without portfolio. Reeling from their losses to the SdP, a younger generation of German activists promoted German interests more vigorously.
In late January 1937, they demanded more public-sector jobs for Germans, public works contracts for local contractors and labor in the border regions, and linguistic concessions in local administration. Hodža's
government accepted on February 18, and in March 1938 committed
itself to proportional minority representation in the civil service.

These concessions could not resolve Czechoslovakia's German question, because the SdP now represented the majority of the Germans.
Whether Henlein and the SdP ever accepted Czechoslovakia is not
clear—Henlein's role in weakening and destroying both democracy and
the republic gives the lie to his protestations of loyalty. Apologies that
blame the stiff-necked Czechs for driving Henlein into the Nazi embrace
are clearly specious. To see the SdP as Hitler's fifth column and Henlein
as the Führer's stooge right from 1933, however, oversimplifies both the
German and the SdP situations.[51] Ties between Henlein and the Reich
offices for Germans abroad existed from the start, and his 1935 election
campaign was largely funded from the Reich. The SdP became only a
tool of Hitler's foreign policy because of complicated political conflict
in the Reich and within the SdP. In the Reich the old-fashioned "tradi-
tionalists" were outmaneuvered by radical Nazis, in particular Himmler's SS and the SD under Reinhard Heydrich. Within the SdP Henlein's
inability to control internal quarrels forced him to seek support abroad,

initially from "traditionalist" organizations in the Reich. After their defeat, and with radical dissent threatening to destroy his own party, he turned directly to Hitler in November 1937, placing his movement and his own political fate in the Führer's hands.

On New Year's Day, 1938, Beran published an article hinting that the SdP and the HSL'S should join the coalition, and urging a direct agreement with Germany. The German activists, and the Czech social democrats and national socialists, felt betrayed. Their mood darkened further when Hitler spoke on February 20 of protecting the ten million Germans living next to the Reich.[52] The Austrian Anschluss of March 11 precipitated the collapse of the German agrarians and Christian socialists and their merger with the SdP. The German Social Democratic minister, Czech, resigned, but the party refused to dissolve and supported the state. The National Democrats, without Kramář who had died in 1937, rejoined the government on March 19.

On March 28 Henlein met with Hitler, who confirmed Henlein's leadership of the SdP (calling him "my viceroy"), and advised making impossible demands on Prague. Henlein repeated, "We must therefore always demand so much that we cannot be satisfied," and the Führer agreed.[53] Henlein now had to appear to negotiate without destroying his party's support or letting his own radicals provoke a Czechoslovak crackdown, while avoiding a final agreement. In a speech in Karlovy Vary (Karlsbad) on April 24 Henlein spelled out a program demanding recognition of the Sudeten Germans as a collective legal personality equal to the Czechs, demarcation of the German areas and the establishment of German-controlled local government there, and most ominously the full freedom to profess membership in the German race and the German world view—a thinly veiled statement of adherence to Nazi ideology.[54]

The HSL'S lost its leader on August 16, 1938.[55] The party confirmed Tiso as chairman on August 31, 1938, and on September 8 he took part in a meeting organized by the SdP. He probably only intended to force Beneš to meet with him again (previous discussions had ended without results early in 1938). Beneš did summon him for discussions, and the Slovak populists and the government maintained their dialogue through the tense days of September.

The Czechoslovak government faced these challenges feeling isolated. In theory it should have been secure: it had treaties with France and the Soviet Union, and behind France stood Great Britain. Reality was less promising than theory. The British were pursuing appeasement, attempting to contain Hitler by meeting his legitimate demands. To avoid another war, blundered into through treaty obligations and misunderstandings, the British would accept peaceful changes in Central Europe—a view communicated to Hitler by Lord Halifax in November 1937. Henlein's propaganda had convinced many British that Prague's "intransigence" was the source of any tension. The Soviet alliance did not endear Czechoslovakia to London, either. The British government was willing to pressure the French to choose between Czechoslovakia and continued British support. As if these developments were not ominous enough, by 1937 Soviet purges in the Red Army raised doubts about its effectiveness.

Tomáš G. Masaryk died on September 14, 1937, leaving his hand-picked successor to steer the Czechoslovak ship of state through the dangerous waters of its anniversary year. German assurances that the Austrian Anschluss in March 1938 was a "family affair" could not lessen the Czechoslovak conviction that they would be next.[56] Hitler's plans for a military operation against Czechoslovakia took shape in the autumn of 1937. They remained flexible and relatively vague, as Hitler let the international tension rise while the SdP and Henlein (seconded by the British, with reluctant French backing) kept up the pressure on Beneš and Hodža.

In this atmosphere of tension, intelligence reports about suspicious German troop movements led the Czechoslovak government to declare "exceptional military measures" on May 20, 1938. This partial mobilization demonstrated Czechoslovakia's determination and ability to defend itself. It now appears, however, that Germany was not in fact preparing for action at that moment. Instead, the May Crisis increased British determination to push France and Czechoslovakia into a position where the threat of war would not arise again. Hitler was also furious, and revised his plans, establishing October 1 as the deadline for final military preparations.[57]

Britain and France forced Beneš to request an impartial mediator between government and SdP, the British shipping magnate Sir Walter Runciman. Runciman, who had few qualifications for his task, arrived in Czechoslovakia on August 3, and departed without success on September 16. In August Beneš personally joined negotiations with the SdP, presenting the so-called Third Plan, and then, on September 7, the Fourth Plan, which effectively accepted the Karlsbad Program's demands. The startled SdP leaders broke off contacts until after Hitler's speech at the Nuremburg Nazi rally on September 12, 1938. In his speech, Hitler thundered, "the Germans in Czechoslovakia are neither defenseless nor are they deserted."[58] After disturbances in Czechoslovakia's German regions, suppressed by firm government action, Henlein fled to Germany. Meanwhile, on September 13, British Prime Minister Neville Chamberlain proposed a personal meeting with Hitler, and on September 15 the two met at Berchtesgaden. In May Hitler had warned his military leaders that a "particularly favorable opportunity" arising unexpectedly might cause him to act precipitately towards Czechoslovakia.[59] That opportunity was about to be handed to him by Czechoslovakia's allies.

AN ISLAND OF DEMOCRACY?

Among the authoritarian regimes and royal dictatorships in its immediate neighborhood, Czechoslovakia seemed like an island of democracy, at least until the tsunami of 1938. The state preserved parliamentary institutions, regular, free elections, and civic freedoms relatively well. Yet in doing so it evolved some features such as the Pětka that undermined genuine parliamentary politics. Elections became a means for distributing power within the ruling coalition, instead of an alternation between government and opposition. The parties carved out fiefdoms in the bureaucracy and institutions, and as their leadership aged, they failed to bring younger figures to the forefront.[60] Masaryk's ideal of humanitarian democracy was tempered by his concern for authority and expertise, and he used every ounce of his formal and informal authority to pursue his goals. Indeed, it has been suggested that one reason Czechoslovakia did not succumb to the local fashion for authoritarian regimes was that, thanks to Masaryk, it was already authoritarian enough to survive.[61]

Evaluating Czechoslovakia's democratic achievement during the interwar years cannot be separated from the question of national minorities. From the start, Masaryk and Beneš were aware that the new state would include minorities. Beneš promised the Paris Peace Conference that Czechoslovakia would become "a sort of Switzerland," taking into account the "special conditions of Bohemia." The minorities committee noted that "the prospects and perhaps almost the existence of the new

State" would depend on how it treated its minorities, especially the Germans.[62] After inital rejection, all German parties except the radical nationalists and communists accepted the state, and between 1926 and 1938 every Czechoslovak government included at least one German minister. Without the Great Depression and Hitler, it is argued, Czech-German cooperation in Czechoslovakia was not doomed. Would Czechoslovak Germans have abandoned the activist parties so dramatically, though, if activism had anything to show beyond mere participation in government? It took two years after the 1935 election's warning for the government to promise action on German grievances, and proportional representation in the civil service as a commitment came only in 1938, just in time to be one of the casualties of Munich.

To an outsider, the Germans in Czechoslovakia did not seem particularly oppressed. They had their own state school system, including schools in Slovakia that had never existed in the old Hungarian kingdom, crowned by the German university in Prague, and a network of voluntary cultural and other associations.[63] Unfortunately, perception is often more important than reality in minority affairs. Czechoslovakia's leaders insisted that it was a product of "Czechoslovak" national self-determination, and had a Czechoslovak identity. For the Germans, used to being the "state-bearing" nation in Austria-Hungary and Bohemia, this was a particularly bitter pill. Many Czechs relished the opportunity to assert the Czechoslovak nature of the new state in various ways. Whatever the official attitude of the leading representatives, individuals in local situations contributed—often detrimentally—to the perception of minority relations.

In 1918, Masaryk referred to Czechoslovakia's Germans as "emigrants and colonists."[64] He chose his words more carefully thereafter, and on the republic's tenth anniversary emphasized that Czechoslovakia was "an ethnically and linguistically mixed state," in which "representation of the minorities is a necessity." Still, the majority "must imprint its own characteristics on society."[65] Defining the lands of the Bohemian crown as a Czech national state made Czechoslovakia's Germans aliens in their own home. Once German Bohemians or Moravians, they now called themselves Sudeten Germans, reflecting a psychological distancing from their ancestors' homelands, as well as the new state they resented.[66] A perfect minority policy would not have prevented Hitler from destroying Czechoslovakia, and in the end many Germans stood ready to defend the republic. There might have been more if Czechs and Slovaks had found more sensitivity, understanding, and will to take political risks on minority issues.

Czechoslovakia's Jews represented both a national and a religious minority. The Czechoslovak census accepted Jewish as a nationality, and in 1921, 180,855 people (1.35 percent) registered their nationality as Jewish. Since 354,342 people (2.42 percent) identified themselves as Jews by religion, over half of Czechoslovakia's Jews considered their identity a national as well as a religious one. Recognition of a separate Jewish nationality reduced the numbers of Germans and Hungarians, but it also obscured the fact that interwar Czechoslovakia had three distinct Jewish communities, each reflecting unique historical experiences.[67]

In Bohemia and Moravia the Jews (just over one percent of the population in 1930) had acculturated and assimilated in the nineteenth century, with full civic equality after 1867. The growth of strong anti-liberal and anti-Semitic attitudes among German nationalists led more Jews to identify as Czechs, but anti-Semitism was also a feature of Czech politics, both before and after independence. The Jews of Slovakia (4.1 percent of the population in 1930) initially adopted German, but later Magyar speech and culture. Jewish identification with Hungary and commercial and professional roles generated Slovak resentment and anti-Semitism. The Jewish community in Ruthenia, mostly Yiddish-speaking and Orthodox with strong Hasidic influence, was the largest (102,542 or 14.12 percent in 1930). Weaker Jewish identification with the Hungarians, and the Ruthenian peasantry's lower level of social and national consciousness, made anti-Semitism in Ruthenia weaker than in Slovakia.

No Czechoslovak government tolerated anti-Semitism, which may help explain the weakness of Zionism in Czechoslovakia. Jews sent their children to Czech or Slovak schools, and they pursued their studies through the university level and into the professions, frequently assimilating into the national culture. The interwar years also saw an erosion of the cultural differences between the Jews of the Czech lands and those of Slovakia and Ruthenia. Overwhelmingly, the Jews accepted and supported the Czechoslovak state, and the alliance between the Jews and the "state-bearing" forces in Czechoslovakia brought positive results.

Czech-Slovak relations provide another measure of interwar Czechoslovakia's success. Slovaks were part of the "state-bearing" Czechoslovak nation, but the term raised the question, were Czechs and

Slovaks two nations or one? Centralists argued that given the level of development in Slovakia, centralism was the only way to protect Slovakia from Hungarian revisionism.[68] They also feared that autonomy for Slovakia would encourage the Germans, threatening the existence of the state. Slovak autonomists saw centralism as the root of all Slovakia's problems, autonomy as the solution, and Slovak centralists as practically national apostates. Religious questions also created friction. The images of Hus, the White Mountain, and the Counter-Reformation provided the myths of Czech national consciousness and became part of the official rhetoric of the new Czechoslovakia. Catholic priests or Lutheran pastors often provided the only nationally conscious intelligentsia in Slovak villages, and society still deferred to them. The anti-clerical strain in Czech nationalism, as well as issues like separation of church and state, parochial schools, and relations with the Vatican, fueled tensions. Slovak Catholics and Slovak Lutherans (traditionally more likely to be "Czechoslovak") were also often at odds.

Slovak industry suffered when it left Hungary and joined more industrialized Bohemia and Moravia. Combined with the depression from 1920 to 1923, this caused a drastic decline in Slovak industrial production, which nationalist rhetoric blamed on Prague's "colonial" policies. Recovery between 1924 and 1929 did not quite reach 1913 levels before the Great Depression hit. Gradual improvement set in only after 1933, partly fueled by the strategic siting of armaments factories in Slovakia, and by 1937, Slovak industrial output had not only exceeded 1929 levels, but finally surpassed 1913.[69]

The school system was a crucial cultural factor in Slovak integration into Czechoslovakia. The schools trained a new Slovak intelligentsia, but ironically in the process students became nationally conscious Slovaks. Nationalist rhetoric complained that they were victims of systematic Czech discrimination, but the problem was more one of perception than reality. Traditionally, education in Hungary had guaranteed state employment and higher social status. Many Slovak graduates thus sought jobs only in the state bureaucracy. The civil service was open to all on merit, however, and the government did not ensure that Slovaks as Slovaks received access to positions of prestige or influence in state institutions. The result was a case of rising expectations exceeding the system's ability to meet them.[70]

In the end, Czechoslovakia did not fulfill the two goals the Slovak nationalists had pursued since the mid-nineteenth century: national recognition and genuine autonomy. Nevertheless, the decision to cast the Slovaks' lot in with the Czechs in 1918 brought them significant gains. They had a distinct territory with its own frontiers, capital, and institutions, and in spite of the state's official ideology, Slovaks "did not sink into the 'Czechoslovak nation,' just as they had previously rejected the enticements of the 'Hungarian political nation.' They were Slovaks even before 1918, but afterwards everyone knew it."[71]

When he resigned as president in 1935, Masaryk asked parliament and all Czechoslovakia's citizens to remember "that states maintain themselves by the ideas from which they were born."[72] How far Czechoslovakia lived and died by Masaryk's ideas may be debated, but their influence on modern Czechoslovak history is undeniably profound. Masaryk's precepts and example helped Czechoslovakia preserve parliamentary institutions, civic freedoms, and a high degree of personal liberty for all its citizens. Under the impact of Munich, Masaryk's ideals were abandoned with unseemly haste by the so-called Second Republic. Vilified by the Nazis, Masaryk quickly became persona non grata under the Communists, too. Nevertheless, his ideas resurfaced in the aftermath of war, revolution, and communist dictatorship, when many Czechs and Slovaks returned to study and debate their significance to their hopes for a better future.

12 From One Totalitarianism to Another

The Munich Conference lives on in international affairs, where "Munich" now stands for misguided, cowardly, or simply stupid appeasement of dictators. For the Czechs, Munich raises questions still debated today. Should Beneš have defied his allies and Hitler? Should Czechoslovakia have fought, even alone, against Nazi Germany? Or was it better for the nation to survive physically by betraying the ideals from which Czechoslovakia was born? Was the lesson of Munich that the Czechs have to submit to Central Europe's dominant power? New research may present better insight into specific aspects of the crisis, but the significance of these questions will not change.[1] Munich and its consequences—the Nazi destruction of rump Czechoslovakia, occupation, liberation and its aftermath, and "Victorious February" of 1948—remain keys in a guide to the modern fate of both Czechs and Sudeten Germans.[2] Yet in 1938, as Europe teetered on the brink of war, these meanings of "Munich" lay in the future. Appeasement was not yet a political obscenity, and those in Britain or France who called it mistaken were crying in the wilderness. The British and French leaders were determined to avoid a war, especially over what the British prime minister called "a quarrel in a far-away country between people of whom we know nothing."[3] Czechoslovakia was to pay the price. After it was paid, war came anyway.

MUNICH AND THE END OF THE CZECHOSLOVAK REPUBLIC

The international crisis that led to the Munich Conference on September 29, 1938, has been analyzed many times. The backdrop included British disenchantment with the Treaty of Versailles, the decline of the League of Nations and collective security, the missed opportunities to check Hitler's revisionist foreign policy, and Britain's commitment to appeasement. Against this backdrop Czechoslovakia, which became the focus of European tensions during 1938, posed a problem. British policy had to consider the possibility that France's 1925 treaty with Czechoslovakia might draw Britain into a European war. Sacrificing Czechoslovak territory, which could be achieved only by France betraying its ally, seemed to be the best way out.

"About Us Without Us": Czechoslovakia and the Munich Conference

Before he flew to Germany on September 15, Chamberlain had already concluded that Czechoslovakia had to cede territory. At Berchtesgaden, he received Hitler's demand for all Czechoslovakia's German-majority districts to convey to the British and French governments. They presented the demands to Prague on September 19, and pressured Beneš to accept, sweetening the pill by promising an international guarantee of the revised borders.[4] Beneš met with Czechoslovak politicians, while trying to find out Moscow's attitude, especially if France failed to honor its treaty. Discussion, and the silence from Moscow, dragged on until late on September 20, when Krofta announced that Czechoslovakia refused the terms, and called for arbitration under the 1925 treaty. The response was a Franco-British ultimatum (delivered at 2:00 A.M. on September 21): if Czechoslovakia refused Hitler's demands, it would stand alone. Ironically, the right-wing National Democrats and the center-right People's Party now urged resistance, even if it meant relying only on the Soviet Union. The Social Democrats, Tradesmen's Party, and Czech and Slovak Agrarians favored accepting the ultimatum.[5] Beneš, deeply upset by the French betrayal and without a clear answer from the Kremlin, argued against fighting alone. At 5:00 P.M. on September 21, Czechoslovakia accepted the Berchtesgaden demands.

That evening crowds poured onto the streets of Prague and other cities. A mob tried to break into the Castle, but was dispersed without waking the exhausted Beneš.[6] A Committee for the Defense of the Republic headed by Ladislav Rašín, Alois Rašín's son, called a demonstration during which 250,000 people gathered in front of parliament, demanding Hodža's resignation and the rejection of the memorandum. Hodža was replaced on September 22 by a hero of the Siberian legion, General Jan Syrový. Syrový's appointment calmed the public by implying that Czechoslovakia would defend itself.

Meanwhile, Chamberlain flew back to Germany to meet Hitler at Godesberg, but instead of being grateful that Czechoslovakia had been forced to give in, Hitler insisted on more. The territory had to be evacuated at once, leaving intact all economic and military assets. Czechoslovakia also had to accept Polish and Hungarian claims advanced on September 21.[7] When the French balked at forcing Prague to accept these new demands, the British reluctantly promised to stand by them. The allies told Beneš on the evening of September 23 that they no longer advised against mobilization. On September 23 Czechoslovakia mobilized, and the next day 1,250,000 men reported to the colors. The army, now over 1.5 million strong, took up its positions on the frontier and in the fortresses.[8] Britain, France, and other powers prepared for war. On September 26, however, Chamberlain decided on a last-ditch effort. He appealed directly to Hitler, as did other world leaders, including President Roosevelt of the United States. On September 28, Hitler agreed to a meeting of Italy, Germany, France, and Britain the next day in Munich.

At the conference on September 29, Chamberlain and French premier Daladier accepted practically all Hitler's demands. Czechoslovakia's representatives, allowed no part in the proceedings, were handed the terms of the final Munich agreement well after midnight on September 30. Between October 1 and 10, Czechoslovakia would surrender its frontier regions to Germany. Britain and France promised to guarantee the new borders, and once the Polish and Hungarian demands were settled, so would Germany and Italy. Public opinion initially welcomed the Munich Conference, and—somewhat to their surprise—Chamberlain and Daladier returned to a hero's welcome. In Czechoslovakia the reaction was quite different. Four leading generals called on Beneš to plead for resistance while the conference at Munich was still meeting. Again, Beneš argued rationally against leading the country into a hopeless struggle alone. In a tense government meeting on September 30 his views prevailed.[9] Krofta announced Czechoslovakia's acceptance of the Munich decision, calling it "a catastrophe we did not deserve," and warning: "we are surely not the last: others will be affected after us."[10]

Beneš viewed Munich as a shortsighted and cowardly betrayal by Czechoslovakia's allies. He was determined to undo it and restore Czechoslovakia's 1938 frontiers, but—whatever he may have thought in private—he never publicly doubted his own conduct. He was convinced that Britain and France would not avoid war, and that Czechoslovakia would reemerge on the side of the victors. Rather than immolate his people, he calculated that it was better to accept the Munich demands and survive. Meeting with Beneš on September 30, Ladislav Rašín stated the other side: "We should have defended ourselves. We have surrendered on our own. . . . It is true that we were betrayed by others, but we are also betraying ourselves."[11]

The Second Republic, October 1938–March 1939

On October 5, President Beneš resigned and went into exile. The country he left behind was also changing dramatically. Czechoslovakia lost approximately one-third of its land, with close to five million inhabitants, 1.25 million of them Czechs or Slovaks (see Map 5, p. 179).[12] Its weakened economy had to absorb 100,000 refugees and the loss of manufacturing capacity and natural resources. Unemployment more than doubled between October 1938 and February 1939. The new frontier interrupted important lines of communication, at one point coming as close as twenty-five miles to Prague.[13] The territorial losses alone made an independent Czechoslovak foreign policy impossible. František Chvalkovský, former ambassador to Rome, replaced Krofta and adapted Czechoslovak policy to the chill winds blowing from Berlin, while doggedly pursuing the promised international guarantees. Czechoslovakia ceded territory to Poland in Těšín and parts of Slovakia, after an ultimatum on October 1. In the First Vienna Award of November 2, 1938, the German and Italian foreign ministers gave Hungary the southern strip of Slovakia and part of Ruthenia.[14] This fulfilled Hitler's conditions, but the Germans still refused the guarantee.

Rudolf Beran's right wing of the Agrarian party was the dominant political force in the Czech lands. In Slovakia all parties except the social democrats and communists accepted a common program at Žilina on October 6 that reflected HSL'S policies. Tiso became head of a Slovak autonomous government on October 7. On October 11, Ruthenia received a similar arrangement. Both the HSL'S and the Ukrainian National Union quickly made themselves the sole legal parties in their regions. On November 18, the Czech right-wing parties and most national socialists merged in a Party of National Unity, while the social democrats and left-wing national socialists established the opposition National Party of Labor on December 11.[15]

Approval of Slovak and Ruthenian autonomy in late November (the country's name officially became Czecho-Slovakia) failed to consolidate the new regime. Emil Hácha, head of the Supreme Administrative Court, was elected president on November 30, and named Beran prime minister and Karol Sidor as vice-premier and minister for Slovak affairs. Beran's government continued to appease Nazi Germany. The relative tolerance and pluralism of the republic's first twenty years gave way to measures against left-wing groups, anti-fascist refugees and activists, and Jews. The KSČ was dissolved on December 27, and Gottwald and his deputy, Rudolf Slánský, left for Moscow. In the post-Munich malaise some Czechs accepted fascist ideology and expressed anti-Semitism with greater openness.[16]

Germany claimed that it could not guarantee the frontiers if the central government was unable to maintain law and order. To establish firmer control, Beran demanded at the end of February 1939 that the Slovak government declare its loyalty to Czecho-Slovakia and renounce separatism. After an evasive Slovak response, Beran and Hácha ordered the army and police to occupy Slovakia, dismissed Tiso, interned the radicals, and announced that Sidor was forming a new Slovak government. Hitler summoned Tiso to Berlin, where he was given a stark choice: proclaim Slovak independence, or be left to Hungarian mercies. On March 14 at Tiso's urging, the Slovak diet declared Slovak independence.[17]

President Hácha, overwhelmed by events, asked to meet Hitler, who received him and Chvalkovský late on the night of March 14–15. After a brutal three-hour interview, Hácha signed a proclamation placing the fate of the Czech nation in Hitler's hands. On March 15 the German army occupied the Czech lands. The next day Hitler's decree created the Protectorate of Bohemia and Moravia. Slovakia was partially occupied by the German army on March 15, and on March 23 the Slovak government signed a treaty making it a German "protected state."

CZECHS AND SLOVAKS IN THE SECOND WORLD WAR, 1939–1945

During his September interview with the generals Beneš assured them: "War—a great European war—will come, with great upheavals and revolutions. [The British and French] do not want to fight now, with us and under favorable conditions; they will have to fight heavily for us when we can no longer fight. . . . Prepare yourselves, we will still play our role."[18] Faced at last with outright German occupation, Czechs interpreted their role in various ways. Some carried the perverse logic of events to the conclusion reached by Emanuel Moravec, the best-known Czech Quisling, and chose collaboration. Some organized resistance, while most, at heart opposed to German domination, hoped to wait out the storm without risking getting into trouble. In Slovakia independence enjoyed the support of the Catholic clergy and at least the acceptance of the great majority of the population. The war eroded that acceptance, while from the beginning some Slovaks worked for the re-creation of a common Czech and Slovak state.

The Protectorate of Bohemia and Moravia

The Protectorate of Bohemia and Moravia was an integral part of the Greater German Reich, though with its own administration, police, gendarmerie, and a tiny ceremonial army. Hácha served as State President to the war's end. Beran's cabinet was replaced on April 27, 1939, by a government headed by General Alois Eliáš. Eliáš maintained contacts with the domestic resistance and the Czechoslovak exile movement, for which the Nazis executed him in 1942. His successors, Jaroslav Krejčí and Richard Bienert, had hardly any real functions.[19] The German Reich controlled foreign affairs, defense, customs, monetary policies, and communications. The Reich Protector could abrogate "in the interests of the Reich" any of the protectorate government's enactments. The first Reich Protector was the former German foreign minister, Baron Konstantin von Neurath, who went on health leave on Sep-

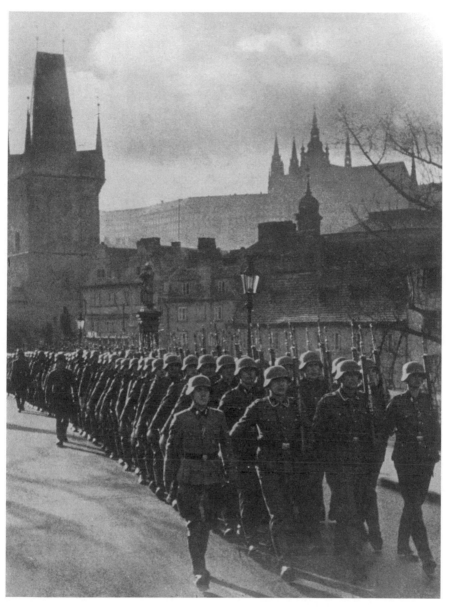

Unwelcome arrivals in Prague, March 15, 1939: the Wehrmacht on Charles Bridge.
(ČTK photo)

tember 27, 1941. His acting replacement was the head of the Reich Security Office, Reinhard Heydrich. After Heydrich's assassination on May 27, 1942, a police general, Kurt Daluege, replaced him as acting Protector. Wilhelm Frick, a former interior minister, was appointed Reich Protector in Neurath's stead on August 20, 1943, but the real power in the Protectorate was the former SdP deputy leader, Karl Hermann Frank. Hitler named Frank to head a newly created German ministry of state for Bohemia and Moravia, making him effectively the chief executive officer in the Protectorate.

The Nazis aimed to Germanize the Protectorate through assimilation, expulsion, and extermination (one of Frank's favorite themes). As long as Germany had not won the war, however, economic needs took priority. Apart from the genuine collaborators, even members of the protectorate government and Czech civil servants tried to protect the interests of their nation as best they could, while cooperating with the Germans as little as possible.[20] Recognizing the line between necessary accommodation and treasonous collaboration became difficult very early. Daily experience demonstrated who was in charge. A geographic location in the heart of the Nazi empire, overwhelming German superiority in force, and no likelihood of quick assistance if war came reinforced the Czechs' difficult situation.

Hitler's decree of March 16, 1939, made all Germans in Bohemia and Moravia Reich citizens, relegating the Czechs to a lower legal status as Protectorate citizens. Hácha dismissed parliament and suspended all political parties on March 21, replacing them with a single National Community, headed by a National Committee. By May the National Community had more than two million members, or nearly 98 percent of those qualified to join.[21] Corporatist organizations replaced the trade unions, and other social, cultural, educational, sporting, and professional groups including the Boy Scouts and the Sokol were suspended or banned.

Already exposed to increased anti-Semitism after Munich, the Jews in Bohemia and Moravia were placed outside the law by a decree of the Reich Protector on June 21, 1939. They could not dispose of their property or buy land, their movements were restricted, they had to wear the yellow Star of David, they received lower food rations, their children could not attend public schools, they could not participate in cultural or athletic activities, and their economic activities were restricted. Jews were now physically separated from Czech society. Transportation to the extermination camps began in October 1941.[22]

The Czech people initially expressed their feelings by passive resistance or symbolic protest. Hopes revived with the outbreak of war in September 1939, but fell as Poland collapsed. Poland's destruction suggested that accepting Munich had at least spared the Czech lands and people similar physical suffering. The patriotic demonstrations climaxed on October 28, Czechoslovak independence day. The police opened fire on the crowds, killing one worker and mortally wounding a medical student, Jan Opletal, who died on November 12. After further demonstrations at Opletal's funeral on November 15, Frank raided the Prague dormitories on the night of November 16–17, arresting over 1,800 students and executing nine arbitrarily chosen ringleaders. More than a thousand students were shipped off to Oranienburg concentration camp. On November 17, Hitler ordered all Czech universities and colleges closed.[23]

These and similar acts of repression suggested that German policy was to leave the Czechs no intellectual leadership. On the other hand, the general population, especially the workers, were to be won over by economic concessions. Food and clothing rationing was introduced later in the Protectorate than in the Reich, a customs union with Germany was not enacted until October 1940, and though the authorities had the power to draft labor after December 1, 1939, they delayed forcing Czech workers to serve outside the Protectorate. Neurath advised that a milder approach would better serve Germany's economic interests.

Domestic resistance groups began to form even before the outbreak of war. Three major organizations early in 1940 formed the Central Committee of Home Resistance (ÚVOD), which the Beneš government-in-exile recognized as representing the home resistance. The Communist Party built up its own underground organization in touch with Gottwald in Moscow. After the Nazi-Soviet Non-Aggression Pact of August 1939, the communists denounced the war as an imperialist conflict and attacked Beneš. The illegal Slovak Communist Party (KSS), which separated from the KSČ after Slovak independence, even called for the inclusion of Slovakia in the USSR. After the Nazi invasion of the Soviet Union in June 1941 the KSČ and KSS returned to the "united front." Negotiations between the KSČ and ÚVOD in the summer of 1941 formed a Central National Revolutionary Committee (ÚNRV) to coordinate the entire resistance.

The outward calm that settled over the Protectorate after the crackdown in November 1939 was broken when two Protectorate government officials sought by the Gestapo fled abroad in January 1940, with the assistance of General Eliáš. When Paris fell in May, the Germans found hard evidence of Eliáš's contacts with the resistance. In the summer of 1941, Hitler abandoned Neurath's line and instituted harsher measures. Heydrich arrived in Prague on September 27, 1941, and declared martial law over most of the Protectorate. He also ordered Eliáš's arrest, and had him condemned to death on October 1, 1941. His execution was postponed, but nearly 200 others were not. By the time martial law was lifted on December 1, the number of victims had risen to some 400. Meanwhile, Heydrich delivered higher wages and better rations to the workers. He applied his carrot and stick policy ruthlessly to keep the Czech workers productive and crush any signs of resistance.[24]

After Eliáš's arrest, the Protectorate government lost any remaining shred of autonomy. All but three of Eliáš's cabinet were replaced. The most infamous new minister was Moravec. A former legionary and enthusiastic supporter of Beneš, his reaction to Munich was a complete about-face. Moravec now urged a Nazi transformation of Czech society from his Office of Public Enlightenment, where he directed a vigorous propaganda campaign extolling the Czech future in Nazi Europe. Heydrich did not permit meetings of the cabinet, whose members now functioned merely as executive agents of the Deputy Reich Protector. The National Community and National Committee also faded into oblivion during 1942.[25]

The success of Heydrich's brutal repression and material incentives concerned the Czechoslovak government-in-exile, lest the Allies think the Czechs were willing collaborators. Teams of specially trained parachutists were sent into Czechoslovakia in 1941 to prepare further resistance acts. On the morning of May 4, 1942, parachutists Jan Kubiš and Jozef Gabčík ambushed Heydrich, who died from his wounds on June 4, 1942. His assassins escaped.[26] Renewed repression and terror followed Heydrich's death. Martial law was reimposed, summary courts ordered the immediate execution of anyone knowing about or approving of the assassination, and Himmler demanded the arrest of 10,000 hostages. Hitler and Frank ordered the destruction on June 10 of the village of Lidice, erroneously supposed to have harbored parachutists. All the adult males were shot, the women sent to concentration camps, the children packed off to foster homes, and the village was razed.[27] The assas-

Deputy Reich Protector Reinhard Heydrich (center) views the Bohemian coronation regalia, symbol of Czech statehood, with State President Emil Hácha (to his left) and other Nazi and Protectorate leaders, November 19, 1941. K. H. Frank is first on the right. (ČTK photo)

sins' hiding place in the Orthodox Church of Sts. Cyril and Methodius was eventually betrayed. Gabčík, Kubiš, and their fellow agents were besieged on June 18 and, after a dramatic battle, were killed or committed suicide. Their helpers, including the priest, elders, and Orthodox Bishop Gorazd, were executed. The terror accounted for more than one thousand victims, and effectively destroyed the ÚNRV. Thereafter there were no similar high-profile acts of resistance. By the summer of 1942, Daluege assured Hitler that German policies after the assassination had been "correct."[28]

Life in the Protectorate continued in spite of war and selective Nazi terror and repression. Even after August 1943, Frank had to concentrate on tapping the Protectorate's economy for the war instead of rooting out the Czechs. By the autumn of 1943, factories in the Reich employed 30,000 forced laborers from Bohemia and Moravia, and Göring's aircraft production lines required an additional 10,000 young conscript workers for six months beginning in the spring of 1944. The Protectorate's value to the German war economy was even higher because it was not a major bombing target until the end of 1944. For most people the need to find food, carry out daily activities, and live their lives under enemy occupation placed them in a grey zone between their circumstances and their preferences.[29] Czechs turned to their native land, its beauties, its history, and its culture for strength and perseverance. Historicism refocused attention on the great figures and moments of the Czech past, reflected in popular historical books, albums, and historical romances.[30] Politically, popular attitudes shifted to the left. The search for why the country collapsed, the experience of occupation and resistance, and the role of the Soviet Union in the anti-Nazi coalition all helped discredit old political parties and the West. The new Czechoslovakia, many insisted, would also be a national state. The idea of expelling at least the pro-Nazi Germans emerged early in the war, and German policies and the role of highly visible Sudeten Germans like Frank only reinforced it. Stored-up resentments would fuel a reckoning in 1945. As the American diplomat George F. Kennan observed as early as May 1939, "if the tide ever turns, Czech retaliation will be fearful to contemplate."[31]

Czech human losses during the war were definitely lower than they would have been had they fought either in September 1938 or March 1939. In fact, thanks to a rising birthrate the Czech population grew during the war. Estimates place the total number of Czechs who were executed or died in concentration camps at between 36,000 and 55,000. These figures represent dreadful human suffering, but the fact is that they are lower than the losses of other nations. Those who suffered the most in the Protectorate were the Jews, whether they had considered themselves Czechs, Germans, or a distinct nationality.

Life in relative freedom ended for the Jews in October 1941. Terezín (Theresienstadt), a fortress town in northwestern Bohemia, was transformed into a ghetto for Jews from Bohemia and Moravia, and some German and Austrian Jews. The first Jews from Prague and Brno were brought to Terezín in January 1942, to be followed during that year by 40,000 more and an additional 37,000 from the Reich (the normal population of Terezín had been 7,000). During the years of horror that followed, life in Terezín, Hitler's showpiece concentration camp, remained privileged only in comparison with other camps—and the greatest "privilege" was the right of the Jewish administration to select candidates for the death camps. Terezín's population fluctuated, and Jews from Bohemia and Moravia were only part of it. In all, some 50,000 Jews from the Protectorate were sent there; another 20,000 were transported directly to other camps by the end of 1942. Several thousand Bohemian and Moravian Jews managed to avoid detention or escaped abroad. When the Red Army finally liberated Terezín on May 7, 1945, only around 8,000 of the Protectorate's Jews sent there still lived. Total losses among Bohemian and Moravian Jews exceeded 75,000, or three-quarters of the total.[32]

After 1943 underground activity in the Protectorate showed new signs of life. The Soviets and the KSČ favored partisan warfare, but Bohemia and Moravia were not well-suited to partisan activities. Further parachute drops of SOE-trained agents tried to restore communications among the domestic resistance movements, the most significant of which was now the Council of Three, led by General Vojtěch Luža until his death in October 1944. The Germans destroyed the underground leadership of the KSČ, leaving individual resistance cells to work independently, directed by the Czechoslovak broadcasts of Radio Moscow. As the war ended, neither the Soviets nor the Western Allies wanted a national uprising.

The Allies finally arrived in April and May 1945, the Americans entering from the west and the Red Army from the east. Its days numbered, the Protectorate government tried and failed to surrender to the Americans instead of the Russians. In the end, the surviving members of the Protectorate government and several leading German officials (including Frank) faced a National Court in a restored Czechoslovakia. Hácha was not among them: he died in prison hospital, an old, sick, and broken man, on June 27, 1945.[33]

The Slovak Republic, 1939–1945

The six-year existence of the Slovak state was tied to the rise and fall of Hitler and the Nazi Third Reich. Outside influences determined its emergence and disappearance, but the Slovak Republic was not simply an artificial Nazi creation. It also built on the autonomist movement led by the HSL'S, the domestic Czechoslovak crisis, and the social and political development of the Slovak nation. The Slovak state's leaders argued that they chose the least evil available alternative in 1939. By the logic of modern nationalism an independent state for the Slovak nation was an absolute value; the question remains whether moral or humanitarian considerations ever could or should limit such a value.[34]

Slovakia was a single-party state. The constitution adopted on July 21, 1939, established a republic, and Tiso became president. Tiso was thus head of state, head of the government, head of the HSL'S, and commander in chief of the armed forces. The constitution was clerical, corporate, and authoritarian on the Italian and Austrian model. It created no institutional counterweight to the HSL'S, yet several factors worked against consolidating a totalitarian single-party state.[35] For one thing, German and Hungarian minority parties existed and had to be respected. For another, the HSL'S was riven by internal rivalries. The clerical and conservative wing backed Tiso, as did the Germans, who preferred reliable and competent partnership to fanatic emulation. The radicals provided a check on Tiso, applied at the Salzburg meeting of July 28, 1940, where the Germans forced Tuka and one of his colleagues into the cabinet. Tiso headed off their challenge, however, by coopting their style and language, proclaiming himself Leader. By 1942 Tiso felt secure against Tuka's challenge, though the Germans still kept the latter around.[36] The party also never completely controlled the Slovak army.

Measures against Slovakia's Jews (89,000 in the territory of the Slovak state according to the 1940 census) initially targeted their position in business, administration, and industry.[37] Later attempts to reduce their representation in the professions threatened the breakdown of essential services such as health care. After September 1941 such Jews could receive presidential exemptions from transportation. The Jewish Codex of September 10, 1941, introduced the Nazi racial definition of Jew and provided the legal foundation for the transportation of Slovakia's Jews. The Slovak ministry of the interior prepared the transportation with SS advice, even paying the Germans 500 Reichsmarks a head for "resettlement" costs. Between March and October 1942 over 56,000 Slovak Jews were transported, until under repeated protests from the Vatican and others, Tiso ordered a halt. Thereafter, the Slovak government interned Jews in relatively more humane work camps, but after the Germans occupied Slovakia in 1944 many of them were transported. Approximately 13,000 more Jews were killed on the spot or sent to the camps. Only a few hundred Jews survived transportation, though by exemptions, by concealment with the aid of sympathetic Slovaks (including government and church functionaries), and by successful flight abroad perhaps one-third of the Slovak Jews lived through the war.[38]

Slovakia's dependence on Germany, hopes of revising the frontiers, and fear of Hungary's intentions determined its foreign policy.[39] It joined Hitler's attack on Poland in 1939, in the fall of 1940 it adhered to the Rome-Berlin-Tokyo Axis, and 50,000 Slovak soldiers went to war with the Soviet Union after June 1941, though after some mass desertions the Slovak contribution was reduced to 16,000.[40] As the tide turned during 1943, elements of the Slovak army contemplated changing sides. At the same time, Slovak resistance became more active. The earliest groups were Czechoslovak in orientation and maintained contacts with London. Lieutenant Colonel Ján Golián recruited members of the Slovak army into a military center, while a more "autonomist" group of Slovak democrats was led by former agrarian Ján Ursíny and Jozef Lettrich. They joined with the KSS leadership under Karol Šmidke, Gustáv Husák, and Ladislav Novomeský to form the Slovak National Council (SNR), in the Christmas Agreement of 1943. Plans began for a national uprising to coincide with the advance of the Red Army in 1944. The SNR and the Military Center had different conceptions of the uprising, coordinating with the Soviet army was difficult, and Soviet-directed partisan activity attracted German attention. On August 29, 1944, Tiso consented to German operations against the partisans, touching off the Slovak national uprising prematurely.

The SNR set up headquarters in Banská Bystrica, where on September 1, 1944, it proclaimed the reestablishment of a common Czechoslovak state. Unfortunately the Germans neutralized the two Slovak divisions that were to open the Carpathian passes for the Red Army, and the garrisons in western Slovakia mostly ignored Golián's call for resistance. A First Czechoslovak Army in Slovakia under General Rudolf Viest, who flew in from London to take command, fielded roughly 60,000 soldiers, supported by another 18,000 partisans. The Red Army opened an offensive toward Dukla pass, but ran into well-prepared German resistance and suffered heavy casualties. Without outside help and heavy weapons, the Slovak national uprising was doomed. After two months the remnants of the First Army retreated into the mountains to continue fighting as partisans. The Germans occupied Banská Bystrica on October 27, 1944. Their reprisals added another 4,000 to the approximately 5,000 Slovak fighters who died in the uprising. The Slovak national uprising failed, but it stated the will of some Slovaks to rejoin the Czechs in a common state, and to do so as national equals.

The Slovak national uprising also ended any autonomy for Tiso's Slovakia. The German army occupied the country, but they could not halt the Soviet advance in the spring of 1945. On April 4, 1945, the Red Army entered Bratislava, while Tiso and the Slovak government retreated into Austria. The Americans interned Tiso in June 1945, and transferred him to Czechoslovakia in October. He was tried and sentenced to death in 1947. The Czech People's Party and the Slovak democrats urged clemency, but the government did not endorse it and Beneš denied it. Tiso was executed on April 18, 1947.[41] In a letter to Pope Pius XII on November 8, 1944, Tiso responded to Vatican criticism of his policies, saying that his government had acted "out of its duty to protect its nation from the enemies who for centuries have been active in its midst. . . . Our fault lies in our gratitude and loyalty to the Germans, who not only recognized and approved the existence of our nation and its natural right to independence and national liberty, but also helped it against the Czechs and Jews, enemies of our nation."[42]

The Czechoslovak Struggle in Exile

When the Germans marched into Prague, Beneš sent a protest telegram to the American president and the British prime minister, announcing his return to politics to work for the re-creation of an independent Czechoslovakia. Czechoslovak diplomats in anti-Nazi countries such as Stefan Osuský, the ambassador to Paris, and Hodža (both Slovaks) disagreed with Beneš's view that the German occupation annulled Munich, and thus Czechoslovakia with its pre-1938 frontiers and political system still legally existed. The differences over the postwar position of Slovakia, the future of the agrarian party, and the alliance with the Soviet Union forced both Osuský and Hodža out of the Czechoslovak government-in-exile, while Beneš's theory was accepted.

Even before September 1939, Czechoslovak exiles organized armed forces, as Masaryk had done during World War I. Between March 15 and September 1 most went to Poland, where army general Lev Prchala tried to organize a Czechoslovak legion.[43] Poland, wary of provoking Hitler, delayed its approval, so many volunteers went on to France. General Sergej Ingr of the home underground went to Paris in June 1939 with messages from Eliáš, and stayed abroad to organize the independent Czechoslovak detachment in France. In October 1939 the French recognized a "Czechoslovak National Committee" as the authority directing these armed units, and the British followed suit in December. The Polish government finally approved the Czechoslovak legion under Lieutenant Colonel Ludvík Svoboda, formally established on September 3, 1939. Most of the Czech and Slovak legion in Poland ended up in Soviet captivity. Others, including the pilots, escaped to the Middle East via Romania, and thence to France.

Two Czechoslovak regiments helped defend France, and some 4,000 soldiers were evacuated to England after the capitulation. Czechoslovak pilots also served in the French Air Force. With the fall of France, the Czechoslovak exile center moved to Great Britain. Czechoslovak fighter squadrons and later a bomber squadron participated in the Battle of Britain and the air war against Germany, and other Czechoslovak pilots served in British or Polish squadrons. The infantry evacuated to England and troops moved from the Middle East formed the Czechoslovak Independent Armored Brigade in September 1943. The brigade landed in Europe in the autumn of 1944, where it blockaded the German forces in Dunkirk. Many other Czechoslovak citizens joined European resistance movements, especially in France, or fought as partisans in Yugoslavia and on the Eastern Front.

After the Nazi invasion of the Soviet Union in 1941 some of the interned Czechoslovaks were released to join the Czechoslovak units forming in the Middle East. The Soviets and Beneš's government-in-exile agreed on July 18, 1941, to organize Czechoslovak forces to fight with the Red Army. In 1943 the First Independent Czechoslovak Regiment entered combat at Sokolov in the Ukraine. The Czechoslovak units in the USSR expanded into the First Czechoslovak Army Group, which under Svoboda fought at Dukla in the Carpathians, and then helped liberate Czechoslovakia from the east.[44]

In London, Beneš concentrated on winning diplomatic recognition. The fall of France removed one obstacle, and when Churchill replaced Chamberlain the "men of Munich" were gone. Beneš gained British recognition as a provisional government (July 21, 1940), and finally as a full-fledged Allied government-in-exile (July 18, 1941). The Soviet Union and the United States also extended full diplomatic recognition. Hand in hand with recognition, Beneš sought repudiation of Munich. The reluctant British had promised Beneš most of what he wanted by July 1942, and Charles de Gaulle for France unequivocally repudiated Munich *ab initio*. Neither the United States nor the USSR had signed the original document, but both Roosevelt and Stalin assured Beneš that they recognized Czechoslovakia in its pre-Munich frontiers.[45]

Beneš's government also developed a policy toward the Sudeten Germans. Beneš initially considered combining border revisions with voluntary and forced expatriation, but gradually shifted his goal to the total removal of all Germans except active anti-fascists.[46] He overcame British reluctance and won American approval for major population transfers after the war, and when Beneš visited Moscow in December 1943, Stalin also agreed. This policy estranged the Czechoslovak government from the democratic Germans, especially the remnants of the Sudeten German Social Democratic Party, led in exile by Wenzel Jaksch.[47]

The KSČ was a potential threat to a democratic Czechoslovakia, which Beneš sought to defuse by actively seeking cooperation. Once the Nazi invasion brought the USSR into the war Beneš contacted the KSČ leadership in Moscow. In discussions with Gottwald and others in Moscow in December 1943, Beneš agreed to exclude from postwar politics the compromised political parties (in the Czech lands primarily the Agrarian party—the backbone of the Pětka in the interwar republic—and in Slovakia the HSL'S), and accept the concept of the National Front, uniting all parties participating in resistance to the Nazis. Other KSČ demands about which Beneš had reservations included national committees to replace local administration, modeled on the soviets of the USSR, and the place of Slovakia and the Slovak nation.

Beneš sought permanent good relations with the Soviet Union for several reasons. Security was one: the expulsion of the Germans would not remove the fact of Czechoslovakia's proximity to Germany, and only the Soviet Union would guarantee Czechoslovakia against a revived Germany. Also, he hoped that the Soviet Union would restrain the KSČ. Finally, Beneš was influenced by the negative example of Soviet relations with the Polish government-in-exile. Thus he eventually accepted Soviet objections to a planned Czechoslovak-Polish federation, and instead signed a Treaty of Friendship, Mutual Assistance, and Postwar Cooperation with the USSR in Moscow in December 1943.[48]

As Soviet armies reached Czechoslovakia's pre-Munich frontiers, such political considerations outweighed military ones, as the case of Ruthenia demonstrated. The London government appointed delegates to establish Czechoslovak control over this, the first liberated Czechoslovak territory, but the Soviet army ignored them. Meanwhile the security apparatus created local soviets that would in due course declare the desire of the local inhabitants to "return" to the Soviet Ukraine. Beneš bowed to Stalin's will in this violation of the pre-Munich frontiers, though he postponed a formal agreement until June 29, 1945. In liberated Slovakia the Soviet army also intervened in internal matters, dissolving and creating local national committees, and arresting and transporting Czechoslovak citizens to Soviet labor camps.

Beneš returned to Moscow in March 1945 to negotiate the makeup of a National Front government for the liberated homeland. During the talks on March 22–29, 1945, Gottwald's communists played their hand well. The London government had no prepared program, and instead discussed a KSČ draft, which decisively shaped the outcome. All agreed that Czechoslovakia's foreign policy was to be based upon the treaty with the Soviet Union. Key points of conflict included the politicization of the army, the national committees, and the Czech-Slovak relationship. Slovak unanimity backed by the KSČ won recognition of Slovak national equality in the new state as "an equal to an equal." By confirming the SNR's functions the agreement created the asymmetrical structure that was a feature of Czechoslovakia for much of the communist era. The program promised retribution to Germans, Magyars, and collaborators, more land reform, and state-directed economic reconstruction.[49]

Each party had three members in the National Front government, but since the KSS and KSČ were counted as separate parties, communists controlled six portfolios. They included two vice-premierships (Gottwald for the KSČ and Viliam Široký for the KSS); the ministry of the interior with its control of the police; information, controlling propaganda and press matters; agriculture, responsible for postwar land reform; and labor and social affairs. Prime Minister Zdeněk Fierlinger was a Social Democrat but a Soviet sympathizer, and Svoboda was minister of defense. On April 5, 1945, the new government proclaimed itself in liberated Košice.

By the end of April the Red Army had cleared Slovakia and most of Moravia, and American General George Patton's Third Army entered Czechoslovakia from the west. Patton had orders not to cross the line of Karlovy Vary–Plzeň–České Budějovice, so that the liberation of Prague would be left to the Red Army. On May 1, a spontaneous uprising broke out at Přerov and spread through the cities and towns of Bohemia and Moravia. On May 5 the rising reached Prague, where a recently formed Czech National Council (ČNR) assumed authority in the name of the Košice government. The Czech insurgents hoped that the Americans, who entered Plzeň on May 6, would come to their aid. Instead, an unexpected ally appeared in the form of Andrei Vlasov's Russian Liberation Army, anti-communist Russians fighting with the Germans against Stalin. Hoping to win their way to American captivity, they turned against the Germans, but negotiations with the ČNR broke down and they withdrew to the west on May 8. That same day the ČNR concluded an agreement on the withdrawal of the German army, whose government had capitulated the day before at Rhiems. Some SS units continued the fight until Red Army tanks entered Prague on May 9, but on that day the war for the Czechs finally ended.

ILLUSIONS AND REALITY, 1945–1948

A week after the guns fell silent in Prague, President Beneš arrived amid great celebration.[50] It quickly became apparent that Czechoslovakia after World War II would not be the same, territorially, demographically, economically, or politically. Czechoslovakia lost Ruthenia and gained a slight extension (at Hungary's expense) south of the Danube at Bratislava. The radical version of population transfer, under which only active anti-Nazi Germans and those needed for economic reconstruction could remain in Czechoslovakia, was applied. Almost all Czechoslovakia's Germans and many of its Hungarians were expelled, and their loss added to the some 250,000 Czechoslovaks who were killed during the war. Reconstruction required state intervention in economic life, and all parties agreed that key industrial and financial institutions would have to be nationalized. The leftward shift in political attitudes visible during the war made banning the old right-wing parties relatively easy. The feeling that lack of national unity had contributed to the Munich disaster made it easy to accept the National Front. The Soviet Union was also popular, though ties to the West were not rejected. The contemporary metaphor was that Czechoslovakia was a bridge between East and West. Whether such a bridge could remain open depended upon maintaining cooperation among the Big Three allies.

A Bridge Between East and West?

The government implemented the Košice program of April 5, 1945, under which the right-wing parties were banned. The only legal political parties were the Social Democrats, the National Socialists, the People's party, the Slovak Democrats, and the Communist party, represented by both the KSČ and the KSS. All parties refused to include the ČNR or other Czech resistance organizations in the government, though the SNR continued to exist in Slovakia. They also rejected the federal structure suggested by the SNR for an asymmetrical pattern, with Slovakia enjoying unique institutions (the SNR and a Board of Commissioners). Three conferences in Prague in June 1945, and April and June 1946, delimited their powers.

All the recognized parties were members of the National Front (NF), which discussed problems and reached decisions binding for parliamentary representatives, party organizations, and the press. The NF also decided what political parties could exist, and since acceptance of the common program was a condition of admission, in effect no opposition was possible. The communists tried to get social interest–group organizations admitted to the front, but the other parties kept it a coalition of political parties. The communists did take over the trade unions, creating a Central Trade-Unions Council (ÚRO) as executive organ of the Revolutionary Trade-Unions Movement (ROH). Antonín Zápotocký headed the ÚRO after May 1945.

The NF somewhat resembled the Pětka in the interwar republic, but it was even less in harmony with parliamentary democracy. In fact the government ruled for several months without a parliament at all, through presidential decrees (ninety-eight between May and October 1945) that significantly altered the shape of the republic. Beneš's decree of October 14, 1945, nationalized major industries, financial institutions, and agriculture, bringing approximately two-thirds of Czechoslovakia's industrial capacity under state control. A decree of June 21, 1945, seized German- or Hungarian-owned lands, as well as the property of accused collaborators or traitors.

Losing their property was only part of the German and Hungarian experience. On June 29, 1945, Beneš signed a decree "on the punishment of Nazi criminals, traitors, and their abettors, and on Extraordinary People's Courts," the Great Retribution Decree.[51] It placed the Germans and Hungarians beyond the law, and stripped them of their citizenship and of civil or even basic human rights. From May until August 1945, a wave of spontaneous and organized acts of violence against Germans swept through the countryside in the so-called "Wild Transfer." Kennan's earlier prediction came true, as the Czechs, caught up on a wave of postwar nationalism, avenged themselves for their prewar and wartime experiences. The worst excesses ceased after August 1945, when the Potsdam Conference accepted the orderly and humane transfer of the Germans. The expulsions affected at least 2.5 million Germans and reduced the German proportion of the population to 1.8 percent.[52]

The Potsdam Conference rejected Czechoslovak proposals to expel the Hungarians, leaving the issue to bilateral negotiations between the two governments. Finally an exchange of populations, involving some 68,000 Czechoslovak Hungarians and a smaller number of Slovaks from Hungary, was agreed. Other Hungarians were forcibly resettled in the now-empty frontier zones of the Czech lands, or subjected to "re-Slovakizing" pressures. The census of 1950 revealed a Hungarian minority that still exceeded 10 percent of Slovakia's population, and whose actual numbers were probably much higher.

The Great Retribution Decree and the Small Retribution Decree of October 27, 1945, also opened up the way for extraordinary trials of collaborators. The extraordinary people's courts had a professional jurist appointed by the president in the chair, with four lay associates nominated by the national committees (where communists had the upper hand), and they imposed sentences from which there was no appeal. The retribution process continued through 1947, enabling the communists to remove or discredit many political opponents.[53] Joining the KSČ, on the other hand, protected even genuine collaborators. Retribution also benefited the communists through control of the distribution of confiscated land from the National Land Fund.

Rule by decree ended when a Provisional National Assembly convened on October 28, the anniversary of Czechoslovak independence. The assembly formally approved all the presidential decrees issued since May 1945. In May 1946, one year after the liberation, it adopted an amnesty for all illegal acts between September 30, 1938, and October 28, 1945, if they were carried out in "the struggle for the reconquest of Czech and Slovak liberty or if they were expressions of longing for a just retaliation for the acts of the occupiers or their abettors." Parliament now legislated, but the National Front still controlled decision-making power.

The American and Soviet armies withdrew in October and November 1945, and as Czechoslovakia regained stability, attention focused on the elections scheduled for May 26, 1946. The National Front members conducted a spirited contest for votes. The KSČ controlled the key positions in the government, had a solid organization, and since war's end had expanded to well over one million members, making it the strongest party, especially among the Czech working class. Its nearest competitor, the National Socialist Party (ČSNS), mustered 520,000 members from the middle levels of society. The People's party (ČSL), still led by Msgr. Šrámek, counted 400,000 members, mainly among committed Catholics. The Social Democrats (ČSD) claimed 350,000 members, but tensions between Fierlinger's pro-communist leadership and the more independent rank-and-file weakened them. The KSS with 120,000 members was merely a branch of the KSČ. The Slovak Democrats (DS) led by Jozef Lettrich tried to attract Slovak Catholics (many of its leaders were Protestants) without collaborating with former l'udáks.

The elections were free, fair, and orderly (see Table 2). The results fulfilled communist expectations in the Czech lands, at least, where the KSČ won just over 40 percent of the popular vote, with the National Socialists at 23.6 percent and the People's Party at just over 20 percent. The Social Democrats received only 15.5 percent of the vote in the Czech lands. In Slovakia the Democratic Party took a full 62 percent of the vote, even though two other parties had emerged months before the election. The Labor Party (SP), former Social Democrats who rejected fusion with the KSS, and the Freedom Party (SS), Slovaks who disagreed with Lettrich's pre-election power-sharing agreement with the Catholics, each received just over 3 percent. The KSS won 30.3 percent. The

TABLE 2

CZECHOSLOVAK ELECTIONS OF 1946

(PERCENT OF POPULAR VOTE)

Parties	KSČ	KSS	ČSNS	ČSL	DS	ČSD	SS	SP
Czechoslovakia	38.12	In KSČ totals	18.37	15.71	13.13	12.1	0.85	0.71
Czech Lands	40.17	–	23.66	20.24	–	15.58	–	–
Slovakia	–	30.37	–	–	62	–	3.37	3.11

SOURCE: Pavel Bělina et al., *Dějiny zemi koruny české, II. Od nástupu osvícenstvi po naši dobu* (Prague: Paseka, 1992), pp. 256–57.

communists' statewide 38 percent of the vote made them the strongest party and the leading force in the new Constituent National Assembly. In the new government the communists controlled nine positions, the National Socialists, populists, and Democrats four each, and the Social Democrats three. Minister of Defense Svoboda was supposedly not a party member. The truly nonpartisan minister was Jan Masaryk, son of the founder of the republic, who was in charge of foreign affairs.

The new government drafted a constitution, set out a two-year recovery plan for 1947–49, and enacted other social and economic measures. The parties were committed to continuing the National Front, but differences between them strained their unity. Publicly, the communists set the goal of winning more than 50 percent of the vote in the next election, due in 1948. Some party leaders genuinely expected to win a majority legally. Gottwald and other leaders also counted on splitting the National Front and securing the support of "left-wing" elements in the other parties to take over power within the government. Many functionaries in the security and intelligence apparatus and activists in the ROH preferred revolutionary action.

The major non-communist parties were rivals for voter support, and Czech parties mistrusted the Slovak democrats. Nevertheless, repeated conflicts with the communists over economic policies, agriculture, actions of the communist-controlled ministry of information, and cultural and censorship policies increasingly brought the national socialists, populists, and Slovak democrats closer together. They still viewed their conflicts with the communists as part of a political and parliamentary struggle. Their opponents, however, controlled a formidable array of extra-parliamentary weapons and used them effectively.

By the middle of 1947, National Front unity was increasingly strained, while the population at large had to accept that the postwar years would not easily fulfill all their hopes and desires. The newly nationalized economy showed signs of sluggishness, competition on the European market revived, and an unexpected drought, coupled with the ending of UNRAA and other postwar relief support, created problems with the food supply. Its attention focused on domestic conditions, the public did not notice the fundamental changes taking place in the international arena. Yet 1947 saw clear signs of the breakdown of the wartime anti-Nazi coalition, whose preservation was crucial to the prospects for democracy in Czechoslovakia.

The Bridge Collapses

Czechoslovakia's postwar foreign policy was anchored in the Soviet alliance.[54] Nevertheless, Beneš and the other Czechoslovak leaders expected that, especially with Jan Masaryk as foreign minister, Czechoslovakia would maintain its traditional friendly ties with Western Europe and the United States. At international meetings, though, the Czechoslovaks loyally supported the Soviet Union's positions. As those positions became more and more hostile to British and American interests, Czechoslovakia's support became correspondingly difficult for Masaryk to explain away in the corridors and antechambers.

Czechoslovakia's dilemma became sharper as 1946 drew to a close. The United States had already prematurely terminated a postwar credit for surplus U.S. equipment, and negotiations with the Export-Import Bank for a $150 million loan stalled. Western doubts about Soviet intentions grew, and the West's response fuelled Stalin's own suspicions. On September 6, 1946, the United States declared that it would keep military forces in Europe "as long as necessary," and in March 1947, President Harry S Truman announced his "Truman Doctrine," promising American aid to free peoples threatened by outside aggression or internal subversion. The European Recovery Program unveiled by George C. Marshall on June 5, 1947, increased this estrangement. The Marshall Plan offered Europe unprecedented U.S. economic assistance, but in a way that would have parted the veil of secrecy around the economic situation in the USSR. Stalin denounced the plan and rejected Soviet participation, a move the rest of the Soviet bloc copied, including Yugoslavia and Poland (who had been interested).

Only Czechoslovakia accepted the invitation to Paris to discuss the European Recovery Program. A delegation including Gottwald and Masaryk flew to Moscow on July 9 to explain this decision. There Stalin made it clear that Czechoslovak participation in the Marshall Plan would be a hostile act contrary to the Czechoslovak-Soviet alliance. When the delegation returned to Prague, the government announced its withdrawal from the Paris conference.[55] The rejection of the Marshall Plan left Czechoslovakia isolated from its former friends among the Western countries, and exposed its dependence on Moscow.

With the lines hardening between East and West in Europe, Stalin moved to establish direct control over the countries he influenced.[56] In September 1947 the European communist parties met in Poland to establish the Communist Information Bureau (Cominform), replacing the Comintern dissolved in 1943. The Cominform's founding congress criticized the French and Italian communists, and urged the Czechoslovak comrades to resolve the power question in Czechoslovakia. The communists' domestic opponents were slow to grasp the changed situation. They continued to view Germany as the main danger to Czechoslovak security, and they remained committed to the Soviet alliance. They believed that international considerations would prevent the Soviet Union from meddling directly in Czechoslovakia, not appreciating the extent to which they were internationally isolated and expendable to Moscow, which was ready to support the KSČ in a bid for total power.

Czechoslovakia's internal situation worsened in step with the worsening international outlook.[57] While the communists in parliament undermined their rivals with demagogic appeals like the "millionaire's tax" proposal, communist-influenced trade union organizations and other mass movements mobilized pressure on the parliament and government. Compromises within the National Front became rarer, and progress toward the new constitution ground to a halt. Public opinion research suggested that support for the KSČ was slipping, which placed the 1948 elections in a new light. The non-communists expected them to sober the KSČ and force it to cooperate with its coalition partners. The communists prepared for a decisive struggle using extra-parliamentary tactics, "the organized movement of the masses." They planned a congress of works councils in Prague on February 22, 1948, and a mass meeting of the peasants' organizations a few days later.

The communist-controlled Ministry of the Interior now played a crucial role in preparations for a showdown. The intelligence service penetrated the other parties to identify and cultivate "left-wing" elements that would align them with the KSČ. Now they planned to destroy the parties where no convenient left-wing leadership was available, above all the National Socialists and the Slovak Democrats. Exposing supposed collaborators or traitors in non-communist coalition parties and then staging their trials had already been used in other people's democracies (the famous "salami tactics"), often with direct Soviet advice. In Czechoslovakia, these tactics were less successful. Minister of Justice Prokop Drtina proved a persistent stumbling bloc.

In January 1948 Drtina exposed two incidents uncovered by his ministry's investigations. One was a fabricated American-run espionage ring, in which leading National Socialists were supposedly to organize anti-communist military officers in the garrison town of Most. The other began in September 1947 when three ministers, Jan Masaryk and two National Socialists, Petr Zenkl and Drtina, received parcels containing explosives. The Ministry of the Interior's investigation was dilatory and inconclusive, but when Drtina ordered his own ministry to investigate, it found clear evidence implicating Communist Party officials in Olomouc. Caches of illegal arms were also linked to ranking communists, including a member of the National Assembly.

Police provocations against the Slovak Democratic Party were more successful. Tiso's trial had been manipulated to inflame opinion against the Democrats. In October the police announced the discovery of a conspiracy involving the Democrats and exiled l'udáks. They arrested nearly 400 people, including Deputy Prime Minister Ursíny's secretary. Citing the supposed conspiracy, the communist chairman of the Slovak Board of Commissioners, Husák, unilaterally announced its dissolution even though the Democrats were in the majority. In the end, Ursíny resigned, but Lettrich remained leader of the Democratic Party, and the reconstituted Board of Commissioners had equal numbers of communists and democrats. After the autumn crisis, however, the communists in Slovakia had the upper hand.

The non-communist parties in the NF, belatedly drawing together in self-defense, were encouraged by events at the Social Democratic party congress in November 1947. After Fierlinger agreed to a pact with the KSČ, the congress rebelled and replaced him as leader. The other non-communist parties saw this result as a signal that the Social Democrats would support reining in the KSČ. Yet no concerted efforts had been made to draw them into a united anti-communist front by the time the final crisis came in February 1948.

When the communist Minister of the Interior transferred the last non-communist police commanders out of Prague in preparation for the "organized movement of the masses," the non-communist ministers passed a resolution on February 13 directing him to rescind the orders. On February 17 ministers from the National Socialist, People's, and Democratic parties agreed that if he refused they would resign. They hoped that the Social Democrat ministers would join them, and that either President Beneš would call elections under a caretaker government or reject the resignations, forcing the KSČ to resume cooperation in the National Front, or take the blame for its collapse. On February 20, twelve ministers handed Beneš their resignations.

The communists could hardly believe their luck. Their opponents had provoked the inevitable clash at a time and in a way that gave the communists practically all the advantages. The ministers who resigned had not brought the Social Democrats with them, nor had they won over Jan Masaryk. As a result a majority of the government remained in office. The communists decided to turn the government crisis into a struggle for power, in which they enjoyed significant advantages. They were united, and directed a numerous and disciplined party. In the background, always a palpable presence, loomed the Soviet Union. Thanks to its control of the interior ministry, the KSČ was firmly in charge of the capital city. The congress of worker's councils and the peasant organizations was already planned; the party summoned crowds of 250,000 to Old Town Square beginning on February 21, and formed a "People's Militia" of armed workers. Gottwald called for the creation of "action committees" within the National Front, which purged non-communists from public functions at all levels. On February 23, a Central Action Committee was created, and General Svoboda assured it that the army was "with the people." A one-hour general strike supporting the communist proposals to "renew" the national front took place on February 24. By then, the struggle for power had effectively already been resolved by a communist coup d'état; there remained now only the government crisis.

Had the non-communists attempted active tactics, they would have had a difficult time: communist-controlled unions kept newsprint from the opponents' presses, the radio was in communist hands, and the police banned non-communist demonstrations. The democratic parties did not attempt to mobilize their supporters until too late, perhaps fearing communist charges of an anti-communist putsch. They appealed for calm and asserted that the crisis would be resolved by constitutional means. Gottwald proposed his "constitutional" solution on February 21. He demanded that Beneš accept the resignations and appoint a reorganized government nominated by him as prime minister. This new government included individuals from the non-communist parties, but except for Masaryk, it was entirely under communist influence. Since a majority of ministers remained, the government had technically not fallen and Gottwald's solution was within the president's constitutional powers. Thus the entire burden of resolving the crisis descended on Beneš, who delayed accepting Gottwald's reorganized government for

President Edvard Beneš approves Prime Minister Klement Gottwald's reorganized government on February 25, 1948. (ČTK photo)

four days, hoping that the non-communist parties could do something to resist the communists' moves to control power. Their failure left him isolated, exposed to pressure from Gottwald and the perfectly organized communist mass demonstrations. Beneš feared conflict splitting Czechoslovak society, perhaps even civil war leading to a Soviet intervention, and in the end, alone and seriously ill, he decided to accept the resignations and the new government on February 25, 1948. That evening Gottwald could proclaim to the cheering throngs on Old Town Square the "defeat of reaction and the victory of the working people."

The struggle to preserve Czechoslovakia as a bridge between East and West, as at least a limited democracy in the part of Europe that had fallen into the Soviet Union's sphere of influence, had failed. Given both the internal and international situation as it had developed since 1945, the struggle could hardly have ended in a victory for the non-communists. Their defeat need not, however, have given the impression that it happened legally, according to the constitution, and with mass popular support.

13 Victorious February and Tragic August

The February coup of 1948 opened the way to Czechoslovakia's full integration into the Soviet bloc, a process marked by two significant deaths. On March 10, 1948, less than two weeks after remaining in Gottwald's new government, Jan Masaryk lay dead beneath his apartment window in the Černín Palace. Whether suicide or assassination, Masaryk's death ended an important personal connection to the First Republic, and removed the one minister with a positive reputation and contacts in the West.[1] As if to reinforce this break with the past, Beneš, after resigning the presidency in June, died on September 3, 1948.

Some observers in 1948 drew parallels with earlier historical disasters that forced Czechs and Slovaks into exile. The U.S. ambassador in Prague noted that under Habsburg rule the Czechs had developed "an ingrained genius for subtle opposition to the existing regime. They are much more adept when in opposition than when they themselves are in control and faced with the problems of construction and positive rule of which they have in modern times had only twenty years of experience."[2] These remarks may only repeat the stereotype of the Czechs as cunning simpletons like Hašek's Josef Švejk. Yet succeeding years saw new waves of emigration, bowing to political storms, and subtle opposition to the regime, before they closed with Czechs and Slovaks once more facing the challenges of construction and positive rule.[3]

CONSOLIDATION
AND STALINISM

The Czechoslovak communists set out to ensure the KSČ's complete dominance in politics, economics, and all other aspects of public life after the February coup. The party leadership spoke at first of a unique Czechoslovak road to socialism, but in the ever darkening atmosphere of the early Cold War, and especially after Gottwald's trip to the Crimea to see Stalin in September 1948, the Czechoslovak communists began to apply Soviet models and practices, frequently with direct Soviet advice.

Building a Monopoly of Power

Political control was already largely consolidated in February.[4] The police arrested non-communist officials even before Beneš's capitulation, and Action Committees purged offices, schools, the workplace, and the National Assembly. The communists formalized these moves by destroying the non-communist parties or bringing them under indirect control. The Social Democratic Party, back under the pro-communist leadership, agreed to merge with the KSČ in June 1948. The other parties shrank drastically through purges, emigration, and resignations. Party leaders were handpicked communist collaborators.[5] The communist-dominated mass organizations joined the National Front, and with the taming of the political parties the NF lost its role as a consensus-building forum. The KSČ tolerated no political rivals, not even the National Front, and eventually it remained active only at the higher levels, where it became a communist-controlled transmission belt to the non-communist political parties. It also gave the system an appearance of pluralism. "We need this façade," Gottwald noted. "We would be stupid to tear down this façade if we already have and are able to have it."[6]

The parliament, purged by the Action Committees, unanimously approved the new government's program in March and a new constitution in May. New parliamentary elections were held on May 30, 1948. In an atmosphere of fear and pressure, the voters were presented with a single list of candidates representing the National Front. Only by publicly requesting a blank ballot, amounting to a risky declaration of opposition, could a voter register disagreement. Official results claimed 89.2 percent of the votes cast for the NF list. The front, itself controlled by the KSČ, held all the seats in parliament.[7]

Neither parliament nor government now functioned as separate organs of legislative and executive power. Parliament, as Slanský told the Central Committee before the elections, would not make any real decisions, for "we decide everything of any importance here."[8] The government was also completely subordinated to the party. Party control over the national committees at the lower levels removed any genuine local self-administration. The independent judicial system was destroyed, and the state prosecutor was now the highest judicial official in Czechoslovakia. What was left of the separate Slovak institutions also withered away, partly because of the built-in centralization of the party system. In addition, the party viewed the Slovak question as an economic one, to be resolved by state-directed development. Finally, the residual Czech nationalism of many functionaries, feeding on the campaign against Slovak "bourgeois nationalists," helped destroy the asymmetrical administrative system.

The KSČ cemented its dominance when the National Assembly elected Gottwald president. The party's power monopoly gave it control of all the state's levers of force. Yet this dictatorial aspect should not hide the fact that elements of Czechoslovak society actively or passively supported the communists. After 1945, a large part of the industrial working class demonstrated left-wing attitudes that sometimes ran ahead even of the KSČ. Though the takeover was not a mass revolution, the communists proved they could mobilize large crowds of supporters. Following the coup, 250,000 workers filled administrative and government posts, creating a hard core of activist party supporters. Small farmers who benefited from the communist-directed postwar land reform also supported the party. As one scholar notes, "an authoritarian state with a public sector much larger than those of the West has rewards as well as punishments to dole out. . . . [T]here were winners as well as losers in the communist takeover."[9]

Foremost among the winners was the Communist Party, whose membership ballooned rapidly. A loyal acolyte of Moscow since its "Bolshevization" in 1929, the KSČ deviated from the Leninist model in its size. After February, party membership reached 2,311,066 by May 1949, or one-sixth of the population. These levels fell during the years of purges and political trials, but the KSČ remained more a mass party than the Soviet or other bloc parties.[10] In spite of its relatively large size, a small group of top officials controlled the KSČ, and through it the state. Communist control also extended to civil society, culture, and the economy.

Immediately after February, the regime drastically reduced the number of voluntary associations and organizations from over 60,000 to only 683. Whatever their interests, their members now not only had to demonstrate public support for official policies, they had to carry them out actively. The Sokol received special attention, especially after the parade to open the Eleventh Sokol Congress (June 19–27, 1948). The marching Sokols openly demonstrated their respect and sympathy for Beneš and their disdain for Gottwald, and the police arrested dozens before the parade ended. On July 9 the government ordered the Sokol organization purged. Beneš's funeral on September 8, 1948, also saw clashes between the security forces and opponents, giving added impetus to the Sokol purges, which ended in November 1948. By then, some 15,000 functionaries had been expelled. Trade unions also changed from organizations defending the workers' interests into transmission belts for the Communist Party's policies, many of which directly harmed the standard of living or working conditions of the working class. The ROH and its constituent branches became essentially part of the state administration.

The Communist Party expertly generated public expressions of approval, which it then touted as proof that the party had popular support. That was for public consumption: within the party, the leaders knew that the communists did not have the "support of the masses." Party leaders sought accurate information about public opinion from the party organizations and the organs of state security. It also tried to shape that opinion. As early as February 24, 1948, the Central Committee presidium banned the import of "reactionary" foreign newspapers and journals, and censored press and radio through its Press Section. The Press Section laid down the line for editors of journals, newspapers, the radio, and the press agency, trusting to party discipline and existential fear (editors were held personally responsible for trespasses) to enforce adherence. Party censorship was replaced in 1953 with a state censorship office, the Main Administration of Press Supervision. With the strictly controlled mass media presenting only the party line, the population had to rely on clandestinely followed broadcasts of Western radio stations such as the BBC, Voice of America, and especially (after 1950) Radio Free Europe.[11]

May Day parade on Wenceslas Square, 1953. (ČTK photo)

After 1948, Czechoslovak scholarship and research was oriented exclusively toward the Soviet example, as the iron curtain cut off contacts with Western scholars. Czechoslovak science was remodeled following Soviet patterns: in 1950 scientific research was centralized, leading to the creation of the Czechoslovak Academy of Sciences (ČSAV) two years later.[12] Soviet-style "socialist realism" now was the measure for all artistic production. The party denounced anything not actively supporting socialist realism as influenced by "class enemies." Independent artistic associations and groups gave way to single organizations, such as the Czechoslovak Writers' Union (March 1949). The Minister of Education and first head of the ČSAV, Zdeněk Nejedlý, presided over a perverse return to earlier attitudes to the role of culture. The officially approved view of Czech history linked the "popular democratic" present with the nationalist past. Nejedlý asserted: "Today Hus would have been the head of a political party, and his tribune would not have been the pulpit, but Prague's Lucerna Cafe or Wenceslas Square. And his party would have been very close, of this we may be certain, to us Communists."[13]

The "Sharp Course Against Reaction"

Force accompanied all these transformations and the inevitable resistance they evoked. The emergence of an economic crisis in the summer of 1948 led Gottwald and Rudolf Slanský to proclaim a "sharp course against reaction." Law 231 of 1948, "for the Protection of the People's Democratic Republic," provided a legal fig leaf for the liquidation of opposition. Loss of employment, forcible relocation, assignment to forced labor camps (TNPs), and trials were the lot of thousands. Estimates place the number sentenced to imprisonment at around 230,000, with another 100,000 sent administratively to the TNPs. The use of illegal methods, trials, and terror remained a feature of the regime throughout its existence, but during the first years they reached unusual proportions, leaving no level of society untouched.

The period of full-scale terror included a series of political trials.[14] One of the earliest involved General Heliodor Píka, leader of the wartime Czechoslovak military delegation to Moscow. His case interested the Soviet Union because he had firsthand knowledge of the situation in Moscow and relationships within the émigré community during the war. Sentenced to death in January 1949, Píka was executed in June. Other military trials and purges followed, accounting for the removal of nearly

5,000 Czechoslovak officers representing "bourgeois elements" by 1950.[15] The major trial of political opponents centered on Milada Horáková, a ranking National Socialist Party official. The trial, from May 31 to June 8, 1950, exhibited all the trappings of earlier Soviet show trials, including extorted confessions and a carefully crafted scenario. It reflected the arrival of the first of many Soviet advisers, sent to help their Czechoslovak comrades search for class enemies.[16] Horáková and three other defendants received the death sentence, carried out on June 27, 1950, in spite of international appeals for clemency.

The year 1950 also saw a crackdown on the Catholic church, which the communist regime viewed as one of its most serious opponents. Originally the communists hoped to create a pliable national Catholic movement, but they were disappointed.[17] On March 13–14, 1950, 429 monastic houses were raided by the police, and some 2,000 former monks were herded off to special prison monasteries. Women's institutions received the same treatment from the end of July to the beginning of August, and 10,000 nuns ended in internment cloisters. Trials of bishops and other church functionaries followed, and even Archbishop Josef Beran was isolated in the archbishop's palace in June 1949. Imprisoned from 1950 until 1963, he was released to go to Rome to receive his cardinal's hat, on condition that he never return.[18]

The true masterpiece among the political trials of this era—and the main objective of the Soviet advisers in Czechoslovakia—was a trial of class enemies within the Communist Party itself. After the Tito-Stalin split in 1948 (in which Czechoslovakia loyally supported the Soviets), Stalin and his local emulators ferreted out actual or potential "Titos" elsewhere. In the process, rivalries and old scores could be settled with Soviet approval and participation. No single pattern holds true for all communist purge trials, but comrades who fought in the Spanish Civil War, Western or domestic resistance, Yugoslav partisan detachments, or had other Western connections were likely candidates for arrest. In Czechoslovakia, "bourgeois nationalism" was also discovered in the KSS. Finally, many of the accused were Jews, reflecting the anti-Semitism (disguised as anti-Zionism or anti-cosmopolitanism) that marked Stalin's last years.

First to fall in Czechoslovakia were the Slovak "bourgeois nationalists," Vladimír Clementis, Husák, Novomeský, and Šmidke, who were dropped from the central committee in 1950 and later expelled. In October 1950, Oto Šling, head of the Brno party organization, was arrested, to be joined by some twenty other local officials. Arrests spread into the ranks of the State Security forces, and by February 1951 swept up such highly placed individuals as Marie Švermová, widow of the communist wartime resistance hero Jan Šverma, and the expelled Slovaks Clementis, Husák, and Novomeský. Further arrests included deputy ministers Bedřich Reicin (Defense), Karel Šváb (Interior), and Josef Smrkovský (Agriculture).

The purge still had not netted a genuine "big fish," a party official significant enough to be the logical key to a conspiratorial organization suitable for a purge trial. Eventually, the choice settled on the general secretary, Slánský, among the most strident in denouncing the comrades arrested earlier. Slánský's arrest at the end of November 1951 completed the cast for the greatest Czechoslovak purge trial. After a year of preparation including extreme physical and psychological torture, the trial opened on November 20, 1952. Slánský and thirteen co-defendants, following a carefully rehearsed scenario, pleaded guilty to an improbable range of treasonous activities, while more than 8,000 resolutions flooded in demanding death for the accused. The sentences did not disappoint the "will of the masses:" eleven defendants, including Slánský, received the death penalty and only three escaped with life imprisonment.[19]

Slánský's execution did not immediately end the Czechoslovak purge trials, which continued through 1953 and 1954. One of the last major purge trials involved the remaining Slovak "bourgeois nationalists" (Clementis had been included in the Slánský trial). Held in April 1954, it resulted in a life sentence for Husák and lengthy prison terms for other defendants. When Stalin and Gottwald died within days of each other in March 1953, however, it was the beginning of the end of the great political trials. The purges left deep traces on Czechoslovak society and the KSČ. In the meantime, the Czechoslovak party leadership had to cope with a second internal crisis, a consequence of the economic transformations under way since 1948.

Transforming the Economy

Immediately after seizing power the communists started dismantling the Czechoslovak private sector. Further nationalization transferred to state ownership enterprises with more than fifty employees as well as all firms in wholesale trade, building, export-import, typesetting, and travel. They joined the heavy-industrial and mining sectors, already nationalized in 1945, and were followed by private craftsmen and traders. By the end of 1949 more than 95 percent of employees in the industrial sector worked for the state. The free market was replaced by the planned economy, following the Soviet example and using Soviet experts. Beginning in February 1949 an extensive economic bureaucracy headed by the State Planning Office replaced the Central Planning Commission set up to direct the two-year postwar recovery program. The ROH worked to ensure that production targets were met, instead of defending the workers. Methods of worker mobilization used during the Soviet Five-Year Plans of the 1930s, such as "socialist competition" and "shock workers" like the Soviet hero Stakhanov, were also introduced.

Gottwald's promise that "we will not build kolkhozes in Czechoslovakia" notwithstanding, the regime began agricultural collectivization in 1949. Private farmers were herded into Unified Agricultural Cooperatives (JZDs) using all methods of persuasion. Renewed pressure in 1952–53 was followed by a third round from 1955 to 1958. As a result, the proportion of small and medium farmers in the population declined from 15.7 percent in the Czech lands and 32.2 in Slovakia in 1948 to only 2.1 and 6.8 percent by 1958. Over 80 percent of all villages had JZDs. Collectivization failed to improve productivity, but its main purpose was political, not economic. It broke the resistance of a recalcitrant social group, while freeing labor for industry.

In 1949 Czechoslovakia adopted its first Five-Year Plan. That same year the Soviet Union created the Council for Mutual Economic Assistance (CMEA or Comecon) to coordinate economic policies and relations among the states in its bloc. In an international atmosphere marked by the Berlin Crisis in 1948–49 and the outbreak of the Korean War in 1950, Czechoslovakia found itself cut off from its remaining Western trading partners and tied to the economies of relatively less developed states. Within the CMEA, Czechoslovakia was to be the machine-building power, emphasizing heavy industry.[20] Stalin also demanded the expansion of bloc military power after 1950. By 1953 the Czechoslovak armed forces had more than doubled in size, to some 230,000 men. The needs of the army had priority during those years, and it remained a significant institution and economic factor even after the creation of the Warsaw Pact in 1955. Between 1950 and 1953 the military ate up approximately one-third of the total production of Czechoslovakia's machine-building sector.

These demands distorted Czechoslovak economic development by creating industrial capacity that far outstripped domestic demand and the supply of raw materials. Scarce investments went into mining coal or other ores that under market conditions would have been unprofitable. Geological research also received support, especially after Stalin informed the Czechoslovak leadership that the country had untapped mineral wealth and should no longer rely on importing raw materials from the West. Finally, resources were poured into developing old and creating new metallurgical complexes. Such enterprises swallowed up capital and energy, leaving other sectors of the economy, especially consumer goods and services, starved for resources and manpower. As a result of these strains and the effects of collectivization, the First Five-Year Plan began to crumble, especially after 1950. By 1952 the party was preparing a currency reform to deal with the looming problems of supplying the population with food and other goods. Against this backdrop of rising economic difficulties, the news arrived that Josef Stalin had died, on March 5, 1953.

SOCIALISM— WITH WHAT KIND OF FACE?

Stalin's death highlighted a paradox in the relationship between the KSČ leadership and its Soviet counterparts. Unswerving obedience to Moscow had been a categorical imperative for the Czechoslovak party for decades, but now the winds from the East were blowing dangerous changes. Separating the high party and state offices was easy enough after Gottwald's convenient death on March 14, and he was replaced by an irreproachably "collective" leadership with Antonín Zápotocký as president, Široký as prime minister, and Antonín Novotný as general secretary. Other aspects of Moscow's "New Course" proved harder to adopt. More emphasis on consumer goods, and especially ending the worst abuses of police power, were popular ideas. But they created difficulties for leaders who had belonged to the top echelons of the party during Czechoslovakia's purges and the first phase of "socialist construction."

After Stalin Without De-Stalinization

Initially the Czechoslovak leaders continued along previously mapped paths. On May 30, 1953, they announced the currency reform.

Each citizen could exchange 300 crowns at a rate of 5:1, the remainder of cash savings at the rate of 50:1, and bank deposits at a somewhat better rate. A single retail price structure was introduced, and wages and prices were converted to the new currency at the rate of 5:1. The currency reform liquidated most people's savings and wiped out the real rise in wages since 1948. The reaction was the widest wave of public protests and strikes against the regime yet seen, affecting more than one hundred factories, including the great Škoda works in Plzeň. Approximately 20,000 people took to the streets there, and the army and People's Militia had to be called out to disperse the demonstrators.

The iron fist suppressed the demonstrations, but the regime ignored this signal that the party was dangerously out of touch with the people. Only after the new Soviet leadership invited Zápotocký to Moscow in July 1953 did the party debate policy changes. In Moscow the Soviets criticized Czechoslovakia for unrealistic planning targets and overemphasis on heavy industry—that is, exactly what they had demanded earlier. When a Czechoslovak "New Course" was finally proclaimed in September it focused largely on the economy. Heavy industry was to be limited, and more attention paid to consumer goods and agriculture to improve the people's living standard. In addition, following the Soviet example, the KSČ promised a more cautious approach to collectivization and a strict observance of "socialist legality."

Zápotocký made critical remarks about collectivization during 1953, and promised that those who wanted to could leave the JZDs. As a result, he became popularly identified with the "New Course," which the central committee confirmed in October. This reorientation, including price cuts on 20,000 items, finally improved ordinary people's living standard. As the last purge trials came to an end, the party successfully staged a mass gymnastics display, the Spartakiáda, which met with a favorable public reaction, even though it was clearly a socialist surrogate for the banned Sokol's congresses.

Hopes for a permanent change were soon disappointed. The New Course did not alter the direction of the Czechoslovak economy, dominated by the machine-building sector, even though demand for arms production and heavy industry within the CMEA declined. Instead, Czechoslovakia had to search for markets elsewhere, especially among developing countries. The political trials continued into 1954. The party presidium did set up an official commission to investigate the purge trials (June 1955), but its main concern was to avoid rehabilitating the leading accused. The farmers who had left the JZDs in droves were driven back into them by the new wave of collectivization beginning in 1955.

As a symbol of continuing commitment to Stalinism, the Czechoslovak party unveiled its socialist-realist masterpiece, a mammoth statue of Stalin overlooking Prague, in May 1955. Speeches eulogized the dear departed for his multifaceted genius, and the new leadership basked in Stalin's reflected glory. Apparently, by making the minimally necessary economic changes they had weathered the effects of Stalin's death. They did not know that Stalin's successor, Nikita S. Khrushchev, was preparing to cause even more serious turmoil. At the Twentieth Congress of the CPSU in February 1956, Khrushchev delivered his famous "Secret Speech" denouncing Stalin's "cult of personality" and abuse of police power. For the Czechoslovak leadership Soviet de-Stalinization came at a most inconvenient time. Adulation and imitation of Stalin's genius legitimized the communist regime in Czechoslovakia: was that now to be taken away? Khrushchev's denunciation focused on Stalin's abuse of the secret police and purges of the Soviet Communist party. When the special commission's report on the trials had not yet been released, when pressure was building from the Czechoslovak victims' relatives, the "Secret Speech" must have seemed like a stab in the back.

It was not long before Khrushchev's speech was widely available via Western radio, clandestine leaflet drops, or other means, so the party could not keep it an internal matter. The response inside the KSČ ranged from outrage on the part of stubborn Stalinists to disillusionment and dismay from former true believers. The CPSU's Twentieth Party Congress stimulated the desire for change in some of the "transmission-belt" organizations. The formally non-communist parties and the Catholic church increased their activity. The trade unions, unimpeachably working class and the largest interest group in the country, raised the need to assert the workers' interests more directly. The Czechoslovak Youth League (ČSM) began to revolt against its insignificant position and the passivity and apathy of the younger generation. The university students demanded freedom of intellectual inquiry, a free press, reduction of required study of Marxism-Leninism, and freedom to travel. They publicized their criticisms in a satirical carnival parade, a threat that finally captured the party's attention.[21]

The Czechoslovak Writers' Union seemed likely to become a significant force for change. Already in 1955 writers had begun questioning party control, calling for creative liberty and an end to censorship. After

While it lasted, the largest monument to Stalin in the Soviet Bloc stood in Prague, photographed May 4, 1955. (ČTK photo)

Khrushchev's speech, their restiveness assumed political tones. The union's second congress met from April 22 to 29, 1956. Poets František Hrubín and Jaroslav Seifert (later a Nobel laureate) demanded not only freedom of artistic expression but the right to criticize political and so cial conditions. As so often in the past, the intellectuals assumed for themselves the role of "conscience of the nation."

Pressure mounted within the KSČ for a special congress to deal with de-Stalinization. The leadership responded by proclaiming at the beginning of May that discussions of the Twentieth Party Congress were over. The party headed off pressure for a special congress by summoning instead a statewide party conference, where delegates were chosen by the apparatus, not elected by the membership. The conference, which met in June, called for a number of cosmetic changes in the bureaucracy, economic administration, and factories.

Events in neighboring Poland and Hungary seemed to confirm that the KSČ had been right to close discussions and limit changes. Riots in

Poland in June led to the "Polish October," bringing the purged Włady-sław Gomułka to power. More seriously, discontent in Hungary erupted in clashes on October 23 between the people and Hungarian security forces, backed by Soviet troops. A full-fledged rebellion followed, as another purge victim, Imre Nagy, tried to steer Hungary out of the War-saw Pact. A Soviet invasion in November crushed Hungary's uprising. Novotný and other KSČ party leaders were in the vanguard of those urging the Soviets to intervene, even offering units of the Czechoslovak army for the purpose. In the autumn of 1956, the Czechoslovak party returned to conservative policies.

The KSČ leadership was too thoroughly and too recently implicated in the purges to accept serious de-Stalinization. The very ferocity of the Czechoslovak purges also meant that no figure with the stature of a Gomułka or Nagy survived to lead a reformist party faction. Wider pop-ular mobilization was also weak: the efforts since 1953 to increase the standard of living for the masses paid off now in their fundamental qui-escence. Thus conflicts between the party and its critics remained rela-tively isolated and never coalesced into nationwide pressure for change. By the autumn of 1957 the party seemed firmly in control.[22]

The fallout of the 1956 events included a campaign against "revi-sionism." Purges of Czech intellectuals and functionaries, of Slovak "Trotskyists," and supporters of Yugoslavia, whose relations with the Soviet bloc worsened after a brief reconciliation in 1955, removed fig-ures who had spoken up too loudly in 1956. The commission's report in 1957 on the trials confirmed the sentences with only a few exceptions. After Zápotocký's death on November 13, 1957, Novotný was elected president while remaining party secretary, concentrating the top offices in one man's hands. A purge of "politically and socially unreliable ele-ments" in economic administration cost thousands of non-party experts their jobs. They would be missed when their "reliable" replacements attempted to carry out the economic reforms of 1958.

These reform proposals, submitted to the Eleventh Party Congress in June 1958, sought to decentralize the economy. The reforms set target figures for vital products, leaving the plant managers to decide how to allocate the rest of their enterprise's productive capacity. Though implic-itly accepting market forces (managers would produce products for which there was demand), the reform concentrated only on the decision-making process, leaving the rest of the command economy untouched. At the same time the last phase of collectivization reinforced centralizing trends. Initially the 1958 reforms had positive results, thanks to investment in production, but they lost momentum in an atmosphere of suspicion of "revisionism" and renewed centralization, and by 1962 they were effectively dead.[23]

Novotný and his fellow leaders celebrated their negotiation of 1956's challenges and getting back in step with the CPSU by approving a new constitution in 1960. Modeled on Stalin's Soviet constitution of 1936, it enshrined the "leading role of the party" in society, the state, and the economy. It also proclaimed that Czechoslovakia had reached socialism (a step beyond "people's democracy") and changed the country's name to the Czechoslovak Socialist Republic (ČSSR). At the same time an administrative reform further reinforced centralization, removing Slovakia's status as a separate administrative unit. The party conference also discussed the Third Five-Year Plan (1961–65), which was to complete constructing socialism. Instead, Czechoslovakia fell into further crises, in which one of the major causes was the failure of the economic plan adopted with such fanfare in 1960.

Pressures for Change

The Czechoslovak reform movement that emerged during the 1960s and swept up the whole society in 1968 did not arise solely out of chronic economic difficulties. Under the rhetoric of building socialism, Czechoslovakia harbored other forces that contributed to the regime's new crisis in 1968. Some of these forces were familiar and had only been covered over by the measures used to survive the crisis of 1956. Others were the logical consequence of processes that the system itself had set into motion.

To a certain extent the outward calm of the years between 1958 and 1967 corresponded to life as lived by Czechoslovak citizens.[24] Certainly their lives were becoming safer. Though political arrests continued at a relatively high rate, and the organs of state security observed suspicious persons and groups assiduously, the irrational terror of the worst Stalinist years receded. In addition to becoming somewhat more secure, life was becoming more comfortable. Personal consumption per capita had risen yearly since 1953, and by the middle of the decade food consumption exceeded prewar levels. The system of medical care and health insurance was nearly universal by the end of the 1950s. In spite of efforts since 1955 to undo wage equalization, Czechoslovak society still reflected narrow income differentials.

Lifestyles, too, were basically similar. Goods were scarce and limited in variety and quality, except for the lucky few who, thanks to position or connections, had access to the stores called Darex (later Tuzex) where Western goods could be purchased for special coupons. Family income depended basically on the number of employed family members. Thus not only the regime's official endorsement of gender equality but also economic necessity brought thousands of women into the labor force. Nevertheless, women usually earned lower wages than men and still found themselves primarily responsible for the family and household. State-provided creches and kindergartens helped but were inadequate to meet the need for child care. The insufficient distribution system added to this double burden, since finding even daily necessities frequently became a time-consuming chore, eating into work and family life.

By the 1960s, many Czechoslovak citizens had accumulated savings and could spend them on durable consumables. Labor-saving domestic items or leisure-enhancing products led the way, when available.[25] By the beginning of the 1960s one-third of the nonagricultural population left their homes for the weekend and spent their holidays away. Many of them traveled abroad, even to the West. Czechoslovakia by the 1960s was becoming a modern industrial society—not in consumption but in demand. This failure of a system trumpeted in official propaganda as achieving genuine socialism was a growing contradiction. Unrealized demand for housing, automobiles, and other consumer goods, and a rising savings level were its symptoms, and contributed to public support for reforms as Czechoslovakia's economy stumbled in 1962.

Another source of pressure for change was the arrival in the 1960s of a new generation, growing up under communism. Members of this postwar generation (by 1965, 60 percent of the citizens of employable age and almost half of all citizens) daily faced the contradiction between official slogans and the way the system actually functioned. Official stress on technical and traditional education placed them in influential positions in industrial centers and in the countryside, where new agro-technical professions employed graduates in the JZDs. In its attitudes toward the regime, this generation differed from the "new intelligentsia" that had risen at the beginning of the 1950s directly from the working class, earning its qualifications on the way. The "new intelligentsia" was still a source of system support and a potential brake on reform, but members of the younger generation criticized the contradictions they saw and supported reform. Members of this generation were also too young to have been actively involved in the purge trials whose legacy still hung over the party.

Discussion of the trials was closed, but in an amnesty to mark the 1960 constitution many later victims (including Husák) were released, though not rehabilitated. Then, at the Twenty-second Congress of the CPSU (October 1961), Khrushchev reopened the attack on Stalin, prompting the KSČ leaders to decide to accept Khrushchev's policies— ironically, only shortly before Khrushchev's own ouster in 1964. Their delayed de-Stalinization included the removal of Gottwald's body from its mausoleum, and the destruction in 1962, supposedly because of foundation problems, of the giant Stalin monument in Prague. Streets, squares, and factories named in honor of the Soviet dictator were once more rechristened.

Meanwhile, the purge trials still influenced internal power struggles. In 1962 the head of the trials commission, Rudolf Barák, was arrested and imprisoned for embezzlement. By ousting Barák (who could have collected incriminating material during his investigation), Novotný rid himself of a potentially dangerous challenger. Novotný then appointed a new investigating commission chaired by Drahomír Kolder, central committee secretary. Only a very general preliminary report was presented to the Twelfth Party Congress in December 1962, and when the Kolder commission's final report was released in 1963, it had been repeatedly edited. Novotný survived its revelations and criticisms by sacrificing the remaining pre-1948 Old Guard, among them the KSS leader, whose replacement was Alexander Dubček.[26] Dropping the Old Guard shattered the continuity at the top characteristic of the KSČ since the death of Stalin. Many of the new figures were not bound to Novotný by shared complicity in the purges. This prepared the ground for the emergence of divisions within the party, as the KSČ struggled to cope with the country's economic problems and continuing social pressure for change.

Signs of economic trouble emerged in 1961, and by 1962 Novotný had to admit that the Third Five-Year plan and the economic reforms of 1958 were failures. Novotný blamed the managers, and argued for a complete recentralization of the economy. Economic growth slowed drastically under provisional one-year plans until in 1963 and 1964 it declined. Novotný blamed the Cuban and Berlin crises (1961 and 1962), declining world prices for uranium, and the collapse of trade with China after the Sino-Soviet split.[27] Within the party, however, the idea grew that the problem lay deeper, within the planned economy itself. Economic criticism had been voiced for some time, frequently (because of press controls) in magazines supposedly covering literature and the arts. Now the leadership turned to its critics to help it out of the crisis. One of the most critical economists, Ota Šik, headed a commission to prepare a new economic reform.

Šik's commission produced a New System of Economic Management, which was approved by the party central committee in 1965. The commission had to decide whether to reform the existing management system or create a new one, and whether market forces could be adapted to the socialist planned economy. Supporters of adapting the market won the argument, and the proposals approved in 1965 left the plan deciding only the basic direction of the economy, with market forces replacing the previous detailed instructions. Enterprises were to be granted freedom to compete, and their production was to be influenced by factors like demand and production costs. Fulfillment of the plan no longer constituted managerial success, which together with wages would now be measured by gross enterprise income.[28]

Adopting the reform program proved easier than putting it into effect. Initial measures in industry and construction were implemented in 1966, and restructuring of wholesale prices in 1967. When the immediate results were negative, the government responded with administrative interventions, and opponents of reform returned to the offensive. Šik's commission never completely implemented its reforms, but they were one of the most daring efforts to combine planning and the market in the entire Soviet bloc. The economic debates and public discussions also raised awareness of the political obstacles to reform.[29]

In Slovakia the economic situation interacted with other sources of discontent. Slovak industrialization was one aim of the government's economic policy. After early gains, the doldrums arrived in the early 1960s, and Novotný's reputation for having a personal antipathy to Slovakia and Slovaks made the situation seem another example of the Czechs' colonial attitude. The released "bourgeois nationalists," especially Husák, bitterly resented Novotný's continued hold on power. The removal of the Old Guard Slovaks opened the way for new faces such as Dubček and Jozef Lénart, the prime minister, to rise to leading positions. These Slovak leaders placed themselves at the head of pressures from Slovak society demanding changes.[30]

Under this combination of pressures, the Czechoslovak regime underwent a hesitant and reluctant liberalization. The KSČ maintained the appearance of unity and its own centralized control, but in reality it was a fragile structure. By the mid-1960s even party members in government positions quarreled with Novotný over the makeup and duties of their offices, the parliament asserted more power, and the non-communist parties in the National Front tried to stretch their atrophied muscles. Similar attitudes appeared in the national committees, the churches, the trade unions, the ČSM, among the national minorities, and the students.

The fourth congress of the Writers' Union in June 1967 gave concrete expression to the desire for change. Already young people, at the fifth congress of the ČSM earlier that month, had complained about the youth organization's monopoly. The Arab-Israeli Six-Day War led to an official anti-Israeli campaign, following Moscow's line against the public's sympathies. In protest the popular Slovak journalist and writer Ladislav Mňačko refused to return to Czechoslovakia from a visit to Israel. His colleagues at the fourth congress attacked the regime's policies, its record during the 1950s, its claim to absolute authority, and its monopoly of cultural life. Milan Kundera bluntly declared that "any interference with freedom of thought and words . . . is a scandal in the twentieth century and a shackle on our emerging literature." Ludvík Vaculík claimed that "not a single human problem . . . has yet been solved" by communism in Czechoslovakia.[31] The party's official delegation walked out. Novotný's response was to punish individual writers and transfer the union's journal, *Literární noviny* (Literary News), to the Ministry of Culture. Divisions in the party leadership showed, however, when at the Central Committee meetings on September 26–27, 1967, four members voted against a crackdown.[32]

Novotný's supporters saw excessive liberalization, the machinations of émigrés and foreign intelligence agencies, and a few intellectual malcontents as the problem. Their solution was a return to strict centralized control by the party. The alternative response focused on defects in the system, and claimed that the party had to "lead, not direct" society.[33] Novotný bluntly expressed his views during a number of speeches beginning in 1966 and continuing through 1967. When Dubček contradicted some of their key themes at the Central Committee meetings on October 30–31, Novotný accused him of being "in the grip of certain narrow national interests."[34] Other Central Committee members criticized Novotný's own leadership, however, and only the decision to adjourn and reconvene in December cut short the chorus. A showdown over power loomed, with Novotný facing an unlikely coalition of the entire KSS apparatus, the regional party organizations in Moravia, and a large part of the apparatus in Bohemia. Behind them stood the disaffected intellectuals, the Slovaks, and the economic reformers. No single party institution fully supported Novotný.

The public, unaware of what was happening, paid more attention to the "Strahov events." Repeated cuts in electric power sparked off a spontaneous demonstration on October 30 by the students housed in the dormitories on Strahov hill, overlooking the Lesser Town. Students took to the streets with candles in their hands to protest the conditions under which they lived and studied.[35] Police forcibly broke up the march, provoking waves of student meetings that spread to other educational institutions. The press and even the Prague newsreels began to cover these events with an openness unthinkable even a few months before.

Novotný could not respond with force, at least until the internal party power struggle was resolved. Novotný's opponents, for their part, found this public discontent potentially useful. With the battle lines clearly drawn, Novotný sought Soviet support. CPSU General Secretary Leonid I. Brezhnev visited Prague on December 8 and 9, just before the meeting of the presidium. Brezhnev discovered that the divisions within the KSČ top echelons ran deeper than he had been led to believe. He decided, after private consultations with a range of Czechoslovak party leaders, that Novotný's position was untenable, but he declined to anoint a successor in advance, reportedly saying *"Eto vashe delo* (It's your affair)."[36]

The next meeting of the central committee began on December 19, 1967. The discussions proved that there was a significant group in favor of what was delicately termed the "division of functions." Novotný would have to give up either his party position or the presidency. The meeting in December postponed a decision until January 3, 1968, by which time the presidium and a newly formed central committee consultative group should have agreed on Novotný's successor. They settled on a dark horse candidate, Alexander Dubček. On January 5, 1968, he was duly elected first secretary of the KSČ.[37]

THE PRAGUE SPRING, 1968

Dubček's election in January 1968 symbolizes the beginning of the Czechoslovak experiment in reformed socialism known as the

"Prague Spring." At first glance, Dubček might seem an unlikely person to become the embodiment of efforts to create a humane form of socialism in keeping with Czechoslovak political and cultural traditions. Born in 1921 in eastern Slovakia, Dubček was taken as a child to the Soviet Union where his communist parents emigrated to help construct "Socialism in One Country." Returning to Czechoslovakia in 1938, he joined the illegal Communist Party and served in the underground and the Slovak National Uprising. By 1951 he was a member of the KSS central committee, and after studies in Moscow he became a member of the KSČ central committee and leader of the KSS in 1962. Little-known to the public at large, his lack of personal ostentation and genuine sincerity won him wide support from a citizenry that was initially highly skeptical.[38]

Reform and Its Limits

Novotný's opponents had removed him from the top party post, but their position was far from dominant. It strengthened somewhat when Novotný resigned the presidency on March 22 (on May 30 he was formally expelled from the party), to be replaced by Svoboda. More importantly, Dubček's leadership replaced many Novotný supporters at the local and regional levels. Once again a commission, headed by presidium member Jan Piller, was set up to review the Czechoslovak political trials. Its recommendations included the immediate dismissal of those implicated in the purges, and the dropping of anyone who had been in the central leadership since the Ninth Party Congress (1949).[39] The culmination of personnel changes would have come at the extraordinary Fourteenth Party Congress, but events changed that.

Dubček's leadership took a dramatic step when on March 4, 1968, it adopted several decrees affecting censorship. The Main Administration of Press Supervision, whose purview had been extended in 1966 to include radio and television, lost control of the broadcast media. The party also ordered it to apply the strict letter of the press law, which made editors-in-chief responsible for content. This measure dismantled prior censorship, and the mass media, carefully and then increasingly enthusiastically, took advantage of the change to discuss many previously taboo subjects. As a result, not only the party rank-and-file but the general non-party public began to take notice. What had seemed originally to be little more than an internal party power struggle began to look like a genuine change.[40]

Reformists had to control and direct this growing public support, while setting out a program that would not provoke a Hungarian-style Soviet response. With Novotný out of the way, Lenárt was replaced as prime minister by Oldřich Černík, reputed to be a pragmatic economic reformer, and Smrkovský, jailed for "economic sabotage" during the purges of the 1950s, became speaker of the national assembly. The Central Committee adopted the blueprint for the new policies, the "Action Program," on April 5, 1968, and the National Assembly approved it at the beginning of May.

The Action Program called for the revival of the National Front and the acceptance of disagreement and debate within it, the legal guarantee of "freedom of speech for minority views and opinions," freedom of movement including travel abroad, and better legal guarantees of the personal rights and property of citizens. It also called for the full rehabilitation of victims of "legal transgressions in previous years." In spite of these calls for a more pluralistic political order, however, the Action Program (as well as speeches by party leaders in April and succeeding months) also reflected the limits in the party's approach to change. The Action Program reaffirmed the "leading role of the party," though now the party was to "win over all workers by systematic persuasion and the personal examples of communists."[41] Thus the KSČ's Action Program did not accept any challenge to the monopoly of the Communist Party. That said, the idea that the party's leading role would rest on the voluntary cooperation of the people was drastic enough to upset conservatives in Czechoslovakia and its neighbors.[42]

The Action Program's economic clauses called for returning initiative to the enterprises, liberalizing foreign trade, and reducing the role of state planning. It also called for attention to the "right of consumers to determine their consumption patterns and lifestyles," as well as workers' rights to defend their interests.[43] But nothing like a return to capitalism was envisioned. Economic planners thus faced the challenge of how to square the circle, harmonizing market forces with elements of the centrally planned system. Šik proposed using interest rates and credit to influence enterprise behavior, while gross enterprise income (not gross output, as heretofore, or profit, as under capitalism) would measure performance. The Action Program allowed a limited return to small-scale private enterprise, but larger enterprises remained state-owned. Workers' councils would provide the entrepreneurial spirit in these enterprises, though Šik and his supporters initially favored the managerial, white-collar workers. Šik's team expected some unemployment from the shift to consumer goods, but hoped it could be absorbed by the expanded service sector. This threat of unemployment, together with the renewed move away from equalized wages, prompted some negative workers' reactions. No final set of policies had been established before the invasion, and in the end the reform economists' proposals for market socialism remained unrealized.[44]

The Action Program also addressed the Slovak question. It called for a "socialist federal arrangement" establishing the "legal coexistence of two equal nations in a common socialist state."[45] Such calls had already come from the SNR on March 14 and were echoed by the KSS on April 10. The Slovak comrades abandoned the asymmetrical system of administration and demanded a full federation. The Czech side saw federation as a way of resolving the Slovak question, giving greater weight to the other problems of reform. Most Slovak supporters of the Dubček regime put federation and national recognition at the top of their agenda.[46] Legislation federalizing the state was passed in the summer and went into effect on October 28, 1968.

The first months changed the public's initial reserved reaction to Dubček. The media, reveling in its new freedom, encouraged general engagement in society's problems. Intellectuals, including party members, issued statements supporting reforms and calling for further democratization. In contrast to 1956, when the intellectuals did not evoke a popular response, in 1968 civil society reemerged from the communist eclipse. The ROH replaced its pro-Novotný leadership under pressure from lower-level organizations, and new trade union branches proliferated under the old umbrella. Inside the ČSM and the NF things became lively again, and many new organizations sprang up. Some, such as the Sokol and the Scouts, had been outlawed by the party after 1948. Others reflected post-1948 experiences, such as Club 231, named after the law under which political victims were sentenced. The Club of Engaged Nonpartisans (KAN) represented Czechoslovakia's non-party activists, and the Preparatory Committee for the Czechoslovak Social Democracy set out to restore the social-democratic party.[47]

By May the original anti-Novotný coalition in the party no longer held together. Faced with the rapid reemergence of civil society and early signals of disquiet from abroad, some of the post-January leadership emphasized the dangers from the right. Vasil Bil'ak, Drahomír Kolder, and Alois Indra led the way. Against this backdrop of threatening sig-

Alexander Dubček's reception among the workers at the ČKD factory in 1968 reflected his genuine popularity among Czechoslovak citizens. (ČTK photo)

nals, Ludvík Vaculík published a manifesto entitled, "Two Thousand Words that Belong to Workers, Farmers, Officials, Scientists, Artists, and Everybody." The text, signed by seventy prominent writers and intellectuals, Olympic athletes, scientists, but also ordinary citizens, appeared on June 27, 1968, in three dailies and the Writers' Union weekly *Literární listy*.

The "Two Thousand Words" criticized the Communist Party for creating the crisis in Czechoslovakia, but also recognized that the party had begun the process of reform and renewal. It warned that lower-echelon leaders who still clung to power would resist changes, and urged citizens to put pressure on opponents of democratization by "public criticism, resolutions, demonstrations, demonstrative work brigades, collections to buy presents for them on their retirement, strikes, and picketing at their front doors." It also noted gathering clouds outside Czechoslovakia, but it promised the government that its citizens would "stand by it, with weapons if need be, if it will do what we give it a mandate to do."[48]

Such calls for grass-roots activity outside the party, and the audacious summons to armed support for the reform government, shocked even members of the Dubček leadership. The party condemned the manifesto and began a campaign against it and its signatories. This response did little to appease the even more shocked leaders of the Warsaw Pact, much less the Soviet Union. The "Two Thousands Words" acted as a catalyst for the Warsaw Pact meeting of July 1968, probably the point of no return for the Soviet determination to end the Prague Spring.[49] "By winter we will know all," the manifesto concluded. Events proved its forecast accurate.

The Road to Intervention

The "Two Thousand Words" may have marked the point of no return, but the "erosion of Soviet trust" in Dubček had begun long before.[50] When he replaced Novotný, Dubček was not well known either in the USSR or in the other Warsaw Pact countries. Initial reactions to his election were positive if for no other reason than his Russian childhood and his party studies in Moscow. First contacts with the bloc leaders also proceeded smoothly, although Dubček did not immediately go to Moscow. Before visiting the Soviets on January 29–30, Dubček met with Hungarian party leader János Kádár, whose skill at mollifying his own people while not running afoul of the Soviet Union he admired. Kádár, favorably impressed, called Dubček "a communist on every major issue without exception," but warned him that the Czechoslovak situation was viewed with concern in other quarters.[51]

Fortified by Kádár's support, Dubček flew to Moscow to meet with Soviet leaders who had already visited Poland and East Germany, where Gomułka and Ulbricht expressed concern over the situation in Czechoslovakia. Dubček reassured the Soviets that the party based all its policies on "friendship and alliance with the Soviet Union," and would protect the leading role of the party and preserve democratic centralism. Brezhnev for his part offered Dubček "total and absolute support" in coping with the "acutely critical internal problems" he and the party faced.[52]

With the Soviet and Czechoslovak leadership in apparent harmony, Dubček returned to Czechoslovakia. An early hint of dissonance came in late February, when Czechoslovakia celebrated the twentieth anniversary of "Victorious February." Dubček showed his speech to Brezhnev in advance, and the Soviet leader demanded changes. The final version was a tame affair, less critical of Novotný's regime and more restrained about mentioning new domestic or international departures.[53] At a Warsaw Pact meeting in Bulgaria on March 6–7, Dubček reassured his critics that the party had matters in hand. At the next meeting, in Dresden on March 23–24, the Soviet Politburo (alarmed by the collapse of censorship in Czechoslovakia and by Novotný's resignation) stepped up the pressure.[54] The Czechoslovak delegation was unprepared to discover that their country was the main item on the agenda. Gomułka and Ulbricht again voiced the harshest criticism, but even Kádár compared the Czechoslovak situation to "the Hungarian counter-revolution when it had not yet become a counter-revolution." Dubček denied that "counter-revolution" was imminent. The Polish and East German leaders' "bad cop" comments allowed the Soviet position to seem reasonable. Brezhnev hoped that Dubček would have "the desire, the willpower, and also the courage to implement the necessary actions" to prevent a deterioration of the situation.[55] A warning had been given in terms that no communist trained in the school of party life since Stalin could have missed.

Dubček concealed the shock of the Dresden meeting from the public and the party Presidium. Of course he did not want to add to public ferment when he and his leadership had to convince the Soviets that they were firmly in control. On the other hand, Dubček and his supporters therefore had to face rising external pressure, contain the most radical reformists, and head off their conservative domestic foes, without the support of an aroused citizenry behind its government. External pressure continued both publicly, as in East German ideologue Kurt Hager's speech on March 27, and privately, as in the personal letter to Dubček in April, supposedly from Brezhnev himself. Hager's speech caused a diplomatic protest, but the Presidium did not publicize the Soviet letter even within the party. It stepped up warnings against "anti-socialist excesses," trying to blunt the concerns of other Warsaw Pact members. Meanwhile, internal change was alarming local and regional potentates who felt threatened. The crowd's behavior at the traditional communist May Day parade reflected Dubček's personal popularity, but also the extent that civil society had reemerged outside the party's direct control.

Prompted by such visions, the Soviet Politburo held another round of consultations with Dubček, Černík, Bil'ak, and Smrkovský in Moscow on May 4–5. Brezhnev, Alexei Kosygin, and Nikolai Podgorny repeatedly asked what specific steps the Czechoslovak leaders would take to meet the threat of counter-revolution. Taken aback, the Czechoslovak leaders could only repeat that the party would control the situation through persuasion. The Soviets and Czechoslovaks also agreed on military exercises in Czechoslovakia in June. The Presidium meeting after Dubček's return resolved that the party had to regain control over the media and use the upcoming personnel changes at the Central Committee to eliminate "hostile elements."

On May 17, Kosygin arrived at Karlovy Vary, supposedly to take the mineral water cure, but actually to meet with virtually all leading party and state officials. Apparently favorably impressed, Kosygin approved the early summoning of the next party congress. Almost all the KSČ leaders were agreed on the need for an extraordinary congress, though they expected different outcomes. As delegate selection proceeded, however, it became clear that conservatives might have difficulty remaining in the leadership. The May plenum of the KSČ Central Committee formally called the congress for September 9, while promising to struggle against both the sins of "dogmatism" and the "rightist threat."

The Soviets considered the May plenum's results positive, and they approved the steps Dubček took to rein in the media, the NF, and other organizations. May had seen student demonstrations and other protest meetings, but nothing like the violent upheavals then convulsing Paris. The planned military exercises on Czechoslovak territory, code named "Šumava," took place officially from June 21 to June 30. In the end, some 24,000 men were involved, with the Soviet contingent numbering about 16,000.[56] The withdrawal of the Soviet troops dragged out until early August, contributing to the timing and impact of Vaculík's "Two Thousand Words."

The "Two Thousand Words" proved to the USSR that the situation had deteriorated since the end of May. On July 4 the Politburo invited the KSČ leadership to another summit in Warsaw. This harshly worded invitation called for the "normalization" of the situation, a phrase ominous in retrospect. Dubček declined, proposing instead a series of bilateral meetings. Eventually the five Warsaw Pact allies met without Czechoslovakia on July 13–14. They prepared a common letter echoing the concerns and language of the Soviet invitation, which the Soviet ambassador presented to Dubček on July 16. Two days later they published it, but only the Czechoslovak press carried Czechoslovakia's response, which refuted the charges of counter-revolution and proposed bilateral discussions.

The KSČ Presidium finally accepted a Soviet Politburo offer to meet at the Slovak village of Čierna nad Tisou, on the frontier with Soviet Ukraine, on July 29. The Čierna meetings went badly, as the Soviets attempted to break down the Presidium's unity. The invective from Ukrainian party leader Pyotr Shelest was so fierce that Dubček was reduced to tears and the Czechoslovak side left the room. In the end all agreed to hold a meeting of all six party leaderships to clear up the tension created by the Warsaw letter. This meeting, in Bratislava on August 3, adopted a joint communique expressing the right of socialist states to pursue their own road to socialism, while asserting that a threat to socialism in one state was a threat to all. During the meeting Bil'ak handed Shelest a secret letter, signed by five hardline KSČ members, calling on the Soviets to intervene in Czechoslovakia "with all the means at your disposal."[57]

In the ensuing days neither Brezhnev's personal appeals to Dubček nor visits by Ulbricht and Kádár worked a last-minute miracle. Convinced at last that Dubček could not be trusted, the Soviet leaders decided to intervene by force. On the night between August 20 and 21, military units of five Warsaw Pact states—East Germany, Poland, Hungary, Bulgaria, and the USSR—crossed Czechoslovakia's borders, while special Soviet forces seized the airport in Prague. "Operation Danube" had begun.

14 The Gray Years

As a purely military exercise, Operation Danube was a resounding success. If armed force is supposed to be deployed for political ends, however, the Warsaw Pact invasion of Czechoslovakia was at best only a qualified success, and only in the long run. In the short run it was a political disaster. The invasion masqueraded as "fraternal assistance" to Czechoslovak party officials who had appealed to the Soviet Union, with the support of the "healthy elements of the working masses." In fact, in a breathtaking display of national unity and resolve, ordinary Czechs and Slovaks met the invasion with nonviolent resistance on a scale that excited admiration the world over. In the days after August 21, none of the signers of the secret letter of invitation was willing publicly to assume the role of a Czechoslovak Kádár, and plans to install a new government had to be dropped. Instead, the Soviet leaders found themselves negotiating with the people they had invaded the country to overthrow. Eventually Dubček's team returned to their posts, but under military occupation and Soviet pressure there was little they could do to prevent the destruction of the Czechoslovak experiment in "socialism with a human face."

THE ONSET OF NORMALIZATION

The Warsaw Pact invasion of Czechoslovakia was the largest military operation in Europe since World War II, involving more than half a million soldiers, over 6,000 tanks, 800 airplanes, and some 2,000 artillery pieces, double the force used to crush the Hungarian revolution of 1956.[1] Entering the country by land and air, the invaders quickly neutralized the Czechoslovak army—which had received orders not to resist in any case—and seized their major objectives.[2] By the end of August 21, Czechoslovakia was in Soviet hands.

The Failure of Force

The invasion was planned to coincide with the usual KSČ Presidium meeting, scheduled for August 20. Bil'ak's hardline group planned to introduce a resolution of no-confidence in Dubček. If everything had gone as planned, the Presidium would have approved the intervention and announced a "Revolutionary Government of Workers and Peasants." Dubček stuck with the prepared agenda, however, which left Bil'ak's motion for later discussion. As a result, when news began to reach the Presidium about the invasion late on the night of August 20, heated arguments were still raging. Instead of approving Bil'ak's motion, the Presidium adopted a statement condemning the intervention as a contravention of "all principles governing relations between socialist states," and a violation of "the fundamental provisions of international law."[3]

Czechoslovak Radio broadcast the Presidium's statement, and it was published the next day. A flood of denunciations of the invasion followed, from such institutions as the National Assembly, the trade union organization, the Academy of Sciences, the Czechoslovak Union of Journalists, the Prague city organization of the KSČ, and others. The Soviet news agency countered with a statement (broadcast by the occupiers on their station, Radio Vltava) claiming that Czechoslovak "party and government figures" had asked the USSR and its allies for "immediate fraternal assistance," against "counter-revolutionary forces" and "external powers hostile to socialism."[4] The Czechoslovak declarations reinforced public opposition and gave the lie to the Soviet proclamation.

Bil'ak's failure on August 20–21 complicated the political progress of the invasion. The Soviets rounded up Dubček, Smrkovský, Černík, and František Kriegel, and spirited them out of the country. Fearing the attitude of the Czechoslovak people, the party hardliners hesitated to organize a collaborationist government. In mass demonstrations, as well as in spontaneous acts of wit and will, removing street names, house numbers, telephone books, or anything else that could help the occupiers locate their targets or control communications, the people expressed support for Dubček and his team. After their initial outrage, the public avoided all contact with the invaders, as expressed in the new-style Ten Commandments: "I don't know, I'm not acquainted, I won't tell, I don't have, I don't know how, I won't give, I cannot, I won't sell, I won't show, I won't do."[5] Czechs and Slovaks put their compulsory Russian study to use, arguing with the occupation soldiers and covering Prague and other towns with inscriptions and posters in Russian. Some reports claimed that the front-line troops had to be withdrawn and replaced with more reliable elements after a few days of such psychological warfare.[6]

The media, especially radio, supported the public's nonviolent but far from passive resistance. After the Soviets seized Czechoslovak Ra-

Soviet soldiers listen to Czech protests on Prague's streets, August 21, 1968. (ČTK photo)

dio's headquarters, broadcasters went underground, using regional broadcasting networks and systems prepared for civil defense. Underground newspapers also sprang up to challenge the occupiers' *Zprávy* (News). The free media played a key role in encouraging the people, publicizing foreign and domestic reactions to the invasion, calling for calm or summoning people to specific protest actions as necessary.[7]

A culminating act of defiance was the hasty convoking, under the nose of the occupying forces, of the Extraordinary Fourteenth Party Congress, which gathered in the ČKD works in Vysočany the day after the invasion. The Prague party organization summoned the delegates via clandestine radio broadcasts, and over 1,200 (more than half of the full complement) arrived. The Congress repudiated the "fraternal assistance" and demanded the immediate release of the interned government and party leaders. It called for a one-hour general strike the next day, and appealed to the world's communist parties for their support. Delegates elected a new, reformist Central Committee, with Dubček unanimously returned as party First Secretary.[8]

The total failure of the plan for a collaborationist government emerged during meetings called by Soviet Ambassador Chervonenko at the Soviet Embassy in Prague on August 22. The pro-Moscow leaders held a second meeting in the president's office in the Castle late that evening, at which Svoboda declared his willingness to go to Moscow to negotiate the return of the detained Czechoslovak leaders. Svoboda defended this as a tactical move, pointing out that Dubček and his supporters could be dismissed after they returned.[9] The Soviets had no acceptable alternative to discussions with the very leadership they had set out to remove.

Dubček Dismantles His Own Reform

After the invasion, Dubček and the other captured leaders were held incommunicado by the KGB, first in Poland and then in Ukraine. They reached Moscow on August 23, unaware that Svoboda's group had also arrived. Brezhnev and Kosygin tried to convince Dubček to accept the intervention, but he refused.[10] Dubček did not speak with the Soviet leaders again until August 26, but already on August 23 the Soviets held talks with Svoboda's delegation. They accepted Svoboda's demand that Dubček's team be returned, but insisted on repudiating the Fourteenth Party Congress. Kosygin spoke ominously of a "civil war" for which

Dubček and the other Czechoslovak leaders would be solely responsible.[11] Talks continued on August 26, this time including the imprisoned reformers (except Kriegel, who refused to participate) and more newly arrived Czechoslovak leaders, most of them hardliners. Angrily Brezhnev and Kosygin dismissed Dubček's and Černík's criticism of the invasion, and insisted on an agreement.

The Moscow Protocol was eventually signed on August 26, 1968, after negotiations in which the Soviets held every trump. The Czechoslovak side won some verbal concessions, but the fifteen-point document annulled the Extraordinary Fourteenth Party Congress, it promised to reimpose censorship and purge the party and state offices, it promised that there would be no reprisals against supporters of the invasion, and most significantly it made no mention of a timetable for troop withdrawals. Thus, although Dubček and his allies returned to their positions, the Moscow Protocol established a basis for achieving the political aim of the intervention: removing Dubček and dismantling the reform program.[12]

As they returned to Czechoslovakia on August 27, the party leaders stressed the need for unity and order. They presented the Moscow agreement in the best possible light, while keeping the full text secret. Dubček and Svoboda addressed the nation on the radio on the day of their return. President Svoboda spoke briefly, admitting that the last few days "have not been easy either for us or for you," and calling on the people to recognize the "political reality" of the occupation forces until conditions had become "normalized."[13] Dubček spoke several hours later, to an expectant audience. His words were heartfelt, broken by long pauses while he wrestled with his emotions, but his message was not reassuring. What Czechoslovakia needed, he said, was rapid "consolidation and normalization of conditions," a prerequisite for any change in the occupation. Dubček called on the people to show realism, "even if we have to carry out some temporary measures, limiting the degree of democracy and the freedom of speech that we have already achieved."[14] This was a call for the people to continue trusting their leaders, while also accepting the loss—temporarily, they were assured—of key aspects of the reforms.

Over the next two days, Černík and Smrkovský also addressed the public. Both emphasized order, discipline, and realism. Smrkovský in particular spoke plainly about the negotiations, called the "fraternal assistance" an occupation, and drew historical parallels: "Such things have happened more than once in Czech and Slovak history, and actually this is the second time it has happened in this century." The comparison to the Nazi occupation was obvious.[15]

In spite of this bitter pill, the population stayed remarkably united behind its leaders. Public opinion polls from September 1968 showed more than 90 percent of the people affirming their "complete confidence" in Svoboda, Dubček, Černík, and Smrkovský. They also supported preserving the Action Program and the post-January policies, expecting only minor changes. Even in Slovakia over 90 percent of the people rejected a return to the situation under Novotný.[16] However reluctantly, most Czechs and Slovaks conceded that there was little alternative to the results of Moscow. Hoping that Dubček and the other leaders would honor their people's trust in them, they ended their week of nonviolent resistance.

The immediate sacrifices paid for the leaders' return seemed bearable: KAN and K231 were closed down, control over the media tightened, and the Fourteenth Party Congress, which had concluded its work in one dramatic day, August 22, was declared invalid. Considering the conditions, it truly was "extraordinary," but it was—unavoidably— attended mostly by delegates from the Czech lands. Thus the separate congress of the Slovak party, scheduled for August 26, assumed great importance. It began the day before the delegation returned from Moscow, and at first approved the actions of the congress in Prague. Then Husák arrived. While calling the previous eight months "a great and bright period in the development of our party and our peoples," Husák insisted that the Vysočany congress could not be recognized because it lacked Slovak representation. In the end, the Slovak congress confirmed Husák as KSS secretary-general and disavowed the Fourteenth Party Congress. Nevertheless, Husák reaffirmed his support for Dubček, saying "either I will back him, or I will leave."[17]

In Prague on August 31, the plenum of the Central Committee of the KSČ "postponed" the Fourteenth Party Congress, leaving a final decision on a new date to the Presidium. It also approved several changes in the makeup of the top party organs and the government, changes that seemed to leave the reformers strengthened. The plenum itself had been enlarged by coopting many of the delegates to the Fourteenth Congress. The new presidium and secretariat sacrificed the most prominent reformists; Hájek, Šik, and others left the government; and the heads of Czechoslovak Radio and Television were also dropped. Yet the dogmatic hardliners saw their representation shrink too, while the

Presidium included thirteen members, and the Central Committee forty-eight, who had been elected to the same posts by the Vysočany congress.[18]

This qualified collaboration incensed the Soviets, but they pursued a long-term strategy spelled out in a meeting of the "Five" in Moscow on August 27. Their priority was to "break the resistance of Dubček" to normalization. A steady barrage of hostile press criticism focused on Dubček and Černík, accompanied by frequent demands that the most high profile reformists should be dropped. Meanwhile the Soviets searched for "realists" who would abandon the attempt to save the "post-January course." The Soviets counted on the influence of their occupying armies, so ensuring a permanent Soviet military presence was a key Soviet goal, one that simultaneously further undermined Dubček.[19]

At the beginning of October, the Soviet leaders met in Moscow with Dubček, Černík, and Husák, to discuss the "temporary" stationing of Soviet armed forces in Czechoslovakia. The Czechoslovaks were forced to accept a treaty stationing approximately 80,000 Soviet soldiers on their soil, signed by Kosygin and Černík in Moscow on October 16. The agreement was kept secret until just before its ratification by the National Assembly, where only four delegates voted against it (ten abstained and sixty were absent).[20] The treaty was valid "for the duration of the temporary deployment of Soviet forces on Czechoslovak territory," and could only be changed with the agreement of both parties, so it formally ratified a permanent Soviet military presence.[21]

This outcome was a bitter blow for the public as well as for the leaders. Repeated compromises had been accepted to ensure the withdrawal of the invading armies, and now they were "temporarily" going to stay. Not everything that had been accomplished during the reform months had yet died, however. On October 28, 1968—the fiftieth anniversary of Czechoslovak independence—the federalization law was passed, to take effect on January 1, 1969.[22] Debates continued on legal reforms, the rehabilitation of purge victims, and economic policy. The press, though subject to censorship, urged maintaining the Action Program, and several journals published critical articles. The mass organizations, trade unions, the Academy of Sciences (whose Historical Institute prepared a documentary collection cited here), and party organizations still reflected the Prague Spring's quickening of intellectual and civic life. University students led a three-day occupation strike of their faculties in late November to demand the continuation of reforms. The trade unions, especially the Metalworkers' Union, supported the strikes. General discontent filled the streets on the October 28 and November 7 anniversaries.

The Central Committee's plenum meeting from November 14 to 17 created a new eight-man Presidium executive committee, of whom only Dubček and Smrkovský were reformists. It also set up a Bureau for the Direction of Party Work in the Czech Lands, headed by Lubomír Štrougal, an emerging realist. Štrougal's authority resembled Husák's position in the Slovak party, and with realists in these two key posts Dubček grew correspondingly weaker. The plenum also appointed Bil'ak to the secretariat, returning him to the top echelons of the party.

After the November plenum Dubček's position continued to weaken. The next crisis arose in December, after another meeting with the Soviets in Kiev on December 7–8.[23] On his return, Husák used federalization to attack Smrkovský, chairman of the National, soon to become Federal, Assembly. Husák demanded that the chairman be a Slovak, since the president and prime minister, like Smrkovský, were Czechs. In the Czech lands, Smrkovský was still regarded as the people's tribune, and the trade unions, students, creative intelligentsia, and press rallied to support him, even talking of a general strike. With Husák threatening to resign and organize a campaign in Slovakia for Smrkovský's dismissal, Dubček did not use this public support to defend the last reformist in the top leadership. The Presidium and Smrkovský himself condemned the strike threat, and finally, on January 7, 1969, Smrkovský resigned.[24]

Hard on the heels of Smrkovský's fall came the news, in the middle of a Central Committee meeting on January 16, 1969, that a young man had set himself ablaze on Wenceslas Square. Jan Palach died three days later, sparking mass demonstrations for the first time since August 1968. Over the next few months a handful of followers took the route of self-immolation, but Palach's hopes of defending freedom of expression (his suicide note demanded the lifting of censorship and the suspension of *Zprávy*) were not realized. Palach joined the ranks of Czech martyrs, but his imitators died without general public reaction.[25]

The next explosion proved to be more than Dubček could survive. During March the world ice hockey championships pitted the Czechoslovak national team against a field that included the Soviet Union. The Czechoslovak team won both encounters with the Soviets, on March 21 and 28, and the public reacted with spontaneous celebrations at which they chanted anti-Soviet slogans. On the second weekend, more than 500,000 demonstrated across the country. In Prague several thousand people attacked the offices of the Soviet airline Aeroflot, possibly in a secret police provocation. This "ice-hockey crisis" gave Dubček's opponents their chance. The Soviet Politburo sent a delegation including Marshal Andrei Grechko to Prague to demand the immediate restoration of order and Dubček's ouster. Grechko openly threatened another invasion.[26] Finally, at the Central Committee plenum on April 17, Dubček resigned, proposing that Husák succeed him. The plenum confirmed the change, and a new Presidium, reduced in size to only eleven members, was elected. Dubček (now chairman of the parliament) was the only reformer in the new body. There was little public reaction. What the massive military invasion of August 1968 had failed to accomplish, the long demoralizing months of "normalization" had achieved: the fall of Alexander Dubček.

Husák Takes Charge

Husák emerged as a leading exponent of the "healthy forces" during the August crisis, and gradually won over doubters among the other Warsaw Pact leaders (especially Kádár, who was suspicious of his Slovak nationalism).[27] During the Prague Spring, Husák had been considered a reformist, but over the ensuing months he proved to be what he had apparently always been: a communist with authoritarian preferences and a taste for power, coupled with the political skill to trim his sails to the prevailing winds. His temperament resembled Polish leader Gomułka's more than Kádár's.[28] Husák quickly set about achieving a "normality" acceptable to the Soviet Union. Press and cultural controls were tightened, the reformist journals banned, trustworthy editors placed in charge of other newspapers, and tighter censorship reimposed. Radio and television were also brought to heel, and throughout the newly obedient media attacks on "rightists" and a reevaluation of the whole development since January continued. *Zprávy*, no longer needed, was finally closed down.[29]

In party matters Husák initially proceeded with some circumspection, but in the end, he realized he would have to purge the party itself in order to reestablish party control over society. Renewed signs of discontent and resistance through the summer and into the autumn reinforced this message. From August 19–21 demonstrations marked the first anniversary of the invasion, and prompted legislation "to protect and strengthen public order," under which many people were later "legally" persecuted. Kohout, Vaculík, Havel, and other intellectuals issued a "Ten Points Manifesto" on the anniversary of the invasion, condemning normalization.[30] In response, at the September plenum, Dubček was dropped from the Presidium, and seven others including Smrkovský were expelled from the central committee. In October, Dubček, Smrkovský, and others were removed even from their positions in the parliament.

These steps at the top were quickly followed by a thorough purge of the party apparatus down to the rank-and-file. By screening party members, Husák aimed to remove remaining "rightists," but also to energize the party and to shift representation away from the white-collar, technocratic managers and back to the working-class core. In January 1970 the central committee began the mass screening, starting at the top. Dubček resigned from the central committee to become ambassador to Turkey, and Černík was dismissed as prime minister (Štrougal replaced him) and expelled from the Presidium. From there, the purge continued downward through 1970. It returned to Dubček in May, when he was recalled from Ankara and a month later expelled from the party. According to Husák's report at the December plenum, over 78 percent of the screened party members remained in the party, while nearly 17 percent had their membership canceled and nearly 5 percent were expelled. Estimates of those affected by the purge reach more than 600,000.[31]

The federal parliament was well in hand already, and neither the SNR nor its Czech counterpart mustered significant resistance. The trade union movement proved more difficult, since the decision at the ROH's congress in September 1968 to allow autonomous trade unions had weakened the center. The newly formed metalworkers' union led the campaign against Smrkovský's dismissal, and at its statewide congress in March 1970 the unions reiterated their support for reform. Nevertheless, the ROH felt the bite of the purges, with about 20 percent of the functionaries of its central council dismissed. Eventually its leadership backtracked on earlier promises, without saving their careers.

The youth organizations were also recentralized, and the ČSM, which had effectively disintegrated, was replaced. The Scouts and Sokol vanished once more, as did the autonomous student associations and the leading student newspaper, Studentské listy (banned in May 1969). A centralized Socialist Union of Youth (SSM) replaced the proposed fed-

Leading normalizers at an NF meeting on January 27, 1971: from left to right, Gustav Husák, Ludvík Svoboda, and Lubomír Štrougal. (ČTK photo)

eration of youth and children's organizations in the autumn of 1970. Its membership of about 300,000 was only one-third the size of its predecessor before 1968. With time, however, and because it was the sole sponsor of social or extracurricular activities for young people, the SSM's membership increased.

Institutions of education, research, and culture were purged with such gusto that the new minister of education was dropped in July 1971 as an ultra-leftist. Nine hundred university professors lost their jobs, including two-thirds of all faculty of the departments of Marxism-Leninism (which were abolished and replaced by Institutes). Five university departments, including sociology, were abolished altogether. The Academy of Sciences lost 1,200 scholars and its research institutes were reorganized. Dismissals reached all the way down to the secondary and elementary schools, which lost one-fourth of their teachers. The culture ministry in the Czech lands reined in the creative artists and their organizations. Fifteen hundred employees of Czechoslovak Radio in Prague were sacked, and all twenty-five of the cultural and literary journals were closed. Artists who had supported reform were blacklisted, unable to publish or have their works performed. During 1970 the artists' unions were abolished and replaced by new unions led by trustworthy but undistinguished hacks. By the time of the new unions' founding congresses in 1972, their membership approximated a quarter of their pre-invasion size.[32]

The normalizers rapidly returned to the central command model of the economy. Compulsory targets were reimposed in July 1969, shortly after the government withdrew its approval of enterprise councils, and price controls at the beginning of 1970. Thanks to the positive impact of earlier reforms, however, the Czechoslovak economy continued to grow into the 1970s, with agriculture performing better than expected. As one observer summed it up a decade later, "three things helped the new leaders survive with flying colours: the Czechoslovak economy was strong, the agricultural results were good, and the workers were not Polish."[33]

Calculating the total impact of the purges connected with Husák's normalization is made more difficult by the fact that many people resigned from their jobs voluntarily and left the country, to be officially dismissed later. Total figures for emigration connected with the Prague Spring can only be estimates. Nor can we know all the motives prompting people to leave their homeland. Nevertheless, as many as 130,000 to 140,000 Czechs and Slovaks left the country by the end of 1971.[34] The most significant effect of this cumulative brain drain was to deplete the pool of technical experts and experienced people in public policy, while reinforcing the sullen passivity and apathy of those who remained.[35]

In his efforts to satisfy Moscow, Husák also had to defend himself against attacks from the "leftist" camp. The invasion had reinvigorated the party hardliners, who had begun to organize immediately after the arrival of Warsaw Pact troops. During the course of the purges of 1970 and into 1971, however, Husák consolidated his position by removing some of the leading ultras and by subsuming the ultra organizations into the SSM and the Socialist Academy. Husák assiduously courted the Kremlin, traveling to the Soviet Union five times in 1969 and four times in 1970. He stressed the need for unity in the leadership and signaled his discontent with the hardliners within the party. The Soviet Union, for its part, wanted a clear statement on the reform period to coincide with Soviet views. A new Czechoslovak-Soviet treaty on friendship and mutual cooperation signed on May 5–6, 1970, showed that the Soviets would stick with Husák, and the December plenum meeting reinforced that outcome.[36]

The plenum also put the capstone on the process of normalization by giving the Soviets the statement they wanted, the "Lessons from the Crisis Development in the Party and Society after the Thirteenth Congress of the KSČ." It reflected the Soviet line, dismissed the Action Program as "revisionist," accepted that by August of 1968 there was a "counter-revolutionary" situation, and accused Dubček, Černík, and Smrkovský of treason. The "Lessons"—distributed throughout the country for compulsory study—also committed the Husák leadership to reject a future return to reform.[37] Though the ultras were chastened, Bil'ak's presence in the top party ranks provided a vigorous and persistent, if always circumspect, hardline presence. This situation suited Moscow, as the stability at the top of the KSČ over the next fifteen years showed.[38]

"REAL EXISTING SOCIALISM"

The victors in the struggle for "normalization" celebrated at the official Fourteenth Congress of the KSČ, replacing the disavowed Vysočany congress, in May 1971. Gracing the podium were the leaders of the five invading Warsaw Pact allies: Brezhnev, Gierek (replacing Poland's Gromułka), Honecker (replacing East Germany's Ulbricht), Kádár, and Zhivkov. Brezhnev called it the "Congress of Victory over the Enemies of Socialism," and it also represented Husák's victory over his potential rivals.[39] Until he relinquished the party leadership to his protegé Miloš Jakeš in 1987, Husák balanced atop a leadership composed of two sorts of "normalizers." There were reformers who had seen which way the wind was blowing after August 1968, and there were hardliners like Bil'ak, who would have been in the political wilderness had the Prague Spring not been crushed. As this leadership aged in office even the grudging admission that Husák was better than the alternatives faded, and society regarded its political heads as traitors and careerists. People reserved their strongest disdain for President Svoboda, whose status as national hero tarnished as he clung to his office.

The KSČ once again proved that surmounting its latest crisis hampered its ability to face new challenges. Basing its legitimacy on the "Lessons," the regime could not reach a Hungarian-style accommodation with society. Instead, the Czechoslovak party had to keep constant vigilance against "rightist" tendencies, and quash any suggestion of reforms. It demanded that its citizens give outward, public expressions of support, and in return offered them selective repression, coupled with a decent level of consumption, which sufficed on the whole to keep society passive and apathetic. Renewed dissent achieved international renown but had limited domestic influence until changes in the Soviet Union undermined the stability of the Soviet bloc.

The Powerful: The Communist Party Under Husák

Under Husák the KSČ remained the dominant political force in Czechoslovakia, but it was transformed by the crisis. Voluntary resignations or purges removed thousands of highly qualified members, and there were few prospective new members with equivalent qualifications. After the end of the purge in 1971, the party's membership recovered from its low point of 1.2 million. By 1976 it had reached 1,382,860 members, in 1981 it had 1,538,179, in 1986, 1,675,000, and in May 1988 it boasted 1,717,000 members, once more approaching 12 percent of the population and its highest absolute membership since 1950.[40] Party members reacted to the bewildering sequence of changes with apathy and cynicism. A confidential report from 1972 claimed that one-third of the total membership had not taken part in any organized party activity during the preceding year, and many cells had not held even a fraction of the obligatory ten meetings.[41] The purges decimated the intelligentsia, but many working-class members also left or were expelled. Nevertheless, the party maintained a base among workers, who with "agricultural workers" numbered just over 50 percent of its total membership in 1988. Efforts to recruit youth succeeded so that by 1988, 51 percent of members had joined the party after 1968, and one-third was under age thirty-five.[42]

Comparing the rapid recovery of party membership with its earlier period of growth between 1945 and 1948, one difference stands out: many members from the earlier period, especially among the intelligentsia, genuinely thought they were struggling for a better society. After 1968, the true believer practically disappeared from the Czechoslovak party, surviving only among the expelled reformers of the "parallel party" underground.[43] Existential considerations were practically the only reason to join the party. The party controlled the citizens' prospects, through the network of positions (550,000 in the 1980s) that required party approval or membership, through access to higher education, employment, promotion—in short, to any form of advancement. Anyone with talent was sooner or later faced with pressure to join, while for those without talent, membership in the KSČ went a long way toward making up for that lack.[44]

The party controlled other levers of coercion, including a numerous and active secret police, special riot police, and auxiliary police forces. The party's own special force, the People's Militia (some 120,000 men) was also reinvigorated after normalization. Regular armed forces numbered about 200,000, with approximately two-thirds consisting of conscripts serving two-to-three-year terms of national service. The military forces were under close party control, with between 80 and 90 percent of the officer corps party members.[45] Looming behind the Czechoslovak People's Army was also the Soviet Central Group of Forces, a continuous, not-so-subtle reminder of the ultimate sanction that maintained the Czechoslovak status quo.

While Husák maintained himself at the top of the KSČ, he added the office of state president in 1975, as senility overcame Ludvík Svoboda's resistance to resigning. This accumulation of offices did not mean, however, that Husák's position was secure. Unlike the most successful general secretary of them all, Stalin, he was not surrounded by his own men. Husák's position was solidified by the protective mantle of Soviet approval, which never slipped from his shoulders while Brezhnev was head of the CPSU. Nevertheless, as economic difficulties accumulated, tensions within the KSČ leadership grew more visible.

By the early 1980s, these tensions produced two reactions within the presidium. The hardliners led by Bil'ak urged greater political and ideological mobilization. Cautiously at first, and then more boldly, Štrougal called for technocratic innovation (the word "reform" was scrupulously avoided). Jakeš emerged as a member of the leadership with excellent connections in Moscow and increasing economic responsibility.[46] Husák shepherded this leadership through the twists and turns of Soviet policy following Brezhnev's death in 1982. Matters became even more interesting when Mikhail Gorbachev became general secretary of the CPSU. Once again, as during de-Stalinization, the KSČ found itself discomfited by changes in Moscow, while its response was limited by the means it had used to surmount the previous crisis: in this case the dead hand of the "Lessons."

The Powerless: Society and the New Social Contract

The collapse of their hopes left Czechs and Slovaks embittered and exhausted. Even more painful was the feeling of betrayal stemming from Dubček's failure to protect anything from the Prague Spring. Though coercion was one prong of the regime's approach to reestablishing party control, the massive application of force was not necessary to cow society: "normalization" was characterized by "civilized violence."[47] The purges of 1970–71 were sufficient to subdue the population without resort to exemplary show trials and death sentences. Moreover, the crackdown on active dissent, and the veiled but pervasive threat of the secret political police, enforced outward conformity thereafter. That this use of force was "civilized" did not make it any less coercive. As Václav Havel pointed out in a letter to Husák in 1975, the question is *"why* are people in fact behaving the way they do? . . . For any unprejudiced observer, the answer is, I think, self-evident: they are driven to it by *fear."*[48] And of course for people to fear the consequences of disobedience, they must have something to lose. Thus the second prong of the regime's policy focused on the consumer economy.

The end of the Prague Spring also meant the end of Šik's economic reforms. Orthodox economic policies, including the prescriptive five-year plan, returned.[49] Husák's regime was blessed with good fortune from 1971 to 1976, the most successful plan during Czechoslovakia's communist era. Net material product grew by 32 percent, personal consumption by 27 percent, and real wages by over 5 percent.[50] The emphasis on consumption allowed the regime to trumpet the success of "real existing socialism," while the people focused on material comfort. To tackle an acute housing crisis, the state constructed sprawling prefabricated concrete apartment blocks on the outskirts of cities and towns. Production of the domestic Škoda automobile, as well as imports of the Soviet-built Fiat, the Lada, increased. In 1969 Czechoslovakia had one car per 21 people, one for every 15 in 1971, one for every 10 in 1975, and one for every 7 in 1981.[51] The cottage outside of town came to symbolize the flight into internal migration that was the popular adaptation to "real existing socialism." In the Czech lands alone, the number of cottages increased from 128,000 in 1969 to 160,000 in 1973 and 225,000 by 1981.[52] Indeed, the "three keys" to happiness in Husák's Czechoslovakia, as the joke had it, were the key to the apartment, the key to the car, and the key to the cottage.

Government policies equalized income levels across society, giving most people a reasonably comfortable standard of living.[53] But Czechoslovakia's shabby socialist consumer paradise did not enjoy good fortune for long. The OPEC oil crisis of 1974 had no immediate effect, since a 1966 agreement tied deliveries of machine products to fixed Soviet oil prices, but with prices skyrocketing on the world market, the Soviet Union increased its prices too. By 1975, Czechoslovakia paid nearly double what it had in 1970 for Soviet oil, and in 1981 more than five times as much. At the same time, Czechoslovakia consumed twice as much Soviet oil in 1981 as it had in 1970.[54] Other raw material prices were rising also, and the value of Czechoslovak manufactured products could not make up the difference. Economic growth actually reversed in 1980 and improved only fractionally in 1981.[55] In response, Czechoslovak policy stressed conservation while developing new supplies. Investment in Soviet or CMEA energy projects was a significant part of the planned overall investment strategy up until 1981–85. Though still counting on Soviet oil and natural gas, the state also invested in domestic brown coal and nuclear energy projects. The party also raised retail prices, with the first round of price hikes taking effect in January 1981.[56]

To protect its "social contract," the party adopted the "Set of Measures to Improve the System of Planned Management of the National Economy."[57] The "Set of Measures" sought to improve the use of raw materials and raise quality, but it only called for limited changes, similar to the Brezhnev-style economic tinkering attempted in the Soviet Union in 1979. The measures did not allow any departure from centralized planning.[58] They failed to solve Czechoslovakia's economic dilemma, not only because they relied on planning without market incentives but because implementing them ran into resistance from managers and workers. Amendments in 1983 and 1984 came to nothing, and finally the whole program was quietly abandoned.[59]

After Gorbachev began his twin projects of *perestroika* and *glasnost* in the Soviet Union, critical voices in Czechoslovakia became bolder. The Institute for Economic Forecasting of the ČSAV formed a center of reform thinking that influenced Czechoslovakia's economic policy after

1989. As Czechs and Slovaks waited to see what impact *přestavba*, the Czech version of *perestroika*, would have on their lives, their tolerance for the shortcomings of the economy was wearing thin. It was not good enough that life was better than it had been under the Nazis or during the First Republic. Nor did Czechs and Slovaks compare their lives with their neighbors in the Soviet bloc, but with what they saw on German and Austrian television. Popular attitudes in the 1980s were summed up in another joke, the Five Laws of Socialist Economics: (1) Though nobody does any work, the plan is always fulfilled; (2) though the plan is always fulfilled, there is nothing in the stores; (3) though there is nothing in the stores, everyone has everything; (4) though everyone has everything, everyone steals; (5) though everyone steals, nothing is ever missing. The question of how much longer Husák's "social contract" would function under such conditions reared its head ever more insistently during the 1980s. Though there was as yet no sign of a mass workers' repudiation of the system as in Poland, Czechoslovaks showed more willingness to challenge the regime in various ways as they entered the second half of the decade.

Culture and Dissent

Protests and opposition to the restoration of "order" after 1968 existed, but isolated acts of self-sacrifice like Palach's suicide did little to affect developments. A group of "workers and students" issued a widely circulated pamphlet that influenced the popular response to the first anniversary of the invasion in 1969.[60] Radical former party members joined with students to organize more lasting, but eventually ineffectual, opposition. A group called the Movement of Revolutionary Youth (HRM), later renamed the Revolutionary Socialist Party, attempted to organize against the Husák regime. Led by Petr Uhl and influenced by Trotsky and the West German New Left, the HRM was quickly infiltrated by the secret police, and in December 1969 its leaders were arrested and placed on trial in 1971.[61] Another group, the Socialist Movement of Czechoslovak Citizens, issued its first manifesto on October 28, 1970. The authorities refrained from attacking it until after November 1971, when the Socialist Movement urged people to boycott the general elections. Between December 1971 and January 1972, they arrested more than 200 individuals and conducted ten political trials at which 47 defendants were sentenced to a total of 118 years in prison.[62] Organized political opposition from the "party of the expelled" died down after 1972.[63]

The next several years were a time of "general atomization or disintegration," as Havel later recalled. Informal meetings and contacts among intellectuals helped keep alive a cultural alternative to the "gray, everyday totalitarian consumerism" of Husák's Czechoslovakia.[64] Vaculík established a Czechoslovak version of *samizdat*, the Padlock Editions (*Edice petlice*) in 1972, and similar undertakings followed. In time, even journals and anthologies on economic theory, history, religion, and philosophy joined the works of independent literature.[65] This cultural activity kept alive independent Czech and Slovak literature, and also forged links between former communists and the non-communists who became signers of Charter 77. The Helsinki Final Act in 1975, which in spite of its limitations bound the USSR and its allies to respect publicly stated norms of human rights, influenced the emergence of Charter 77. So did Czechoslovakia's ratification in 1976 of the two United Nations conventions on human rights, which were published as part of the code of laws of the ČSSR. These developments increased the contradiction between the Husák regime's words, and its actions against its citizens.

In March 1976 twenty-two young musicians associated with a counter-culture rock group, Plastic People of the Universe, were arrested.[66] For Havel and other leading intellectuals who rallied to their defense, the state's actions were deeply threatening precisely because the "criminals" were not political opponents of the regime. The intellectuals' fear, as Havel expressed it, was that "the regime could well start locking up everyone who thought independently and who expressed himself independently, even if he did so only in private."[67] The Plastic People's defenders organized protests at home and abroad, involving non-communists and former communists. The cause brought together dissidents of differing backgrounds and political experiences, forging a sense of common purpose that found expression in December 1976 in several meetings involving Havel and other dissident intellectuals. In their agreement that "something must be done" lay the germ of the civic initiative, Charter 77.[68]

Charter 77 announced its existence on January 1, 1977. It was not a single protest on a specific issue, though the Plastic People case helped it crystallize, nor did it pursue the political struggle. Reflecting the alienation of normalized society, Charter 77 was an example of "antipolitics," not politics.[69] In the words of its inaugural document, "Charter

77 is not an organization; it has no rules, permanent bodies or formal membership. It embraces everyone who agrees with its ideas, participates in its work, and supports it. It does not form the basis for any oppositional political activity."[70] Charter 77 based its approach on the demand that the authorities respect the words of their own constitution, laws, and international agreements.

Charter 77 called for dialogue with the authorities and issued documents detailing specific violations of human rights. Of course, Husák's regime ignored dialogue, attacked Charter 77 in the media, and harassed and arrested its members. An "Anti-Charter" pushed by organized campaigns in the workplace had some success, and the movement remained numerically small (by 1985 only about 1,200 people had signed it). They came from all age groups, political persuasions, and religious convictions, and young people (including some who were only children in 1968) predominated among the later signers. Workers made up a significant proportion of signers, though the leadership remained in the hands of intellectuals, and few Slovaks were active Chartists.

Charter 77's strength was not in numbers, but in the moral importance of what it did, illustrated in Havel's most influential essay, "The Power of the Powerless" (1978). Havel wrote about a greengrocer who places the motto "Proletarians of the world, unite!" in his shop window. He argued that this powerless individual, who would undoubtedly suffer serious consequences if he chose not to participate in the regime's lie, nevertheless did have power—the power of exposing the lie simply by opting to "live in truth." Charter 77 was an attempt to live in truth, and Havel argued that behind it lay the "independent life of society," like "the proverbial one-tenth of the iceberg visible above the water." The highly visible dissidents, Havel claimed, were not different from the unnoticed thousands who lived this independent life of society. "The original and most important sphere of activity . . . is simply an attempt to create and support the 'independent life of society' as an articulated expression of 'living within the truth.' "[71]

Havel recognized that such an attempt might lead to more political actions, and Charter 77 reflected that in its own activities. It branched out from concerns with abuses of citizens' legal rights (where the related Committee to Defend the Unjustly Persecuted, VONS, took over) to take in other areas. Charter documents dealt with issues the regime ignored, such as minority questions, environmental pollution, and nuclear safety. Independently of Charter 77, other forms of alternative action and living became more visible during the 1980s. In a running battle with the Ministry of Culture, the Jazz Section of the official Musicians' Union created space for alternative forms of youth music. In 1985 the regime arrested its seven-member executive committee, prompting protests from Western artists.[72] Young people in particular were also active in informal groups supporting peace and nuclear disarmament, as well as in groups focusing on ecological problems created by socialism's disregard for pollution, its technologically outmoded industry, and its intensive chemical agriculture.[73]

Religious life also demonstrated a quickening during the 1980s.[74] The Archbishop of Prague, František Cardinal Tomášek, assumed a higher profile, criticizing the regime's front organization, Pacem in Terris. The celebrations in June 1985 of the 1,100th anniversary of the death of St. Methodius drew from 150,000 to 250,000 people to a weekend festival addressed by Cardinal Tomášek and others. Slovak pilgrimage sites also saw more visitors. On March 6, 1988, Cardinal Tomášek celebrated a special mass in honor of the Blessed Agnes in St. Vitus's cathedral in front of 8,000 worshipers. Afterward they chanted slogans under his windows in support of religious freedom. By early 1988, as many as 600,000 had signed a petition demanding greater religious rights, begun by a group of Moravian Catholics and publicly supported by the cardinal-archbishop.[75] As in Poland, the organization of such undertakings by Czechoslovak Catholics was one of the first laboratories of autonomous civic activity for the participants.

By the later 1980s the "independent life of society" was increasingly manifesting itself in ways that challenged the regime. The social contract of normalization, that political passivity and formal support for the public rituals of communism would be repaid by a shabby but comfortable standard of living, was breaking down as the economy continued to falter. And if under Brezhnev Husák could always count on the Soviet Union's support—with the ultimate sanction, the Soviet troops on Czechoslovak soil, held in implicit reserve—after his death the external climate for normalized Czechoslovakia was changing dramatically.

THE GORBACHEV FACTOR

One of the eternal verities shaping Husák's policies was the Brezhnev Doctrine, the USSR's interpretation of the sovereign rights of states in the "Socialist Commonwealth," promulgated after the 1968 invasion. *Pravda* on September 26, 1968, stated plainly that "the sovereignty of individual socialist countries cannot be set against the interests of world socialism. . . . To fulfill their internationalist duties to the fraternal nations of Czechoslovakia and to defend their own socialist gains, the Soviet Union and the other socialist states were forced to act and did act in decisive opposition to the anti-socialist forces in Czechoslovakia."[76] Husák, bereft of almost all domestic legitimacy, was both threatened and reassured by the Brezhnev doctrine. What it did not state, however, was what would happen if Soviet policies themselves changed. The question did not arise under Brezhnev's successor, Yurii Andropov, nor under Andropov's successor, Konstantin Chernenko. Gorbachev was a different matter.

Gorbachev's concern for the Soviet economy, with spillovers into CMEA and bilateral economic relations, put economic changes suddenly back on the agenda. In Czechoslovakia this ran counter to the "Lessons," but the KSČ Central Committee adopted a new economic approach in January 1987, calling for decentralization of decision-making and introducing some market mechanisms. Specialists at the ČSAV's Institute for Economic Forecasting criticized these measures because of their limited use of market mechanisms and because they allowed no change in the political factors affecting economic performance. Thus by the late 1980s the Czechoslovak economy had returned party specialists to the same place as before 1968: to the realization that real economic reform implied political change.[77]

Though Gorbachev was scrupulously careful not to address the Brezhnev doctrine directly, he tolerated enough diversity in bloc relations to imply changes. He was also aware of the threat to the Czechoslovak regime if he forced it to adopt policies similar to his. After a visit in 1987, Gorbachev noted that evaluating the Prague Spring was "above all a matter for the Czechoslovak comrades themselves." He did not push the KSČ leadership on the economy, either, saying "we have seen that the Czechoslovak comrades in accordance with their own conditions are also looking for ways of improving socialism." Ironically, this acceptance of "separate roads to socialism" in a new guise suited hardliners like Bil'ak, who insisted that "one should not copy something blindly," and reasserted the validity of the "Lessons."[78] Czechoslovakia joined East Germany as the Soviet bloc states least thrilled by the Gorbachev phenomenon.

Gorbachev, meanwhile, found himself driven by the logic of *perestroika* to gamble on the emergence of reformist communist leaders, capable of meeting public demands without losing control. Thus he tolerated changes in Hungary and Poland late in 1988 that began the negotiated transfer of power in those countries from the communists to other forces. That, in turn, opened up the floodgates for further change, and the torrent that led from Warsaw to Budapest to Dresden and Berlin, finally swept up Prague and Bratislava on its way to Sofia, Timişoara, and Bucharest. The fall of communism in Czechoslovakia would have been impossible without the coming together of both internal and external forces in 1988–89. The end of the forty-year communist experiment in Czechoslovakia opened up new prospects for Czechs and Slovaks—new prospects, and new challenges and responsibilities.

15 Velvet Revolution to Velvet Divorce

On November 17, 1989, an officially approved demonstration commemorating Jan Opletal and the Nazi destruction of the Czech universities in 1939 was attacked by riot police in a downtown Prague street. The attacks sparked off a wave of protest and demonstration that led to the rapid toppling of the communist government. Truly, it seemed (as contemporary posters stated) that what had taken ten years in Poland, ten months in Hungary, and ten weeks in East Germany had only taken ten days in Czechoslovakia. The collapse of communism in Czechoslovakia did not entirely resemble the negotiated handovers achieved in Poland and Hungary, nor did it result in the mass violence that riveted world attention on Bucharest in December. For its peaceful, even good-humored qualities it was quickly dubbed "The Velvet Revolution."[1]

THE FALL OF COMMUNISM IN CZECHOSLOVAKIA

The Velvet Revolution surprised many, not only by its particular characteristics but by the rapidity and drama of the changes. Outside observers—and many Czech and Slovak dissidents—found it hard to believe that the Husák regime or its Jakeš-led epigone would change quickly. Nevertheless, by 1988 there were signs that under the ice things were finally stirring, as a younger generation that had not directly experienced the 1968 intervention reached maturity. The lip service the Czechoslovak authorities paid to Gorbachev's policies of openness may also have contributed to people's willingness to speak, or even act out.

Signs of the Times

During 1988 more independent initiatives joined Charter 77 and other long-standing dissident groups.[2] The general public also showed a greater willingness to participate in public expressions of discontent. On the twentieth anniversary of the invasion of 1968, more than 10,000 mostly young people gathered in Prague, shouting support for Gorbachev and greater freedom until dispersed with tear gas. To their surprise, the authorities discovered that hardly any well-known dissidents were involved, evidence that the "social contract" was losing effectiveness. October 28 was declared a public holiday for the first time since 1968, but in spite of the temptation to spend the weekend at their cottages, about 5,000 people met on Wenceslas Square to chant Masaryk's name and call for freedom. On December 10 another demonstration, this time with official permission, marked the fortieth anniversary of the Universal Declaration on Human Rights. French President François Mitterrand was visiting Prague, which may explain the official sanction. Nevertheless, the presence of 5,000 demonstrators suggested that Czechoslovakia's party bosses were unsure how to respond to their society while under pressure on human rights from both the Soviet Union and the West.

In 1989 the party evidently decided to show a firmer hand. During January demonstrations on the anniversary of Palach's suicide, the authorities attacked protesters with water cannon and tear gas. They arrested several leading dissidents, including Havel, who was sentenced to nine months in jail. Havel's arrest and sentencing set the stage for the publication of "A Few Sentences," a statement that began circulating at the end of June and by September had 40,000 signatures. "A Few Sentences" called on the regime to honor its words about *perestroika* and democratization, to release all political prisoners, to implement basic human rights, and to reevaluate the events of 1968.[3]

Events moved dramatically in September when Hungary began to allow East German citizens "vacationing" in Hungary to leave for West Germany. Thousands of East Germans clambered into the West German embassy in Prague, too. On September 30, Erich Honecker announced that the East Germans in the Prague embassy would be expelled to West Germany. The battered Trabants and scattered windrows of East German marks left by the jubilant "expellees" suggested to many Czechs and Slovaks that their own regime might not be permanent, either. If October 28 seemed quieter in 1989 than in 1988, international events, especially the fall of the Berlin Wall on November 10, countered any resulting pessimism. Many Czechs also took the elevation of the Blessed Agnes to full sainthood by the Polish pope, John Paul II, on November 12 as an omen that change had to come.[4]

The Velvet Revolution

The demonstration that triggered change in Czechoslovakia was co-sponsored by the SSM and an independent students' union the authorities had approved only weeks earlier. The occasion was the fiftieth anniversary of the Nazi destruction of Czech universities, celebrated as International Students' Day.[5] Gathered where Opletal's funeral procession had begun fifty years before, 10,000 to 15,000 youthful demonstrators listened to speakers calling for democratization and Jakeš's dismissal. Then they proceeded to a candle-lighting ceremony at the Slavín cemetery, a shrine of national heroes at Vyšehrad. Several thousand decided to move the demonstration to Wenceslas Square, the traditional site of political protests in Prague. When they found the direct route blocked by riot police, they proceeded along the embankment toward National Avenue (Národní třída), where they turned right past the National Theater. As the crowd, now perhaps as many as 55,000 strong, approached the narrow head of the street, it came face to face with a phalanx of policemen equipped with the helmets, plexiglass shields, and truncheons of the riot squads. After a long standoff, the riot police began systematically beating the 5,000 demonstrators at the head of the procession. Their only exit was past cordons of police and special "Red Beret" anti-terrorist forces, who continued to beat them as they fled.

This brutal end to the student-led demonstration was the catalyst that transformed Czechoslovakia. In response the students called for strikes at the faculties of higher education. On Saturday, November 18, theater students took their strike proclamation to a meeting of the capital's stage actors and directors, who supported them. Thus when the afternoon audiences gathered across Prague, they were treated to read-

Students and riot police face off on National Avenue, November 17, 1989. (ČTK photo)

ings of the students' proclamation and the suspension of performances in sympathy. In many cases, the audience reacted with spontaneous applause and their own complaints. The theater strike rapidly spread to other towns, including Brno and Bratislava, creating a vital link between the students, the actors, and the general public and a source of information when official control of the media was still effective.

The theaters also provided the milieu from which Civic Forum (OF) emerged. Havel, who had returned to Prague from his cottage on November 18, met with other dissidents on the afternoon of November 19, and they decided to create a single opposition organization, Civic Forum. The formal foundation of OF took place that evening in a Prague theater. In its first proclamation, OF declared that it legitimately represented the wishes of the people. It issued specific demands, including Husák's resignation, the removal of the Prague party chief, and an investigation into police action on November 17, and announced its support for a general strike called by the students for two hours on November 27.[6]

Civic Forum was an unknown quantity to most Czechoslovaks for several days after its formation. The communications media, both print and broadcast, remained under official censorship until after November 19, when the SSM's *Mladá fronta* (Young Front) broke the restrictions. Control over distribution still allowed the party to ensure that only its *Rudé právo* reached the provinces. Czechoslovak television and radio also stayed under party control for several more days. Thus knowledge about OF and its position was difficult to gain. Adding to these difficulties was the perception that OF represented the attitudes of a few dissident intellectuals and the widespread political cynicism and apathy created by the normalized regime.

To counter suspicion, OF insisted that it was not a party, but "simply an open association of those who feel responsible for the positive resolution of the present unbearable political situation, who want to unite the strength of all decent and democratically thinking citizens—artists, students, workers, all people of good-will."[7] OF's headquarters, in Prague's Laterna magica (Magic Lantern) theater, became the revolution's general headquarters and a clearinghouse for uncensored information. In Slovakia on November 20 a group of democratic activists laid the groundwork for OF's Slovak counterpart, Public Against Violence (VPN). In the ensuing days, VPN would come to hold a position in Slovakia analogous to OF's in the Czech lands, and the two established direct contacts on November 21.[8]

Meanwhile, demonstrations continued. Spontaneously, groups of citizens and students met in Wenceslas Square on the afternoon of November 18, and the next day's gatherings there and in Charles Square (Karlovo náměstí) were larger and more self-confident. That afternoon several thousand demonstrators set off toward the Castle, but their way was blocked by police. By the afternoon of Monday, November 20, nearly 200,000 demonstrators had gathered at the statue of St. Václav, filling the square and listening as best they could to the speakers who addressed them from the base of the statue. Once again they attempted to march to the Castle, and again they were met by police. As rumors spread the next day that further demonstrations would be broken up with massive force, the student strike coordinating committee issued a proclamation to world governments.[9]

The reaction to the events of November 17 exposed the KSČ's weakness. The SSM pressured Jakeš and Prague party boss Miroslav Štěpán to resign, fearing that the self-organizing students would simply sweep it aside as representative of "youth." It never could overcome its long association with the stagnant normalized party, but in the crucial early days the SSM provided legitimacy to the unofficial student strike committees, logistical assistance by making typewriters and mimeograph machines available to them, and an establishment ally within the party.[10]

The pressure from without also increased. On Tuesday afternoon, November 21, more than 200,000 people in Wenceslas Square listened to Civic Forum speakers from the balcony of the Melantrich building, headquarters of the Czechoslovak Socialist Party, whose newspaper *Svobodné slovo* (Free Word) now joined *Mladá fronta* in breaking the censorship. Crowds of similar size continued to gather on succeeding days, to hear speakers from various groups, listen to updates on the talks between the government and OF, and revel in the falling away of habits of caution and fear. Pop star Marta Kubišová's singing of her 1968 hit, a setting of Comenius's words promising the Czech people that control of their affairs would return to their own hands, stirred memories of the Prague Spring. The celebration of 1968 culminated on Friday, November 24, when Alexander Dubček joined Havel on the Melantrich balcony. The meeting broke up with chants of "Dubček to the Castle!" and calls for another mass demonstration, this time on the larger surface of Letná plain.[11]

These repeated popular demonstrations could hardly be dispersed by the rapidly demoralized People's Militia, and although the party considered applying a "Tiananmen Square" solution using the Czechoslovak People's Army, that option failed in the Central Committee. Workers in large numbers participated in the demonstration on Thursday afternoon, November 23, and thereafter. Petr Miller, a worker from the ČKD factory, was coopted to the Civic Forum's leadership. His colleagues at the ČKD works demonstrated their attitude dramatically when Štěpán visited the factory to rally the workers against the students' strike demand. When he intoned, "We will not be dictated to by children," meaning the students, the workers roared back, to his visible discomfiture, "We are not children!"[12]

The federal government under Ladislav Adamec had been in contact with the OF leaders since November 21, and on Sunday, November 26, Adamec even addressed the crowds on Letná. By this time the KSČ had finally met in a twice-postponed emergency session, on Friday, November 24. After trying to ditch only the most prominent "normalizers," Jakeš resigned. Other party leaders tainted by normalization remained in their functions, to the manifest discontent of OF and the people at the mass demonstrations. Under increasing pressure both from within the party and from the streets, on November 26 the party dropped Štěpán (who also left his Prague district party functions), Lenárt, and other compromised figures.[13]

Both government and party were still vainly attempting to undermine the general strike with promises of dialogue and concerns over lost production. OF adopted a masterful strategy to counter appeals to economic worries. The strike would be symbolic, lasting two hours at midday, and students volunteered to man crucial shift work or emergency services so that production and public safety would not suffer. The general strike on November 27 was a great success. Surveys by an official institute indicated that countrywide almost half the population stopped work to some extent, the great majority of them for the full two hours. Another quarter publicly supported the strike in ways that OF and VPN had recommended short of a work stoppage. About 10 percent were prevented from showing support, and the remainder chose not to take part. Participation in Prague reached 57 percent.[14] Public support made the strike the incontrovertible proof that the regime lacked all legitimacy. As the leaders of party and government absorbed that lesson, the pace of change quickened. On November 29, the Federal Assembly formally abrogated the constitutional guarantee of the "leading role" of the KSČ, and removed the political monopoly of the NF and the ideological monopoly of Marxism-Leninism in national life.

The government reorganization proceeded more slowly. The new cabinet announced on December 3 fell far short of meeting the public's wishes. Of the 21 members, 16 were communists, 2 were from the tame NF political parties, and 3 had no formal party membership. Even the government's statement condemning the 1968 invasion as a "violation of the norms of relations between sovereign states," won little favor. Several more days of mass demonstrations, together with OF's refusal to support the new government, forced Adamec to resign on December 7. The Slovak communist and former deputy prime minister, Marián Čalfa, unveiled a new "government of national understanding" on December 10. For the first time since 1948, the communists were in a minority (9 out of 21 members). Celebrated dissidents who had been in prison or banished to manual labor weeks before, such as Jiří Dienstbier, Jan Čarnogurský, and Miroslav Kusý, also took roles in the new government.[15] It was a caretaker regime that would prepare for a freely contested election to be held by June 1990.

OF and the other opponents of the regime felt that as long as Husák

Václav Havel addressing the crowds on Wenceslas Square with the news of the first non-communist government since 1948, December 10, 1989. (ČTK photo)

was still president, there could be no guarantee that the changes would last. Thus while concentrating on the new government, they also called for Husák's resignation and "Havel to the Castle!"[16] On December 10, after swearing in the new government, Husák finally resigned. By this time Havel was the leading candidate to succeed him, both inside OF and on the streets. Dubček was Havel's likeliest rival, and the communists seized upon his candidacy as a way of dividing the Czech and Slovak leaders.[17] In the end, with grace, Dubček accepted the post of chairman of the Federal Assembly on December 28, 1989. The next day he presided over the ceremony in the Vladislav Hall in which the same body elected Havel ninth president of the republic.

The "Velvet Revolution" seems, even after more than a decade, to have an almost absurd or surrealist character. A small group of dissidents, together with the students and supported by growing masses of ordinary citizens at the public demonstrations, confronted a regime that had lost legitimacy. Neither side had a clear picture of what to do next. After years of principled but apparently fruitless opposition, dissident figures seemed at times bemused by the growing sense of their own power. Stories such as those told of Dienstbier, who overnight went from boiler stoker to foreign minister, emphasize the strangeness these dissidents felt at being catapulted from irrelevance to positions of real authority and responsibility.[18] As it became convinced that it would be possible to push for more, OF gained confidence and increased its demands, while the party increasingly lost its bearings. The continued presence of thousands of ordinary Czechs and Slovaks at the demonstrations provided crucial leverage, while bringing more people into the movement as the costs of joining decreased with the decreasing likelihood of massive repression.[19] Yet, while the crowds knew what they were against, they did not always have a clear picture of where they wanted to go. As Czechoslovakia entered the year 1990 under a non-communist government, the question that faced it and its new leaders was "where to now?"

THE SHORT LIFE AND HARD TIMES OF THE CZECH AND SLOVAK FEDERATIVE REPUBLIC

During the decade after the Velvet Revolution one of the most used (and overused) words applied to all the countries in East Central

Europe was "transition." Among the many faces of the transition, three led the way: transition to democratic political systems, to free-market economies, and to pluralistic civil societies. This threefold transition was complicated by other concerns, including security questions after the Warsaw Pact dissolved, future relations to the USSR (itself disintegrating), and internal ethnic and national minority issues. As Czechoslovakia faced all these challenges, the underlying question of future relations between Czechs and Slovaks within the state gave them each added complexity.

The Triple Transition in the ČSFR

Practically everyone in Czechoslovakia by the end of 1989 was definite about one thing: they wanted to live in a genuine democracy, without adjectives like "people's" or "socialist," with which they had had such unhappy historical experiences. Thus Čalfa's government saw its raison d'être in carrying out free elections for a truly democratic parliament. Aware of their tenuous legitimacy, the representatives in the two National Councils and the Federal Assembly agreed that they should change the constitution only with an electoral mandate. As a result, the transition to democracy began using the pseudo-democratic constitution of the ČSSR after 1969. Between April and May 1990, the assembly passed laws guaranteeing civic and economic freedoms such as freedom of association, assembly, and petition, establishing the legal equality of different forms of property, and allowing the creation of limited-liability companies and economic contacts with foreign firms. The assembly also adopted an electoral law with proportional representation and fixed party lists, as in the first republic.

Czechoslovakia's first free, democratic elections were duly held on June 8–9, 1990. Voters elected delegates to both the Federal Assembly and the ČNR and SNR. The result, following the pattern of most of Czechoslovakia's neighbors in the northern tier of the former Soviet bloc, was a massive repudiation of the communists.[20] After some hesitation, OF and VPN contested the elections as "movements," still chary of the label "parties." Three distinct groups cooperated in these movements. The dissidents who had opposed the regime in earlier years were joined by others who had occupied what one analyst called "parking orbits" in the old system: places where they built professional experience and expertise, developing skills needed now, while not openly opposing the regime.[21] Finally there were communists or former communists who also had desperately needed skills and were willing to repudiate the party.[22]

Together OF and VPN polled nearly half of the votes cast (47 percent), which translated into 170 seats out of the 300-member Federal Assembly (itself divided into the House of Nations and the House of the People). The communists garnered 47 seats, with the Christian Democrats third with 40 seats.[23] In the simultaneous voting for the ČNR, OF's predominance was even greater, with a total of 127 mandates out of 200 going to its candidates. The communists followed far behind with 32 seats, while the autonomist coalition for Moravia and Silesia won 22 seats and the Christian Democrats won 19.[24] VPN and its allies in the Christian Democratic Movement similarly controlled the SNR.

One distinctive feature of Czechoslovakia's political landscape emerged already in the first free elections. In spite of the cooperation between OF and VPN, Czechoslovakia lacked any genuine statewide political movement or party. Even the KSČ was on its way to separating into two distinct parties. Instead, political forces organized themselves distinctly in each republic, a feature that influenced the institutional choices made by the three governments functioning on the basis of the 1990 elections, the federal, the Czech, and the Slovak.[25]

The electoral law established the proportional system, which encouraged party proliferation, making it difficult for any single party to form a majority government. The system was also parliamentary, not presidential. The historical traditions of the first Czechoslovak state included Masaryk's powerful moral authority, but even his constitutional powers were limited. Havel, who for now enjoyed something like Masaryk's moral stature among his fellow citizens, wielded even less formal political power. Elected by the legislature and subject to its recall, he had no popular electoral legitimacy. Executive power rested with the prime minister, and as a nonpartisan figure, the president had to avoid openly supporting any party's political ideas.[26]

During these first years of transition the political spectrum was unstable. The umbrella "movements" that won the 1990 elections sheltered a broad range of political views.[27] Predictably, once the elections were over and the communists repudiated, they began to reveal internal tensions, and finally broke up into more "normal" political parties. Attitudes to economic reform were a catalyst for the emergence of political parties, though personalities also played a role.

In February 1991 the Civic Forum formally split into political parties, the strongest of which was Václav Klaus's Civic Democratic Party (ODS). Two smaller parties with similar philosophies but incompatible personalities and ideas on organization also kept the "civic" label, the Civic Democratic Alliance (ODA) and the Civic Movement (OH), led by Foreign Minister Dienstbier. These three parties cooperated in government until 1992. The center was held by a party with roots going back to the prewar People's party, the Christian and Democratic Union–Czechoslovak People's Party (KDU-ČSL). On the left the Communist Party of Bohemia and Moravia (KSČM), as the KSČ eventually rechristened itself, stubbornly refused to become a social-democratic party of the Western European type. The KSČM initially overshadowed the revived Czechoslovak, later Czech, Social-Democratic Party (ČSSD). There was also an autonomist Moravian-Silesian coalition, and the Republican Party on the radical fringe.

The internal tensions within the VPN and between it and its coalition partner, the Christian Democratic Movement (KDH), led by Čarnogurský, increasingly focused on the VPN prime minister, Mečiar. When he was forced from office in 1991 and Čarnogurský took over, Mečiar turned his supporters into a new party, the Movement for a Democratic Slovakia (HZDS). The HZDS advocated preserving the social networks of the socialist regime and going slowly on privatization. The Party of the Democratic Left (SDL') re-created the Slovak communists as a mainstream European-style left-wing party. On the right the Slovak National Party (SNS) sometimes cooperated with Mečiar and sometimes criticized him. Slovakia's Hungarian minority had its own Christian-Democratic movement and a coalition entitled Coexistence, which later split into separate Hungarian parties and then recoalesced into another coalition.

Economic reform was central to all three government programs. Transition to a market economy was the accepted goal, but exactly how to achieve it remained debatable. One group of Czech government advisers favored a gradual approach. State-owned enterprises would be restructured under government supervision, and privatization would follow by finding private, possibly foreign, investment for the restructured companies. The classic example of this approach was the sale of a share of the flagship automobile company, Škoda-Mladá Boleslav, to Volkswagen in 1991. Potential problems with this approach included its slow pace and abuse by managers of state-owned companies, who might privatize them in their own interests or try not to compete with newly established private firms under their control. The advantage was to minimize the impact of the economic transformation on the population.

Klaus as federal finance minister argued that there was no alternative to rapid economic transformation. Klaus carried through some macroeconomic measures to begin the transformation, including currency devaluations in 1990, the removal of state control over most wholesale and retail prices on January 1, 1991, and the pursuit of restrictive monetary policies to restrain inflation. Transformation to a free market, however, required a fundamental shift to private ownership. Klaus and his advisers developed a plan featuring "coupon privatization" to change the structure of ownership in the country as rapidly as possible. All Czechoslovak citizens who paid a nominal fee received booklets of coupons, which they could exchange for shares in privatized enterprises, making the majority of citizens direct part-owners of the economy.[28]

One unexpected feature of the coupon privatization was the emergence of investment funds. The brainchild of Viktor Kožený, a twenty-eight-year-old entrepreneur whose example was rapidly followed by banks and other institutions, the investment funds purchased citizens' coupon booklets for a fixed sum, promising impressive rates of return.[29] The investment funds with their guarantee of high returns for little outlay greatly stimulated the sales of coupon booklets, and the first wave of coupon privatization, initiated in May 1992, was considered a great success. Approximately 8.5 million citizens took part, either individually or through investment funds.

Though perhaps the gaudiest, the coupon scheme was not the only string to the privatization bow. More traditional means were also used, in the "great" and "small" privatizations. The small privatization sold small, service-oriented enterprises by auction beginning in January 1991. The great privatization sold selected large-scale manufacturing enterprises to concrete investors on the basis of government-approved plans, or to the highest bidder beginning in October 1991. One other privatization method was restitution, an effort to undo some of the injustices of the communist regime. Private real property seized by the state after February 25, 1948, was to be returned to its original owners or their heirs. Restitution raised uncomfortable issues with an international dimension, because the regime specifically drew the line at the communist seizure of power in 1948. This choice avoided the problem of restitution to Germans expelled from Czechoslovakia after 1945, but it also left unresolved the issue of Jewish property seized by the Germans after 1939. In the end the government reached a compromise with Jewish property owners that returned their properties as fulfillment of promises made, but never carried out, by postwar governments. Restitution also raised the question of returning church holdings in arable and forest land, as well as the fate of monuments such as St. Vitus's cathedral in Prague.

In spite of these controversies, both the domestic and international response to the Czechoslovak economic program was positive. The economy did show a jump in inflation and negative GDP growth rate (see Table 3). The loss of the former CMEA market caused balance-of-trade problems as the ČSFR sought to reorient its trade to the West, but unemployment remained comparatively low, reflecting in part the government's slowness to close down large state-owned enterprises and in part the ability of the growing service sector to absorb workers. Tourism, focused largely on Prague but taking in other parts of the country

TABLE 3

ECONOMIC INDICATORS IN CZECHOSLOVAKIA, 1990–1992 (ANNUAL % CHANGE)

Czechoslovakia	*1990*	*1991*	*1992*
Inflation	10.0	57.9	11.8
Unemployment	1.7	6.6	5.5
GDP growth	−0.4	−16.4	−7.2
Industrial growth	−3.7	−23.1	−10.0
Czech Lands	*1990*	*1991*	*1992*
Inflation	9.9	56.6	12.7
Unemployment	1.1	4.4	2.6
GDP growth	−1.9	−14.5	−10.6
Industrial growth	—	−25.0	−10.6
Slovakia	*1990*	*1991*	*1992*
Inflation	10.3	61.2	10.0
Unemployment	2.3	11.8	10.4
GDP growth	−2.0	−15.8	−7.0
Industrial growth	−2.7	−24.9	−13.7

SOURCE: Carol Skalnik Leff, *The Czech and Slovak Republics: Nation Versus State* (Boulder, Colo.: Westview Press, 1997), p. 183.

as well, also provided jobs as it blossomed. In comparison with its neighbors, especially Poland and Hungary where "shock therapy" approaches to the economic transition won out, Czechoslovakia initially looked very successful.

Czechoslovakia's foreign policy, as elsewhere in the region, was expressed in the slogan "back to Europe." Symbolically this return to Europe was contraposed to the forty years of integration into foreign, economic, and security policy structures dominated by the Soviet Union. Czechoslovakia contributed to the dissolution of the Warsaw Pact on July 1, 1991, and on July 27 the last of the Soviet troops stationed on Czechoslovak soil after 1968 left. The CMEA was wound up in the same year. Czechoslovakia, which had been one of the founding members of the IMF and the International Bank for Reconstruction and Development, rejoined those bodies on September 20, 1990. As early as February 21, 1990, Czechoslovakia became a member of the Council of Europe, and it signed an association agreement with the European Union on December 16, 1991. Regional initiatives, such as the "Visegrád Three," christened at a meeting there between the presidents of Poland, Hungary, and the ČSFR on February 15, 1991, always played second fiddle to the longed-for return to "Europe."[30] Nevertheless, the Visegrád states created the Central Europe Free Trade Agreement (CEFTA) in 1992.

Standing astride the road back to "Europe" was Germany. The German question interconnected problems of foreign affairs, national identity, and Czech-Slovak relations: Germany was the economic model of what most Czechs aspired to, and also the likeliest foreign investor in their privatizing economy. The German issue also opened memories of the Czech and Slovak experience in World War II, especially the Munich conference and the destruction of Czechoslovakia, the wartime Slovak state, and the postwar expulsion of the Germans. The German question raised issues about what kind of society the Czechs and Slovaks were forming, and whether their attitude to this complicated past said anything about their present-day ability to create a pluralistic, civil society.

Already before the fall of communism, dissident circles had discussed the expulsion.[31] In a gesture that unleashed media debate on the same issues, at Christmas 1989 Havel sent a letter to West German president Richard von Weizsäcker in which he called the expulsion "a deeply immoral act," for which he apologized.[32] The ensuing public reaction demonstrated how sensitive the Sudeten German question remained, with opinion firmly against Havel. In March 1990, von Weizsäcker returned Havel's gesture during a state visit to Prague on the anniversary of the Nazi occupation.[33] Negotiations on a treaty of friendship and mutual cooperation proceeded over the next year and a half. Then at the last minute, Slovak politicians objected to language in the preamble recognizing that "the Czechoslovak state has never ceased to exist since 1918," which ignored the Slovak state from 1939 to 1945. Nevertheless, Chancellor Helmuth Kohl and President Havel finally signed the treaty on February 27, 1992.[34]

Because the treaty specifically left property questions outside its scope, however, the Czech-German relationship was not definitively settled by its ratification. On the Czech side, the government refused to negotiate directly with representatives of the expelled Sudeten Germans.[35] On the German side, the political significance of the Sudeten German organizations, especially to the Bavarian Christian Social Union, the federal Christian Democratic Union's partners, gave them leverage that they used to keep the issue open.

These issues of retribution and restitution had a broader counterpart in a more general need to overcome the past, specifically the communist past. They also had a personal dimension for individual Czechs and Slovaks. During the twenty years of normalization, only a relative handful of people became active dissidents. Others made the personal compromises necessary to pursue education, a career, protect their family, and gain access to scarce goods or other benefits. Still others opportunistically supported and participated in the regime. The psychological fallout from this situation added a painful and embarrassing undertone to the problem of what to do with the major Czechoslovak communist leaders. There were calls to try those who collaborated with the Soviet invasion in 1968, but although the Czechoslovak government publicly identified twenty-one party officials (five of them already deceased) as traitors, for the moment no trials ensued. Only Štěpán was tried and sentenced to two and a half years for ordering the November 17, 1989, attack.[36] Trying the former KSČ leadership did not, in any case, address another troubling aspect of the past, the network of informers and collaborators controlled by the secret police (StB).

Though the StB was abolished in January 1990, its files still existed like unexploded land mines buried under the political landscape. Thousands of people were named in its registers of agents. This situation drove the interest in "lustration," a term with roots in Classical Latin, where it refers to a sacrifice of ritual purification. Lustration involved many motives, not all of them praiseworthy. In addition to the desire to deal with the past, there were fears that compromised politicians would be subject to blackmail. Political calculations also played a part, beginning just before the first free elections in 1990 when the leader of the People's Party was exposed as an StB agent, ending his political career and damaging the KDU-ČSL.[37] A parliamentary commission took up the lustration of members of parliament, and presented its findings on live television, but without the desired effect.[38] The case of Jan Kavan illustrates the ambiguities of relying on secret police records to document collaboration. Kavan, who for twenty years had actively opposed the regime and supported dissidents from his British exile, formally cleared his name only in 1996, but in 1998 became Czech foreign minister.

In an attempt to regularize the situation, the federal parliament passed a lustration law in October 1991. For a period of five years no one who had joined or collaborated with the StB, or had held a high party position, could serve in elected or appointed office in the government or administration, or on companies in which the state held a stake. Critics of the law spoke of witch hunts and suggested that its aim was to rid the ODS of rivals such as the dissident-dominated OH, as well as the Slovak center-left and Vladimir Mečiar (against whom unsubstantiated allegations of collaboration were in fact raised).[39]

Czech-Slovak Relations and the Velvet Divorce

As these problems illustrate, the transition in almost all its facets involved Czech-Slovak relations. Initially, placing these relations on a new footing looked no more difficult than other challenges facing the Czechs and Slovaks. Both sides agreed that the 1969 federalization was unsatisfactory, but were confident that a new, more enduring relationship would be attained. Signs that it would not be that easy emerged early in 1990 with the "hyphen war." When President Havel proposed that "Socialist" be dropped from the country's official name, Slovak representatives suggested spelling the reborn state's name "Czecho-Slovak Republic." After much apparently needless wrangling, the assembly approved the use of the hyphen in Slovakia and no hyphen in the Czech lands. This unwieldy solution was replaced with a completely new name, the Czech and Slovak Federative Republic.[40] Symbols matter, and behind the "hyphen war" lay a history of unresolved questions about the Czech-Slovak relationship.

How did it come about that the resolution eventually chosen was to separate into two independent states? On the one hand, the international setting, for once in the history of this bumpy relationship, was not one of threatening crisis. The Soviet Union was focused on internal concerns, and indeed it also eventually dissolved. Germany's postwar democratization and integration into Western Europe lessened the threat from that side. Thus, unlike in 1938 and 1968, discussions of the Czech-Slovak relationship did not take place in an atmosphere of imminent crisis. On the other hand, the international considerations that had brought Czechs and Slovaks together in 1918 and again after 1945 had lost their potency. After the expulsion of the Germans, the Czechs no longer needed the Slovaks to offset an internal minority. The ČSFR still contained a significant Hungarian population, but Slovak fears of Hungarian revisionism (though never absent) were dulled by the sense that the international system would not allow Hungary to expand against its neighbors.[41] Historical memories of previous critical moments in the relationship were thus more likely to reinforce negative images and expectations (for the Czechs, that the Slovaks "always" took advantage of their life-or-death crises, for the Slovaks, that the Czechs would never take them seriously until the knife was against their throats).[42]

Another fateful historical legacy was the federal structure inherited from the communist ČSSR, which remained in effect while the first freely elected parliament prepared a new Czechoslovak constitution within its two-year term. The federal institutions in the ČSSR constitution had existed in a centralized one party dictatorship where they were actually irrelevant. Now these institutions operated in a free, contested, and multiparty environment. The structure of the legislature, with federal, Czech, and Slovak parliaments sharing power, has already been described. Let us look more closely at the Federal Assembly. It consisted of a 150-member upper house, the Chamber of the People, elected by the total population through proportional representation, and a lower house, the Chamber of the Nations, composed of seventy-five representatives from the Czech lands and seventy-five from Slovakia.[43] Both houses had to approve legislation, and on certain key issues, such as constitutional amendments, declarations of war, and the election of the president, majority rule was suspended. Such legislation required not only a three-fifths majority in the upper house, but a similar majority in *both* national sections of the lower house. Thus only thirty-one Slovak or Czech deputies could block any constitutional amendment, a feature that could make passing constitutional legislation extremely difficult.[44]

The structure of the state also contributed to the emergence of separate Czech and Slovak party systems after 1990.[45] The leaders of the ČNR and SNR and their respective governments tended to seek first the interests of "their" constituency and not the federation. Discussions over the relative competence of the federal and republic institutions—in which Czech premier Petr Pithart and his Slovak counterpart Mečiar stressed "strong republics" as the foundation for a strong federation—led in December 1990 to the passage of a constitutional amendment under which the federation retained control of defense, foreign affairs, monetary and economic policies, and ethnic minority questions, but the republics gained broad economic powers. The republics continued to exist within the federal structure but increasingly went their own ways.[46]

Still other institutional factors contributed to the competitive behavior of the political elites. The lability of voter allegiances meant that nearly all votes were up for grabs and encouraged politicians to seek vote-getting issues. Appeals to national sentiment worked well. The lack of a strong tradition of elite cooperation also played a role. Under communism, even within the party, elites tended to circulate within either the Czech lands or Slovakia. Some extra-party cooperation among dissidents did exist, but such ties were occasional and limited. The role of the former dissidents also declined, especially after the 1992 elections.[47] All these factors made negotiations between representatives of the federal, Czech, and Slovak governments over the form of an "authentic federation" a recurrent source of disagreement.

These negotiations began as early as April 1990 and continued through several rounds, until just before the elections in June 1992.[48] The two sides approached the concept of the federation from fundamentally different positions. From the Czech perspective, Czechoslovakia already existed as a federation and the question was to determine what competencies it could transfer without rendering it incapable of functioning as an effective state. Thus Czechs favored a strong federation with significant powers reserved for the central authorities. From the Slovak side this attitude smacked of the stereotypical "Pragocentrism," and their starting point was the existence of two states, Slovakia and the Czech lands. The question was what of their own powers these two states would give up to the central institutions. In some Slovak versions the Czech-Slovak federation resembled a confederation or even just a loose commonwealth with a minimum of power granted to the federal level.[49]

Mečiar's dismissal in April 1991 changed the faces at the table, but it did not alter the issues.[50] In conversations with Pithart, Čarnogurský maintained that an agreement between the two republics should take the form of a state treaty, preceding any new federal constitution. The Czechs considered a treaty acceptable as a political initiative, but felt it would not be internationally binding because the federation already existed.[51] In continuing discussions Pithart's government agreed to accept a treaty, and in January 1992 both national councils created commissions to draft it. In February, these commissions and representatives from all three governments hammered out a text, which was to be submitted to the ČNR and SNR for approval. At the SNR presidium meeting on March 12, the proposal failed to reach the agenda for the full council by a single vote. Both sides agreed to postpone further discussions until after the 1992 elections.[52]

TABLE 4
CZECH AND SLOVAK OPINION
ON THE PREFERRED FORM
OF STATE (PERCENT)

In favor of (percent)	*Unitary State*	*Federa-tion*	*Confedera-tion*	*Indepen-dence*	*Other/Don't Know*
June 1990					
Czech Republic	30	45	—	12	13
Slovakia	14	63	—	13	6
November 1991					
Czech Republic	39	30	4	5	22
Slovakia	20	26	27	14	13
March 1992					
Czech Republic	34	27	6	11	22
Slovakia	13	24	32	17	12

SOURCE: Carol Skalnik Leff, *The Czech and Slovak Republics: Nation Versus State* (Boulder, Colo.: Westview Press, 1997), p. 138.

The 1992 elections were fought primarily on economic issues, though in Slovakia the right to sovereignty was also significant. Nevertheless, questions about the economic transformation of the ČSFR necessarily also influenced Czech-Slovak relations. Klaus, contesting the elections as head of the ODS, continued to argue that a rapid economic restructuring program was necessary. In Slovakia, economic fears stemming from Slovakia's reliance on the arms industry and other heavy industries in large factories made Slovak politicians favor a slower-paced reform with more concern for the social consequences. In Czech eyes, the Slovak reluctance to bite the bullet fitted the stereotype of Slovakia as a recipient of Czech investment and resources. Slovaks pointed out that they suffered disproportionately from the economic changes already and could only expect it to get worse under Klaus's proposals (see Table 3).[53] Thus economic policies and economic fears also played a role in the impending dissolution of the federation. Deadlocked political institutions prevented a resolution of economic policy questions without a resolution of the question of Czech-Slovak relations.

The results of the elections, held on June 5–6, 1992, were a victory for Klaus and the ODS in the Czech lands, and for Mečiar and HZDS in Slovakia, each with approximately 30 percent of the vote.[54] The voters had spoken: what they had said was not clear. The outcome of the 1992 elections was not an endorsement for the eventual dissolution of the federation. All public opinion research carried out at the time suggested that the majority of both Czechs and Slovaks wanted to live in a common state. These results fueled calls for a referendum, some from President Havel himself. It is probable that opponents of a referendum did fear to put the question to the test of a general vote. On the other hand, the public opinion evidence says nothing about *what kind* of common state the Czechs and Slovaks imagined living in. As Table 4 shows, changes in support for different forms of state over time included a small but regular increase in Slovak sentiment for independence, a dramatic collapse of Slovak support for a federation, but no clear preference on the form of a common state. Clearly, however, the majority of Czechs in 1992 joined their leaders in favoring a strong centralist form (either unitary or federal) while the Slovaks similarly supported in greatest numbers a looser, confederal structure. Since this was precisely the issue on which political discussion continually foundered, a public vote that returned such a result would in effect have resolved nothing.

Immediately after the elections, President Havel asked Klaus, as leader of the strongest party, to form the federal government.[55] Mečiar insisted on negotiations with Klaus first about the government's composition. After several meetings, Klaus announced that he was uninterested in becoming federal prime minister, since the Slovak side viewed the government's role as liquidating the federation. Eventually, the two parties agreed on the composition of a caretaker federal government. Mečiar became Slovak prime minister; Klaus headed a Czech coalition government.[56] Not only did the federal government have fewer ministries than the Czech and Slovak governments, they also were led by second-level politicians.

In the initial post-election meetings, while Mečiar and Klaus were meeting privately, Michal Kováč described to the rest of the Czech delegation the Slovak plans to return to the 1968 concept of an economic and defense union. When this indiscretion was relayed to Klaus in the plenary meeting, Mečiar turned "pale, then ashen, apparently crumbling on the inside. . . . The battle was over before it had begun. It was time to haggle and to sign a peace treaty."[57] That haggling still took several weeks, during which Havel's term as president expired. The HZDS refused to back his reelection bid on July 3, which failed as a result, though legally he was still president for five months. In fulfillment of the Slovak government program, the SNR overwhelmingly adopted a declaration of sovereignty on July 17, stating that "the thousand-year-long struggle of the Slovak nation for identity has been fulfilled."[58] Within hours, Havel tendered his resignation to the federal assembly, effective July 20. Havel denied that he resigned in protest against the Slovak declaration, but stated that he could not fulfill the oath he took to the ČSFR by remaining in office.[59] Czechoslovakia spent its last months without a president.

As the ČSSD led efforts to head off the dissolution, it appeared that Mečiar and the HZDS were hesitating, hoping to prepare for statehood under some form of arrangement with the Czech lands. Klaus and the ODS now became the ones pushing for a radical resolution. A basic agreement on the end of the federation as of December 31, 1992, reached at a meeting in Brno on August 26, was eventually presented to the Federal Assembly on October 27. Meanwhile, the SNR had adopted a new constitution for Slovakia. The Czech government moved more slowly, but it submitted a draft constitution to the ČNR on November 10. The federal parliament approved the law ending the federation on November 25. The Czech constitution was finally adopted on December

16, and the final session of the federal parliament was held on December 17. At midnight, as 1992 turned to 1993, the Czechoslovak state formally ceased to exist.

The dissolution of Czechoslovakia was thus not quite as "velvet" as the label suggests. The Czech-Slovak "divorce" did, however, take place in a legislative, orderly, and nonviolent way. In spite of friction during their more than seven decades of shared statehood, Czechs and Slovaks had never used violence against each other. Neither the Czech lands nor Slovakia had large settled populations of the other nationality. Instead of demands for border revisions or saber-rattling threats to protect "fellow-nationals" under alien oppression, the question of Czechs in Slovakia and Slovaks in the Czech lands was therefore simply another item to be settled by mutual agreement.[60] Even the institutional arrangements that contributed to the eventual Czech-Slovak "divorce" also contributed to the peaceful dissolution of the federation and the resolution of the questions arising from it. Thus if the failure of the seventy-three-year Czechoslovak experiment in sharing a common state highlights the problems of democracy in a multinational setting, at least it also suggests that—given the right conditions—democratic institutions can help a peaceful resolution of those problems through separation.[61]

16 Alone at Last

On October 24, 1992, the Czech government held a solemn ceremony at Vyšehrad, seat of the Přemyslid dukes. It began with the hymn "Hospodine, pomiluj ny," evoking memories of the Cyrilo-Methodian mission to the Slavs. Following appropriate speeches, the dignitaries laid a wreath at the plaque commemorating Vratislav I, the first king of Bohemia, who had died 900 years before.[1] In this way the politicians who would in a few weeks bear responsibility for the newly emerging Czech Republic anchored its statehood in the history of medieval Bohemia. At the same time, however, they also anchored it in the history of Czechoslovakia, which Klaus claimed in his remarks as "an inseparable part of Czech history, . . . at the time of its birth the logical culmination of the Czech liberal and democratic tradition, created jointly by such personalities as Palacký, Havlíček, Masaryk."[2]

Yet the new Czech Republic would also be significantly different. As one historian commented, "we cannot hark back to history—this state has never been a Czech state, it has always been mixed."[3] Now it was less mixed than ever before. In Pithart's words, the Czechs' "housemates" had been removed from their home: first the Jews and Germans, then the Ruthenians, finally the Slovaks and the Hungarians. Thus the civic principle, "instead of being a demanding and praiseworthy value toward which we strive, is the only practical possibility: we Czechs (and Moravians and Silesians) are after all here by ourselves."[4] The Czechs were not quite "by themselves" in their new state, but they continued in traditions marked out by both Czechoslovakia and the Czech national renascence as they pursued this "only practical possibility."[5] Selecting and commemorating traditions helps define the nature of the state, so perhaps the appropriation of the democratic traditions of the first Czechoslovak Republic can serve to anchor and legitimize democracy in its Czech successor.[6]

GOING IT ALONE

As they began life in their new state, the Czechs could find security in a sense of continuity. Klaus's ODS led the coalition government, Havel returned—this time as Czech president—to the Castle, and the government pursued continued economic transformation.[7] Further privatization, including coupon privatization, had been postponed by the conflict over the state. Now it could be undertaken with renewed gusto.[8] Beginning in April 1994, a second wave unfolded, involving fewer enterprises owing to the loss of Slovakia, but attracting more Czech participants. By the end of 1994, more than 80 percent of the country's GNP was produced by the private sector.[9] It seemed that coupon privatization was going to work.

The Economic Transformation: Success?

The Czech government certainly viewed the transformation as a success. Its leaders preached a neo-liberal, free market message that won them the favorable regard of Western financial actors, and the Czech reputation as the leader among the transforming economies had more behind it than rhetoric. Geography placed the Czech economy between two advanced Western economies, Austria and Germany. History gave the Czechs the interwar republic's industrial reputation, suggesting that they could reclaim that status. Normalization gave them low foreign debt, since Husák's regime had been loath to borrow abroad. Klaus's government served out its full term, which created an impression of stability.[10] Fiscal responsibility, avoiding deficit budgets—Klaus even suggested a balanced budget law—maintaining a stable currency, and striving to control inflation encouraged investors. By the end of 1994, Klaus was speaking of the "post-transformation" stage in the Czech economy.[11] The Czech Republic's entry in 1995 to the OECD (which the Czech press referred to as "the rich mens' club") was touted as recognition of success.[12]

Through the mid-1990s the Czech Republic's economic performance suggested that it had successfully met the initial challenges of transformation (see Table 5). It was cited as evidence that radical reform not only succeeded, but also reaped political benefits.[13] Klaus's government enjoyed popular support that other post-communist governments could only envy.[14] Yet some analysts pointed out that this apparent success could be explained by other factors. In spite of his Thatcherite rhetoric, Klaus postponed badly needed structural reorganization of state-controlled enterprises while preserving a significant level of social support.[15] Low unemployment was thus not evidence of success, but a symptom that the reckoning had been postponed. Optimists suggested that the Czechs might get away with it, if the private sector could absorb the unemployment created by eventual restructuring. Other critics drew attention to the rising trade imbalance. Only the explosion of tourism to the Czech Republic, and the intangible asset of Prague, prevented the budget from being in the red.[16]

Not by Bread Alone

Klaus's coalition had to settle two constitutional "leftovers" from the breakup of Czechoslovakia. The Czech constitution provided for an upper house, the Senate, which Klaus was in no hurry to create. Under

TABLE 5

SELECTED ECONOMIC INDICATORS
FOR THE CZECH REPUBLIC, 1993–1997

Year	1993	1994	1995	1996	1997
GDP growth (percent)	−0.9	2.6	4.8	4.1	0.3
Unemployment (percent)	3.5	3.2	2.9	3.5	5.2
Consumer price inflation (percent)	20.8	10.0	9.1	8.8	8.5
Trade balance (US$ billions)	0.34	−0.44	−3.8	−5.8	−4.4

SOURCE: Compiled from the U.S. State Department, Bureau of Economic and Business Affairs, *Country Reports on Economic Policy and Trade Practices* <http://www.state.gov>.

the constitution, if the lower house were dissolved, the Senate remained in session to provide continuity. Without a Senate, therefore, theoretically the government could not be dismissed. After three unsuccessful drafts, parliament passed legislation creating the Senate in the autumn of 1995, though arguments over when to hold the elections continued. Elections were finally held in November 1996.

The second "leftover" involved setting up a regional administration between the central government and the local communities. Such structures had been common in Bohemian and Moravian history, and in Czechoslovakia the introduction of land-based administrative units had recognized Bohemia, Moravia-Silesia, Slovakia, and Ruthenia. Setting up regional governments, whether at the land level or in districts, might have undone the balance of power in the Czech system, which favored Klaus's coalition. Given separate Moravian political sentiment and strong regional disparities in unemployment, a regional challenge to Klaus could not be discounted. Therefore, he remained adamantly opposed to any change in the centralized administration. He proposed more numerous small units, the opposition supported larger units, and the issue was not resolved before the elections of 1996.

Klaus's preference for centralization shaped his attitude to civil society, setting him at odds with President Havel. In separate speeches on the anniversary of the "Velvet Revolution" in 1994, they stated their positions. Havel argued against relying on the political and economic system to stabilize itself. "Parties and power are only the means to fulfill the goals of the common good," he insisted. "Parties should listen to the multifaceted opinions of a pluralistic civil society, as expressed by all individuals, groups, and organizations, including educated people, experts, academics, and intellectuals."[17] Klaus, pointing to the democratic political system with independent parties and a free market, continued: "Nothing else needed to be done. Some people, however, still want to take advantage of the collapse of communism to create something more than 'just' a free society. . . . For them, it is not enough that our country has free citizens—they would like it to have better citizens."[18] The practical problem involved was establishing nonprofit status for churches and other organizations involved in public interest activities. At the end of September 1995 a bill finally created legal foundations for "organizations for the public benefit." It granted exemptions from property, inheritance, and gift taxes as well as a 30 percent income tax write-off to organizations engaged in charitable, educational, social, and similar activities.[19]

Other issues also continued beyond the breakup of the federation. The lustration law passed in 1991 remained valid in the Czech Republic, and in the autumn of 1993 another law declared the communist regime illegal and unjust, opening up the possibility of prosecutions for crimes committed in service to the regime in spite of the standard statute of limitations. An Office for the Documentation and Investigation of the Crimes of Communism (ÚDV) was set up, but its work went very slowly. The ÚDV brought charges of treason against five former leading party officials, as well as a group of police and secret police officers, in 1995, but the state prosecutor's office sent them back as incomplete.[20]

The once and future Czech presidents: President Václav Havel and Prime Minister Václav Klaus at a government meeting, April 1993. (ČTK photo)

As the five-year term of the lustration law approached its end in 1996, parliament approved its extension to the year 2000, overriding Havel's veto.[21] Both issues provoked discussions about the past, guilt, collaboration, and resistance, but little progress toward trials and their potential catharsis.

The communist past was linked to the problem of corruption. The public believed that former managers and communist officials benefited from the economic transformation, parlaying their connections into a lateral move into the economy, where they were doing very well as "red capitalists." Probably the most notorious privatization scandal was the Lizner Affair, which began in October 1994 when the head of the Center for Coupon Privatization, Jaroslav Lizner, was arrested with 8,334,500 crowns in cash in his briefcase. He was accused of taking it as a bribe from a company wanting to buy a stake in one of the major dairies. Lizner was convicted and sentenced to six years in prison (he was released three years early for good behavior). To the end he denied any wrongdoing, and hinted that he was the victim of intrigues from high places.[22]

Since privatization was so intimately bound up with Klaus and the ODS, the Lizner affair had political repercussions. So did scandals over party financing. Each party had funding difficulties, since they almost all started from nothing and ran up significant debts in the earliest political campaigns. Even before the breakup of the federation, the ODS, ODA, and KDU-ČSL had been involved in dubious loan transactions, and the ČSSD suffered from bad bookkeeping and high debts. In November 1994, the ODS organized a fund-raising dinner with Klaus at the Prague Žofín for heads of businesses, many of them state-owned. The reservation fee was 100,000–250,000 crowns. Quickly dubbed the "Meal of Fortune," the affair sparked legislation forbidding state-owned firms from donating to political parties.[23]

In spite of these and similar scandals, Klaus approached the upcoming elections in 1996 with his customary conviction that he was on the right course. The elections, he said, would decide whether or not the Czech Republic would continue down the path of economic growth, low unemployment, political stability, and an increasing standard of living. "We are the only country of the former Eastern bloc in which the post-communist left wing has not returned to power. I believe that it will still be so after the elections."[24]

THE "CZECH ROAD" BITES BACK

The results of the elections, held on May 31 and June 1, 1996, proved Klaus right—barely. The governing coalition lost thirteen seats and fell two seats short of a majority in the Chamber of Deputies. The ODS was still the strongest party, with about 29.6 percent of the vote, but many discontented voters had rallied around the ČSSD, which gained almost 26.4 percent, or three times as many votes as in 1992.[25] To form a majority government without the ČSSD would have necessitated cooperating with the Republicans, and all parties treated them, and the KSČM, as "untouchables." Eventually, Havel brokered an agreement that the ČSSD would "tolerate" a Klaus-led minority coalition government. The socialists received key positions in parliamentary committees and the post of chairman of the Chamber of Deputies for party leader Miloš Zeman.

The rise of the ČSSD appeared to be a Czech version of a regional pattern in which reforming governments had been thrown out and the left returned to power. As early as 1994 the ratio of contented to discontented voters in Czech society was nearly equal, and that discontented vote swung behind the Social Democrats—not toppling the right-wing reformers but limiting their freedom of movement. In any case the ČSSD differed from the other regional left-wing parties in that it was not a successor to the former communists, though Zeman had been a KSČ member. The elections of 1996 seemed to be a step toward consolidating the Czech party system, offering voters a clearer and more stable choice between left and right alternatives.[26]

The Economic Transformation: Failure?

Klaus faced the Czech Republic's increasing economic difficulties at the head of a minority government. Though the 1996 figures were not very different from the previous year, the trade deficit continued to grow, and the structure of GDP growth (driven by consumption, not capital investment) was worrying. The closing of the Privatization Ministry in July 1996 was thus not the triumph it should have been.[27] August brought signs of trouble in the banking industry, as the country's sixth-largest bank, Kreditní Banka Plzeň, collapsed, and the government had to take over Agrobanka Praha, the largest private bank and fifth-largest overall, the next month. Nevertheless, at the beginning of 1997 Klaus sounded his usual self-confident tone, remarking that "you can say anything about the Czech economy except that it is stagnating," and predicting GDP growth of 5 percent for the coming year.[28]

Instead, the continuing high current account deficit forced Klaus's government in April and May 1997 to unveil two economic reform "packages" limiting wages in the state sector, social support payments, and government investments. The government also introduced import deposits, provoking threats of legal action from the European Union. At the end of May, the international financial markets passed their verdict on Klaus's packages, which had not addressed his policy of a strong crown. Under their pressure, the central bank was forced to float the currency. The crown suffered a sharp drop, but within several months had returned to its previous levels. The deeper, structural problems contributing to the balance-of-trade deficit remained.[29]

What had happened to Klaus's economic miracle, when it seemed to have been so successful for so long? Coupon privatization failed to generate capital for the newly privatized companies or the state; it simply transferred nominal ownership to holders of investment coupons or the funds. Companies therefore lacked capital for badly needed modernization, and had to turn to the banks to find it.[30] The coupon privatization also could not ensure effective ownership and management of the privatized concerns. Very few individual investors could take an active role in running the companies in which they invested. The investment funds could not do so either, since the law governing them made it difficult for them to exercise effective corporate governance.[31] The way was open for unscrupulous managers to siphon off the firm's capital assets into dummy enterprises and eventually into their own pockets, a practice the Czechs called "tunneling." Finally, the investment funds themselves tended to be owned or controlled by banks, again because of the shortage of capital. The major shareholder in the banks was the state, which created a different, but tangible, form of state control over the supposedly privatized companies. As a result, many managers ran up debts and losses as they had in the old days.[32]

Klaus repeatedly stated that it was not possible to choose the perfect new owner, and that in fact the *first* owner of a newly privatized company was not important. He counted on the market to force owners to strive for efficiency and a profit. If they failed, more effective managers would buy them out, or, in the worst case, they would go bankrupt.

The market would ensure that in the end, the entire economy benefited. Criticisms of Klaus's approach focus on his lack of understanding for the conditions a functioning free-market economy requires.[33] He had a visceral dislike for any form of regulation, which matched the rhetoric of his self-proclaimed mentors like Milton Friedman and his admirers like Margaret Thatcher, who once called Klaus "my other favourite prime minister."[34] But he failed to appreciate that their attacks on regulation assumed long-standing rules and legal frameworks that clearly defined private property and protected the rights of property owners. Klaus rapidly transferred titular ownership into private hands, but without creating a regulated capital market, civil law agencies to enforce contracts, or efficient bankruptcy legislation. As one writer puts it, Klaus created private *possession* without creating private *property*.[35] And in such a system, the big fish eat the little fish. To quote a critical editorial, "Klaus's concept that the 'first owners' are not important, that the market will transfer property rights to 'responsible owners' was ridiculous: if Mr. Novák is the first owner of a lemon and he squeezes it dry, then the second owner does not get a lemon, but a lemon rind."[36]

Klaus's difficulties dissolved the glue binding the coalition together. As long as Klaus was the economic miracle-worker, putting up with his autocratic manner to stay in the coalition was worth it. Now, he was losing support even among ODS stalwarts. In the end, another financing scandal brought about Klaus's downfall. Amid media accounts of donations from nonexistent foreigners behind which lurked shady privatization dealings, Foreign Minister and party co-founder Josef Zieleniec resigned. Further press rumors of a secret ODS bank account in Switzerland brought calls from Finance Minister Ivan Pilip and Interior Minister Jan Ruml for Klaus to step down. After the ODA and KDU-ČSL announced they were leaving the coalition, on November 30, 1997, Klaus submitted his government's resignation.[37]

At this point Havel stepped in, fulfilling his constitutional duties by appointing a reluctant Josef Tošovský, head of the Czech National Bank, to lead a caretaker government. Havel entered the party strife in an address on December 9, 1997, in which he subjected Klaus's entire record as prime minister to thorough criticism. The problem, Havel asserted, was that transformation "stopped halfway, which is possibly the worst thing that could have happened to it." Only now had efforts begun to bring the economy's legal framework and the capital market into order. How could restructuring succeed, he asked, "when there are so few clear owners, and when so many of those who represent the owners see their role not as a task, mission or commitment but simply as an opportunity to transfer the entrusted money somewhere else and get out?" Klaus, stony-faced, did not applaud, and afterward said that Havel "showed how deep is his ignorance of the workings of the market economy and a free society eight years after the fall of communism."[38] Havel's departure from a nonpartisan position resolved the immediate problem, but his open conflict with Klaus made it more difficult for him to return to that role afterward.

From Klaus to Zeman

Tošovský's cabinet finally won approval in mid-January, by promising to hold early elections in June.[39] During this transitional period, the political spectrum further reoriented itself. At the ODS party congress the rebels failed to unseat Klaus, who mobilized his supporters in lower party organizations. Most of the anti-Klaus ODS figures formed a new party, the Freedom Union (US), headed by Ruml. Opinion polls in mid-spring put the US ahead of ODS by several points, but during the campaign Klaus rallied once more, campaigning on the "threat from the left." In the elections on June 19–20, 1998, the ODS failed to overtake the ČSSD (which emerged the clear winner with 32 percent of the vote), but Klaus's party came second with 28 percent. The KSČM gained 11 percent, leaving US trailing the KDU-ČSL by 9 percent to 8.6 percent.[40] The extremist Republican Party failed to clear the 5 percent parliamentary hurdle.

Otherwise, the situation resembled 1996. The socialists could not rule alone, so a coalition with one of the center-right parties was necessary. Yet Ruml steadfastly refused, even though Zeman eventually offered not to take the post of prime minister. The KDU-ČSL rank-and-file refused to allow their leader, Josef Lux, to support the socialists. A coalition of ODS, US, and KDU-ČSL was theoretically possible, but the personal antipathies left by the way the coalition had come apart in 1997 prevented it. In the end the ODS and the ČSSD reached an "opposition agreement," in which the ODS tolerated a minority ČSSD government, receiving in return control of key parliamentary committees and the chairmanship of both chambers. They also agreed on proposing constitutional amendments to benefit the larger parties.[41] The other parties denounced the agreement, and Havel openly expressed his own reservations. In the end, however, he accepted Zeman as prime minister in a "hidden silent grand coalition."[42]

The 1998 elections marked the first time since 1989 that there had been an alternation between government and opposition in the Czech Republic. In this respect, though undeniably the system still had problems electing a stable majority government, the elections were a signpost in the consolidation of democracy in the Czech Republic. The ČSSD government served out its statutory four-year term, and the Czech public has now seen that a left-wing government could be in power without the world coming to an end.[43]

Zeman might have thought the world *was* coming to an end in 1998, considering the recession into which the Czech economy plunged. GDP growth slowed significantly in 1997 (ending the year at 0.3 percent), and in 1998 it contracted by 2.3 percent (see Table 6). The trade balance ended the year in the red at $2.6 billion, while unemployment pushed double digits (on the year it ended at 9.4 percent, but in many localities it was much higher). Inflation broke the 10 percent level. Tošovský's government had already amended the bankruptcy law in January 1998, hoping to clear at least part of the three- or four-year backlog of unresolved cases. In April, a Securities Commission was established for the capital market, and banking legislation increased the Central Bank's powers to separate the banks from investment funds and enterprises. Nevertheless, the ongoing debt crisis forced major Czech banks to post record losses.[44] These difficulties, with the arrears in tax collections and the government's pledge to support social welfare and investment programs, drove the budget into deficit.

One of the ČSSD programs was a plan to revitalize key industries. The list of affected companies sounded like a roll call of the great names of Czechoslovakia's industrial past. There was Brno's Zetor enterprise, once a worldwide tractor exporter; Tatra-Kopřivnice, once maker of the black limousines favored by the communist bigwigs and still producer of heavy-duty trucks; Škoda-Plzeň, the heavy-machine branch of Emil Škoda's industrial empire; the metallurgical concern Vítkovice; and others. The program established a Revitalization Agency, which developed recovery plans in cooperation with a newly established Konsolidační Banka (KoB) under the direction of a consortium of the international financial companies, Lazard Frères and Latona. The program failed to reach its goals, partly because of divisions within the government and partly because of the reluctance of the foreign firms to invest capital in the project. Though Tatra in particular demonstrated some promising signs of recovery, the whole program was wound up in 2001 and revitalization efforts continued through the Consolidation Agency, created from the KoB but operating without the restrictions imposed by a banking license.[45]

Zeman's government also set about the delayed privatization of the banking sector. Speedy privatization, Zeman asserted, was the only way to drag banking out of its crisis. In the process, the government would have to separate commercial and investment banking, and "untangle the absolutely non-transparent ownership structure created by the ridiculous and dangerous coupon privatization."[46] The government planned to sell Československá Obchodní Banka, followed by Česká Spořitelna and finally Komerční Banka. Interested international financial institutions such as the EBRD saw the program as a way to move forward on restructuring as well as avoiding an Asian-style bad debt spiral.[47]

To encourage foreign direct investment, the socialist government introduced an incentive package in 1998, later enhanced in May 2000. Both foreign and domestic companies that invested $10 million or more through newly registered companies received tax breaks and other incentives. The enhancements lowered the investment required to $5 million for regions where unemployment was 25 percent higher than the national average. These incentives attracted foreign direct investment: $4.9 billion in 1999, $4.6 billion in 2000, and $2.3 billion by midway through 2001.[48] The Czech Republic showed reasonable economic growth starting in 2000, but it is vulnerable to world economic trends

TABLE 6

SELECTED ECONOMIC INDICATORS
FOR THE CZECH REPUBLIC, 1998–2001

Year	1998	1999	2000	2001
Real GDP growth (percent)	−2.3	−0.2	2.9	3.3
Unemployment (percent)	7.5	9.4	8.8	8.5
Consumer price inflation (percent)	10.7	2.1	3.9	6.0
Trade balance (US$ billion)	−2.6	−2.06	−3.5	−2.3
Current account deficit (% of GDP)	1.9	1.5	4.8	5.0

SOURCE: U.S. Department of State, Bureau of Economic and Business Affairs, *2001 Country Reports on Economic Policy and Trade Policies: Czech Republic* (Washington, D.C.: U.S. Department of State, 2001) <http://www.state.gov>.

and the consequences of its own deficit and continuing balance-of-trade problems (see Table 6).

For the Czech Republic to integrate into the European Union, it will have to move away from the heavy industries and other traditions of the industrial age toward high-tech and service industries.[49] As anyone who experienced the communist era service standards can attest, there have been many changes, especially in retail services and in larger tourist localities. It is not easy to overturn two generations of conditioning, however, and many observers argue that the Czechs still have much to learn about service and entrepreneurship. And since by such measures as availability of consumer goods, comfortable lifestyle, and fundamental freedoms they are much better off than under communism, the incentive to change may be too weak to make a difference, at least in the short run.[50] It is, in any event, one of the barriers the Czech Republic will have to break through in order to move from being a leading post-communist state to being a standard Western economy and society.

Blbá nálada

The economic crisis into which the Czech Republic plunged in 1998 deepened a public sense of frustration and discontentment already visible in 1997. Havel during a television address in April referred to a "blbá nálada" (bad-tempered mood) taking hold among the population. At the time, the expression seemed to capture something about Czech society's attitude. Ten years after the "Velvet Revolution," it seemed that all the Czechs had accomplished was to end up where they had started. Had they really achieved so little, or was it rather that expectations for a rapid, decisive transformation had been too high?[51]

Certainly aspects of the political, economic, and social transformation could be criticized. Corruption and financial scandals helped bring down Klaus's government. The ČSSD (which itself had a financing scandal in early 1998) seized upon corruption as one of its election themes, unveiling a "Clean Hands" campaign, and swearing that it would get to the bottom of allegations of corruption in privatization.[52] Other aspects of the "Clean Hands" campaign targeted the civil service. Public perceptions changed little: Czechs were becoming less willing to pay bribes, but they still believed that corruption was a fact of life.[53] According to Transparency International, an anticorruption organization, the Czech Republic ranked behind Slovenia, Estonia, and Hungary among other

EU candidates in a "Corruption Perceptions Index" (thirty-ninth place out of ninety-nine countries). By 2001 the Czech Republic had slipped into a tie with Bulgaria and Croatia in forty-seventh place.[54] The index measured perceptions, which would change only slowly even if the situation improved, but these results were not encouraging for the "Clean Hands" campaign. Accusations of corruption continued to dog the ČSSD government.[55]

Lustration returned to public attention in 2000. As the social-democratic government prepared a new civil service law, parliament extended the original 1991 legislation again, this time without specifying an end date, but exempting anyone born after December 1, 1971. Again parliament overrode Havel's veto of the new extension.[56] A new lustration scandal broke when it was revealed that during the early 1990s the Ministry of the Interior had issued more than a hundred false lustration certificates. Since the ČSSD was divided on continuing the lustration law, some suggested that publicizing this problem was intended to convince the public and legislators that the lustration process was too flawed to continue. In the end, however, the new civil service law confirmed the lustration law's provisions.[57]

The communists attacked the lustration laws as a form of discrimination, but there were other areas where more pervasive and troubling discrimination ran deep in Czech society. The most sensitive area continued to be the relations between the majority Czech society and the 200,000–250,000 Czech Roma (Gypsies).[58] Subjected under communism to efforts to integrate them into socialist society, Roma lost traditional social customs and networks, while receiving greater security, employment, and pressure to send their children to school. The transformation hit them hard. Since most Roma workers were unskilled, their unemployment figures dwarfed the statistics for the population at large. Funding for social workers and the educational system dried up. The Roma organized politically, but their organizations fractured into competing, smaller groups until their political clout was completely dissipated. Without employment, with limited prospects for exerting political influence, and subject to regular discrimination and acts of ostracism or violence by the majority society, many Roma slid into crime and prostitution.

Havel has frequently spoken out on Roma issues, though his appeals met with "a stony public response."[59] The central government is usually less sympathetic, since it is in frequent contact with local authorities who not only are more likely to express prejudices but also have to deal on a daily basis with the problems between the Roma and their neighbors. Local authorities are often openly hostile to the Roma and resent what they see as the do-gooder attempts of the president or central authorities to instruct them on how to deal with a situation with which they, so the local officials argue, have no experience.

After the dissolution of the ČSFR, the law on Czech citizenship stipulated that applicants had to show a clean police record for the last five years, a provision referred to as the "Gypsy clause." Many Roma in the Czech lands moved there from Slovakia after World War II, so they had to apply for Czech citizenship. Given their community's statistically higher crime rates, proving a clean police record would be difficult for some of them. Under international criticism, the time period was reduced to two years in 1996. In 1999 a further change allowed former Czechoslovak citizens living in the Czech Republic since 1993 to gain citizenship by declaration. This change was intended to resolve the situation of the estimated 10,000–20,000 stateless persons (mostly Roma) still in the Czech Republic.[60]

The town council in Ústi nad Labem provoked an international outcry over the "ghettoization" of the Roma by a plan to erect a wall separating Roma-inhabited apartment blocks from their neighbors, supposedly as a noise barrier. That plan was dropped, but at the local level town councils still try to deal with the "Roma problem" by moving Roma families out of central locations into housing in surrounding localities. This physical separation makes it harder for the Roma to find what meager opportunities for work or schooling exist.

Physical separation may also make them more vulnerable to the attacks, sometimes resulting in death, to which Roma have been subject. After several years of complaints that police were slow to investigate racially motivated attacks on Roma, the situation has improved. Nevertheless, fear and their hopeless economic conditions have driven thousands of Roma to seek asylum abroad, most dramatically in 1997 after a television documentary showed successful Roma immigrants in Canada. The asylum movement created bad publicity for the Czech Republic and the intended countries of asylum, resulting in the reintroduction of visa requirements in some cases.[61] The Czech government created a commission on Roma affairs and a commissioner for human rights, and stepped up efforts to recruit and train Roma for the police force. Meanwhile, some Roma sum up their situation like this: "The communists took away our violin and gave us a pickax; democracy has taken the pickax away and given us back the violin."[62]

The Roma are not the only victims of violence, often perpetrated by skinheads and other movements actively promoting neo-Nazi ideology and anti-Semitism. Arab, Indian, and African or Afro-Czech residents have also been skinhead targets. The government follows the radical movements with concern, but also has to define the line between guaranteed freedom of expression and propagating openly racist hatred. There are some 5,000 to 7,000 active members of skinhead groups, and the police have been criticized for not intervening more vigorously to stop anti-Semitic or other pro-Nazi utterances at their concerts and meetings.[63] Before the 2002 elections, some skinhead groups attempted to create a registered political party. Public opinion research indicated that in the event of an economic depression, a socially radical, ultra-nationalist movement could attract close to 20 percent of the vote.[64] Thus, the decline of the Republican Party after the 1998 elections may not mean an end to the threat from the far right to Czech democracy. Equally troubling is that, although only a tiny proportion of the population would condone the murders and other skinhead attacks, the racial prejudice behind them is much more widespread. On a more optimistic note, research has shown that Czech attitudes to the Roma are significantly better among Czechs who live in daily contact with them.[65]

Czech women experience a different kind of discrimination, usually in the workplace. During the transformation women became unemployed at a much higher rate than men, though some Czech women were happy to get rid of the double burden.[66] Those who do seek employment often run into difficulties. In spite of legal prohibitions of discrimination on the basis of sex or appearance, women in traditionally patriarchal Czech society end up in lower paid, lower status jobs. Their role in political life has also declined: over 29 percent of the parliament members in the ČSSR were women, but in the Czech Republic only 15 percent after the 1998 elections. Of course under the old regime their position was a formality, not a sign of real influence, and the old communist women's organizations quickly folded up after 1989. The KSČM currently has the highest proportion of women in its parliamentary delegation, which may cause an "allergic reaction" toward women in other parties. Nevertheless, there are popular female political figures and the role of women in politics may increase.[67]

Does this admittedly incomplete catalogue of challenges and problems mean that the Czech Republic has failed to navigate the third aspect of the triple transition, to a pluralistic civil society? Certainly many high hopes from the 1989 revolutions have been disappointed, and the need for a civil society remains one of Havel's recurrent themes.[68] If membership in organizations indicates civil society's strength, then the Czech Republic does have a weak civil society.[69] Czechs, it seems, are not "joiners"—and who can blame them, when one considers how the communist regime controlled such groups and used them to mobilize society for its ends? Instead of joining organizations, many Czechs still rely on the networks of friends that helped them during the communist regime. The Zeman government took steps to try to aid the development of civil society, creating a 500 million crown endowment to support NGOs in 1999, and in 2000 announcing that it would give another 1.5 billion crowns to groups dealing with human rights and the environment through its Council for Non-Governmental Organizations.[70] It also set up an office of "Public Rights Protector" to receive citizens' complaints of government violations of their rights. Such policies, and a scaling down of 1989's unrealistic expectations, helped some NGO activists in the Czech Republic to affirm that they are now "on the right path."[71]

The Czechs' "bad-tempered mood" of the late 1990s may have been born of transformational exhaustion, but they knew where they wanted to go, even if the shortest way there was not clear. One letter to a newspaper put it plainly:

> Personally, I am in a good mood, but it could be better, if the political parties at least sometimes fulfilled their promises and politicians caught lying and cheating resigned on their own, if these parties had more decent people and fewer crooks among their candidates, if the civil service actually worked according to the valid laws, if the police began to catch thieves, tunnelers, and other criminals and the courts actually sentenced them, if the army was not impoverished, if the state would guarantee the security of the citizens and public order, if debtors had to return the money they borrow, if they succeeded in instituting a market economy, if the schools and the media would raise young people according to classical values, if the advertising agencies did not brainwash us, if the state actually took care of the environment and cultural monuments and at the same time prevented the development of prostitution and corruption, if someone would actually start to work on our laws so that they corresponded to the legal norms valid in the EU, if the Supreme Court would dissolve political parties that break the law, and finally if Article I of the constitution would take

effect and we would have a legally based and democratic state founded on respect for the rights of man and the citizen.[72]

Yes, this is a bilious diatribe on the contemporary state of the Czech Republic, but it is also a satisfactory description of a democratic, free-market, civil society. Knowing where one wants to go is part of making a successful journey. As the "bad-tempered mood" lifted early in the new millennium, it seemed that the Czech Republic would get there in the end.[73]

BACK TO EUROPE?

On March 12, 1999, in Independence, Missouri, the Czech Republic, Hungary, and Poland formally joined the North Atlantic Treaty Organization. Twelve days later NATO began bombing Yugoslavia. The Czechs, whose sympathy for the Serbs dates back to the nineteenth century, were reminded that joining the institutional structures of Europe might impose obligations, sometimes onerous ones, as well as confer benefits.[74] Nevertheless, in keeping with the slogan "Back to Europe," the Czech Republic seeks continued integration into the economic, political, and security structures of Europe. Because these institutions in turn demanded specific Czech behavior and policy choices, going "back to Europe" had foreign policy and internal dimensions, playing a direct role in the process of Czech transformation.

Joining the Clubs

The ČSFR pursued membership in international organizations while leaving the Soviet embrace. After the breakup of the federation, the Czech Republic succeeded to the ČSFR's membership in the United Nations, the Council of Europe, and the Organization for Security and Cooperation in Europe (OSCE). In October 1994 it signed an association agreement with the European Union, and at the end of 1995 it became a member of the OECD. If Czechs as individuals were not "joiners," the same could not be said about their state, at least as far as European institutions were concerned.[75]

The ČSFR's acceptance into the Council of Europe confirmed that it had the minimum democratic institutions required for membership.[76] But Council membership went beyond a seal of approval; it imposed obligations and allowed the Council to criticize domestic Czech policies in the light of its 150 conventions. Under the European Convention on Human Rights, for instance, a member of a minority could appeal to the Human Rights Committee and to the European Court of Human Rights, and the Council has not hesitated to speak up on Roma issues. Thus membership was an ongoing process of developing democratic institutions and practices, as defined by the Council's members over its half century of existence, not just a reward for initial good behavior. Membership in the Council of Europe was also important for the Czech Republic as a validation of acceptability to NATO and the European Union.

Even before the breakup of the federation, the ČSFR authorized the participation of Czechoslovak military units in the former Yugoslavia within UNPROFOR. When two Czech soldiers were killed in 1995, the Czech minister of defense spelled out the mission's political significance bluntly: Czech participation was "an investment in our own future security, in the sense that in case of a threat we will not remain isolated."[77] Czech cooperation with the international community in the former Yugoslavia, this time under NATO leadership, continued in IFOR and SFOR, adding to the more than 400 military observers who had served since 1989 in ten countries under UN, EU, or OSCE auspices.[78] Czech participation also reinforced the message that the Czechs were a realistic future member of the NATO alliance.

The ČSFR was one of the most enthusiastic Visegrád states in pursuing NATO membership, and when the alliance unveiled its Partnership for Peace program in 1994, the Czech Republic signed on with alacrity.[79] However, it viewed the Partnership only as a "first step" toward eventually joining the alliance as a full-fledged member.[80] Two lines of argument dominated Czech public pronouncements on NATO enlargement. The security argument frequently referred directly to the historical memories of Munich and similar past traumas. The fact that NATO decisions required consensus meant that "no decisions about us will ever again be made without us."[81] The other argument was based on shared values. As might be expected, Havel expressed this approach to NATO membership many times. In a speech in Cracow in June 1996 he pointed out that, although the specific postwar strategic situation that had created NATO had changed, its other source, "the concept of the common defense of the values of the democratic, Western world against any threat," was just as valid today.[82]

When the Czech Republic, Poland, and Hungary formally joined NATO in 1999, Kavan, Zeman, and Havel all stressed Czechoslovakia's unhappy history in the twentieth century. They welcomed NATO enlargement not only as a security guarantee but as a commitment to the values of democracy and an open society embodied not only in NATO but also in the European Union. Zeman linked NATO and EU membership explicitly when he noted that "since the emergence of the Czech Republic in 1993, our integration into NATO and the European Union was confirmed as the strategic foreign policy objective of every government in power regardless of its political orientation."[83] Frequently seen as two sides of one coin, in the end the process of joining NATO and the EU affected domestic aspects of the transition as well as foreign policy.

The Thorny Road to the European Union

When Czechoslovakia signed its association agreement with the European Community in 1991, it was hailed as "perhaps the most important agreement Czechoslovakia has concluded since the war."[84] Yet in 1999, as NATO membership arrived and the EU accession process progressed, another article began with the words: "Do we want to enter Europe at all?"[85] Were the Czechs really losing their desire to go "back to Europe?" How far along the road to the goal of EU entry had they progressed, and what was now making them question whether they should complete the journey?

The initial phase of the journey unfolded in a way similar to NATO expansion.[86] Under pressure from the new democracies of Eastern Europe and wanting to stabilize them, the European Community sought to avoid a flat refusal to new members. Thus the association agreements, like the Partnership for Peace, sought to keep everyone happy without a binding commitment to enlargement. The associated countries received trade and customs concessions (though key EC industries still had protection), and were given a ten-year period in which to manage their economic transformations and bring their legal systems into line with the community's.[87]

None of the hopeful associated states was content with this halfway house status, and they lobbied for binding promises of future membership. At the Copenhagen Council meeting in 1993, the EU adopted three general conditions for future membership: stable democratic institutions, the rule of law, and human and minority rights; a market economy able to withstand competition from the EU economies; and the ability to take on the obligations of membership, including the EU common law, the *acquis communautaire*. Matters were delayed while the EU absorbed Austria, Sweden, Norway, and Finland. After the EU published clearer guidelines in May 1994, the Central and Eastern European countries were able to apply formally. The Czech Republic submitted its application in January 1996, and in 1997 the EU included it together with Poland, Hungary, Slovenia, Estonia, and Cyprus among the countries on a "fast track" to membership. Negotiations began in 1998, and since then the Czech government has insisted that early accession to the EU is its goal.

The negotiations proceeded on the basis of an "accession partnership" setting out the specific preparation strategy for each country. The European Commission publishes a yearly progress report in which the priorities in the accession partnership are evaluated, and areas for further work identified. Applicant countries also present a specific program outlining how they will prepare to adopt the *acquis*.[88] Since 1997, EU aid to the Czech Republic through the PHARE program (Polish and Hungarian Assistance for the Reconstruction of Europe) has been specifically targeted to help it meet these goals.

Preparation for EU membership thus involved complicated and coordinated reshaping of legislation, administration, and economic policies. The *acquis* are set out in twenty-nine chapters covering the entire gamut of public legal, administrative, and economic life. The annual progress reports evaluate not only the broad Copenhagen requirements for admission, but specifically address each chapter of the *acquis*, setting out the extent to which each requirement has been fulfilled and identifying specific priorities for further effort. The Czech Republic has met the first two criteria (democracy and market economy), if restructuring continues successfully, while in applying the *acquis* the most recent report lists many areas fully, largely, or partially fulfilled.[89] Entry into the "Europe" represented by the EU, then, begins to look like an incredibly intrusive, expensive, and bureaucratic exercise of "meddling in the internal affairs" of the applicant countries.

Expansion is not only a technical question; it also has a political side. Experience has shown that integration has to begin before admission and will continue afterward, no matter how well prepared a new member may be. Although the applicant countries may need transition periods and exemptions, the EU must also ensure that current member states accept expansion, or it risks loosening the European integration already achieved. One issue already creating some difficulty is the free movement of labor. Germany raised the possibility of delaying this EU norm for the new member states for a period of eighteen years, later reduced to seven. Current member states also fear increased taxes if the economies of the newly admitted countries have to be raised to the EU standard. Current net recipients from the EU budget would prefer not to see aid from Brussels totally diverted to the East.[90] The applicant countries worry about their agricultural sectors, domestic small and medium-sized enterprises, and the need to put their financial houses in order. All this costs money, and adapting to the EU may last for years after formal admission. Nevertheless, expansion has built up its own logic, resources have been invested, hopes have been raised, and the EU is now at a point where it must accept at least some applicant states in the near future. The Czech Republic claimed to be prepared for admission by January 1, 2003.

Environmental and energy policy shows how EU accession is caught in a web of foreign and domestic concerns. Czechoslovakia received EC support for the environment through the PHARE program, continued after 1993. It helped install better monitoring systems, upgrade sewage treatment, and refit factories and power plants with scrubbing technology to reduce air pollution. PHARE also subsidized the contract with Westinghouse to improve safety and reliability at the Temelín nuclear plant.[91] In 1999, Austria led an effort in the European Parliament against completion of the plant, whose original Soviet design (although different from the reactor at Chernobyl and modified by Westinghouse) was considered suspect. Austrian politicians warned that Temelín could endanger the Czech Republic's EU entry.[92] In January 2002 Jörg Haider, leader of the Austrian right-wing Freedom Party, launched a petition campaign against bringing the completed reactor online.[93] The EU has called for the highest standards of safety in the Czech nuclear industry, and also facilitated agreements between the Austrian and Czech governments over voluntary environmental impact studies on the Czech side, but the problem of nuclear power and related environmental issues remains.[94]

Another example of how EU admission intertwines domestic politics, public opinion, and foreign policy is that hardy perennial, Czech-German relations. At the Sudeten German organization's annual meeting in 1996, while Czech-German negotiations over a joint parliamentary declaration were taking place, German Finance Minister Theo Waigel demanded that the Czech government repudiate the "Beneš Decrees" of 1945 that stripped the Germans and Hungarians of their property and citizenship. He implied that Czech EU accession could be jeopardized if Prague refused, another demonstration of the Sudeten German organization's clout.[95] The declaration, ratified after nasty debates in 1997, affirms that "the entry of the Czech Republic into the European Union and free movement within this space will further ease the coexistence of Czechs and Germans." Critics called it flawed from the start, and on the most important questions, such as restitution or the Beneš decrees, simply an agreement to disagree.[96]

In the midst of the German election campaign in the summer of 1998, rookie Prime Minister Zeman criticized the presence of representatives of the Sudeten German organization at the Czech-German forum, comparing them to the Republicans and the KSČM in the Czech Republic. Chancellor Kohl reacted very strongly, and the exchange cast a pall over Kavan's first official visit to Germany.[97] When a Social-Democrat–led coalition replaced the conservatives after the German elections and the Czech government turned to pressing domestic matters, the situation stabilized—until, that is, another election year for both countries.

Interviewed in an Austrian magazine at the height of the anti-Temelín drive in 2002, Zeman referred to Haider as a "post-Nazi" politician and to the former Czechoslovak Germans as "traitors" and "Hitler's fifth column." Klaus entered the fray with the suggestion that the Beneš decrees should be written into the accession treaty.[98] The EU's official position was that accession was not linked to the decrees.[99] During a trip to Russia in April, Zeman got a statement of support from President Vladimir Putin, and once the Hungarian prime minister raised the issue, the Slovak government also backed the Czechs.[100] The Czech parliament, in an unusual display of unanimity, reaffirmed that the results of the decrees were "unquestionable, inviolable and unchangeable."[101] At the annual Sudeten German rally in May 2002, the CDU/CSU candidate for chancellor, Bavaria's Günter Stoiber, called on the Czechs to repeal the decrees, stopping just short of making it a precondition for EU admission.[102]

As the increasingly technical and difficult EU accession collected neuralgic points of international and domestic politics, public enthusiasm for the project fluctuated. The early euphoria of "back to Europe" had long since vanished in the mundane details of 80,000 specific aspects of the *acquis*. One commentator compared the process to a poorly served wedding banquet, where the guest is forced like a child to eat bite after bite "for Daddy" (the EU) without ever seeing the whole menu, or enjoying the meal "for himself."[103] The situation offered possibilities for a Euroskeptic, and Klaus seized them. He began insisting on protecting "national interests" and refusing to surrender sovereignty to the EU, and ODS voter support increased by three to four percent.[104] It seems certain that Czech EU accession will happen, whatever the exact date. But this step "back to Europe" is now taking place under the sign of fears that EU regulations will cause the adulteration of Czech slivovice or the death of guláš as we know it, instead of as an affirmation that the Czechs belong to Europe.[105]

Thus at the end we return to where we started: the Czech location on the map of Europe. In the arguments over EU accession strong echoes of earlier symbols, rhetorical images, and historical myths resound. One of them is the "dream of Europe," as a positive value, something to which the Czechs by culture, tradition, and history belong. That dream fueled the eagerness with which Czechoslovakia and its neighbors dismantled the CMEA, fled the Warsaw Pact, and knocked on the doors of Western Europe's institutions. One editorial insisted that the Czechs should accept EU norms "so that we could become a standard European country, in which no solid investor, employer, or customer would have any reason to worry."[106] The other echo recalled the dedication in 1910 of a plaque on Vítkov (Žižkov) hill outside Prague, on which these words were inscribed: "An insignificant handful of people overcame the serried armored ranks, because they were convinced of their truth. Then there were two sides. Europe and ourselves. And that Europe was pale, ghastly."[107] This Europe was outside, alien, and potentially hostile, against which the Czechs had to defend "their truth," standing alone against all.

These images of Europe defined Czech identity, either as the essence of Europe (democracy, freedom of thought, Masaryk's concept of humanism), or as defending a Czech truth against the armored ranks of the "pale, ghastly" Europe (again, the Hussite period provides the myths). Alternatives to Europe were in a similar way a search for a Czech identity. Slavdom identified the Czechs as Western outliers of a new, better, purer Europe—the unspoiled Slavic world. Another alternative, so strong in the discussions of Central Europe before 1989, was the search for a lost center, where everything naturally tended to synthesis, diversity, and tolerance. These two symbolic images seem to have exhausted their attractiveness. The Slavic identity was undermined by communist manipulation of its symbols and the experience of Soviet domination, though Zeman did seek Putin's support over the Beneš decrees in 2002. The idea of the lost center probably died with the general rejection of any "third way" in the rush to enter the West after 1989, and the historical record of the preceding century and a half did not support the tolerant, synthetic, and diverse image of Central Europe. There remains the temptation to use Europe to separate Czech identity from those beyond Europe's pale: Russia, the Balkans, "Asia."[108]

Images of smallness and powerlessness also resounded in comments about EU accession. Klaus played on the nationalist note into the election campaign of 2002, but never said staying outside the EU was a viable option. Still, his attitude smacked of cooperating with the inevitable, resonating with historical interpretations of the Czech fate going back to Václav and Boleslav.[109] The counterargument appeals to opposing myth-images. Accepting that the Czech Republic will give up some formal sovereignty to join the EU, supporters claimed that in return it would gain much more. "The Czechs have often waited outside the doors while their affairs were decided, and most often during periods when they were 'sovereign'," wrote one editorial. "EU entry means never being outside the doors again."[110]

In 1848 František Palacký made the famous statement that if Austria had not existed for centuries, it would be necessary to create it. He did not mean the dynastic monarchy that did not survive World War I, but a federal Austria of free and equal nations. Perhaps, after the harsh schooling of the twentieth century, Europe may be ready to realize Palacký's dream on an even wider scale. The Czechs and the Czech Republic have the opportunity to be co-authors of that new Europe, and their own fate. Masaryk, were he alive today, might paraphrase one of his famous sayings and assert: "The European question must be a Czech question."

Notes

CHAPTER 1

1. Poland, too, likes to see itself in this guise. See Norman Davies, *Heart of Europe: The Past in Poland's Present* (Oxford: Oxford University Press, 2001).

2. Vladimír Macura, *Znamení zrodu: České obrození jako kulturní typ*, 2d ed. (Jinočany: H&H, 1995), pp. 170–77; Milan Kundera, "A Kidnapped West or Culture Bows Out," translated by Edmund White, *Granta* 11 (1984): 93–122.

3. See František Palacký, *Dějiny národu českého v Čechách a na Moravě* (1848; Prague: B. Kočí, 1908), pp. 7–8, and Vladimír Macura, *Český sen* (Prague: Nakladatelství Lidové noviny, 1999), pp. 63–77.

4. See Derek Sayer, *The Coasts of Bohemia: A Czech History* (Princeton, N. J.: Princeton University Press, 1998).

5. See: John M. Kramer, "The Environmental Crisis in Eastern Europe: The Price for Progress," *Slavic Review* 42, no. 2 (Summer 1983): 204–20; Kramer, "Chernobyl' and Eastern Europe," *Problems of Communism* 35 (November-December 1986): 42, 47–50; Radio Free Europe/Radio Liberty, *Newsline, Central and Eastern Europe*, May 5, 2000 <http://www.rferl.org/newsline/2000/05/3-cee/cee-030500.html>, and chapter 17.

6. Miroslav Vaněk, "Porobení přírody," in *Proč jsme v listopadu vyšli do ulic*, compiled by Jiří Vančura (Brno: Doplněk, 1999), pp. 133–54.

7. Ivan Rada et al., *Dějiny zemí koruny české, I: od příchodu slovanů do roku 1740* (Prague: Paseka, 1992), pp. 11–18; Karel Sklenář, *Památky pravěku na území ČSSR: Od lovců mamutů ke státu Přemyslovců* (Prague: Orbis, 1974); Radomír Pleiner and Alena Rybová, eds., *Pravěké dějiny Čech* (Prague: Academia, 1978).

8. Sklenář, *Památky pravěku*; Traian Stoianovich, *Balkan Worlds: The First and Last Europe* (Armonk, N.Y., and London: M. E. Sharpe, 1994), pp. 13–16.

9. Jan Filip, *Keltská civilizáce a její dědictví*, 5th ed. (Prague: Academia, 1996).

10. The Greek "barbarian" has a similar sense. See Josef Holub and Stanislav Lyer, *Stručný etymologický slovník jazyka českého se zvláštním zřetelem k slovům kulturním a cizím* (Prague: Státní pedagogické nakladatelstvi, 1967), pp. 333, 442, 461.

11. John A. Armstrong, *Nations Before Nationalism* (Chapel Hill: University of North Carolina Press, 1982), pp. 128–67

12. *Kosmova kronika česká*, 6th ed., edited by Karel Hrdina and Marie Bláhová, translated by Zdeněk Fiala and Marie Bláhová (Prague: Svoboda, 1975), pp. 12–13.

13. See Jiří Sláma, "Boiohaemum-Čechy," in *Bohemia in History*, edited by Mikuláš Teich (Cambridge: Cambridge University Press, 1998), p. 37.

14. Michal Lutovský and Naďa Profantová, *Sámova říše* (Prague: Academia, 1995). Czechs and Slovaks view Samo's empire as a forerunner of their states: see Peter A. Toma and Dušan Kováč, *Slovakia: From Samo to Dzurinda* (Stanford: Hoover Institution Press, 2001).

15. This account relies on Rada et al., *Dějiny zemí koruny české, I*, pp. 24–27; but compare Dušan Třeštík, *Počátky Přemyslovců: vstup Čechů do dějin (530–935)* (Prague: Lidové noviny, 1997), pp. 17–53, who argues that the Czechs were a single tribe with several rulers.

16. Rada et al., *Dějiny zemí koruny české, I*, p. 26; Třeštík, *Počátky Přemyslovců*, pp. 76–78.

17. Many Slavic languages derive their word for "king" from Charlemagne's name "Carolus," in Czech, *král*. See Holub and Lyer, *Stručný etymologický slovník*, p. 266.

18. This account reflects the views of most scholars. See *Magna Moravia: Sborník k 1100. výročí příchodu byzantské míse na Moravu* (Prague: Státní pedagogické nakladatelství, 1965); Josef Poulík and Bohuslav Chropovský, *Velká Morava a počátky československé státnosti* (Prague and Bratislava: Academia and Obzor, 1985); and Třeštík, *Počátky Přemyslovců*, pp. 263–96; but see also the revisionist works of Imre Boba, *Moravia's History Reconsidered: A Reinterpretation of Medieval Sources* (The Hague: Martinus Nijhoff, 1971);

Charles Bowlus, *Franks, Moravians, and Magyars: The Struggle for the Middle Danube, 788–907* (Philadelphia: University of Pennsylvania Press, 1995); and Martin Eggers, *Das grossmährische Reich: Realität oder Fiktion? Eine Neuinterpretation der Quellen zur Geschichte des mittleren Donauraumes im 9. Jahrhundert* (Stuttgart: Anton Hiersemann, 1995).

19. Třeštík, *Počátky Přemyslovců*, pp. 74–98.

20. *The Vita of Constantine and the Vita of Methodius*, translated by Marvin Kantor and Richard S. White, with an introduction by Antonín Dostál (Ann Arbor: University of Michigan Press, 1976), p. 75.

21. Martin Eggers, *Das Erzbistum des Method: Lage, Wirkung und Nachleben der kyrillomethodianischen Mission* (Munich: Otto Sagner, 1996).

22. Třeštík, *Počátky Přemyslovců*, pp. 348–74; Rada et al., *Dějiny zemí koruny české, I*, pp. 34–35.

23. See Pavla Obrazová and Jan Vlk, *Maior Gloria svatý kníže Václav* (Prague and Litomyšl: Paseka, 1994), esp. pp. 192–217 and 228–230; and Robert B. Pynsent, *Questions of Identity: Czech and Slovak Ideas of Nationality and Personality* (Budapest: Central European University Press, 1994), pp. 196–98.

24. Václav Novotný, *Od nejstarších dob do smrti knížete Oldřicha*, vol. 1, part 1 of *České dějiny* (Prague: Jan Laichter, 1912), pp. 554–73.

25. Třeštík, *Počátky Přemyslovců*, pp. 437–40.

26. See Obrazová and Vlk, *Svatý kníže Václav*, pp. 111–41.

27. Novotný, *České dějiny*, vol. 1, part 1, pp. 512–17.

28. Ivan Hrbek, "Ibráhím ibn Jákúb v Praze, Čechách a jiných slovanských zemích," *Český lid* 6 (1951): 267–71.

29. Novotný, *České dějiny*, vol. 1, part 1, pp. 582–92.

30. Ibid., pp. 627–52; Rudolf Turek, *Slavníkovci a jejich panství* (Hradec Králové: Kruh, 1982).

31. The Polish Piasts also claim descent from a peasant. See Paul W. Knoll, *The Rise of the Polish Monarchy: Piast Poland in East Central Europe, 1320–1370* (Chicago: University of Chicago Press, 1972), p. 3.

CHAPTER 2

1. Ivan Rada et al., *Dějiny zemí koruny české, I*, pp. 47–49; Josef Žemlička, *Čechy v době knížecí (1034–1198)* (Prague: Lidové noviny, 1997), pp. 53–68.

2. Václav Novotný, *Od Břetislava I. do Přemysla I.*, vol. 1, part 2 of *České dějiny* (Prague: Jan Laichter, 1913), pp. 3–27.

3. Žemlička, *Čechy v době knížecí*, pp. 69–76.

4. Ibid., pp. 104–18.

5. Ibid., pp. 221–30.

6. Ibid., pp. 328–64.

7. Ibid., pp. 201–8; Tomáš Pěkný, *Historie Židů v Čechách a na Moravě* (Prague: Sefer, 1993), pp. 14–16.

8. This section relies on Václav Novotný, *Čechy královské za Přemysla I. a Václava I., 1197–1253*, vol. 1, part 3 of *České dějiny* (Prague: Jan Laichter, 1928).

9. See *Minulost našeho státu v dokumentech*, compiled and edited by Státní ústřední archiv v Praze (Prague: Svoboda, 1971), pp. 35–36.

10. Žemlička, *Čechy v době knížecí*, pp. 386–401.

11. The classic study of this period is Josef Vítězslav Šimák, *Středověká kolonisace v zemích českých*, vol. 1, part 5 of *České dějiny* (Prague: Jan Laichter, 1938), esp. pp. 503–37.

12. What follows draws on Václav Novotný, *Rozmach české moci za Přemysla II. Otakara, 1253–1271*, vol. 1, part 4 of *České dějiny* (Prague: Jan Laichter, 1937).

13. See Dobroslava Menclová, *České hrady* (Prague: Odeon, 1972), p. 67.

14. Josef Šusta, *Soumrak Přemyslovců a jejich dědictví*, vol. 2, part 1 of *České dějiny* (Prague: Jan Laichter, 1935), p. 275, citing Rudolf's own account to the pope.

15. Jiří Rak, *Bývali Čechové: české historické mýty a stereotypy* (Jinončany: H&H, 1994), pp. 67–82.

16. Paul W. Knoll, *Rise of the Polish Monarchy*, pp. 18–27.

17. *Pokračovatelé Kosmovi*, 1st ed., translated by Karel Hrdina et al. (Prague: Svoboda, 1974), pp. 39–40.

18. Arne Novák and Jan V. Novák, *Přehledné dějiny literatury české od nejstarších dob až po naše dny*, 4th ed. (1936; Brno: Atlantis, 1995), pp. 11–14.

19. Pěkný, *Historie Židů*, pp. 17–26.

20. Novák and Novák, *Přehledné dějiny literatury české*, pp. 18–24.

CHAPTER 3

1. Jiří Rak, *Bývali Čechové*, pp. 9–33.

2. Josef Šusta, *Král cizinec*, vol. 2, part 2 of *České dějiny* (Prague: Jan Laichter, 1939); Jiří Spěváček, *Král diplomat (Jan Lucemburský, 1296–1346)* (Prague: Panorama, 1982).

3. Jaroslav Mezník, *Čechy a Morava v 14. století* (Prague: Státní pedagogické nakladatelství, 1991), pp. 15–17; Jiří Spěváček, *Jan Lucemburský a jeho doba, 1296–1346: K prvnímu vstupu českých zemí do svazku se západní evropou* (Prague: Svoboda, 1994), pp. 137–58.

4. See Jiří Daňhelka, Karel Hádek, Bohuslav Havránek, and Naděžda Kvítková, eds., *Staročeská kronika tak řečeného Dalimila* (Prague: Academia, 1988), pp. 8–9.

5. Zdeněk Fiala, ed., *Zbraslavská kronika: Chronicon Aulae Regiae*, translated by František Heřmanský and Rudolf Mertlík (Prague: Svoboda, 1976), pp. 356–60.

6. Otfrid Pustejovsky, *Schlesiens Übergang an die böhmische Krone: Machtpolitik Böhmens im Zeichen von Herrschaft und Frieden* (Cologne: Böhlau Verlag, 1975).

7. Spěváček, *Jan Lucemburský*, pp. 495–512.

8. Karel IV, "Vlastní životopis," in *Kroniky doby Karla IV*, edited by Marie Bláhová, translated by Jakub Pavel (Prague: Svoboda, 1987), pp. 27–28.

9. Beneš Krabic z Weitmile, "Kronika pražského kostela," in *Kroniky doby Karla IV*, translated and edited by Marie Bláhová (1987), p. 224.

10. Karel IV, "Vlastní životopis," p. 27.

11. Jiří Spěváček, *Karel IV. Život a dílo, 1316–1378* (Prague: Svoboda, 1979), pp. 304–7.

12. František Kavka, *Vláda Karla IV. za jeho císařství (1355–1378): Země České koruny, rodová, říšská a evropská politika* (Prague: Univerzita Karlova, 1993), p. 10.

13. See Tomáš Pěkný, *Historie Židů*, pp. 34–36, and the literature cited there.

CHAPTER 4

1. Jiří Rak, *Bývali Čechové*, pp. 49–66; František Šmahel, "The Hussite Movement: An Anomaly of European History?" in *Bohemia in History*, edited by Mikuláš Teich (Cambridge: Cambridge University Press, 1998), pp. 79–97.

2. Petr Čornej, *Lipanské ozvěny* (Prague: H&H, 1995), pp. 183–85.

3. See Alexander Patschovsky, *Die Anfänge einer ständigen Inquisition in Böhmen. Ein Prager Inquisitoren-Handbuch aus der ersten Hälfte des 14. Jahrhunderts* (Berlin: W. de Gruyter, 1975); Alexander Patschovsky, *Quellen zur böhmischen Inquisition im 14. Jahrhundert* (Weimar: Böhlau, 1979); also Alexander Patschovsky, "Ketzer und Ketzerverfolgung in Böhmen im Jahrhundert vor Hus," *Geschichte in Wissenschaft und Unterricht* 32 (1981): 261–72.

4. See František Šmahel, *Doba vymknutá z kloubu*, vol. 1 of *Husitská revoluce* (Prague: Historický stav Akademie věd České Republiky, 1993), pp. 220–33.

5. On these issues see Matthew Spinka, *John Hus' Concept of the Church*

(Princeton, N.J.: Princeton University Press, 1966), pp. 11–12, 22–36. See also, Howard Kaminsky, "Wyclifism as Ideology of Revolution," *Church History* 32 (1963): 57–74.

6. Brian Tierney, *Foundations of Conciliar Theory* (Cambridge: Cambridge University Press, 1955).

7. František Šmahel, *Husův proces v Kostnici* (Prague: Melantrich, 1988).

8. Peter z Mladoňovic, *Zpráva o mistru Janu Husovi v Kostnici*, translated by František Heřmanský (Prague: Universita Karlova, 1965), p. 173; Matthew Spinka, *John Hus at the Council of Constance* (New York: Columbia University Press, 1965), p. 233.

9. Vavřinec z Březové, *Husitská kronika, Píseň o vítězství u Domažlic*, edited by Marie Bláhová, translated by František Heřmanský and Jan Blahoslav Čapek (Prague: Svoboda, 1979), pp. 30–33.

10. This section uses František Šmahel, *Kronika válečných let*, vol. 3 of *Husitská revoluce* (Prague: Historický stav Akademie věd České Republiky, 1993), and Ivan Rada et al., *Dějiny zemí koruny české, I*, pp. 163–78.

11. Petr Čornej, *Tajemství českých kronik* (Prague: Vyšehrad, 1987), and Petr Čornej, *Lipanská křižovatka. Příčiny, průběh a historický význam jedné bitvy* (Prague: Panorama, 1992).

12. Rada et al., *Dějiny zemí koruny české, I*, pp. 178–87; František Šmahel, *Epilog bouřlivého věku*, vol. 4 of *Husitská Revoluce* (Prague: Historický ústav Akademie věd České Republiky, 1993).

13. *Ze starých letopisů českých*, translated and edited by Jaroslav Porák and Jaroslav Kašpar (Prague: Svoboda, 1980), p. 182.

14. Petr Chelčický, *Petr Chelčický: Treatises on Christianity and the Social Order*, translated and edited by Howard Kaminsky (Lincoln: University of Nebraska Press, 1964).

CHAPTER 5

1. The tutor to the Pernštejns, Jan Češka, once said, "If a peasant were made a burgher today, tomorrow he would want to be a page, being a page he would want to be a lord, being a lord, he would desire the kingship." Cited in Josef Macek, *Hospodářská základná a královská moc*, vol. 1 of *Jagellonský věk v českých zemích* (Prague: Academia, 1992), pp. 175–76. This section also draws from Jaroslav Purš and Miroslav Kropilák, gen. eds., *Přehled dějin Československa do r. 1526*, vol. 1, part 1 of *Přehled dějin Československa* (Prague: Academia, 1980), pp. 525–27.

2. Macek, *Jagellonský věk*, vol. 1, pp. 170–79.

3. František Šmahel, "The Hussite Movement," pp. 94–96.

4. For a detailed dissection of the nobility during the Jagiellonian age see Josef Macek, *Šlechta*, vol. 2 of *Jagellonský věk v českých zemích* (Prague: Academia, 1994), pp. 9–90.

5. *Ze starých letopisů českých*, p. 221.

6. Robert A. Kann and Zdeněk V. David, *The Peoples of the Eastern Habsburg Lands, 1526–1918*. A History of East Central Europe (Seattle: University of Washington Press, 1984), pp. 24–28.

7. Josef Macek, "The Monarchy of the Estates," in *Bohemia in History*, edited by Mikuláš Teich (Cambridge: Cambridge University Press, 1998), pp. 98–103.

8. Kann and David, *Peoples of the Eastern Habsburg Lands*, pp. 37–43.

9. See Jaroslav Krejčí, *Czechoslovakia at the Crossroads of European History* (London: I. B. Tauris, 1990), p. 60. See also, Purš and Kropilák, *Přehled dějin Československa do r. 1526*, pp. 538–40.

10. *Ze starých letopisů českých*, p. 411.

11. Macek, *Jagellonský věk*, vol. 1, pp. 292–318.

12. J. V. Polišenský, *The Thirty Years War*, translated by Robert Evans (Berkeley: University of California Press, 1971), pp. 23–52. See also, Jaroslav Purš and Miroslav Kropilák, gen. eds., *Přehled dějin Československa, 1526–1848*, vol. 1, part 2 of *Přehled dějin Československa* (Prague: Academia, 1982), pp. 9–11.

13. Macek, "Monarchy of the Estates," pp. 106–8.

14. Ivan Rada et al., *Dějiny zemí koruny české, I*, pp. 217–20; Purš and Kropilák, *Přehled dějin Československa, 1526–1848*, pp. 16–22.

15. Purš and Kropilák, *Přehled dějin Československa, 1526–1848*, p. 61.

16. Ibid., pp. 62–63.

17. Rada et al., *Dějiny zemí koruny české, I*, pp. 220–24; Jaroslav Pánek, *Zápas o Českou konfesi* (Prague: Melantrich, 1991), pp. 29–34 and 63–67.

18. The best study in English of the monarch and his time is still R. J. W. Evans, *Rudolf II and His World: A Study in Intellectual History, 1576–1612* (Oxford: Clarendon Press, 1973).

19. This section relies on Rada et al., *Dějiny zemí koruny české, I*, pp. 240–54, and Purš and Kropilák, *Přehled dějin Československa, 1526–1848*, pp. 70–78.

20. Purš and Kropilák, *Přehled dějin Československa do r. 1526*, pp. 546–47.

21. Rada et al., *Dějiny zemí koruny české, I*, pp. 240–54; Ivana Čornejová, *Tovaryšstvo Ježíšovo: jezuité v Čechách* (Prague: Mlada fronta, 1995), pp. 59–73.

22. Josef Janáček, *Rudolf II. a jeho doba* (Prague and Litomyšl: Paseka, 1997), pp. 244–66; Josef Válka, "Rudolfine Culture," in *Bohemia in History*,

edited by Mikuláš Teich (Cambridge: Cambridge University Press, 1998), pp. 130–32.

23. Válka, "Rudolfine Culture," pp. 132–33.

24. Janáček, *Rudolf II*, pp. 515–26.

25. Purš and Kropilák, *Přehled dějin Československa, 1526–1848*, pp. 82–94.

26. Janáček, *Rudolf II*, pp. 376–438.

27. Ibid., pp. 439–58.

28. Polišenský, *Thirty Years War*, pp. 49–51.

29. Rada et al., *Dějiny zemí koruny české, I*, pp. 224–29.

30. See Charles Ingrao, *The Habsburg Monarchy, 1618–1815* (Cambridge: Cambridge University Press, 1994), pp. 28–31; and Purš and Kropilák, *Přehled dějin Československa, 1526–1848*, pp. 95–97.

31. Rada et al. *Dějiny zemí koruny české, I*, pp. 230–34.

CHAPTER 6

1. Josef Petráň, *Staroměstská exekuce*, 3d revised and expanded ed. (Prague: Brána, 1996).

2. J. V. Polišenský, *Thirty Years War*, pp. 178–81; Ingrao, *The Habsburg Monarchy*, pp. 34–35.

3. This section relies on Jaroslav Purš and Miroslav Kropilák, *Přehled dějin Československa, 1526–1848*, pp. 182–90.

4. Robert Kann and Zdeněk David, *Peoples of the Eastern Habsburg Lands*, pp. 117–22; Ivan Rada et al., *Dějiny zemí koruny české, I*, p. 276; figures given in Purš and Kropilák, *Přehled dějin Československa, 1526–1848*, p. 190, differ slightly but suggest a drop of similar proportions.

5. See Robert Joseph Kerner, *Bohemia in the Eighteenth Century: A Study in Political, Economic, and Social History with Special Reference to the Reign of Leopold II, 1790–1792* (New York: Macmillan, 1932), pp. 66–71.

6. Kann and David, *Peoples of the Eastern Habsburg Lands*, p. 111.

7. Ibid., pp. 107–10.

8. Ibid., pp. 115–18; Purš and Kropilák, *Přehled dějin Československa, 1526–1848*, pp. 226–28.

9. Rada et al., *Dějiny zemí koruny české, I*, pp. 277–79; Purš and Kropilák, *Přehled dějin Československa, 1526–1848*, pp. 237–46.

10. Rada et al., *Dějiny zemí koruny české, I*, pp. 279–81.

11. Eduard Maur, *Kozina a Lomikar* (Prague: Melantrich, 1989).

12. Jiří Rak, *Bývali Čechové*, pp. 127–33; Ivana Čornejová, *Jezuité v Čechách*, pp. 92–94.

13. Josef Petráň and Lydia Petráňová, "The White Mountain as a Symbol in Modern Czech History," in Mikuláš Teich, ed., *Bohemia in History*, pp. 143–63; Victor S. Mamatey, "The Battle of the White Mountain as Myth in Czech History," *East European Quarterly* 15 (1981): pp. 335–45.

14. See John Comenius, *The Labyrinth of the World and the Paradise of the Heart*, translated by Howard Louthan and Andrea Sterk, with a preface by Jan Milič Lochman (New York and Mahwah, N.J.: Paulist Press, 1998). See also, Josef Válka, "Rudolfine Culture," pp. 138–39.

15. Jiří Mikulec, *Pobělohorská rekatolizace v českých zemích* (Prague: Státní pedagogické nakladatelství, 1992); Purš and Kropilák, *Přehled dějin Československa, 1526–1848*, pp. 190–96.

16. Rada et al., *Dějiny zemí koruny české, I*, pp. 285–86; Čornejová, *Jezuité v Čechách*, pp. 110–19.

17. See Vít Vlnas, *Jan Nepomucký: česká legenda* (Prague: Mladá fronta, 1993).

18. Josef Pekař, *Postavy a problemy českých dějin* (Prague: Vyšehrad, 1990), p. 195.

19. Jiří Rak and Jan P. Kučera, *Bohuslav Balbín a jeho místo v české kultuře* (Prague: Vyšehrad, 1983).

20. See Robert A. Kann, *A History of the Habsburg Empire, 1526–1918* (Berkeley: University of California Press, 1974), pp. 37–60.

21. Otto Urban, *České a slovenské dějiny do roku 1918* (Prague: Svoboda, 1991), pp. 120–21.

22. Kann, *Habsburg Empire*, pp. 93–96; Ingrao, *Habsburg Monarchy*, pp. 142–49.

CHAPTER 7

1. Charles Ingrao, *The Habsburg Monarchy*, pp. 105–49.

2. Louis Eisenmann, *Le compromis austro-hongrois de 1867: Étude sur le dualisme* (1904; Hattiesburg, Miss.: Academic International, 1971), pp. 22–25; Gerhard Hanke, "Das Zeitalter des Zentralismus (1740–1848)," in *Handbuch der Geschichte der böhmischen Länder*, edited by Karl Bosl (Stuttgart: Anton Hiersemann, 1974), pp. 436–68.

3. This section relies on Pavel Bělina et al., *Dějiny zemí koruny české, II. Od nástupu osvícenství po naši dobu* (Prague: Paseka, 1992), pp. 18–22; Otto Urban, *České a slovenské dějiny* (1991), pp. 126–28.

4. Ingrao, *Habsburg Monarchy*, pp. 155–56; Horst Haselsteiner, "Cooperation and Confrontation Between Rulers and the Noble Estates, 1711–1790," in *A History of Hungary*, Peter F. Sugar, gen. ed., edited by Péter Hánák, assisted by Tibor Frank (Bloomington: University of Indiana Press, 1990), p. 147.

5. Ingrao, *Habsburg Monarchy*, pp. 152–59; Robert Kann, *The Habsburg Empire*, pp. 96–101.

6. See František Martin Pelcl, *Paměti*, translated and edited by Jan Pan, with a foreword by Jiří Černý (Prague: Státní nakladatelství krásné literatury, hudby a umění, 1956), pp. 88–89.

7. See Herman Freudenberger, "State Intervention as an Obstacle to Economic Growth in the Habsburg Monarchy," *Journal of Economic History* 27, no. 4 (December 1967): 495; and Otto Urban, *České a slovenské dějiny do roku 1918*, 2d ed. (Prague: Aleš Skřivan ml., 2000), pp. 150–60.

8. Eisenmann, *Le compromis austro-hongrois*, pp. 22–25.

9. Jaroslav Purš and Miroslav Kropilák, *Přehled dějin Československa, 1526–1848*, p. 332.

10. Herman Freudenberger, "The Woolen-Goods Industry of the Habsburg Monarchy in the Eighteenth Century," *Journal of Economic History* 20, no. 3 (September 1960): 383–406.

11. Robert Kann and Zdeněk David, *Peoples of the Eastern Habsburg Lands*, pp. 204–5.

12. Ibid., p. 205.

13. Purš and Kropilák, *Přehled dějin Československa, 1526–1848*, pp. 347–49.

14. This section draws from William E. Wright, *Serf, Seigneur, and Sovereign: Agrarian Reform in Eighteenth-Century Bohemia* (Minneapolis: University of Minnesota Press, 1966).

15. Purš and Kropilák, *Přehled dějin Československa, 1526–1848*, pp. 350–55.

16. Stefan Plaggenborg, "Maria Theresia und die böhmischen Juden," *Bohemia* 39, no. 1 (1998): 1–16.

17. Hugh LeCaine Agnew, "Josephinism and the Patriotic Intelligentsia in Bohemia," *Harvard Ukrainian Studies* 10 (1986): 577–97; Purš and Kropilák, *Přehled dějin Československa, 1526–1848*, pp. 413–22.

18. Robert Kerner, *Bohemia in the Eighteenth Century*, remains an invaluable account of this process in Bohemia.

19. Hugh LeCaine Agnew, "Ambiguities of Ritual: Dynastic Loyalty, Territorial Patriotism, and Nationalism in the Last Three Royal Coronations in Bohemia," *Bohemia* 41, no. 1 (2000): 3–22.

20. Éva H. Balázs, *Hungary and the Habsburgs, 1765–1800: An Experiment in Enlightened Absolutism*, translated by Tim Wilkinson (Budapest: Central European University Press, 1997). See also, Ernst Wangermann, *From Joseph II to the Jacobin Trials: Government Policy and Public Opinion in the Habsburg Dominions in the Period of the French Revolution* (Oxford and London: Oxford University Press, 1969).

21. This section is based mostly on Hugh LeCaine Agnew, *Origins of the Czech National Renascence* (Pittsburgh: University of Pittsburgh Press, 1993).

22. Miroslav Hroch, *Social Preconditions of National Revival in Europe: A Comparative Analysis of the Social Composition of Patriotic Groups Among the Smaller European Nations*, translated by Ben Fowkes (Cambridge: Cambridge University Press, 1985).

23. Bělina et al., *Dějiny zemí koruny české, II*, p. 45.

24. Antonín Kostlán, "Kralovská česká společnost nauk a počátky nové tolerance," in *Mezi časy . . . Kultura a umění v českých zemích kolem roku 1800*, edited by Zdeněk Hojda and Roman Prahl (Prague: KLP-Koniasch Latin Press, 2000), pp. 98–105.

25. Bělina et al., *Dějiny zemí koruny české, II*, pp. 48–52.

26. Agnew, "Josephinism."

27. Franz Joseph Kinský, *Erinnerung über einen wichtigen Gegenstand, von einem Böhmen*, vol. 3 of *Des Grafen Kinskýs gesamelte Schriften* (Vienna: Wappler, 1786), p. 57.

28. Karel Hynek Thám, *Obrana jazyka českého proti zlobivým jeho utrháčům, též mnoha vlastencům v cvíčení se v něm liknavým a nedbalým* (Prague: Schönfeld, 1783), p. 21.

29. Vladimir Macura, *Znamení zrodu*, pp. 42–60.

30. Hugh LeCaine Agnew, "Enlightenment and National Consciousness: Three Czech 'Popular Awakeners'," in *Nation and Ideology: Essays in Honor of Wayne S. Vucinich*, edited by Ivo Banac, John G. Ackerman, and Roman Szporluk (Boulder, Colo.: East European Monographs, 1981), pp. 201–26.

CHAPTER 8

1. Clemens Wenzel Lothar Fürst von Metternich, *Memoirs of Prince Metternich, 1815–1829*, vol. 1, edited by Prince Richard Metternich, papers classified and arranged by M. A. de Klinkowstrom, translated by Mrs. Alexander Napier (New York: Harper & Brothers, 1881), pp. 333–34.

2. See Jan Nejedlý, "O lásce k vlasti," *Hlasatel Český* 1, no. 1 (1806): 3–5.

3. See Karel Sklenář, *Obraz vlasti: Příběh Národního muzeum* (Prague: Paseka, 2001), pp. 58–62.

4. Hugh Agnew, "Ambiguities of Ritual."

5. Antonín Okáč, *Český sněm a vláda před březněm 1848: kapitoly o jejich ústavních sporech* (Prague: Nákladem Zemského Národního výboru, 1947).

6. Robert Kann and Zdeněk David, *Peoples of the Eastern Habsburg Lands*, pp. 206–9.

7. See William O. McCagg, *A History of the Habsburg Jews, 1670–1918* (Bloomington: Indiana University Press, 1989), pp. 76–81.

8. Robert W. Seton-Watson, *A History of the Czechs and Slovaks* (1943; Hamden, Conn.: Archon Books, 1965), p. 165.

9. Joseph Matthias Graf von Thun-Hohenstein, *Der Slawismus in Böhmen* (Prague: J. G. Calve, 1845), p. 17.

10. Bernard Bolzano, *Über das Verhältniss der beiden Volkstämme in Böhmen* (Vienna: Wilhelm Braumüller, 1849), pp. 40–45.

11. Milan Řepa, *Moravané nebo Češí? Výjoj českého národního vědomí na Moravě v 19. století* (Brno: Doplněk, 2001), pp. 39–76.

12. Jiří Pernes, *Pod moravskou orlici aneb dějiny moravanství* (Brno: Barrister & Principal, 1996), pp. 81–102.

13. This section relies on Miroslav Hroch, "The Social Composition of the Czech Patriots in Bohemia, 1827–1848," in *The Czech Renascence of the Nineteenth Century; Essays Presented to Otakar Odložilik in Honour of His Seventieth Birthday*, edited by Peter Brock and H. Gordon Skilling (Toronto: University of Toronto Press, 1970), pp. 33–52.

14. Josef Jungmann, "O jazyku českém. Rozmlouvání druhé," *Hlasatel Český* 1, no. 3 (1806): 344.

15. Miroslav Hroch, *Na prahu národní existence: touha a skutečnost* (Prague: Mladá fronta, 1999), pp. 228–33.

16. František Palacký, *Dějiny národu českého v Čechách a na Moravě*, p. 8.

17. See Jiří Rak, *Bývali Čechové*, pp. 101–2; and "Rukopisy Královédvorský a Zelenohorský. Dnešní stav poznání," *Sborník Národního muzea* Řada C, no. 13–14 (1969).

18. Jiří Rak, "Tylova píseň v dobovém politickém kontextu," in *Locus amoenus—Místo líbezné: Symposium o české hymně, 27. X. 1993*, edited by Jiří K. Kroupa, compiled by Jiří Šubrt (Prague: KLP-Koniasch Latin Press, 1994), pp. 37–40.

19. See Karel Sabina, *Vzpomínky* (Prague: František Borovy, 1937), pp. 20–24.

20. Cited in Pavel Bělina et al., *Dějiny zemí koruny české, II*, p. 81.

21. See Alexander Schwan, "German Liberalism and the National Question in the Nineteenth Century," in *Nation-Building in Central Europe*, edited by Hagen Schulze (Leamington Spa: Berg, 1987), pp. 73–75, and Jan Křen, *Konfliktní společenství: Češi a Němci* (Prague: Academia, 1990), pp. 26–36.

22. See Jan Heidler, *Čechy a Rakousko v politických brožurách předbřeznových* (Prague: František Řívnác and Matice česká, 1920); also Křen, *Konfliktní společenství*, pp. 80–82.

23. Karel Havlíček, *Dílo*, vol. 2, edited by Alexander Stich, with a foreword by Alexander Stich (Prague: Československý spisovatel, 1986), p. 57.

24. See ibid., pp. 81–83.

25. Jonathan Sperber, *The European Revolution, 1848–1851* (Cambridge:

Cambridge University Press); Arnošt Klima, *Češi a Němci v revoluci, 1848–1849* (Prague: Nebesa, 1994); Stanley Z. Pech, *The Czech Revolution of 1848* (Chapel Hill: University of North Carolina Press, 1969).

26. The following discussion rests on Pech, *The Czech Revolution of 1848*, and Klima, *Češi a Němci v revoluci, 1848–1849*.

27. See: Křen, *Konfliktní společenství*, pp. 113–14; Otto Urban, *Česká společnost, 1848–1918* (Prague: Svoboda, 1982), pp. 22–29.

28. Urban, *Česká společnost, 1848–1918*, p. 33. See also, C. A. Macartney, *The Habsburg Empire, 1790–1918* (New York: Macmillan, 1969), pp. 322–50.

29. Havlíček, *Dílo*, pp. 143–44.

30. See: Franz Palacký, "Eine Stimme über Österreichs Anschluss an Deutschland," in *Gedenkblätter: Auswahl von Denkschriften, Aufsätzen und Briefen aus den letzten fünfzig Jahren* (Prague: Tempsky, 1874), pp. 150–52; Jiří Kořalka, *Tschechen im Habsburgerreich und in Europa, 1815–1914: Sozialgeschichtliche Zusammenhänge der neuzeitlichen Nationsbildung und der Nationalitätenfrage in den böhmischen Ländern* (Vienna: Verlag für Geschichte und Politik and R. Oldenbourg, 1991), pp. 29–31; Joseph Frederick Zacek, *Palacký: The Historian as Scholar and Nationalist* (The Hague: Mouton, 1970), pp. 24–25.

31. Urban, *Česká společnost, 1848–1918*, p. 37.

32. Macartney, *The Habsburg Empire, 1790–1918*, p. 354.

33. See Zdeněk Tobolka, *Politické dějiny československého národa od r. 1848 až do dnešní doby*, vol. 1 (Prague: Československý kompas, n.d.), pp. 51–55.

34. Zdeněk Tobolka, *Slovanský sjezd v Praze roku 1848* (Prague: Šimáček, 1901), pp. 51–53.

35. Urban, *Česká společnost, 1848–1918*, pp. 40–41.

36. Seton-Watson, *A History of the Czechs and Slovaks*, pp. 188–89.

37. Among the farsighted who realized the threat was Franz Schuselka. See Franz Schuselka, *Das Revolutionsjahr, März 1848–März 1849* (Vienna: Jasper, Hügel & Manz, 1850), p. 185.

38. See Pech, *The Czech Revolution of 1848*, p. 286; also Jerome Blum, *Noble Landowners and Agriculture in Austria, 1815–1848* (Baltimore: Johns Hopkins University Press, 1948).

39. Pech, *The Czech Revolution of 1848*, pp. 275–76.

40. Istvan Deak, *The Lawful Revolution: Louis Kossuth and the Hungarians, 1848–1849* (New York: Columbia University Press, 1979).

41. Robert Sak, *Rieger: Příběh Čecha devatenáctého věku* (Semily: Město Semily, 1993), p. 103.

42. Andreas Gottsmann, *Der Reichstag von Kremsier und die Regierung Schwarzenberg: die Verfassungsdiskussion des Jahres 1848 im Spannungsfeld zwischen Reaktion und nationaler Frage* (Vienna: R. Oldenbourg, 1994).

CHAPTER 9

1. Alan Sked, *The Decline and Fall of the Habsburg Empire, 1815–1918* (New York and London: Longman, 1989), pp. 101–18; A. J. P. Taylor, *The Habsburg Monarchy, 1809–1918: A History of the Austrian Empire and Austria-Hungary* (1948; Harmondsworth: Penguin Books, 1985), pp. 84–85.

2. C. A. Macartney, *The Habsburg Empire, 1790–1918*, pp. 433–37.

3. Ibid., pp. 430–31.

4. Otto Urban, *Česká společnost, 1848–1918*, pp. 81–84.

5. Vladimir Macura, *Český sen*, pp. 119–28.

6. Marcela C. Efmertová, *České země v letech 1848–1918* (Prague: Nakladatelství Libri, 1998), pp. 346–47.

7. Robert A. Kann, *Empire Reform*, vol. 2 of *The Multinational Empire: Nationalism and National Reform in the Habsburg Monarchy, 1848–1918* (New York: Columbia University Press, 1950), pp. 115–25.

8. See Robert Kann and Zdeněk David, *Peoples of the Eastern Habsburg Lands*, p. 298.

9. Pavel Cibulka, *Politické programy českých národních stran, 1860–1890* (Prague: Historický Ústav AV ČR, 2000), pp. 45–47.

10. Hugh LeCaine Agnew, "Noble *Natio* and Modern Nation: The Czech Case," *Austrian History Yearbook* 23 (1992): 50–71.

11. Milan Řepa, *Moravané nebo Češí? Vývoj českého národního vědomí na Moravě v 19. století*, pp. 106–36.

12. See Macartney, *The Habsburg Empire, 1790–1918*, p. 543.

13. Cited in ibid., pp. 562–63.

14. Pavla Vošahlíková, "Vliv Národních listů na utváření českého veřejného mínění ve 2. polovině 19. století," in *Bratří Grégrové a česká společnost v druhé polovině 19. století*, edited by Pavla Vošahlíková and Milan Řepa (Prague: Dr. Eduard Grégr a syn, 1997), pp. 39–48.

15. Efmertová, *České země v letech 1848–1918*, pp. 293–307.

16. František Palacký, "Idea státu rakouského," *Národ* II, no. 132 (May 16, 1865).

17. Cibulka, *Politické programy národních stran*, p. 131; Jaroslav Purš, "Tábory v českých zemích v letech 1868–1871 (Příspěvek k problematice národního hnutí)," *Československý časopis historický* 6 (1958): 234–66, 446–70, 661–90.

18. Edmund Bernatzik, ed., *Die österreichischen Verfassungsgesetze mit Erläuterungen* (Vienna: Manz, 1911), pp. 1087–91.

19. Robert A. Kann, *Empire and Nationalities*, vol. 1 of *The Multinational*

Empire: Nationalism and National Reform in the Habsburg Monarchy, 1848–1918 (New York: Columbia University Press, 1950), pp. 181–91.

20. Urban, *Česká společnost, 1848–1918*, p. 251.

21. Macartney, *The Habsburg Empire, 1790–1918*, pp. 583–85; Urban, *Česká společnost, 1848–1918*, pp. 248–57.

22. William Alexander Jenks, *Austria Under the Iron Ring, 1879–1893* (Charlottesville: University Press of Virginia, 1965).

23. Quoted in Macartney, *The Habsburg Empire, 1790–1918*, p. 615.

24. Cibulka, *Politické programy národních stran*, pp. 306–15.

25. This section draws on Kann and David, *Peoples of the Eastern Habsburg Lands*, pp. 312–18.

26. Ibid., pp. 314–15. See also, Efmertová, *České země v letech 1848–1918*, pp. 182–85.

27. This section draws on Efmertová, *České země v letech 1848–1918*, pp. 232–45.

28. See Macartney, *The Habsburg Empire, 1790–1918*, pp. 622–23.

29. Istvan Deak, *Beyond Nationalism: A Social and Political History of the Habsburg Officer Corps, 1848–1918* (New York: Oxford University Press, 1990).

30. Vlastislav Lacina, *Hospodářství českých zemí, 1880–1914* (Prague: Historický ústav ČSAV, 1990), p. 22; Urban, *České a slovenské dějiny*, 2d ed., p. 253.

31. David F. Good, *The Economic Rise of the Habsburg Empire, 1750–1918* (Berkeley: University of California Press, 1979), p. 256.

32. Efmertová, *České země v letech 1848–1918*, pp. 224–27; Lacina, *Hospodářství českých zemí, 1880–1914*, pp. 74–77.

33. Lacina, *Hospodářství českých zemí, 1880–1914*, pp. 69–70.

34. Peter Prokš, ed., *Politické programy Českoslovanské a Československé sociálně demokratické strany dělnické, 1878–1948* (Prague: Historický ústav AV ČR, 1999), pp. 13–14.

35. See ibid., pp. 20–22.

36. Macartney, *The Habsburg Empire, 1790–1918*, pp. 631–11.

37. Prokš, *Politické programy strany dělnické*, pp. 26–36.

38. Urban, *České a slovenské dějiny*, 2d ed., pp. 225–26.

39. Stanley B. Winters, "T. G. Masaryk and Karel Kramář: Long Years of Friendship and Rivalry," in *Thinker and Politician*, vol. 1 of *T. G. Masaryk (1850–1937)*, edited by Stanley B. Winters (New York: St. Martin's Press, 1990), pp. 155–56.

40. Karel Sklenář, *Obraz vlasti*, pp. 275–84.

41. Cited in Pavel Bělina et al., *Dějiny zemí koruny české*, II, p. 137.

42. Pieter Judson, " 'Not Another Square Foot!': German Liberalism and the Rhetoric of National Ownership in Nineteenth-Century Austria," *Austrian History Yearbook* 26 (1995): 83–97.

43. Catherine Albrecht, "The Rhetoric of Economic Nationalism in the Boycott Campaigns of the Late Habsburg Monarchy," *Austrian History Yearbook* 32 (2001): 47–67; Gary B. Cohen, *The Politics of Ethnic Survival: Germans in Prague, 1861–1914* (Princeton, N.J.: Princeton University Press, 1981).

CHAPTER 10

1. Theodore Mills Kelly, "Czech Radical Nationalism in the Era of Universal Manhood Suffrage, 1907–1914," Ph. D. diss., George Washington University, 1995.

2. Richard Charmatz, *Das politische Denken in Österreich: Geschichtliche Betrachtungen*, 2d ed. (Vienna: Verlag des Volksbildungshauses Wiener Urania, 1917), p. 70. See also, C. A. Macartney, *The Habsburg Empire, 1790–1918*, pp. 637–38.

3. See Karen Johnson Freeze, "The Young Progressives: The Czech Student Movement, 1887–1897," Ph. D. diss., Columbia University, 1974; and Jan Havránek, "Počátky a kořeny pokrokového hnutí studentského na počátku devadestátých let 19. století," *Acta Historia Universitatis Carolinae Pragensis* 2, no. 1 (1961): 5–33.

4. Bruce Garver, *The Young Czech Party, 1874–1901, and the Emergence of a Multi-Party System* (New Haven, Conn.: Yale University Press, 1978), pp. 182–86.

5. See Alois Rašín, *Paměti dr. Aloiše Rašína*, 2d ed., compiled by Ladislav Rašín, Memorabilia (Brno: Bonus A, 1994), pp. 67–90. See also, Jan Havránek, "Protirakouské hnutí dělnické mládeže a studentů a události roku 1893," *Acta Historia Universitatis Carolinae Pragensis* 2, no. 2 (1961): 21–81, and Jiří Pernes, *Spiklenci proti Jeho Veličenstvu: historie tzv. spiknutí Omladiny v Čechách* (Prague: Mladá fronta, 1988).

6. Stanley B. Winters, "T. G. Masaryk and Karel Kramář: Long Years of Friendship and Rivalry," pp. 161–63.

7. See Tomáš Garrigue Masaryk, René Wellek, ed., *The Meaning of Czech History*, translated by Peter Kussi (Chapel Hill: University of North Carolina Press, 1974), and Miloš Havelka, ed., *Spor o smyslu českých dějin, 1895–1938* (Prague: Torst, 1995).

8. Otto Urban, *České a slovenské dějiny*, 2d ed., p. 233.

9. A currency reform in 1892 replaced the gulden with the crown (*Krone*) at the rate of two to one, so the tax hurdle was actually lowered to eight crowns. See Macartney, *The Habsburg Empire, 1790–1918*, p. 671.

10. Peter Prokš, *Politické programy strany dělnické*, p. 45.

11. Cited in Garver, *Young Czech Party*, p. 252.

12. This section rests on Urban, *České a slovenské dějiny*, 2d ed., pp. 235–38.

13. Josef Harna, ed., *Politické programy českého národního socialismu* (Prague: Historický ústav AV ČR, 1998), pp. 36–39.

14. Prokš, *Politické programy strany dělnické*, pp. 50–51; Robert Kann, *Empire and Nationalities*, pp. 155–57.

15. Andrew G. Whiteside, *The Socialism of Fools: Georg Ritter von Schönerer and Austrian Pan-Germanism* (Berkeley: University of California Press, 1975); Carl E. Schorske, *Fin-de-Siècle Vienna: Politics and Culture* (New York: Knopf, 1980), pp. 116–33.

16. Schorske, *Fin-de-Siècle Vienna*, pp. 133–46.

17. See Macartney, *The Habsburg Empire, 1790–1918*, pp. 668–69.

18. Kann, *Empire and Nationalities*, pp. 207–9.

19. Macartney, *The Habsburg Empire, 1790–1918*, pp. 758–59.

20. The negotiations are covered in detail in William A. Jenks, *The Austrian Electoral Reform of 1907* (1950; New York: Octagon Books, 1974), pp. 27–62.

21. Jan Havránek, *Boj za všeobecné, přímé a rovné hlasovací právo roku 1893*, Rozpravy ČSAV, Řada společenských věd, 74, sešit 2 (Prague: ČSAV, 1964).

22. Comparing machine horsepower per capita: the Czech lands, 60.4 hp; Great Britain, 180.2 hp; Germany, 82.5 hp; France, 51.2 hp; Austro-Hungarian average, 32.2 hp. Russia's figure was 10.1 hp. See Urban, *České a slovenské dějiny*, 2d ed., p. 231.

23. Marcela Efmertová, *České země v letech 1848–1918*, pp. 190–202.

24. Urban, *České a slovenské dějiny*, 2d ed., p. 253.

25. Mark Cornwall, "The Struggle on the Czech-German Language Border, 1880–1940," *English Historical Review* 109 (September 1994): 914–30.

26. Urban, *České a slovenské dějiny*, 2d ed., pp. 256–57; Efmertová, *České země v letech 1848–1918*, p. 126.

27. And not just Czech society: see Gary B. Cohen, *Education and Middle-Class Society in Imperial Austria, 1848–1918* (West Lafayette, Ind.: Purdue University Press, 1996).

28. Comparable statistics for other nationalities were: Poles, 40.82; Ukrainians, 23.92; Slovenes, 23.92; Serbs and Croats, 74.14; Romanians, 71.61; Magyars, 56.72. See Urban, *České a slovenské dějiny*, 2d ed., p. 237.

29. See Hillel J. Kieval, *Languages of Community: The Jewish Experience in the Czech Lands* (Berkeley: University of California Press, 2000), pp. 181–97, and H. Gordon Skilling, "Masaryk: Permanent Dissenter: The Hilsner Case and Anti-Semitism," *Cross Currents* 8 (1989): 243–60.

30. Scott Spector, *Prague Territories: National Conflict and Cultural Innovation in Kafka's Fin de Siècle* (Berkeley: University of California Press, 2000);

Scott Spector, "Německá, židovská a česká identita v Praze. Felix Weltsch a Egon Erwin Kisch," *Slovanský přehled* 84, no. 1 (1998): 39–46.

31. Katherine David-Fox, "Prague-Vienna, Prague-Berlin: The Hidden Geography of Czech Modernism," *Slavic Review* 59, no. 4 (2000): 735–60.

32. Stanley B. Winters, "Jan Otto, T. G. Masaryk, and the Czech National Encyclopedia," *Jahrbücher für Geschichte Osteuropas* 31, no. 4 (1983): 516–42.

33. Milan Hlavačka, *Jubilejní výstava 1891* (Prague: Techkom, 1991); Catherine Albrecht, "Pride in Production: The Jubilee Exhibition of 1891 and Economic Competition Between Czechs and Germans in Bohemia," *Austrian History Yearbook* 24 (1993): 101–18.

34. Cited in Efmertová, *České země v letech 1848–1918*, pp. 133–34.

35. This section relies on Francis R. Bridge, *The Habsburg Monarchy Among the Great Powers* (New York: Berg, 1991).

36. See Macartney, *The Habsburg Empire, 1790–1918*, pp. 785–86, and Arnold Suppan, "Masaryk and the Trials for High Treason Against the South Slavs in 1909," in *Thinker and Politician*, vol. 1 of *T. G. Masaryk (1850–1937)*, edited by Stanley B. Winters (New York: St. Martin's Press, 1990), pp. 210–24. Masaryk's speech is reprinted in Czech translation in Jiří Kovtun, *Slovo má poslanec Masaryk* (Prague: Československý spisovatel, 1991), pp. 254–71.

37. See R. W. Seton-Watson, *The Southern Slav Question and the Habsburg Monarchy* (1911; New York: H. Fertig, 1969), and Kovtun, *Slovo má poslanec Masaryk*, pp. 279–311.

38. Ladislav Hladký, "T. G. Masaryk a Bosna a Hercegovina: příspěvek k historii českojihoslovanských vztahů," *Slovanské historické studie* 20 (1994): 33–55.

39. Theodore Mills Kelly, "The Czech National Council and the Slovaks, 1900–1914," *Kosmas: Czechoslovak and Central European Journal* 12, no. 2 (Fall 1997): 99–118.

40. Paul Vyšný, *Neo-Slavism and the Czechs, 1898–1914* (Cambridge: Cambridge University Press, 1977).

41. Kann, *Multinational Empire*, vol. 2, pp. 187–96.

42. Macartney, *The Habsburg Empire, 1790–1918*, pp. 810–12.

43. Cited in Milada Paulová, *Dějiny Maffie: Odboj Čechů a Jihoslovanů za světové války, 1914–1918* (Prague: Československá grafická unie, 1937), pp. 205–6.

44. Urban, *Česká společnost, 1848–1918*, p. 588.

45. Efmertová, *České země v letech 1848–1918*, pp. 139–40.

46. See Hans Lemberg, "Masaryk and the Russian Question Against the Background of German and Czech Attitudes to Russia," in Winters, ed., *Thinker and Politician*, pp. 283–301.

47. Victor S. Mamatey, "The Establishment of the Republic," in *A History*

of the Czechoslovak Republic, 1918–1948, edited by Victor S. Mamatey and Radomír Luža (Princeton, N.J.: Princeton University Press, 1973), p. 14.

48. Ibid., p. 15.

49. This text was drafted by Czernin. See Urban, *České a slovenské dějiny*, 2d ed., p. 249.

50. Peter Heumos, "'Kartoffeln her oder es gibt eine Revolution': Hungarkrawalle, Streiks und Massenproteste in den böhmischen Ländern, 1914–1918," *Slezský sborník* 97, no. 2 (1999): 81–104.

51. Jan Heidler, *1917, projevy českých spisovatelů* (Prague: Vesmír, 1921), pp. 75–78.

52. Milada Paulová, *Tajný výbor Maffie a spolupráce s Jihoslovany v letech 1916–1918* (Prague: Academia, 1968), pp. 227–28; Jan Galandauer, "Prohlášení českého svazu z 30. května 1917: Zapomenutá programová revoluce," *Český časopis historický* 91, no. 4 (1993): 582–93.

53. Robert F. Hopwood, "The Conflict Between Count Czernin and Emperor Charles in 1918," *Austrian History Yearbook* 4–5 (1968–69): 28–43; Edward P. Kelleher, "Emperor Karl and the Sixtus Affair: Politico-Nationalist Repercussions in the Reich German and Austro-German Camps, and the Disintegration of Habsburg Austria, 1916–1918," *East European Quarterly* 26, no. 2 (1992): 163–84.

54. Victor S. Mamatey, "The Czecho-Slovak Agreement of Pittsburgh (May 30, 1918) Revisited," *Kosmas* 2, no. 2 (1983): 41–48; Antonín Klimek, Helena Nováčková, Milada Polišenská, and Ivan Šťovíček, eds., *Vznik Československa 1918* (Prague: Ústav mezinárodních vztahů, 1994), p. 123.

55. Betty Miller Unterberger, *The United States, Revolutionary Russia, and the Rise of Czechoslovakia* (Chapel Hill: University of North Carolina Press, 1989).

56. Mamatey, "The Establishment of the Republic," pp. 21–22.

57. Edvard Beneš, *Světová válka a naše revoluce: Vzpomínky a úvahy z boju za svobodu národa, III, Dokumenty* (Prague: Orbis & Čin, 1928), pp. 318–21.

58. Klimek et al., *Vznik Československa 1918*, pp. 245–46.

CHAPTER 11

1. Josef Korbel, *Twentieth-Century Czechoslovakia: The Meanings of Its History* (New York: Columbia University Press, 1977), pp. 82–84; Robert Kann and Zdeněk David, *Peoples of the Eastern Habsburg Lands*, pp. 325–27.

2. Karel Čapek, *Talks with T. G. Masaryk*, edited by Michael Henry Heim, translated by Dora Round (New Haven, Conn.: Catbird Press, 1995), p. 244.

3. The story that Rašín threw back in the Social-Democrat leader Josef Seliger's face the remark by Windischgärtz in 1848, "I do not negotiate with rebels," is a fabrication. See Jaroslav Valenta, "Legenda o 'rebelech, s nimíž se nevyjednává'," *Moderní dějiny* 2 (1994): 197–214. See also, Jaroslav Valenta, "Nezdařený pokus o jednání mezi Čechy a Němci na přelomu let 1918–1919," ibid. 3 (1995): pp. 229–40.

4. J. W. Breughel, "The Germans in Pre-War Czechoslovakia," in Victor Mamatey and Radomír Luža, eds., *A History of the Czechoslovak Republic*, pp. 168–69.

5. See Rudolf Laun, *Les prétentions des Tchécoslovaques á des territoires allemands* (The Hague: Martin Nijhoff, 1919). See also, Zdeněk Karník, *České země v éře První republiky, díl první, Vznik, budování a zlatá léta republiky (1918–1929)* (Prague: Libri, 2000), pp. 37–44.

6. Peter Pastor, *Hungary Between Wilson and Lenin: The Hungarian Revolution of 1918–1919 and the Big Three* (Boulder, Colo.: East European Quarterly, 1976); Jörg Hoensch, "Tschechoslowakismus oder Autonomie. Die Auseinandersetzungen um die Eingliederung der Slowakei in die Tschechoslowakische Republik," in *Das Jahr 1919 in der Tschechoslowakei und in Ostmitteleuropa*, edited by Hans Lemberg and Peter Heumos, Bad Weisseer Tagungen des Collegium Carolinum, 17 (Munich: R. Oldenbourg, 1993).

7. Late in 1918, hoping to prevent its inclusion in Czechoslovakia, the city fathers decided to rename it Wilsonov, but Wilson declined and the modern Slovak version, Bratislava, was fixed. It became the Slovak capital on January 16, 1919. See Marián Hronský, "Bratislava či Wilsonov? Město na Dunaji pred trištvrte storočím," *Historická revue* 3, no. 6 (1992): 13–15.

8. Rudolf L. Tökés, *Bela Kun and the Hungarian Soviet Republic: The Origins and Role of the Communist Party of Hungary in the Revolutions of 1918–1919* (New York: Published for the Hoover Institution on War, Revolution and Peace by F. A. Praeger, 1967).

9. Zdeněk L. Suda, *Zealots and Rebels: A History of the Communist Party of Czechoslovakia* (Stanford: Hoover Institution Press, 1980), pp. 23–33. See also, Vladislav Zapletál, "K událostem roku 1919," *Acta Universitatis Palackianae Olomucensis: Historica*, no. 21 (1981): 25–43, and Marián Hronský, "Slovenská republika rád (vojenskopolitická situacia)," *Historie a vojenství* 37, no. 4 (1988): 36–52.

10. Paul Robert Magocsi, *The Shaping of a National Identity: Subcarpathian Rus, 1848–1948* (Cambridge, Mass.: Harvard University Press, 1978), pp. 76–102. See also, Victor S. Mamatey, "The Slovaks and Carpatho-Ruthenians," in *The Immigrants' Influence on Wilson's Peace Policies*, edited by Joseph P. O'Grady (Lexington: University of Kentucky Press, 1967), pp. 239–49.

11. Zbyněk Zeman, *The Life of Edvard Beneš, 1884–1948: Czechoslova-*

kia in War and Peace, in collaboration with Antonín Klimek (Oxford: Clarendon Press, 1997), pp. 38–46.

12. This section is based on Dagmar Perman, *The Shaping of the Czechoslovak State: Diplomatic History of the Boundaries of Czechoslovakia, 1914– 1920* (Leiden: E. J. Brill, 1962).

13. Ibid., pp. 153–55.

14. This section uses Hans Lemberg, "Die Tschechoslowakei im Jahr 1. Der Staatsaufbau, die Liquidierung der Revolution und die Alternativen 1919," in *Das Jahr 1919 in der Tschechoslowakei un in Ostmitteleuropa*, edited by Hans Lemberg and Peter Heumos (Munich: R. Oldenbourg, 1993), pp. 225–48; and Václav L. Beneš, "Czechoslovak Democracy and Its Problems, 1918–1920," in Mamatey and Luža, *A History of the Czechoslovak Republic*, pp. 39–98.

15. The text of the constitutional law, 121/1920 Sb., may be found at the Web site of the Parliament of the Czech Republic, "Zákon ze dne 29. února 1920, kterým se uvozuje Ústavní listina Československé republiky," Electronic Library of the Chamber of Deputies, Czech Republic <http://www.psp.cz/docs/ texts/constitution.1920.html>.

16. Daniel E. Miller, *Forging Political Compromise: Antonín Švehla and the Czechoslovak Republican Party, 1918–1933* (Pittsburgh: University of Pittsburgh Press, 1999).

17. Stanley B. Winters, "Passionate Patriots: Czechoslovak National Democracy in the 1920s," *East Central Europe/L'Europe du Centre-Est* 18, no. 1 (1991): 55–68.

18. See Suda, *Zealots and Rebels*, pp. 113–19.

19. See Ferdinand Peroutka, *Rok 1918*, vol. 1 of *Budování státu: Československá politika v letech popřevratových*, 2d ed. (Prague: František Borový, 1933), pp. 253–55; also Čapek, *Talks with TGM*, pp. 240–49.

20. See Václav L. Beneš, "Czechoslovak Democracy and Its Problems, 1918–1920," pp. 88–89.

21. F. Gregory Campbell, *Confrontation in Central Europe: Weimar Germany and Czechoslovakia* (Chicago: University of Chicago Press, 1975), p. 208.

22. Zdeněk Kárník, "Ustavení ČSR jako parlamentní demokracie v podmínkách národněpolitické a sociálněpolitické krize střední Evropy (jaro-léto 1920): Události, jijich důsledky a širší souvislosti," in *Československo 1918–1938: Osudy demokracie ve střední Evropě*, edited by Jaroslav Valenta, Emil Voráček, and Josef Harna (Prague: Historický ústav AV ČR, 1999), pp. 90–110; Antonín Klimek, "Počátky parlamentní demokracie v Československu," in ibid., pp. 111–22.

23. The following paragraphs draw from Vlastislav Lacina, *Zlatá léta československého hospodářství 1918–1929* (Prague: Historický ústav AV ČR, 2000), pp. 28–39.

24. Mark Cornwall, " 'National Reparation?' The Czech Land Reform and the Sudeten Germans, 1918–38," *Slavonic and East European Review* 75, no. 2 (1997): pp. 259–80.

25. Suda, *Zealots and Rebels*, pp. 38–42.

26. Victor S. Mamatey, "The Development of Czechoslovak Democracy, 1920–1938," in Mamatey and Luža, *A History of the Czechoslovak Republic*, pp. 102–6; Nancy Meriwether Wingfield, "Conflicting Constructions of Memory: Attacks on Statues of Joseph II in the Bohemian Lands After the Great War," *Austrian History Yearbook* 28 (1998): 147–71.

27. Suda, *Zealots and Rebels*, pp. 45–49.

28. Karel Sommer, "Zatčení a internace Andreje Hlinky," *Slezský sborník* 96, no. 2 (1988): 106–18.

29. Lacina, *Zlatá léta*, 82.

30. Eduard Kubů and Jana Šetřilová, "Hrad a Alois Rašín v letech 1922–1923: zápas o deflaci a omluvu legionářům," *Český časopis historický* 93, no. 3 (1995): 451–69; Vlastislav Lacina, "Měnová politika v prvním desetiletí Československé republiky," ibid. 91, no. 1 (1993): 1–17.

31. Miloš Trapl, "Začlenění římskokatolické církve do české společnosti po roce 1918," in Valenta, Voráček, and Harna, eds., pp. 145–46.

32. Manfred Alexander, "Proces s Vojtechom Tukom zo spravodajstva nemeckého konzulátu bratislave," *Historický časopis* 40, no. 5 (1992): 609–24; Carol Skalnik Leff, *National Conflict in Czechoslovakia: The Making and Remaking of a State, 1918–1987* (Princeton, N.J.: Princeton University Press, 1988), pp. 82–83.

33. Paul E. Zinner, "Czechoslovakia: The Diplomacy of Edvard Benes," in *The Diplomats, 1919–1939*, edited by Gordon A. Craig and Felix Gilbert (Princeton, N.J.: Princeton University Press, 1953), pp. 100–122; Zeman, *Beneš*, pp. 59–85.

34. The following relies on Piotr S. Wandycz, "Foreign Policy of Edvard Beneš, 1918–1938," in Mamatey and Luža, *A History of the Czechoslovak Republic*, pp. 216–38.

35. See Campbell, *Confrontation in Central Europe*.

36. Igor Lukes, "Czechoslovak-Soviet Relations from the End of World War I to Adolf Hitler's Machtergreifung," *Diplomacy and Statecraft* 5, no. 2 (1994): 248–86.

37. See the indispensible Piotr S. Wandycz, *France and Her Eastern Allies, 1919–1925* (Minneapolis: University of Minnesota Press, 1962), and Piotr S. Wandycz, *The Twilight of French Eastern Alliances, 1926–1936: French-Czechoslovak-Polish Relations from Locarno to the Remilitarization of the Rhineland* (Princeton, N.J.: Princeton University Press, 1988).

38. Piotr Wandycz, "The Little Entente: Sixty Years Later," *Slavonic and East European Review* 59, no. 4 (1981): 548–64.

39. Lacina, *Zlatá Léta*, pp. 41–47.

40. Mamatey, "Development of Czechoslovak Democracy," p. 143.

41. Zora P. Pryor, "Czechoslovak Economic Development in the Interwar Period," in Mamatey and Luža, *A History of the Czechoslovak Republic*, pp. 209–10.

42. Mamatey, "Development of Democracy," p. 143.

43. See Karl J. Crosby, "Leading Figures of the Hlinka Slovak People's Party," *Kosmas* 5, no. 2 (1986): 57–69.

44. Mamatey, "Development of Democracy," p. 150.

45. Lubomír Slezák, "Sudetští Němci a hospodářství první republiky," *Moderní dějiny* 2 (1994): 123–41; Ladislav Lipscher, "Beschwerden der Sudetendeutschen im wirschaftlichen Bereich während der ersten tschechoslowakischen Republik," *Jahrbuch für Zeitgeschichte* (1982–83): 33–57.

46. Ronald M. Smelser, "Nazis Without Hitler: The DNSAP and the First Czechoslovak Republic," *East Central Europe/L'Europe du Centre-Est* 4, no. 1 (1977): 1–19.

47. Keith Hamilton, "Old Adam and Five Beggars: British Reaction to the Tardieu Plan," *Revue d'Europe Centrale* 5, no. 2 (1997): 95–115.

48. Igor Lukes, *Czechoslovakia Between Stalin and Hitler: The Diplomacy of Edvard Beneš in the 1930s* (New York: Oxford University Press, 1996), pp. 43–49.

49. Zeman, *Beneš*, pp. 95–116.

50. This section relies on Mamatey, "Development of Democracy," pp. 152–61.

51. Ronald M. Smelser, "At the Limits of a Mass Movement: The Case of the Sudeten German Party, 1933–1938," *Bohemia* 17 (1976): 240–66.

52. Norman H. Baynes, ed., *The Speeches of Adolf Hitler, April 1922–August 1939*, Royal Institute for International Affairs (London and New York: Oxford University Press, 1942), pp. 1404–6.

53. Ronald M. Smelser, *The Sudeten Problem, 1933–1938: Volkstumspolitik and the Formulation of Nazi Foreign Policy* (Folkestone: Dawson, 1975), pp. 217–18.

54. Ibid., p. 222.

55. Mamatey, "Development of Democracy," pp. 160–61.

56. Lukes, *Between Stalin and Hitler*, pp. 125–27.

57. Igor Lukes, "The Czechoslovak Partial Mobilization in May 1938: A Mystery (Almost) Solved," *Journal of Contemporary History* 31, no. 4 (1996): 699–720.

58. Baynes, *Speeches of Hitler*, pp. 1488–97.

59. Smelser, *The Sudeten Problem*, p. 225.

60. Joseph Rothschild and Nancy M. Wingfield, *Return to Diversity: A Political History of East Central Europe Since World War II*, 3d ed. (New York: Oxford University Press, 2000), p. 235.

61. F. Gregory Campbell, "Central Europe's Bastion of Democracy," *East European Quarterly* 11, no. 2 (1977): 171.

62. Breughel, "The Germans in Pre-War Czechoslovakia," p. 172.

63. Ibid., pp. 186–87; Gottfried Schramm, "Tschechen und Deutsche in der ersten Republik," *Bohemia* 29, no. 2 (1988): 383–90.

64. T. G. Masaryk, *Cesta demokracie I: Soubor projevů za republiky, 1918–1920*, Spisy T. G. Masaryka, 3 (Prague: Čin, 1933), p. 20.

65. T. G. Masaryk, *Cestá demokracie III: projevy, články, rozhovory, 1924–1928*, Spisy T. G. Masaryka, 35 (Prague: Ústav T. G. Masaryka, 1994), pp. 328–29.

66. Karl F. Bahm, "The Inconveniences of Nationality: German Bohemians, the Disintegration of the Habsburg Monarchy, and the Attempt to Create a 'Sudeten German' Identity," *Nationalities Papers* 27, no. 3 (1999): 375–405.

67. Beneš, "Czechoslovak Democracy and Its Problems, 1918–1920," p. 41. For the following discussion see Ezra Mendelsohn, *The Jews of East Central Europe Between the World Wars* (Bloomington: Indiana University Press, 1983), pp. 132–42.

68. See Vavro Ján Šrobár, *Osvobodené Slovensko: pamäti z rokov 1918–1920* (Prague: Čin, 1928), p. 36.

69. Jozef Faltus and Václav Průcha, *Prehl'ad hospodárskeho vývoja na Slovensku v rokoch 1918–1945* (Bratislava: Vydavatel'stvo politickej literatúry, 1969).

70. Owen V. Johnson, *Slovakia, 1918–1938: Education and the Making of a Nation* (Boulder, Colo.: East European Monographs, 1985).

71. "Nedotknutel'né piliere padli: Slovenský a český historik hodnotia význam 28. októbra 1918," *Pravda*, October 27, 1992 (Bratislava).

72. T. G. Masaryk, *Cestá demokracie IV: projevy, články, rozhovory, 1929–1937*, Spisy T. G. Masaryka, 36 (Prague: Ústav T. G. Masaryka, 1997), p. 451.

CHAPTER 12

1. For a defense of Beneš based on newly available Czechoslovak archives, see Igor Lukes, "Stalin and Beneš at the End of September 1938: New Evidence from the Prague Archives," *Slavic Review* 52, no. 1 (1993): 28–48; and Igor Lukes, "Stalin and Czechoslovakia in 1938–39: An Autopsy of a Myth," *Diplomacy and Statecraft* 10, no. 2–3 (1999): 13–47. Joseph Kalvoda, "Munich: Beneš and the Soldiers," *Ukrainian Quarterly* 47 (1991): 153–69, gives a critical view.

2. Pavel Tigrid, *Kapesní průvodce inteligentí ženy po vlastním osudu*, 2d ed. (Prague: Odeon, 1990).

3. Igor Lukes, *Czechoslovakia Between Stalin and Hitler*, p. 247.

4. This section relies on Keith Eubank, "Munich," in Mamatey and Luža, *A History of the Czechoslovak Republic, 1918–1948*, pp. 239–52.

5. Victor S. Mamatey, "The Development of Czechoslovak Democracy," pp. 162–63; Zbyněk Zeman, *The Life of Edvard Beneš*, pp. 124–27.

6. Lukes, *Between Stalin and Hitler*, pp. 230–31.

7. Ladislav Deák, "Polské územní nároky vôčí Slovensku v roku 1938," *Historický časopis* 39 (1991): 12–27; Eubank, "Munich," p. 248.

8. Lukes, *Between Stalin and Hitler*, pp. 236–38.

9. Ibid., pp. 251–55; Zeman, *Beneš*, pp. 134–37.

10. Cited in Edvard Beneš, *Mnichovské dny. Paměti* (Prague: Svoboda, 1968), p. 346.

11. Cited in Pavel Bělina et al., *Dějiny zemí koruny české, II*, p. 191.

12. Theodor Procházka, "The Second Republic, 1938–1939," in Mamatey and Luža, *A History of the Czechoslovak Republic*, pp. 256–60.

13. Ibid., p. 261. See also, Zdeněk Štěpánek, "Péče o utečence z okupovaného pohraničí Moravy a Slezska v letech 1938–1939," *Časopis Matice moravské* 112 (1993): 43–54.

14. See Procházka, "Second Republic," pp. 257–58; Juraj Zudel, "Zmeny československo-maďarských hranic v dôsledku viedenskej arbitráže," *Slovenská archivistika* 26 (1991): 34–43.

15. Jan Gebhart and Jan Kuklík, "Pomnichovská krize a vznik Strany národní jednoty," *Český časopis historický* 90 (1992): 365–93.

16. Jan Rataj, "O rasový národ: k proměnám nacionalismu v druhé republice," *Historie a vojenství* 42 (1993): 80–94.

17. An interesting firsthand account is Martin Sokol, "Ako došlo k vyhlášeniu Slovenského Štátu? Moje poznámky k marcovým udalostiam 1939," *Historický časopis* 39 (1991): 323–29. See also, Procházka, "Second Republic," pp. 264–68.

18. Beneš, *Mnichovské dny. Paměti*, p. 342.

19. The following discussion relies on Gotthold Rhode, "The Protectorate of Bohemia and Moravia, 1939–1945," in Mamatey and Luža, *A History of the Czechoslovak Republic*, pp. 296–321. See also, Tomáš Pasák, *Pod ochranou Říše* (Prague: Práh, 1998).

20. Petr Němec, "Das tschechische Volk und die nationalsozialistische Germanisierung des Raumes," *Bohemia* 32 (1991): 424–55; Petr Němec, "Die Lage der deutschen Nationalität im Protektorat Böhmen und Mähren unter dem Aspekt der 'Eindeutschung' dieses Gebiets," ibid., pp. 39–59.

21. The Czech joke compared the National Community to a cemetery: "Sooner or later everyone ends up in it." Cited in Rhode, "The Protectorate of Bohemia and Moravia," pp. 302–3. See also, Jan Gebhart and Jan Kuklík, "Po-

čátky Národního souručenství v roce 1939," *Český časopis historický* 91 (1993): 417–41.

22. Miroslav Kárný, "Die Protektoratsregierung und die Verordnungen des Reichsprotektors ber das jüdische Vermögen," *Judaica Bohemiae* 29 (1993): 54–66.

23. After the war, November 17 was declared International Students' Day. See Karel Litsch, "K výročí 17. listopadu 1939," Acta Universitatis Carolinae, *Historia Universitatis Carolinae Pragensis* 29 (1989): 9–13.

24. Miroslav Kárný, "Die materiellen Grundlagen der Sozialdemagogie in der Protektoratspolitik Heydrichs," *Historica* 29 (1989): 123–59.

25. Vojtěch Mastný, *The Czechs Under Nazi Rule: The Failure of National Resistance, 1939–1942* (New York: Columbia University Press, 1971).

26. Symbolically, Kubiš was a Czech and Gabčík a Slovak. Radomír Luža, "The Czech Resistance Movement," in Mamatey and Luža, *A History of the Czechoslovak Republic*, pp. 351–54.

27. Unlike similar or even more horrific actions in occupied Poland or the Soviet Union, the Nazis publicized this one widely themselves.

28. Rhode, "The Protectorate," pp. 313–15.

29. Dana Musilová, "Zásobování a vyživa českého obyvatelstva v podminkách válečného řízení hospodářství (1939–1945)," *Slezský sborník* 89 (1991): 255–66.

30. Typical examples: Vilém Mathesius, ed., *Od slovanských věrozvěstů k národnímu obrození*, vol. 1 of *Co daly naše země Evropě a lidstvu* (Prague: Evropský literární klub, 1940); Vilém Mathesius, ed., *Obrozený národ a jeho země na fóru evropském a světovém*, vol. 2 of *Co daly naše země Evropě a lidstvu* (1940); and Jan Blahoslav Čapek, gen. ed., *Kde domov můj?: památník věnovany naší vlasti a hymne národa českého* (Prague: Čin, 1940).

31. George F. Kennan, *From Prague After Munich: Diplomatic Papers, 1938–1940* (1968; Princeton, N.J.: Princeton University Press, 1971), p. 178.

32. Miroslav Kárný, "Lidské ztráty československých židů v letech 1938–1945," *Český časopis historický* 89 (1991): 410–20.

33. Tomáš Pasák and Robert Kvaček, *JUDr. Emil Hácha* (Prague: Horizont, 1997).

34. Jörg K. Hoensch, "The Slovak Republic, 1939–1945," in Mamatey and Luža, *A History of the Czechoslovak Republic*, pp. 271–95, and Yeshayahu Jelinek, *The Parish Republic: Hlinka's Slovak People's Party*, East European Monographs, 14 (Boulder, Colo.: East European Quarterly, distributed by Columbia University Press, 1976).

35. Hoensch, "Slovak Republic," pp. 272–73. See also, Ivan Kamenec, *Slovenský stát* (Prague: Anomal, 1992), pp. 25–36.

36. See Jelinek, *Parish Republic*, pp. 93–95; and L'ubomír Lipták, ed., *Politické strany na Slovensku, 1869–1989* (Bratislava: Archa, 1992), p. 223. For

the Salzburg meetings, see L'ubomír Lipták, "Príprava a priebeh salzburských rokovaní roku 1940 medzi prestavitel'mi Nemecka a slovenského štátu," *Historický časopis* 13 (1965): 329–65.

37. Land reform was also directed against Jews. See Samuel Cambel, "Arizácia a dalšie zmeny v pozemkovej držbe na Slovensku do leta 1944," *Historický časopis* 43 (1995): 69–88.

38. See Ivan Kamenec, "Deportácie židovských občanov zo Slovenska roku 1942," in *Tragédia slovenských židov*, edited by Dezider Tóth (Banská Bystrica: DATEI, 1992), pp. 77–100, and Kamenec, *Slovenský stát*, pp. 107–16.

39. Kennan, *From Prague After Munich*, p. 135. See also: L'ubomír Lipták, "Mad'arsko v politike slovenského štátu v rokoch 1939–1943," *Historický časopis* 15, no. 1967 (1967): 1–35; and Miroslav Tejchman, "Slovensko-Rumunsko-Chorvatská spolupráce v letech druhé světové války a Mad'arsko," *Slovanský přehled* 78 (1992): 158–70.

40. See Hoensch, "Slovak Republic," p. 289. See also, Charles K. Kliment, *Slovenská armáda, 1939–1945* (Plzeň: Mustang, 1996).

41. Bradley F. Abrams, "The Price of Retribution: The Trial of Jozef Tiso," *East European Politics and Societies* 10 (1996): 255–92.

42. Secrétairerie d'État de sa Sainteté, *Le Saint Siège et les victimes de la guerre, Janvier 1944–Juillet 1945*, Actes et documents du Saint Siège relatifs á la Seconde Guerre Mondiale, 10 (Città del Vaticano: Libreria Editrice Vaticana, 1980), pp. 476–77.

43. See Jan Němeček, "Armadní general Lev Prchala a československý odboj v Polsku," *Historie a vojenství* 43 (1994): 107–32.

44. Luža, "The Czech Resistance Movement," pp. 353–54. See also, Jiří Kocian, "Program obnovy Československa v českém politickém spektru v letech 1939–1945," *Moderní dějiny* 2 (1994): 163–70.

45. Edward Taborsky, "Politics in Exile, 1939–1945," in Mamatey and Luža, *A History of the Czechoslovak Republic*, pp. 322–42. See also, Harry Hanak, "President Beneš, Britové a budoucnost Československa, 1939–1945," *Historie a vojenství* 44 (1994): 13–39.

46. For Beneš's thinking in 1941, see Detlef Brandes, "Eine verspätete tschechische Alternative zum Münchener 'Diktat.' Edvard Beneš und die sudetendeutsche Frage, 1938–1945," *Vierteljahrshefte für Zeitgeschichte* 42 (1994): 221–41.

47. Wenzel Jaksch, *Europas Weg nach Potsdam: Schuld und Schicksal im Donauraum* (Stuttgart: Deutsche Verlags-Anstalt, 1958).

48. Piotr S. Wandycz, *Czechoslovak-Polish Confederation and the Great Powers, 1940–43*, Indiana University Publications, Slavic and East European Series, 3 (Bloomington: Indiana University Press, 1956). See also, Detlef Brandes, "Konfederace nebo východní pakt?" *Slovanský přehled* 78 (1992): 436–48.

49. *Program československé vlády Národní fronty Čechů a Slováků přijatý*

na první schůzi vlády dne 5. dubna 1945 v Košicích (Prague: Ministerstvo informací, 1945).

50. For this section, in addition to other cited works, see Zeman, *Beneš*, pp. 239–59.

51. The full text of this and other key decrees, and a complete list of their titles, may be found on the Czech Parliament's Web page <http://www.psp.cz/docs/laws/dek>.

52. Eagle Glassheim, "National Mythologies and Ethnic Cleansing: The Expulsion of Czechoslovak Germans in 1945," *Central European History* 33, no. 4 (2000): 463–86; Tomáš Staněk, *Odsun Němců z Československa 1945–1947* (Prague: Naše vojsko, 1991).

53. Karel Kaplan, ed. and comp., *Dva retribuční procesy: komentované dokumenty (1945–1947)* (Prague: Ústav pro soudobé dějiny ČSAV, 1992).

54. Zeman, *Beneš*, pp. 260–82.

55. Jan Masaryk remarked, "I went to Moscow as the Foreign Minister of an independent sovereign state; I returned as a lackey of the Soviet government." Cited in Zbyněk Zeman, *The Masaryks: The Making of Czechoslovakia* (London: Weidenfeld & Nicolson, 1976), p. 208.

56. Vojtěch Mastný, "Stalin and the Militarization of the Cold War," *International Security* 9, no. 3 (1984): 109–29.

57. This section is based on Karel Kaplan, *Pět kapitol o únoru* (Brno: Doplněk, 1997); and Radomír Luža, "Czechoslovakia Between Democracy and Communism," in Mamatey and Luža, *A History of the Czechoslovak Republic*, pp. 387–415.

CHAPTER 13

1. Zbyněk Zeman, *The Masaryks: The Making of Czechoslovakia*, pp. 210–13, leans toward suicide, an explanation still hotly rejected by some. See, e.g., Jindřich Grulich, *Smrt Jana Masarkya-nebyla to nešťastná náhoda* (Karvín: Jindřich Grulich, 2001).

2. Ambassador Lawrence A. Steinhardt to Secretary of State, April 30, 1948, in United States Department of State, *Foreign Relations of the United States, 1948. Volume IV. Eastern Europe and the Soviet Union* (Washington, D.C.: United States Government Printing Office, 1974), pp. 747–48.

3. See Ladislav Holý, *The Little Czech and the Great Czech Nation: National Identity and the Post-Communist Transformation of Society* (Cambridge: Cambridge University Press, 1996).

4. The following draws from Karel Kaplan, *Zakladatelské období komunistického režimu*, vol. 2 of *Československo v Letech 1948–1953* (Prague: Státní pedagogické nakladatelství, 1991).

5. Zdeněk Suda, *Zealots and Rebels*, pp. 224–25; Kaplan, *Zakladatelské období*, pp. 16–23.

6. Cited in Kaplan, *Zakladatelské období*, p. 25.

7. Suda, *Zealots and Rebels*, pp. 226–27.

8. Cited in Kaplan, *Zakladatelské období*, p. 42.

9. Carol Skalnik Leff, *The Czech and Slovak Republics: Nation Versus State* (Boulder, Colo.: Westview Press, 1997), p. 50.

10. By 1951 purges had reduced the total membership to 1,677,433, a drop of one-third but still 12 percent of the Czechoslovak population. Suda, *Zealots and Rebels*, p. 233.

11. Karel Kaplan and Dušan Tomášek, *O cenzuře v Československu v letech 1945–1956: Studie* (Prague: Ústav pro soudobé dějiny AV ČR, 1994).

12. Stanley B. Winters, "The Period of Transition from the ČAVU to the ČSAV (1945–1952)," *Historická Olomouc* 9 (1998): 293–308.

13. Zdeněk Nejedlý, *Komunisté dědici velkých tradic českého národa*, 3d ed. (1946; Prague: Československý spisovatel, 1950), p. 46.

14. Karel Kaplan, *K politickým procesům v Československu, 1948–1954: dokumentace komise ÚV KSČ pro rehabilitaci 1968* (Prague: Ústav pro soudobé dějiny AV ČR, 1994).

15. Píka was fully rehabilitated in 1968. Before his execution, he vigorously denied the charges in a letter to Gottwald: Věra Brachová, "Dopis generala H. Piky prezidentu Gottwaldovi (I)," *Historie a vojenství* 41, no. 1 (1992): 112–39; Věra Brachová, ed., "Dopis generala H. Piky prezidentu Gottwaldovi (II)," *Historie a vojenství* 41, no. 2 (1992): 115–49.

16. Karel Kaplan, *Sovětští Porádci v Československu, 1949–1956* (Prague: Ústav pro soudobé dějiny, 1993).

17. Karel Kaplan, *Stát a církev v Československu v letech 1948–1953* (Brno: Doplněk, 1993); Jaroslav Cuhra, "KSČ, stát a římskokatolická církev (1948–1989)," *Soudobé dějiny* 8, no. 2–3 (2001): 267–80.

18. See Václav Vaško, "Kardinál Beran a jeho zápas s totalitou: Portrét osobnosti," *Soudobé dějiny* 8, no. 2–3 (2001): 384–408.

19. Karel Kaplan, *Report on the Murder of the General Secretary*, translated by Karel Kovanda (Columbus: Ohio State University Press, 1990), provides a study of the trial in English.

20. Karel Kaplan, *Československo v RVHP 1949–1956* (Prague: Ústav pro soudobé dějiny AV ČR, 1995).

21. John P. C. Matthews, *Majales: The Abortive Student Revolt in Czechoslovakia in 1956*, Cold War International History Project Working Papers, 24 (Washington, D.C., 1999) <http://cwihp.si.edu/publications.htm>. Majáles parades were held in both Prague and Bratislava.

22. Muriel Blaive, *Promarněná příležitost: Československo rok 1956* (Prague: Prostor, 2001).

23. Suda, *Zealots and Rebels*, pp. 283–86.

24. This section draws on Karel Kaplan, *Československo v letech 1952–1966* (Prague: Státní pedagogické nakladatelství, 1991).

25. Ibid., p. 100.

26. See Carol Skalnik Leff, "Inevitability, Probability, Possibility: The Legacies of the Czech-Slovak Relationship, 1918–1989, and the Disintegration of the State," in Michael Kraus and Allison Stanger, eds. and trans., *Irreconcilable Differences? Explaining Czechoslovakia's Dissolution* (Lanham and Oxford: Rowman & Littlefield, 2000), p. 33.

27. Kaplan, *Československo v letech 1952–1966*, p. 104.

28. Ota Šik, *Plán a trh za socialismu*, 3d ed. (Prague: Academia, 1967).

29. H. Gordon Skilling, *Czechoslovakia's Interrupted Revolution* (Princeton, N.J.: Princeton University Press, 1976), pp. 57–62.

30. Ibid., pp. 49–56.

31. Jaromír Navrátil, comp. and ed., *The Prague Spring 1968: A National Security Archive Documents Reader*, edited by Antonín Benčík, Václav Kural, Marie Michálková, and Jitka Vondrová, translated by Mark Kramer et al. (Budapest: Central European University Press, 1998), pp. 8–10.

32. Navrátil, *Prague Spring 1968*, p. 12; Skilling, *Czechoslovakia's Interrupted Revolution*, pp. 62–72.

33. Karel Kaplan, *Československo v letech 1967–1969* (Prague: Státní pedagogické nakladatelství, 1991), pp. 9–10. See also, Kieran Williams, *The Prague Spring and Its Aftermath: Czechoslovak Politics, 1968–1970* (Cambridge: Cambridge University Press, 1997), pp. 4–20.

34. Navrátil, *Prague Spring 1968*, pp. 13–17.

35. See Skilling, *Czechoslovakia's Interrupted Revolution*, pp. 79–82.

36. See Miklós Kun, *Prague Spring—Prague Fall: Blank Spots of 1968* (Budapest: Akadémiai Kiadó, 1999), p. 10; also Navrátil, *Prague Spring 1968*, pp. 18–19.

37. Suda, *Zealots and Rebels*, pp. 319–21.

38. Alexander Dubček, *Hope Dies Last: The Autobiography of Alexander Dubček*, edited and translated by Jiří Hochmann (London: HarperCollins, 1993). See also, William Shawcross, *Dubček*, revised and updated ed. (1970; New York: Simon & Schuster, 1990).

39. The Piller Commission report is available in English: Jiří Pelikán, ed., *The Czechoslovak Political Trials, 1950–1954: The Suppressed Report of the Dubček Government's Commission of Inquiry, 1968* (Stanford: Stanford University Press, 1971).

40. Williams, *Prague Spring and Its Aftermath*, pp. 67–69; Frank Kaplan, *Winter Into Spring: The Czechoslovak Press and the Reform Movement, 1963–1968* (Boulder, Colo.: East European Quarterly, 1977).

41. See the excerpts of the Action Program, in Navrátil, *Prague Spring 1968*, pp. 90–94.

42. Suda, *Zealots and Rebels*, pp. 326–31; Skilling, *Czechoslovakia's Interrupted Revolution*, pp. 217–21.

43. Navrátil, *Prague Spring 1968*, p. 94.

44. Ota Šik, *The Third Way: Marxist-Leninist Theory and Modern Industrial Society*, translated by Marian Sling (London and New York: Wildwood House and International Arts and Sciences Press, 1976); Williams, *Prague Spring and Its Aftermath*, pp. 20–25.

45. Navrátil, *Prague Spring 1968*, p. 94.

46. Skilling, *Czechoslovakia's Interrupted Revolution*, pp. 451–65. See also, Leff, *National Conflict in Czechoslovakia*, pp. 170–76.

47. Navrátil, *Prague Spring 1968*, pp. 177–81, and Skilling, *Czechoslovakia's Interrupted Revolution*, pp. 546–48. See also, Otakar Rambousek and Ladislav Gruber, comps. and eds., *Zpráva dokumentační komise K 231* (Louvain: Členové dokumentační komise K 231 v exilu, 1973).

48. Citations to "Two Thousand Words" from Navrátil, *Prague Spring 1968*, pp. 179–81.

49. Williams, *Prague Spring and Its Aftermath*, pp. 89–91.

50. The phrase comes from ibid.; see esp. pp. 29–39, 63–111. For analyses from various perspectives, see Jiří Valenta, *Soviet Intervention in Czechoslovakia, 1968: Anatomy of a Decision*, rev. ed. (1979; Baltimore: Johns Hopkins University Press, 1991), and Karen Dawisha, *The Kremlin and the Prague Spring* (Berkeley: University of California Press, 1984). See also, Dimitri K. Simes, "The Soviet Invasion of Czechoslovakia and the Limits of Kremlinology," *Studies in Comparative Communism* 8 (1975): 174–80.

51. Navrátil, *Prague Spring 1968*, pp. 37–41; also Williams, *Prague Spring and Its Aftermath*, p. 65.

52. Navrátil, *Prague Spring 1968*, pp. 42–44; see also, Williams, *Prague Spring and Its Aftermath*, p. 66.

53. Williams, *Prague Spring and Its Aftermath*, p. 66; Navrátil, *Prague Spring 1968*, pp. 51–54.

54. Williams, *Prague Spring and Its Aftermath*, pp. 70–71.

55. Navrátil, *Prague Spring 1968*, pp. 64–72.

56. Williams, *Prague Spring and Its Aftermath*, p. 117.

57. Navrátil, *Prague Spring 1968*, pp. 324–25.

CHAPTER 14

1. Philip Windsor and Adam Roberts, *Czechoslovakia 1968: Reform, Repression, and Resistance* (New York: Columbia University Press, 1969), pp. 107–11; Karen Dawisha, *The Kremlin and the Prague Spring*, pp. 319–20; Hans Renner, *A History of Czechoslovakia Since 1945*, translated by Evelien Hurst-Buist (London: Routledge, 1989), pp. 71–72.

2. Defense Minister Martin Dzúr not only ordered the Czechoslovak People's Army not to resist, he enjoined them to provide "maximum all-round assistance" to the Warsaw Pact troops. See Jaromír Navrátil, *Prague Spring 1968*, pp. 411–13.

3. Ibid., pp. 414–15.

4. The statement is included in Historický ústav ČSAV, *Sedm pražských dnů, 21.–27. srpen 1968: dokumentace*, edited by Josef Macek (Prague: Academia, 1990), pp. 28–29. The Soviet news agency TASS also published a declaration supposedly issued by these (unnamed) leaders calling on the citizens to rally around the "realistically thinking core" of the party. Ibid., pp. 29–32.

5. Ibid., pp. 275, 369. The slogan is pithier in Czech because, thanks to the verb structure, each sentence is actually a single word.

6. Windsor and Roberts, *Czechoslovakia 1968*, pp. 127–28.

7. H. Gordon Skilling, *Czechoslovakia's Interrupted Revolution*, pp. 776–80.

8. Ibid., pp. 764–72; Jiří Pelikán, ed., *The Secret Vysočany Congress: Proceedings and Documents of the Extraordinary Fourteenth Congress of the Communist Party of Czechoslovakia, 22 August 1968*, translated by George Theiner and Deryck Viney (New York: St. Martin's Press, 1971); Historický ústav ČSAV, *Sedm pražských dnů*, pp. 84–87.

9. See Navrátil, *Prague Spring 1968*, pp. 460–64.

10. Dubček called it "the greatest political mistake and one that will have tragic consequences." Ibid., pp. 465–68.

11. Ibid., pp. 469–71.

12. The text of the agreement is given in ibid., pp. 477–80.

13. Historický ústav ČSAV, *Sedm pražských dnů*, pp. 299–300.

14. Ibid.

15. Ibid., pp. 313–18.

16. Jaroslaw A. Piekalkiewicz, *Public Opinion Polling in Czechoslovakia* (New York: Praeger, 1972), pp. 262–64; Skilling, *Czechoslovakia's Interrupted Revolution*, pp. 808–10; Renner, *Czechoslovakia Since 1945*, pp. 82–83.

17. Navrátil, *Prague Spring 1968*, pp. 487–88.

18. Pelikán, *Secret Vysočany Conference*, pp. 96–97; Renner, *Czechoslovakia Since 1945*, p. 87.

19. See Navrátil, *Prague Spring 1968*, pp. 506–7.

20. Skilling, *Czechoslovakia's Interrupted Revolution*, pp. 814–15; Renner, *Czechoslovakia Since 1945*, pp. 88–89.

21. Text of the treaty in Navrátil, *Prague Spring 1968*, pp. 533–36.

22. Jozef Zatkuliak, ed., *Federalizácia československého štátu 1968–1970: vznik československej federácie roku 1968* (Prague: Ústav pro soudobé dějiny AV ČR, 1996).

23. See Navrátil, *Prague Spring 1968*, pp. 555–60.

24. Skilling, *Czechoslovakia's Interrupted Revolution*, p. 818; Kieran Williams, *Prague Spring and Its Aftermath*, pp. 183–88.

25. Jiří Lederer, *Jan Palach. Zpráva o životě, činu, a smrti českého studenta* (Prague: Novinář, 1990); Renner, *Czechoslovakia Since 1945*, pp. 93–94; Williams, *Prague Spring and Its Aftermath*, pp. 188–91.

26. Navrátil, *Prague Spring 1968*, pp. 564–70.

27. See ibid., pp. 504–12.

28. Skilling, *Czechoslovakia's Interrupted Revolution*, pp. 820–21; Renner, *Czechoslovakia Since 1945*, p. 96.

29. Skilling, *Interrupted Revolution*, p. 821; Vladimir V. Kusin, *From Dubček to Charter 77: A Study of "Normalization" in Czechoslovakia, 1968–1978* (New York: St. Martin's Press, 1978), pp. 99–102.

30. Jiří Pelikán, *Socialist Opposition in Eastern Europe: The Czechoslovak Example*, translated by Marian Sling, V. Tosek, and R. Tosek (New York: St. Martin's Press, 1976), pp. 117–24.

31. Compare Williams, *Prague Spring and Its Aftermath*, p. 234, with Kusin, *From Dubček to Charter 77*, pp. 84–86, and Vladimir V. Kusin, "Husák's Czechoslovakia and Economic Stagnation," *Problems of Communism* 31 (May-June 1982): 29.

32. Kusin, *From Dubček to Charter 77*, pp. 102–6; Renner, *Czechoslovakia Since 1945*, pp. 99–101.

33. Kusin, *From Dubček to Charter 77*, p. 134; Martin Myant, *The Czechoslovak Economy, 1948–1988* (Cambridge: Cambridge University Press, 1989), p. 183.

34. See Renner, *Czechoslovakia Since 1945*, p. 101; Kusin, *From Dubček to Charter 77*, pp. 173–75.

35. Renner, *Czechoslovakia Since 1945*, p. 101; Sharon L. Wolchik, "The Scientific-Technological Revolution and the Role of Specialist Elites in Policy-Making in Czechoslovakia," in *Domestic Policy in Eastern Europe in the 1980s: Trends and Prospects*, edited by Sharon L. Wolchik and Michael J. Sodaro (New York: St. Martin's Press, 1983), pp. 111–32.

36. Williams, *Prague Spring and Its Aftermath*, pp. 244–49; Kusin, *From Dubček to Charter 77*, pp. 135–39.

37. Komunistická strana Československa, *Poučení z krizového vývoje straně a společnosti po XIII. sjezdu KSČ. Rezoluce k aktuálním otázkám jednoty strany: schváleno na plenárním zasedání ÚV KSČ v prosinci 1970* (Prague: Svoboda, 1988).

38. Williams, *Prague Spring and Its Aftermath*, pp. 248–49; Renner, *Czechoslovakia Since 1945*, pp. 102–5.

39. Renner, *Czechoslovakia Since 1945*, p. 105.

40. Sharon L. Wolchik, *Czechoslovakia in Transition: Politics, Economics, and Society* (London: Pinter Publishers, 1991), p. 89.

41. Renner, *Czechoslovakia Since 1945*, p. 109.

42. Wolchik, *Czechoslovakia in Transition*, pp. 90–91.

43. Milan Kundera, *The Book of Laughter and Forgetting*, translated by Michael Henry Heim (New York: Knopf, 1980); Derek Sayer, *The Coasts of Bohemia: A Czech History*, pp. 313–21; Kusin, *From Dubček to Charter 77*, pp. 26–29.

44. Kusin, "Husák's Czechoslovakia," p. 26.

45. Ibid.

46. See ibid., p. 36.

47. Milan Šimečka, *The Restoration of Order: The Normalization of Czechoslovakia, 1969–1976*, translated by A. G. Bain, with a preface by Zdeněk Mlynář (London: Verso, 1984), pp. 72–79.

48. Václav Havel, "Letter to Dr. Gustáv Husák," in *Václav Havel: Living in Truth*, edited by Jan Vladislav (London: Faber & Faber, 1986), p. 4.

49. Myant, *Czechoslovak Economy*, pp. 176–85; Judy Batt, *Economic Reform and Political Change in Eastern Europe: A Comparison of the Czechoslovak and Hungarian Experiences* (New York: St. Martin's Press, 1988).

50. *Statistická ročenka Československé socialistické republiky, 1980* (Prague: Státní nakladatelství technické literatury, 1980), p. 538; Kusin, "Husák's Czechoslovakia," pp. 27, 31; Jaroslav Krejčí and Pavel Machonin, *Czechoslovakia, 1918–1992: A Laboratory for Social Change* (New York: St. Martin's Press, 1996), pp. 197–98.

51. *Statistická ročenka Československé socialistické republiky 1973* (Prague: Státní nakladatelství technické literatury, 1973), p. 472; *Statistická ročenka Československé socialistické republiky 1982* (Prague: Státní nakladatelství technické literatury, 1982), p. 550.

52. Šimečka, *Restoration of Order*, pp. 137–45; Kusin, "Husák's Czechoslovakia," p. 28; Bernard Wheaton and Zdeněk Kavan, *The Velvet Revolution: Czechoslovakia, 1988–1991* (Boulder, Colo.: Westview Press, 1992), p. 9.

53. Krejčí and Machonin, *Czechoslovakia, 1918–1992*, pp. 128, 197–98.

54. Kusin, "Husák's Czechoslovakia," p. 31.

55. Renner, *Czechoslovakia Since 1945*, p. 114.

56. Wolchik, *Czechoslovakia in Transition*, p. 242; Sharon L. Wolchik, "Economic Performance and Political Change in Czechoslovakia," in *Prospects for Change in Socialist Systems: Challenges and Responses*, edited by Charles J. Bukowski and Mark A. Cichock (New York: Praeger, 1987), pp. 40–42; Jan Vaňous, "East European Economic Slowdown," *Problems of Communism* 31 (July-August 1982): 1–19.

57. "Soubor opatření ke zdokonalení soustavy plánovitého řizení národního hospodářství po roce 1980," in *Příloha hospodářských novin* (1980).

58. Ibid; Wolchik, *Czechoslovakia in Transition*, pp. 242–43.

59. Myant, *Czechoslovak Economy*, pp. 209–13.

60. Kusin, *From Dubček to Charter 77*, pp. 148–49; Pelikán, *Socialist Opposition*, pp. 117–224.

61. Kusin, *From Dubček to Charter 77*, pp. 149–50; Renner, *Czechoslovakia Since 1945*, pp. 120–21.

62. Pelikán, *Socialist Opposition*, pp. 125–59; Kusin, *From Dubček to Charter 77*, pp. 156–60.

63. Vladimir V. Kusin, "Dissent in Czechoslovakia After 1968," in *Dissent in Eastern Europe*, edited by Jane Leftwich Curry (New York: Praeger, 1983), p. 49.

64. Václav Havel, *Disturbing the Peace: A Conversation with Karel Hvížďala*, translated by Paul Wilson (New York: Vintage Books, 1991), pp. 119–21.

65. H. Gordon Skilling, "Independent Currents in Czechoslovakia," *Problems of Communism* 34 (January-February 1985): 38–40; Kusin, "Dissent in Czechoslovakia," pp. 53–54.

66. Timothy W. Ryback, *Rock Around the Bloc: A History of Rock Music in Eastern Europe and the Soviet Union* (New York: Oxford University Press, 1990), pp. 146–48; H. Gordon Skilling, *Charter 77 and Human Rights in Czechoslovakia* (London: Allen & Unwin, 1981), pp. 7–16.

67. Havel, *Disturbing the Peace*, p. 128.

68. Ibid., pp. 132–34; Renner, *Czechoslovakia Since 1945*, pp. 132–33.

69. George Konrád, *Anti-Politics* (New York: Harcourt Brace Jovanovich, 1984); Gale Stokes, *The Walls Came Tumbling Down: The Collapse of Communism in Eastern Europe* (New York: Oxford University Press, 1993), pp. 21–23.

70. Skilling, *Charter 77*, pp. 211–12.

71. Václav Havel, "The Power of the Powerless," translated by Paul Wilson, in *The Power of the Powerless: Citizens Against the State in Central-Eastern Europe*, edited by John Keane (New York: M. E. Sharpe, 1985), pp. 64–69.

72. Josef Škvorecký, "Hipness at Dusk," *Cross Currents* 6 (1987): 53–62; Skilling, "Independent Currents," pp. 41–43.

73. Skilling, "Independent Currents," pp. 45–48; John M. Kramer, "Chernobyl' and Eastern Europe," *Problems of Communism* 35 (November-December 1986): 40–43; John Kramer, "The Environmental Crisis in Eastern Europe: The Price for Progress."

74. Jaroslav Cuhra, "KSČ, stát a římskokatolická církev (1948–1989)," pp. 288–93.

75. Stokes, *The Walls Came Tumbling Down*, p. 152; Paul Wilson, "Religious Movement in Czechoslovakia: Faith or Fashion?" *Cross Currents: A Yearbook of Central European Culture* 7 (1988): 109–19; Skilling, "Independent Currents," pp. 43–45.

76. Navrátil, *Prague Spring 1968*, p. 502.

77. Wolchik, *Czechoslovakia in Transition*, pp. 40–41, 245–48; Myant, *Czechoslovak Economy*, pp. 250–56.

78. Both citations from Wheaton and Kavan, *Velvet Revolution*, p. 18.

CHAPTER 15

1. Timothy Garton Ash, *The Magic Lantern: The Revolution of '89 Witnessed in Warsaw, Budapest, Berlin, and Prague* (New York: Random House, 1990), p. 78.

2. Bernard Wheaton and Zdeněk Kavan, *The Velvet Revolution: Czechoslovakia, 1988–1991*, pp. 24–30; Gale Stokes, *The Walls Came Tumbling Down*, pp. 153–54; Sharon Wolchik, *Czechoslovakia in Transition*, pp. 47–49.

3. See Wheaton and Kavan, *Velvet Revolution*, pp. 27–28.

4. Carol Skalnik Leff, *The Czech and Slovak Republics*, pp. 76–79.

5. The Czechoslovak regime had also named its party-led university for foreign students the University of 17 November. See Edward Taborsky, "Czechoslovakia's 'University of November 17th'," *East Europe* 21, no. 4 (1972): pp. 7–11.

6. Jiří Suk, comp. and ed., *Občanské fórum, listopad—prosinec, 1989. 2. díl—dokumenty* (Prague and Brno: Ústav pro soudobé dějiny AV ČR and Doplněk, 1998), pp. 13–14.

7. Ibid., p. 14.

8. Jiří Suk, comp. and ed., *Občanské fórum, listopad—prosinec, 1989. 1. díl—události* (Prague and Brno: Ústav pro soudobé dějiny AV ČR and Doplněk, 1997), pp. 51–52.

9. Wheaton and Kavan, *Velvet Revolution*, p. 70; Suk, *Občanské fórum—dokumenty*, p. 55.

10. Wheaton and Kavan, *Velvet Revolution*, pp. 58–60.

11. Ash, *The Magic Lantern*, pp. 94–96.

12. Wheaton and Kavan, *Velvet Revolution*, pp. 70–72, 79–80.

13. Suk, *Občanské fórum—události*, p. 82.

14. Dragoslav Slejška and Jan Herzmann, *Sondy do veřejného mínění (Jaro 1968, Podzim 1989)* (Prague: Svoboda, 1990), p. 47; Wheaton and Kavan, *Velvet Revolution*, p. 95.

15. Ash, *The Magic Lantern*, pp. 123–25.

16. Tony R. Judt, "Metamorphosis: The Democratic Revolution in Czechoslovakia," in *Eastern Europe in Revolution*, edited by Ivo Banac (Ithaca: Cornell University Press, 1992), pp. 99–100.

17. See Leff, *Czech and Slovak Republics*, p. 82. See also, Ash, *The Magic Lantern*, p. 125.

18. Judt, "Metamorphosis," pp. 100–101.

19. Rasma Karklins and Roger Petersen, "Decision Calculus of Protestors and Regimes: Eastern Europe, 1989," *Journal of Politics* 55, no. 3 (August 1993): 588–614; Leff, *Czech and Slovak Republics*, pp. 82–83.

20. Keith Crawford, *East Central European Politics Today: From Chaos to Stability?* (Manchester: Manchester University Press, 1996), pp. 189–90.

21. Róna-Tas Ákos, "The Selected and the Elected: The Making of the New Parliamentary Elite in Hungary," *East European Politics and Societies* 5, no. 3 (Fall 1991): pp. 369–72.

22. Leff, *Czech and Slovak Republics*, pp. 84–85.

23. See ibid., pp. 96–97. See also the analysis of elections, Český statistický úřad, *Volby v ČR, 1990–1999*, online document, 4201–00 <http://www.czso.cz>.

24. Český statistický úřad, *Volby v ČR, 1990–1999*, analysis of elections to the ČNR in 1990.

25. Leff, *Czech and Slovak Republics*, pp. 97–99.

26. Ibid., pp. 108–9.

27. Crawford, *East Central European Politics*, pp. 228–30; Robin H. E. Shepherd, *Czechoslovakia: The Velvet Revolution and Beyond* (London and New York: Macmillan and St. Martin's Press, 2000), pp. 55–57.

28. Zdislav Šulc, "Systemové základy ekonomické transformace," in *Transformace české společnosti, 1989–1995*, edited by Vlasta Šafaříková (Brno: Doplněk, 1996), pp. 119–21.

29. Ivan Svítek, "Každý bude investovat," *Respekt*, June 24, 1991, p. 4.

30. jaš, "Nechcceme žádné bloky (Velvyslanci Maďarska a Polska k Visegrádu)," *Lidové noviny*, February 15, 1991, p. 1; Jiří Forejt, "Nejde o nový blok (Náš zpravodaj z třístranného setkání ve Visegrádu," ibid., February 16, 1991, p. 1.

31. Bradley F. Abrams, "Morality, Wisdom, and Revision: The Czech Opposition of the 1970s and the Expulsion of the Sudeten Germans," *East European Politics and Societies* 9, no. 2 (Spring 1995): 234–55.

32. Jiří Ruml, "Předvolební (Každá mince mívá dvě strany)," *Lidové noviny*, January 9, 1990, p. 1.

33. Celestine Bohlen, "Upheaval in the East: 51 Years After Hitler Marched in, Prague Welcomes a German Chief," *New York Times*, March 16, 1990, p. A1; "West German President Visits on 51st Anniversary of Nazi Invasion," *Associated Press Wire Reports, International News*, March 15, 1990.

34. Zbyněk Petráček, "Zástupný problém právní kontinuity," *Respekt*, September 23, 1991, p. 2; Jan Metzger, "Nejasno až do konce: Prezidenti Havel a von Weizsäcker podepíší čs.-německou smlouvu," ibid., October 7, 1991, p. 3; LN, "Smlouva ČSFR-SRN," *Lidové noviny*, October 11, 1991, p. 12; ČTK Czechoslovak News Agency, "German Chancellor Stresses Historic Significance of New Treaty," *CTK National News Wire*, February 26, 1992.

35. British Broadcasting Corporation, "Czech Premier Rejects Sudeten German Call for Commission," *BBC Summary of World Broadcasts* EE/1109/B/1 (June 27, 1991); ČTK Czechoslovak News Agency, "ČSFR Threatens to Counter Sudeten Claims with Own from WW Two," *ČTK National News Wire*, June 11, 1992.

36. Shepherd, *Czechoslovakia*, pp. 112–13; Leff, *Czech and Slovak Republics*, pp. 85–86.

37. See two articles by Bohumil Pečinka: "Lustrace stále přítomné," *Lidové noviny*, February 10, 1995, p. 5; and "Lustrace ovlivnily volby," ibid., April 2, 1996, p. 2.

38. David Franklin, "A Velvet Purge in Prague: The Exposure of Alleged Secret Police Collaborators Is Threatening Czechoslovakia's Fragile Democracy," *The Guardian*, June 5, 1991.

39. Pečinka, "Lustrace stále přítomné"; Catherine Monroy, "Czechoslovakia Asks Whether Its Purge Has Gone Too Far," *Manchester Guardian Weekly*, March 15, 1992, p. 15.

40. Václav Žák, "The Velvet Divorce—Institutional Foundations," in *The End of Czechoslovakia*, edited by Jiří Musil (Budapest: Central European University Press, 1995), pp. 150–51.

41. Michael Kraus, "The End of Czechoslovakia: International Forces and Factors," in Michael Kraus and Allison Stanger, eds., *Irreconcilable Differences?*, pp. 200–203.

42. Leff, *National Conflict in Czechoslovakia*, p. 177; Carol Skalnik Leff, "Inevitability, Probability, Possibility," in Kraus and Stanger, eds., *Irreconcilable Differences?*, pp. 36–37.

43. Eight electoral districts in the Czech lands sent 101 members to the Chamber of the People and four Slovak districts sent 49 delegates. See Petr Kopecký, "From 'Velvet Revolution' to 'Velvet Split': Consociational Institutions and the Disintegration of Czechoslovakia," in Kraus and Stanger, eds., *Irreconcilable Differences?*, pp. 73–74.

44. Allison Stanger, "The Price of Velvet: Constitutional Politics and the Demise of the Czechoslovak Federation," in ibid., p. 143.

45. Leff, *Czech and Slovak Republics*, pp. 134–35.

46. Ivan Jemelka and Jana Šmídová, "Pozice-kompromisy-shoda? (Mečiar: Pocity jsou zlé, Kučerák: Obavy postupně mizí, Klaus: Republika se nerozpadne, Čalfa: Tři vlády v ofenzivě," *Lidové noviny*, November 14, 1990, p. 1; Alena Slezáková, "Most přes rozbouřené vody (Na pořadu v parlamentu kompetenční zákon)," ibid., December 11, 1990, p. 1; Alena Slezáková and Martin Daneš, "Pozvání na brynzové halušky (Poslanci Federálního shromáždění schválili kompetetnční zákon)," ibid., December 13, 1990, p. 1.

47. Kopecký, "Consociational Institutions," pp. 76–79.

48. This account relies on Jan Rychlík, "The Possibilities for Czech-Slovak

Compromise, 1989–1992," in Kraus and Stanger, eds., *Irreconcilable Differences?*, pp. 52–57.

49. Leff, *Czech and Slovak Republics*, p. 135.

50. Already the previous fall, Čarnogurský said, "in the future Europe we would like to have our own chair and our own star on the European flag." FBIS, "Interview with Jan Carnogursky," *Daily Reports, Eastern Europe* FBIS-EEU–90–200 (October 16, 1992): 33–34.

51. Petr Brodský and Eva Koubová, "Státní smlouva," *Respekt*, May 12, 1991, p. 2; Jiří Kabele, "Od pomlčky ke smlouvě," ibid., June 3, 1991, p. 2.

52. Milan Zemko, "Domestic and International Aspects of the Czechoslovak State's Crisis and End," in Kraus and Stanger, eds., *Irreconcilable Differences?*, pp. 247–57; Roman Krasnický, "Bez halušek," *Lidové noviny*, March 12, 1992, p. 1; rk, "Sbohem volby (Závěrečné setkání předsedů české a slovenské národní rady," *Lidové noviny*, March 12, 1992, p. 1.

53. Leff, *Czech and Slovak Republics*, pp. 135–36; Petr Kopecký, "Consociational Institutions," pp. 79–80.

54. jaš et al., "Česko-Slovenskso '92: Vpravo-Vlevo," *Lidové noviny*, June 8, 1992, p. 1.

55. Rychlík, "The Possibilities for Czech-Slovak Compromise," pp. 58–64.

56. rk, "Českým premiérem Václav Klaus, slovenským Vladimír Mečiar," *Lidové noviny*, June 18, 1992, p. 1.

57. Miroslav Macek, "Fragments from the Dividing of Czechoslovakia," in Kraus and Stanger, eds., *Irreconcilable Differences?*, p. 245.

58. LN, "Deklarace SNR o svrchovanosti," *Lidové noviny*, July 18, 1992, p. 3.

59. Václav Havel, "Hovory z Lán: Hovory devadesáté deváté a zatím poslední," ibid., July 20, 1992, p. 8. See also, Petr Janyška, Lampcr Ivan, and Martin Weiss, "Nebudu druhým Benešem: Rozhovor s Václavem Havlem," *Respekt*, February 25, 1991, p. 4.

60. Leff, *Czech and Slovak Republics*, pp. 141–42; Stephen Denyer and Martin Šolc, "Czechoslovakia: What's in the Divorce Settlement?" *International Financial Law Review* 12, no. 2 (February 1993): 28.

61. Leff, *Czech and Slovak Republics*, pp. 143–44; Kopecký, "Consociational Institutions," pp. 81–83.

CHAPTER 16

1. "Tradice humanity a democracie: Slavnost k obnově českého státu," *Český denik*, October 26, 1992.

2. "'Budujeme stát pro sebe': Václav Klaus na Vyšehrad, 24. 10. 1992," ibid., October 27, 1992.

3. Otto Urban, "Byli jsme před Československem," *Lidové noviny*, July 24, 1992.

4. Petr Pithart, "Paradoxy rozchodu: Filozofické a mravné hlediska a evropské paralely," in *Rozloučení s Československem: Příčiny a důsledky československého rozchodu*, edited by Rüdiger Kipke and Karel Vodička (Prague: Československý spisovatel, 1993), pp. 119–20.

5. See Dušan Třeštík, *Češi: Jejich národ, stát, dějiny a pravdy v transformaci. Texty z let 1991–1998* (Brno: Doplněk, 1999), pp. 151–84.

6. See Hugh LeCaine Agnew, "Old States, New Identities? The Czech Republic, Slovakia, and Historical Understandings of Statehood," *Nationalities Papers* 28, no. 4 (2000): 619–50.

7. This section relies on Robin H. E. Shepherd, *Czechoslovakia*, pp. 75–102, and Carol Skalnik Leff, *Czech and Slovak Republics*, pp. 186–96, in addition to other cited literature.

8. Silvia Cambie, "Czech Privatization Moves Into High Gear with Second Wave," *Central European* 4, no. 5 (May 1994): 25 ff.

9. Michal Achremenko, "Po poslední, druhé vlně přišla třetí," *Lidové noviny*, August 13, 1996, p. 5.

10. Peter Kysel, "Czech Market Takes Pride of Place in European Emerging Markets," *Central European* Emerging Securities Market Supplement (October 1994), p. 10.

11. FBIS, "Klaus Discusses Mandatory Balanced Budget," *Daily Reports, Eastern Europe* FBIS-EEU-94-173 (September 5, 1994); FBIS, "Klaus Discusses Economic Successes, Concerns," *Daily Reports, Eastern Europe* FBIS-EEU-94-231 (December 23, 1994).

12. Pavel Novotný, "Česko v klubu bohatých," *Lidové noviny*, September 15, 1995, p. 5; am, "The European: Češi vyhrali," ibid., November 28, 1995, p. 12.

13. Anders Aslund, Peter Boone, and Simon Johnson, "How to Stabilize: Lessons from Post-Communist Countries," *Brookings Papers on Economic Activity*, no. 1 (1996): 217–313.

14. The New Democracy Barometer surveys in 1995 (available for searching at the Web site of TARKI, Budapest <http://rs2.tarki.hu:90/ndb-html>) showed that 70 percent of the population evaluated the country's economic performance as positive to some extent, and 87 percent expected better things in five years.

15. "The Czech Republic: Václav Thatcher," *The Economist* 332, no. 7875 (August 6, 1994): p. 42.

16. Martina Rabenseifnerová, "ČR navštívilo 16,6 miliónů turistů," *Lidové noviny*, February 16, 1996, p. 6; Martin Poláček, "Praha trumfla Vídeň," ibid., November 19, 1996, p. 4.

17. Václav Havel and Václav Klaus, Petr Pihart, discussant, "Rival Visions," *Journal of Democracy* 7, no. 1 (1996): 15.

18. Ibid., p. 14.

19. mam, "Sněmovna umožnila vznik obecně prospěšných společnosti," *Lidové noviny*, September 29, 1995, p. 3.

20. Bohumil Pečinka, "Rok 1968 náš úřad neabsolutizuje," ibid., August 7, 1995, p. 16; Radek Adamec, "Brzy se rozhodne o vlastizradě," ibid., June 29, 1996, p. 3.

21. Bohumil Pečinka, "Lustrace do roku 2000," ibid., September 28, 1995, p. 1; Vojtěch Cepl and Mark Gillis, "Making Amends After Communism," *Journal of Democracy* 7, no. 4 (1996): 118–24.

22. Ondřej Neumann, "Aféra Lizner—korupce se nevyhnula ani 'bezpečné' kuponovce," *Lidové noviny*, September 29, 1999, p. 3.

23. Miroslav Korecký, "Stranické peníze—aféry bez konce," ibid., p. 6.

24. Václav Klaus, "Naše třetí svobodné volby," ibid., May 25, 1996, p. 8.

25. rep, "Klaus zvítězil, ale nejvíc získal Zeman," *Mladá fronta dnes*, June 3, 1996, p. 1.

26. Leff, *Czech and Slovak Republics*, pp. 160–61; FBIS, "Research Detects Polarization Within Society," *Daily Reports, Eastern Europe* FBIS-EEU-96-062 (January 25, 1995).

27. "End of the Road for the Privatization Ministry," *Finance East Europe* 6, no. 8 (April 19, 1996): 8; FBIS, "Czech Republic: GDP Growth of 4.4 Percent in 1996 Better Than Forecast," *Daily Reports, Eastern Europe* FBIS-EEU-97-084 (March 25, 1997).

28. FBIS, "Czech Republic: Klaus Views Economic Prospects for 1997," *Daily Reports, Eastern Europe* FBIS-EEU-97-012 (January 10, 1997).

29. Shepherd, *Czechoslovakia*, pp. 98–99; FBIS, "Czech Republic: Daily Views Economic Measures Passed by Cabinet 16 Apr," *Daily Reports, Eastern Europe* FBIS-EEU-97-107 (April 17, 1997); FBIS, "Czech Republic: EU Sets Ultimatum for Abolition of Import Deposits," *Daily Reports, Eastern Europe* FBIS-EEU-97-206 (July 25, 1997).

30. David Ellerman, "Voucher Privatization with Investment Funds: A Sure Way to Decapitalize Industry," *Transition Newsletter* 9, no. 6 (November-December 1998): 10–13.

31. Zdislav Šulc, "Systemové základy ekonomické transformace," pp. 127–40.

32. Shepherd, *Czechoslovakia*, pp. 79–89.

33. Lubomír Mlčoch, "Czech Privatization: A Criticism of Misunderstood Liberalism (Keynote Address)," *Journal of Business Ethics* 17, no. 9–10 (July 1998): 951–59.

34. Cited in Shepherd, *Czechoslovakia*, p. 76.

35. Ibid., pp. 83–84.

36. Václav Žák, "Na co se soustředit 'cestou do Evropy'," *Lidové noviny,* August 7, 1999, p. 10.

37. Steven Saxonberg, "A New Phase in Czech Politics," *Journal of Democracy* 10, no. 1 (1999): 101–2; FBIS, "Czech Republic: Klaus Rejects Criticism from Close Party Colleagues," *Daily Reports, Eastern Europe* FBIS-EEU-97-276 (October 3, 1997); FBIS, "Czech Republic: Josef Zieleniec Announces His Resignation from Czech ODS," *Daily Reports, Eastern Europe* FBIS-EEU-98-021 (January 21, 1998).

38. Citations from Shepherd, *Czechoslovakia,* pp. 48–49. See also, rep, "Prezident podrobil odcházející vládu Václava Klause tvrdé kritice," *Mladá fronta dnes,* December 10, 1997, p. 6.

39. FBIS, "Daily Views Chances, Impact of PM-Designate Tosovsky," *Daily Reports, Eastern Europe* FBIS-EEU-97-351 (December 19, 1997); FBIS, "Daily Sees June Election Date as Victory for Klaus, CSSD," *Daily Reports, Eastern Europe* FBIS-EEU-98-013 (January 14, 1998).

40. Saxonberg, "A New Phase in Czech Politics," pp. 101–2.

41. Ibid., pp. 103–4.

42. Michal Klíma, *Kvalita demokracie v České Republice a volební inženýrství* (Prague: Radix, 2001), pp. 20–21.

43. Saxonberg, "A New Phase in Czech Politics," pp. 106–7.

44. Shepherd, *Czechoslovakia,* pp. 100–101.

45. Jana Frančíková, "Šéf revitalizace: neočekávejte zázraky," *Mladá fronta dnes,* March 2, 2000, p. 15; Jaroslav Bad'ura, "Tatra opět vydělává a zvyšuje výrobu," ibid., November 8, 2000, p. 19; mp, "Revitalizace stála stát přes dvě stě milionů," ibid., July 18, 2001, p. 4.

46. FBIS, "Prime Minister Zeman claims Czech economy in 'crisis'," *Daily Reports, Eastern Europe* FBIS-EEU-98-335 (December 1, 1998).

47. FBIS, "After a slumber, the privatization of the banks is beginning to gather more momentum," *Daily Reports, Eastern Europe* FBIS-EEU-98-279 (October 6, 1998); "Czech Economy: Downgraded Banks but Improved Outlook," *Transition Newsletter* 9, no. 6 (November-December 1998): 10–13.

48. U.S. Department of State, Bureau of Economic and Business Affairs, *2001 Country Reports on Economic Policy and Trade Policies: Czech Republic* (Washington, D.C.: U.S. Department of State, 2001), <http://www.state.gov>.

49. Valter Komárek, "Lepšího života se vám zachtělo, hlupáčkové?" *Lidové noviny,* August 4, 1999, p. 1.

50. Shepherd, *Czechoslovakia,* pp. 119–26.

51. See dub, "Blbá nálada—vděčné téma politických diskusí," *Lidové noviny,* January 18, 1999, p. 3, and ČTK, "Sofres-Factum: Stav ekonomiky vnímají negativně čtyři lidé z pěti," ibid., February 8, 1999, p. 2.

52. Jan Kubita and Miroslav Korecký, "Zemanova vláda vyhlásila boj proti korupci," ibid., February 18, 1999, p. 2.

53. Ondřej Neumann, "Lidí ochotných uplácet je o třetinu méně než před rokem," ibid., October 1, 1999, p. 5.

54. Ondřej Neumann, "Česko je na tom s úplatky podobně jako Maďarsko a Polsko," ibid., October 27, 1999, p. 4. For the 2001 survey, see Transparency International, "New Index Highlights Worldwide Corruption Crisis, Says Transparency International," press release (2001) <http://www.transparency.org/cpi/2001/cpi2001.html>.

55. Jeffrey M. Jordan, "Patronage and Corruption in the Czech Republic (Part 1)," *RFE/RL East European Perspectives* 4, no. 4 (February 20, 2002) <http://www.rferl.org>; Jeffrey M. Jordan, "Patronage and Corruption in the Czech Republic (Part 2)," *RFE/RL East European Perspectives* 4, no. 5 (March 6, 2002) <http://www.rferl.org>.

56. Roman Krasnický and Ondřej Bílek, "Lustrace jsou evergreenem české politiky," *Mladá fronta dnes*, October 26, 2000, p. 4; obi, "Lustrace platí dál," ibid., November 29, 2003, p. 3.

57. Petra Breyerova, "Lustration is Alive, but Kicking in a New Way," *Wall Street Journal Europe*, June 15, 2001, p. 9; British Broadcasting Corporation, "Czech Parliament Passes Civil Service Bill—no Jobs for Life," *BBC Monitoring*, March 12, 2002, ČTK News Agency.

58. This section uses Josef Kalvoda, "The Gypsies of Czechoslovakia," *Nationalities Papers* 19, no. 4 (Winter 1991): 269–96; Zoltan Barany, "Living on the Edge: The East European Roma in Postcommunist Politics and Societies," *Slavic Review* 53, no. 2 (Summer 1994): 321–44; and Zoltan Barany, "Orphans of Transition: Gypsies in Eastern Europe," *Journal of Democracy* 9, no. 3 (1998): 142–56.

59. Leff, *Czech and Slovak Republics*, p. 170.

60. U.S. Department of State, Bureau of Democracy, Human Rights, and Labor, *Country Reports on Human Rights Practices, Czech Republic, 2001* (Washington, D.C.: U.S. State Department, 2001) <http://www.state.gov>.

61. Barany, "Orphans of Transition," p. 147; Shepherd, *Czechoslovakia*, pp. 116–19.

62. Jindřich Šídlo, "Romové nejsou úplně tvárný národ," *Respekt*, February 28, 2000, p. 17. See also: Bureau of Democracy, Human Rights, and Labor, *Country Reports on Human Rights Practices, Czech Republic, 2001*; Pavel Barša, "Nacionalismus, nebo integrace? Romská emancipace a její historické paralely," in *Národnostní politika v postkomuistických zemích*, edited by Břetislav Dančák and Petr Fiala (Brno: Masarykova univerzita, Mezinárodní politologický ústav, 2000), pp. 306–13.

63. FBIS, "Daily Lists Illegally Operating 'Neo-Nazi' Groups," *Daily Reports, Eastern Europe* FBIS-EEU-97-240 (August 28, 1997); FBIS, "Daily Lists Legally Operating 'Extremist' Organizations," ibid.; Magnus Bennett, "Czech Officials Vow Crackdown After Neo-Nazis Rock Near Prague," *Jerusalem Post*,

April 17, 2001, p. 11; Miroslav Mareš, "Pravicový extremismus a romská menšina v České republice," in *Národnostní politika v postkomunistických zemích*, edited by Břetislav Dančák and Petr Fiala (Brno: Masarykova univerzita, Mezinárodní politologický ústav, 2000), pp. 94–123.

64. Josef Bouška, "Jednotni zvítězíme," *Respekt*, April 23, 2001, p. 6.

65. Research shows similarities in Slovak attitudes to the Hungarian minority in Slovakia. See gas, "Pruzkum: soužiti s Romy se zlepsuje," *Lidové noviny*, August 17, 1999, p. 4.

66. Wolchik, *Czechoslovakia in Transition*, pp. 201–3; Leff, *Czech and Slovak Republics*, pp. 198–200; Marianne A. Ferber, "Czech Women in Transition," *Monthly Labor Review* 117, no. 11 (November 1994): 32 ff.

67. Steven Saxonberg, "Women in East European Parliaments," *Journal of Democracy* 11, no. 2 (April 2000): 145–58.

68. rep, "Prezident podrobil odcházející vládu Václava Klause tvrdé kritice."

69. Marc Morjé Howard, "The Weakness of Post-Communist Civil Society," *Journal of Democracy* 12, no. 1 (January 2002): 159.

70. Bureau of Democracy, Human Rights, and Labor, *Country Reports on Human Rights Practices, Czech Republic, 2001*.

71. Martina Macková, "Haken: Občansksá společnost? Jsme na cestě," *Mladá fronta dnes*, April 17, 2002, p. 3.

72. Václav Drbohlav, "Blbá nálada," *Lidové noviny*, January 26, 1999, p. 11.

73. "Člověk by se měl radovat," *Respekt*, July 2, 2001, p. 14.

74. gas, "Spokojenost s členstvím v NATO klésá," *Lidové noviny*, May 25, 1999, p. 2.

75. This section draws on Leff, *Czech and Slovak Republics*, pp. 240–72.

76. nel, "Cesta otevřená (ČSFR a Rada Evropy)," *Lidové noviny*, January 12, 1991, p. 2.

77. Vilém Holán, "Mrtví jsou cenou za obnovenou čest," ibid., August 26, 1995, p. 12.

78. Alexandra Procházková and Michael Hä, "Sněmovna schválila vojenskou misi," ibid., December 9, 1995, p. 1.

79. Petr Janyška, "Střední Evropa do NATO," *Respekt*, October 14, 1991, p. 3.

80. "Partnerství pro mír má rozhodně smysl," *Lidové noviny*, August 23, 1994, p. 7; Jana Blažková, "Krok na cestě k alianci," ibid., October 13, 1994, p. 7.

81. FBIS, "Lobkowicz Views Approval of Republic's NATO Accession," *Daily Reports, Eastern Europe* FBIS-EEU-98-106 (April 16, 1997); FBIS, "Daily Views Tasks Awaiting Republic Before NATO Entry," *Daily Reports, Eastern Europe* FBIS-EEU-97-191 (July 10, 1997).

82. Václav Havel, "Idea NATO nepatří na smetiště dějin," *Lidové noviny*, June 22, 1996, p. 5.

83. "Speech by the Prime Minister of the Czech Republic, Milos Zeman, Brussels, March 16, 1999," online document (1999) <http://www.nato.int/docu/speech.htm>.

84. Petr Janyška, "Naše nejdůležitější dohoda: Dokument o asociaci parafován," *Respekt*, February 12, 1991, p. 2.

85. Miroslav Korecký, " 'Návrat do Evropy' byl zatím ve stínu diskuse o NATO," *Lidové noviny*, January 13, 1999, p. 3.

86. In this section I draw from Leff, *Czech and Slovak Republics*, pp. 254–69.

87. Elena Iankova, *Governed by Accession? Hard and Soft Pillars of Europeanization in Central and Eastern Europe*, East European Studies Occasional Papers, 60 (Washington, D.C.: Woodrow Wilson Center for International Scholars, 2001), pp. 8–10.

88. Ibid., p. 11.

89. Commission of the European Communities, *2001 Regular Report on the Czech Republic's Progress Towards Accession* (Brussels: Commission of the European Communities, 2001), pp. 3–5, 108–15; Leff, *Czech and Slovak Republics*, p. 255.

90. Howard J. Wiarda, *The Politics of European Enlargement: NATO, the EU, and the New U.S.–European Relationship*, East European Studies Occasional Papers, 67 (Washington, D.C.: Woodrow Wilson International Center for Scholars, 2002), pp. 14–15.

91. Leff, *Czech and Slovak Republics*, 204–5, 258–59; Jeffrey D. Pierson, "Changing Czech Energy Policy," *The OECD Observer*, no. 191 (December-January 1994): 35 ff.

92. See two articles by Marek Kerles: "Rozhodnutí o dostavbě vzdaluje Česko od vstupu do Evropské unie, tvrdí Vídeň," *Lidové noviny*, May 14, 1999, p. 3; and "Temelín: Rakušané hrozí vetem v EU," ibid., September 21, 1999, p. 6.

93. Kate Connolly, "Haider Plays Nuclear Power Games," *The Guardian*, January 16, 2002; FBIS, "Czech Foreign Minister Views Austrian Anti-Temelin Petition, Zeman's Statements," *Daily Reports, Western Europe* FBIS-WEU-2002-0124 (January 23, 2002).

94. Commission of the European Communities, *2001 Progress Towards Accession*, pp. 70–73.

95. Timothy W. Ryback, "Dateline Sudetenland: Hostages to History," *Foreign Policy* 105 (Winter 1996): 162–64.

96. Andrew Stroehlein, *The Failure of a New History: Czechs and the Czech-German Declaration* (Telford, Shropshire: Central Europe Review, 2000) <http://www.ce-review.org>.

97. FBIS, "Zeman, Kavan Reject German Politicians' Criticism," *Daily Reports, Eastern Europe* FBIS-EU-98-218 (August 6, 1998); FBIS, "Daily: New Foreign Minister's First Foreign Trip 'Fiasco'," *Daily Reports, Eastern Europe* FBIS-EU-98-219 (August 7, 1998).

98. Jolyon Naegele, "End Note: Postwar Decrees Haunt Czech Relations with Berlin, Vienna," *RFE/RL (Un)Civil Societies* 3, no. 8 (February 20, 2002) <http://www.rferl.org>; Marek Švehla and Eliška Bártová, "Dektrety se trhají," *Respekt*, March 4, 2002, p. 13.

99. FBIS, "EU not Interested in Linking Czech's Accession to Postwar Decrees—Spokesman," *Daily Reports, Eastern Europe* FBIS-EEU-2002-0225 (February 25, 2002); FBIS, "Text of Czech Premier's European Commissioner's Joint Press Release," *Daily Reports, Eastern Europe* FBIS-EEU-2002-0411 (April 11, 2002).

100. "Russian President Supports Prague on Benes Decrees Issue," *RFE/RL Newsline*, April 18, 2002 <http://www.rferl.org>; FBIS, "Slovak, Czech Ministers Agree on Rejecting Abolition of Postwar Decrees," *Daily Reports, Eastern Europe* FBIS-EEU-2002-0513 (May 13, 2002).

101. See the Czech foreign ministry's Web site at <http://www.mfa.cz/decrees>.

102. FBIS, "Candidate for German Chancellor Urges Czechs to Annul Postwar Decrees," *Daily Reports, Eastern Europe* FBIS-EEU-2002-0519 (May 19, 2002); FBIS, "German Government Backs Unconditional Czech EU Entry—Minister," *Daily Reports, Eastern Europe* FBIS-EEU-2002-0518 (May 18, 2002).

103. Jiří Večerník, "Špatně servírovana hostina," *Mladá fronta dnes*, August 16, 2001, p. 2.

104. Jan Herzmann, "Co přinesou Klausovy výroky o Evropské unii?" ibid., June 16, 2000, p. 6; Roman Krasnický, "Do EU chtějí nejvíc ty země, o které Evropa nemá zájem," ibid., November 8, 2000, p. 6.

105. Zbigniew Krzysztyniak, "Threatening Tradition," *The Warsaw Voice*, January 28, 2001.

106. Večerník, "Špatně servírovana hostina," p. 2. See also Holý, *The Little Czech and the Great Czech Nation: National Identity and the Post-Communist Transformation of Society*, pp. 141–56.

107. Vladimír Macura, *Český sen*, p. 63, and Karel Hvížd'ala, "Václav Klaus: moderní manažer z 19. století," *Mladá fronta dnes*, July 14, 2000, p. 7.

108. Macura, *Český sen*, pp. 75–77.

109. Herzmann, "Co přinesou Klausovy výroky o Evropské unii?" p. 6.

110. Kateřina Šafaříková, "Češi do Evropy nechtějí," *Respekt*, May 28, 2001, p. 2.

Bibliography

BOOKS AND ARTICLES

Abrams, Bradley F. "Morality, Wisdom, and Revision: The Czech Opposition of the 1970s and the Expulsion of the Sudeten Germans." *East European Politics and Societies* 9, no. 2 (Spring 1995): 234–55.

———. "The Price of Retribution: The Trial of Jozef Tiso." *East European Politics and Societies* 10 (1996): 255–92.

Agnew, Hugh LeCaine. "Enlightenment and National Consciousness: Three Czech 'Popular Awakeners'." In *Nation and Ideology: Essays in Honor of Wayne S. Vucinich*, edited by Ivo Banac, John G. Ackerman, and Roman Szporluk, pp. 201–26. Boulder, Colo.: East European Monographs, 1981.

———. "Josephinism and the Patriotic Intelligentsia in Bohemia." *Harvard Ukrainian Studies* 10 (1986): 577–97.

———. "Czechoslovakia in American Eyes; 1918 and 1989 Compared." Conference presentation. World Conference of the Czechoslovak Society of Arts and Sciences. Prague, 1992.

———. "Czechs, Slovaks, and the Slovak Linguistic Separatism of the Mid-Nineteenth Century." In *The Czech and Slovak Experience*, edited by John Morison, pp. 21–37. London and New York: Macmillan, 1992.

————. "Noble *Natio* and Modern Nation: The Czech Case." *Austrian History Yearbook* 23 (1992): 50–71.

————. "The Emergence of Modern Czech National Consciousness: A Conceptual Approach." *Ethnic Studies* 10 (1993): 211–22.

————. *Origins of the Czech National Renascence.* Pittsburgh: University of Pittsburgh Press, 1993.

————. "Ambiguities of Ritual: Dynastic Loyalty, Territorial Patriotism, and Nationalism in the Last Three Royal Coronations in Bohemia." *Bohemia* 41, no. 1 (2000): 3–22.

————. "Old States, New Identities? The Czech Republic, Slovakia, and Historical Understandings of Statehood." *Nationalities Papers* 28, no. 4 (2000): 619–50.

Albrecht, Catherine. "Pride in Production: The Jubilee Exhibition of 1891 and Economic Competition Between Czechs and Germans in Bohemia." *Austrian History Yearbook* 24 (1993): 101–18.

————. "The Rhetoric of Economic Nationalism in the Boycott Campaigns of the Late Habsburg Monarchy." *Austrian History Yearbook* 32 (2001): 47–67.

Alexander, Manfred. "Proces s Vojtechom Tukom zo spravodajstva nemeckého konzulátu bratislave." *Historický časopis* 40, no. 5 (1992): 609–24.

————. "Die tschechische Diskussion über die Vertreibung der Deutschen und deren Folgen." *Bohemia* 34, no. 2 (1993): 390–409.

Armstrong, John A. *Nations Before Nationalism.* Chapel Hill: University of North Carolina Press, 1982.

Ash, Timothy Garton. *The Magic Lantern: The Revolution of '89 Witnessed in Warsaw, Budapest, Berlin, and Prague.* New York: Random House, 1990.

Aslund, Anders, Peter Boone, and Simon Johnson. "How to Stabilize: Lessons from Post-Communist Countries." *Brookings Papers on Economic Activity*, no. 1 (1996): 217–313.

Ákos, Róna-Tas. "The Selected and the Elected: The Making of the New Parliamentary Elite in Hungary." *East European Politics and Societies* 5, no. 3 (Fall 1991): 369–72.

Bahm, Karl F. "The Inconveniences of Nationality: German Bohemians, the Disintegration of the Habsburg Monarchy, and the Attempt to Create a 'Sudeten German' Identity." *Nationalities Papers* 27, no. 3 (1999): 375–405.

Balázs, Éva H. *Hungary and the Habsburgs, 1765–1800: An Experiment in Enlightened Absolutism.* Translated by Tim Wilkinson. Budapest: Central European University Press, 1997.

Banac, Ivo, ed. *Eastern Europe in Revolution.* Ithaca: Cornell University Press, 1992.

Barany, Zoltan. "Living on the Edge: The East European Roma in Postcommunist Politics and Societies." *Slavic Review* 53, no. 2 (Summer 1994): 321–44.

———. "Orphans of Transition: Gypsies in Eastern Europe." *Journal of Democracy* 9, no. 3 (1998): 142–56.

Barša, Pavel. "Nacionalismus, nebo integrace? Romská emancipace a její historické paralely." In *Národnostní politika v postkomunistických zemích*, edited by Břetislav Dančák and Petr Fiala, pp. 306–13. Brno: Masarykova univerzita, Mezinárodní politologický ústav, 2000.

Batt, Judy. *Economic Reform and Political Change in Eastern Europe: A Comparison of the Czechoslovak and Hungarian Experiences.* New York: St. Martin's Press, 1988.

Baynes, Norman H., ed. *The Speeches of Adolf Hitler, April 1922–August 1939.* Royal Institute for International Affairs. London and New York: Oxford University Press, 1942.

Bělina, Pavel, et al. *Dějiny zemí koruny české, II. Od nástupu osvícenství po naši dobu.* Prague: Paseka, 1992.

Beneš, Edvard. *Světová válka a naše revoluce: Vzpomínky a úvahy z boju za svobodu národa, III, Dokumenty.* Prague: Orbis & Čin, 1928.

———. *Memoirs of Dr. Edward Beneš: From New War to New Victory.* Translated by Godfrey Lias. Boston: Houghton Mifflin, 1954.

———. *Mnichovské dny. Paměti.* Prague: Svoboda, 1968.

Bernatzik, Edmund, ed. *Die österreichischen Verfassungsgesetze mit Erläuterungen.* Vienna: Manz, 1911.

Blaive, Muriel. *Promarněná příležitost: Československo rok 1956.* Prague: Prostor, 2001.

Blanning, T. C. W. *Joseph II.* London: Longman, 1994.

Blum, Jerome. *Noble Landowners and Agriculture in Austria, 1815–1848.* Baltimore: Johns Hopkins University Press, 1948.

Boba, Imre. *Moravia's History Reconsidered: A Reinterpretation of Medieval Sources.* The Hague: Martinus Nijhoff, 1971.

Bohatá, Marie. "Business Ethics in Central and Eastern Europe with Special Focus on the Czech Republic." *Journal of Business Ethics* 16, no. 14 (1997): 1571–77.

———. "Macroeconomic Situation of the Czechoslovak Economy at the End of the 1980s." *Eastern European Economics* 36, no. 4 (July–August 1998): 75–87.

Bolzano, Bernard. *Über das Verhältniss der beiden Volkstämme in Böhmen.* Vienna: Wilhelm Braumüller, 1849.

Borák, Mečislav. *Spravedlnost podle dektretu.* Ostrava: Tilia, 1998.

Bowlus, Charles. *Franks, Moravians, and Magyars: The Struggle for the Middle Danube, 788–907.* Philadelphia: University of Pennsylvania Press, 1995.

Brachová, Věra, ed. "Dopis generala H. Piky prezidentu Gottwaldovi (I)." *Historie a vojenství* 41, no. 1 (1992): 112–39.

———. "Dopis generala H. Piky prezidentu Gottwaldovi (II)." *Historie a vojenství* 41, no. 2 (1992): 115–49.

Brandes, Detlef. "Konfederace nebo východní pakt?" *Slovanský přehled* 78 (1992): 436–48.

———. "Eine verspätete tschechische Alternative zum Münchener 'Diktat': Edvard Beneš und die Sudetendeutsche Frage, 1938–1945." *Vierteljahrshefte für Zeitgeschichte* 42, no. 2 (1994): 221–41.

Bren, Paulina. "Czech Restitution Laws Rekindle Sudeten Germans' Grievances." *RFE/RL Research Report* 3, no. 2 (January 14, 1994): 17.

Bridge, Francis R. *The Habsburg Monarchy Among the Great Powers.* New York: Berg, 1991.

Bureau of Democracy, Human Rights, and Labor, U.S. Department of State. *Country Reports on Human Rights Practices, Czech Republic, 2001.* Washington, D.C.: U.S. State Department, 2001. <http://www.state.gov>.

Bureau of Economic and Business Affairs, U.S. Department of State. *2001 Country Reports on Economic Policy and Trade Policies: Czech Republic.* Washington, D.C.: U.S. Department of State, 2001 <http://www.state.gov>.

Cambel, Samuel. "Arizácia a dalšie zmeny v pozemkovej držbe na Slovensku do leta 1944." *Historický časopis* 43 (1995): 69–88.

Cambie, Silvia. "Czech Privatization Moves Into High Gear with Second Wave." *Central European* 4, no. 5 (May 1994): 25 ff.

Campbell, F. Gregory. *Confrontation in Central Europe: Weimar Germany and Czechoslovakia.* Chicago: University of Chicago Press, 1975.

———. "Central Europe's Bastion of Democracy." *East European Quarterly* 11, no. 2 (1977): 155–76.

Čapek, Jan Blahoslav, gen. ed. *Kde domov můj?: památník věnovany naší vlasti a hymne národa českého.* Prague: Čin, 1940.

Čapek, Karel. *Talks with T. G. Masaryk.* Edited by Michael Henry Heim. Translated by Dora Round. New Haven, Conn.: Catbird Press, 1995.

Carsten, F. L. "Jan Masaryk Twelve Days Before His Death." *Slavonic and East European Review* 61, no. 2 (1983): 252–53.

Cepl, Vojtěch, and Mark Gillis. "Making Amends After Communism." *Journal of Democracy* 7, no. 4 (1996): 118–24.

Černý, Bohumil. *Vražda v Polné*. Prague: Vydavatelství časopisu Ministry národní obrany, 1968.

Český statistický úřad. *Volby v ČR, 1990–1999*. Online document. 4201–00 <http://www.czso.cz>.

Charmatz, Richard. *Das politische Denken in Österreich: Geschichtliche Betrachtungen*. 2d ed. Vienna: Verlag des Volksbildungshauses Wiener Urania, 1917.

Chelčický, Petr. *Petr Chelčický: Treatises on Christianity and the Social Order*. Translated and edited by Howard Kaminsky. Lincoln: University of Nebraska Press, 1964.

Churaň, Milan, gen. ed. *Kdo byl kdo v našich dějinách ve 20. století*. Prague: Libri, 1994.

Cibulka, Pavel. *Politické programy českých národních stran, 1860–1890*. Prague: Historický Ústav AV ČR, 2000.

Cohen, Gary B. *The Politics of Ethnic Survival: Germans in Prague, 1861–1914*. Princeton, N.J.: Princeton University Press, 1981.

———. *Education and Middle-Class Society in Imperial Austria, 1848–1918*. West Lafayette, Ind.: Purdue University Press, 1996.

Comenius, John. *The Labyrinth of the World and the Paradise of the Heart*. Translated by Howard Louthan and Andrea Sterk, with a preface by Jan Milič Lochman. New York and Mahwah, N.J.: Paulist Press, 1998.

Commission of the European Communities. *2001 Regular Report on the Czech Republic's Progress Towards Accession*. Brussels: Commission of the European Communities, 2001.

Čornej, Petr. *Tajemství českých kronik*. Prague: Vyšehrad, 1987.

———. *Lipanská křižovatka. Příčiny, průběh a historický význam jedné bitvy*. Prague: Panorama, 1992.

———. *Lipanské ozvěny*. Prague: H&H, 1995.

Čornejová, Ivana. *Tovaryšstvo Ježíšovo: jezuité v Čechách*. Prague: Mlada fronta, 1995.

Cornwall, Mark. "The Struggle on the Czech-German Language Border, 1880–1940." *English Historical Review* 109 (September 1994): 914–51.

———. "'National Reparation?' The Czech Land Reform and the Sudeten Germans, 1918–38." *Slavonic and East European Review* 75, no. 2 (1997): 259–80.

Crawford, Keith. *East Central European Politics Today: From Chaos to Stability?* Manchester: Manchester University Press, 1996.

Crosby, Karl J. "Leading Figures of the Hlinka Slovak People's Party." *Kosmas* 5, no. 2 (1986): 57–69.

Cuhra, Jaroslav. "KSČ, stát a římskokatolická církev (1948–1989)." *Soudobé dějiny* 8, no. 2-3 (2001): 267–93.

Curry, Jane Leftwich, ed. *Dissent in Eastern Europe*. New York: Praeger, 1983.

"Czech Economy: Downgraded Banks but Improved Outlook." *Transition Newsletter* 9, no. 6 (November–December 1998): 10–13.

"The Czech Republic: Rejoining the West." *Crossborder Monitor* 4, no. 49 (December 11, 1996): 12.

"The Czech Republic: Václav Thatcher." *The Economist* 332, no. 7875 (August 6, 1994): 42.

Dančák, Břetislav, and Petr Fiala, eds. *Národnostní politika v postkomunistických zemích*. Brno: Masarykova univerzita, Mezinárodní politologický ústav, 2000.

Daňhelka, Jiří, Karel Hádek, Bohuslav Havránek, and Naděžda Kvítková, eds. *Staročeská kronika tak řečeného Dalimila*. Prague: Academia, 1988.

David-Fox, Katherine. "Prague-Vienna, Prague-Berlin: The Hidden Geography of Czech Modernism." *Slavic Review* 59, no. 4 (2000): 735–60.

Davies, Norman. *Heart of Europe: The Past in Poland's Present*. Oxford: Oxford University Press, 2001.

Dawisha, Karen. *The Kremlin and the Prague Spring*. Berkeley: University of California Press, 1984.

Deak, Istvan. *The Lawful Revolution: Louis Kossuth and the Hungarians, 1848–1849*. New York: Columbia University Press, 1979.

———. *Beyond Nationalism: A Social and Political History of the Habsburg Officer Corps, 1848–1918*. New York: Oxford University Press, 1990.

Deák, Ladislav. "Polské zemní nároky vôči Slovensku v roku 1938." *Historický časopis* 39 (1991): 12–27.

Dejmek, Jindřich. "Milan Hodža a československá zahraniční politika v třicátých letech (1935–1938)." *Moderní dějiny* 7 (1999): 65–84.

Denyer, Stephen, and Martin Šolc. "Czechoslovakia: What's in the Divorce Settlement?" *International Financial Law Review* 12, no. 2 (February 1993): 28.

Dubček, Alexander. *Hope Dies Last: The Autobiography of Alexander Dubček*. Edited and translated by Jiří Hochmann. London: HarperCollins, 1993.

"Eastern Approaches." *The Economist* 343, no. 8019 (May 31, 1997): S13–S15.

Efmertová, Marcela C. *České země v letech 1848–1918.* Prague: Nakladatelství Libri, 1998.

Eggers, Martin. *Das grossmährische Reich: Realität oder Fiktion? Eine Neuinterpretation der Quellen zur Geschichte des mittleren Donauraumes im 9. Jahrhundert.* Stuttgart: Anton Hiersemann, 1995.

————. *Das Erzbistum des Method: Lage, Wirkung und Nachleben der kyrillomethodianischen Mission.* Munich: Otto Sagner, 1996.

Eisenmann, Louis. *Le compromis Austro-Hongrois de 1867: Étude sur le dualisme.* 1904. Hattiesburg, Miss.: Academic International, 1971.

Ellerman, David. "Voucher Privatization with Investment Funds: A Sure Way to Decapitalize Industry." *Transition Newsletter* 9, no. 6 (November–December 1998): 10–13.

"End of the Road for the Privatization Ministry." *Finance East Europe* 6, no. 8 (April 19, 1996): 8.

"EU Caution on Czech Economy." *East European Markets* 17, no. 9 (April 25, 1997): 3.

Evans, R. J. W. *Rudolf II and His World: A Study in Intellectual History, 1576–1612.* Oxford: Clarendon Press, 1973.

Faltus, Jozef, and Václav Průcha. *Prehl'ad hospodárskeho vývoja na Slovensku v rokoch 1918–1945.* Bratislava: Vydavatel'stvo politickej literatúry, 1969.

Felak, James Ramon. *At the Price of the Republic: Hlinka's Slovak People's Party, 1929–1938.* Pittsburgh: University of Pittsburgh Press, 1994.

Ferber, Marianne A. "Czech Women in Transition." *Monthly Labor Review* 117, no. 11 (November 1994): 32–36.

Fiala, Zdeněk, ed. *Zbraslavská kronika: Chronicon Aulae Regiae.* Translated by František Heřmanský and Rudolf Mertlík. Prague: Svoboda, 1976.

Filip, Jan. *Keltská civilizace a její dědictví.* 5th ed. Prague: Academia, 1996.

Freeze, Karen Johnson. "The Young Progressives: The Czech Student Movement, 1887–1897." Ph. D. diss., Columbia University, 1974.

Freudenberger, Herman. "The Woolen-Goods Industry of the Habsburg Monarchy in the Eighteenth Century." *Journal of Economic History* 20, no. 3 (September 1960): 383–406.

————. "State Intervention as an Obstacle to Economic Growth in the Habsburg Monarchy." *Journal of Economic History* 27, no. 4 (December 1967): 493–509.

————. "Progressive Bohemian and Moravian Aristocrats." In *Intellectual and Social Developments in the Habsburg Empire from Maria Theresa to World War I*, edited by Stanley B. Winters and Joseph Held, in collaboration with István Deák and Adam Wandruszka, pp. 115–30. Boulder, Colo.: East European Quarterly, 1975.

Frolec, Václav, gen. ed. *Vánoce v české kultuře.* Prague: Vyšehrad, 1989.

Galandauer, Jan. "Prohlášení českého svazu z 30. května 1917: Zapomenutá programová revoluce." *Český časopis historický* 91, no. 4 (1993): 582–93.

Garver, Bruce. *The Young Czech Party, 1874–1901, and the Emergence of a Multi-Party System.* New Haven, Conn.: Yale University Press, 1978.

———. "Czech Cubism and Fin-de-Siecle Prague." *Austrian History Yearbook* 19–20, no. 1 (1983–84): 91–104.

———. "Václav Klofáč and the Czechoslovak National Socialist Party." *East Central Europe/L'Europe Du Centre-Est* 17, no. 2 (1990): 155–78.

Gebhart, Jan, and Jan Kuklík. "Pomnichovská krize a vznik Strany národní jednoty." *Český časopis historický* 90 (1992): 365–93.

———. "Počátky Národního souručenství v roce 1939." *Český časopis historický* 91 (1993): 417–41.

Gitter, Robert J., and Markus Scheuer. "Low Unemployment in the Czech Republic: 'Miracle' or 'Mirage'?" *Monthly Labor Review* 121, no. 8 (August 1998): 31–37.

Glassheim, Eagle. "National Mythologies and Ethnic Cleansing: The Expulsion of Czechoslovak Germans in 1945." *Central European History* 33, no. 4 (2000): 463–86.

Glatz, Ferenc. "Data on Trianon Hungary." In *Hungarians and Their Neighbors in Modern Times, 1867–1950,* edited by Ferenc Glatz, pp. 105–10. Boulder, Colo., and Highland Lakes, N.J.: Social Science Monographs and Atlantic Research and Publications, 1995.

Good, David F. *The Economic Rise of the Habsburg Empire, 1750–1918.* Berkeley: University of California Press, 1979.

Gottsmann, Andreas. *Der Reichstag von Kremsier und die Regierung Schwarzenberg: die Verfassungsdiskussion des Jahres 1848 im Spannungsfeld zwischen Reaktion und nationaler Frage.* Vienna: R. Oldenbourg, 1994.

Gross, Nachum T. "The Industrial Revolution in the Habsburg Monarchy, 1790–1914." In *The Emergence of Industrial Societies,* edited by Carlo M. Cipolla. The Fontana Economic History of Europe, Vol. 4, Part 1. London: Collins/Fontana Books, 1973.

Grulich, Jindřich. *Smrt Jana Masarkya—nebyla to nešťastná náhoda.* Karvín: Jindřich Grulich, 2001.

Ham, John C., Jan Švejnar, and Katherine Terrell. "Unemployment and the Social Safety Net During Transitions to a Market Economy: Evidence from the Czech and Slovak Republics." *American Economic Review* 88, no. 5 (1998): 1117–42.

Hamilton, Keith. "Old Adam and Five Beggars: British Reaction to the Tardieu Plan." *Revue d'Europe Centrale* 5, no. 2 (1997): 95–115.

Hanak, Harry. "President Beneš, Britové a budoucnost Československa, 1939–1945." *Historie a vojenství* 44 (1994): 13–39.

Hanke, Gerhard. "Das Zeitalter des Zentralismus (1740–1848)." In *Handbuch der Geschichte der böhmischen Länder*, edited by Karl Bosl, pp. 413–575. Stuttgart: Anton Hiersemann, 1974.

Harna, Josef, ed. *Politické programy českého národního socialismu.* Prague: Historický ústav AV ČR, 1998.

Haselsteiner, Horst. "Cooperation and Confrontation Between Rulers and the Noble Estates, 1711–1790." In *A History of Hungary*, Peter F. Sugar, gen. ed., edited by Péter Hánák, assisted by Tibor Frank, pp. 138–64. Bloomington: University of Indiana Press, 1990.

Havel, Václav. "The Power of the Powerless." Translated by Paul Wilson. In *The Power of the Powerless: Citizens Against the State in Central-Eastern Europe*, edited by John Keane, pp. 23–96. New York: M. E. Sharpe, 1985.

———. "Letter to Dr. Gustáv Husák." In *Václav Havel: Living in Truth*, edited by Jan Vladislav, pp. 3–35. London: Faber & Faber, 1986.

———. *Disturbing the Peace: A Conversation with Karel Hvížďala.* Translated by Paul Wilson. New York: Vintage Books, 1991.

Havel, Václav, and Václav Klaus, Petr Pithart, discussant. "Rival Visions." *Journal of Democracy* 7, no. 1 (1996): 12–23.

Havelka, Miloš, ed. *Spor o smyslu českých dějin, 1895–1938.* Prague: Torst, 1995.

Havlíček, Karel. *Dílo.* 2 vols. Edited by Alexander Stich. With a foreword by Alexander Stich. Prague: Československý spisovatel, 1985–86.

Havránek, Jan. "Počátky a kořeny pokrokového hnutí studentského na počátku devadesátých let 19. století." *Acta Historia Universitatis Carolinae Pragensis* 2, no. 1 (1961): 5–33.

———. "Protirakouské hnutí dělnické mládeže a studentů a události roku 1893." *Acta Historia Universitatis Carolinae Pragensis* 2, no. 2 (1961): 21–81.

———. *Boj za všeobecné, přímé a rovné hlasovací právo roku 1893.* Rozpravy ČSAV, Řada Společenských Věd, 74, Sešit 2. Prague: ČSAV, 1964.

Haynes, Kathryn. "The FDI Play in Central Europe." *Global Finance* 12, no. 12 (December 1998): 44–48.

Heidler, Jan. *Čechy a Rakousko v politických brožurách předbřeznových.* Prague: František Řivnáč and Matice česká, 1920.

————. *1917, projevy českých spisovatelů*. Prague: Vesmír, 1921.

Heumos, Peter. "'Kartoffeln her oder es gibt eine Revolution': Hungarkrawalle, Streiks und Massenproteste in den böhmischen Ländern, 1914–1918." *Slezský sborník* 97, no. 2 (1999): 81–104.

Historický ústav ČSAV. *Sedm pražských dnů, 21.–27. srpen 1968: dokumentace*. Edited by Josef Macek. Prague: Academia, 1990.

Hladký, Ladislav. "T. G. Masaryk a Bosna a Hercegovina: příspěvek k historii česko-jihoslovanských vztahů." *Slovanské historické studie* 20 (1994): 33–55.

Hlavačka, Milan. *Jubilejní výstava 1891*. Prague: Techkom, 1991.

Hoensch, Jörg. "Tschechoslowakismus oder Autonomie. Die Auseinandersetzungen um die Eingliederung der Slowakei in die Tschechoslowakische Republic." In *Das Jahr 1919 in der Tschechoslowakei und in Ostmitteleuropa*, edited by Hans Lemberg and Peter Heumos. Bad Weisseer Tagungen Des Collegium Carolinum, 17. Munich: R. Oldenbourg, 1993.

Holub, Josef, and Stanislav Lyer. *Stručný etymologický slovník jazyka českého se zvláštním zřetelem k slovům kulturním a cizím*. Prague: Státní pedagogické nakladatelstvi, 1967.

Holý, Ladislav. *The Little Czech and the Great Czech Nation: National Identity and the Post-Communist Transformation of Society*. Cambridge: Cambridge University Press, 1996.

Hopwood, Robert F. "The Conflict Between Count Czernin and Emperor Charles in 1918." *Austrian History Yearbook* 4–5 (1968–69): 28–43.

Howard, Marc Morjé. "The Weakness of Post-Communist Civil Society." *Journal of Democracy* 12, no. 1 (January 2002): 157–69.

Hraba, Joseph, Allan L. McCutcheon, and Jiří Večerník. "Rural and Urban Differences in Economic Experiences: Anxiety and Support for the Post-Communist Reforms in the Czech and Slovak Republics." *Rural Sociology* 64, no. 3 (September 1999): 439–63.

Hrbek, Ivan. "Ibráhím ibn Jákúb v Praze, Čechách a jiných slovanských zemích." *Český lid* 6 (1951): 267–71.

Hroch, Miroslav. "The Social Composition of the Czech Patriots in Bohemia. 1827–1848." In *The Czech Renascence of the Nineteenth Century: Essays Presented to Otakar Odložilik in Honour of His Seventieth Birthday*, edited by Peter Brock and H. Gordon Skilling, pp. 33–52. Toronto: University of Toronto Press, 1970.

————. *Social Preconditions of National Revival in Europe: A Comparative Analysis of the Social Composition of Patriotic Groups Among the Smaller European Nations*. Translated by Ben Fowkes. Cambridge: Cambridge University Press, 1985.

————. *Na prahu národní existence: touha a skutečnost.* Prague: Mladá fronta, 1999.

Hronský, Marián. "Slovenská republika rád (vojenskopolitická situacia)." *Historie a vojenství* 37, no. 4 (1988): 36–52.

————. "Bratislava či Wilsonov? Město na Dunaji pred trištvrte storočím." *Historická revue* 3, no. 6 (1992): 13–15.

Iankova, Elena. *Governed by Accession? Hard and Soft Pillars of Europeanization in Central and Eastern Europe.* East European Studies Occasional Papers, 60. Washington, D.C.: Woodrow Wilson Center for International Scholars, 2001.

Iggers, Wilma, ed. *Die Juden in Böhmen und Mähren: Ein Historisches Lesebuch.* Munich: C. H. Beck, 1986.

Ingrao, Charles. *The Habsburg Monarchy, 1618–1815.* Cambridge: Cambridge University Press, 1994.

Jaksch, Wenzel. *Europas Weg nach Potsdam: Schuld und Schicksal im Donauraum.* Stuttgart: Deutsche Verlags-Anstalt, 1958.

Janáček, Josef. *Rudolf II. a jeho doba.* Prague: Paseka, 1997.

Janák, Jan. "Táborové hnutí na Moravě v letech 1868–1874." *Časopis Matice moravské* 77 (1958): 290–324.

Jelinek, Yeshayahu. *The Parish Republic: Hlinka's Slovak People's Party.* East European Monographs, 14. Boulder, Colo.: East European Quarterly, distributed by Columbia University Press, 1976.

Jenks, William Alexander. *The Austrian Electoral Reform of 1907.* 1950. New York: Octagon Books, 1974.

————. *Austria Under the Iron Ring, 1879–1893.* Charlottesville: University Press of Virginia, 1965.

Johnson, Owen V. "The Slovak Intelligentsia, 1919–1938." *Slovakia* 28, no. 51–52 (1978–79): 25–48.

————. "The Modernization of Slovakia: The Role of Vocational High Schools, 1918–1938." *Slovakia* 31, no. 57 (1984): 59–86.

————. *Slovakia, 1918–1938: Education and the Making of a Nation.* Boulder, Colo.: East European Monographs, 1985.

Jordan, Jeffrey M. "Patronage and Corruption in the Czech Republic (Part 1)." *RFE/RL East European Perspectives* 4, no. 4 (February 20, 2002) <http://www.rferl.org>.

————. "Patronage and Corruption in the Czech Republic (Part 2)." *RFE/RL East European Perspectives* 4, no. 5 (March 6, 2002) <http://www.rferl.org>.

Judson, Pieter. "'Not Another Square Foot!': German Liberalism and the

Rhetoric of National Ownership in Nineteenth-Century Austria." *Austrian History Yearbook* 26 (1995): 83–97.

Judt, Tony R. "Metamorphosis: The Democratic Revolution in Czechoslovakia." In *Eastern Europe in Revolution*, edited by Ivo Banac, pp. 96–116. Ithaca: Cornell University Press, 1992.

Jungmann, Josef. "O jazyku českém. Rozmlouvání první." *Hlasatel Český* 1, no. 1 (1806): 43–49.

———. "O jazyku českém. Rozmlouvání druhé." *Hlasatel Český* 1, no. 3 (1806): 321–53.

Kalvoda, Josef. "The Gypsies of Czechoslovakia." *Nationalities Papers* 19, no. 4 (Winter 1991): 269–96.

Kalvoda, Joseph. "Munich: Beneš and the Soldiers." *Ukrainian Quarterly* 47 (1991): 153–69.

Kamenec, Ivan. "Deportácie židovských občanov zo Slovenska roku 1942." In *Tragédia Slovenských židov*, edited by Dezider Tóth, pp. 77–100. Banská Bystrica: DATEI, 1992.

———. *Slovenský stát*. Prague: Anomal, 1992.

Kaminsky, Howard. "Wyclifism as Ideology of Revolution." *Church History* 32 (1963): 57–74.

———. *A History of the Hussite Revolution*. Berkeley: University of California Press, 1967.

Kann, Robert A. *The Multinational Empire: Nationalism and National Reform in the Habsburg Monarchy, 1848–1918*. Vol. 1, *Empire and Nationalities*. Vol. 2, *Empire Reform*. New York: Columbia University Press, 1950.

———. *A History of the Habsburg Empire, 1526–1918*. Berkeley: University of California Press, 1974.

Kann, Robert A., and Zdeněk V. David. *The Peoples of the Eastern Habsburg Lands, 1526–1918*. A History of East Central Europe. Seattle: University of Washington Press, 1984.

Kaplan, Frank. *Winter Into Spring: The Czechoslovak Press and the Reform Movement, 1963–1968*. Boulder, Colo.: East European Quarterly, 1977.

Kaplan, Karel. *Political Persecution in Czechoslovakia, 1948–1972*. Crises in Soviet-Type Systems, Study No. 3. Cologne: Index, 1983.

———. *Report on the Murder of the General Secretary*. Translated by Karel Kovanda. Columbus: Ohio State University Press, 1990.

———. *Československo v letech 1952–1966*. Prague: Státní pedagogické nakladatelství, 1991.

———. *Československo v letech 1967–1969*. Prague: Státní pedagogické nakladatelství, 1991.

————. *Zakladatelské období komunistického režimu.* Vol. 2 of *Československo v letech 1948–1953.* Prague: Státní pedagogické nakladatelství, 1991.

————. *Poslední rok prezidenta: Edvard Beneš v roce 1948.* Prague: Ústav pro soudobé dějiny AV ČR, 1993.

————. *Sovětští Porádci v Československu, 1949–1956.* Prague: Ústav pro soudobé dějiny, 1993.

————. *Stát a církev v Československu v letech 1948–1953.* Brno: Doplněk, 1993.

————. *K politickým procesům v Československu, 1948–1954: dokumentace komise ÚV KSČ pro rehabilitaci 1968.* Prague: Ústav pro soudobé dějiny AV ČR, 1994.

————. *Československo v RVHP 1949–1956.* Prague: Ústav pro soudobé dějiny AV ČR, 1995.

————. *Pět kapitol o únoru.* Brno: Doplněk, 1997.

————, ed. and comp. *Dva retribuční procesy: komentované dokumenty (1945–1947).* Prague: Ústav pro soudobé dějiny ČSAV, 1992.

Kaplan, Karel, and Dušan Tomášek. *O cenzuře v Československu v letech 1945–1956: Studie.* Prague: Ústav pro soudobé dějiny AV ČR, 1994.

Karel IV. "Vlastní životopis." In *Kroniky doby Karla IV*, edited by Marie Bláhová, translated by Jakub Pavel. Prague: Svoboda, 1987.

Karklins, Rasma, and Roger Petersen. "Decision Calculus of Protestors and Regimes: Eastern Europe, 1989." *Journal of Politics* 55, no. 3 (August 1993): 588–614.

Kavka, František. *Vláda Karla IV. za jeho císařství (1355–1378): Země České koruny, rodová, říšská a evropská politika.* Prague: Univerzita Karlova, 1993.

Kárník, Zdeněk. "Ustavení ČSR jako parlamentní demokracie v podmínkách národněpolitické a sociálněpolitické krize střední Evropy (jaro-léto 1920): Události, jejich důsledky a širší souvislosti." In *Československo 1918–1938: Osudy demokracie ve střední Evropě*, edited by Jaroslav Valenta, Emil Voráček, and Josef Harna, pp. 90–110. Prague: Historický ústav AV ČR, 1999.

————. *České země v éře První republiky, díl první, Vznik, budování a zlatá léta republiky (1918–1929).* Prague: Libri, 2000.

Kárný, Miroslav. "Die materiellen Grundlagen der Sozialdemagogie in der Protektoratspolitik Heydrichs." *Historica* 29 (1989): 123–59.

————. "Lidské ztráty československých židů v letech 1938–1945." *Český časopis historický* 89 (1991): 410–20.

————. "Die Protektoratsregierung und die Verordnungen des Reichsprotektors über das jüdische Vermögen." *Judaica Bohemiae* 29 (1993): 54–66.

Kelleher, Edward P. "Emperor Karl and the Sixtus Affair: Politico-Nationalist Repercussions in the Reich German and Austro-German Camps, and the Disintegration of Habsburg Austria, 1916–1918." *East European Quarterly* 26, no. 2 (1992): 163–84.

Kelly, Theodore Mills. "Czech Radical Nationalism in the Era of Universal Manhood Suffrage, 1907–1914." Ph. D. diss., George Washington University, 1995.

———. "The Czech National Council and the Slovaks, 1900–1914." *Kosmas: Czechoslovak and Central European Journal* 12, no. 2 (Fall 1997): 99–118.

———. "Taking It to the Streets: Czech National Socialists in 1908." *Austrian History Yearbook* 29 (1998): 93–112.

Kennan, George F. *From Prague After Munich: Diplomatic Papers, 1938–1940*. 1968. Princeton, N.J.: Princeton University Press, 1971.

Kerner, Robert Joseph. *Bohemia in the Eighteenth Century: A Study in Political, Economic, and Social History with Special Reference to the Reign of Leopold II, 1790–1792*. New York: Macmillan, 1932.

Kieval, Hillel J. *The Making of Czech Jewry: National Conflict and Jewish Society in Bohemia, 1870–1918*. New York: Oxford University Press, 1988.

———. "Masaryk and Czech Jewry: The Ambiguities of Friendship." In *Thinker and Politician*. Vol. 1 of *T. G. Masaryk (1850–1937)*, edited by Stanley B. Winters, pp. 302–27. New York: St. Martin's Press, 1990.

———. *Languages of Community: The Jewish Experience in the Czech Lands*. Berkeley: University of California Press, 2000.

Kinský, Franz Joseph. *Erinnerung über einen wichtigen Gegenstand, von einem Böhmen*. Vol. 3 of *Des Grafen Kinskýs Gesamelte Schriften*. Vienna: Wappler, 1786.

Kirschbaum, Stanislav J. *A History of Slovakia: The Struggle for Survival*. New York: St. Martin's Press, 1995.

Kisielewski, Tadeusz. "The Problem of a Polish-Czechoslovak and Central European Confederation During World War II." *Polish Western Affairs* (1992): 273–90.

Klima, Arnošt. *Češi a Němci v revoluci, 1848–1849*. Prague: Nebesa, 1994.

Klimek, Antonín. "Počátky parlamentní demokracie v Československu." In *Československo 1918–1938: Osudy demokracie ve střední Evropě*, edited by Jaroslav Valenta, Emil Voráček, and Josef Harna, pp. 111–22. Prague: Historický ústav AV ČR, 1999.

Klimek, Antonín, Helena Nováčková, Milada Polišenská, and Ivan Šťovíček, eds. *Vznik Československa 1918*. Prague: Ústav mezinárodních vztahů, 1994.

Kliment, Charles K. *Slovenská armáda, 1939–1945*. Plzeň: Mustang, 1996.

Klíma, Michal. *Kvalita demokracie v České Republice a volební inženýrství*. Prague: Radix, 2001.

Knoll, Paul W. *The Rise of the Polish Monarchy: Piast Poland in East Central Europe, 1320–1370*. Chicago: University of Chicago Press, 1972.

Kocian, Jiří. "Program obnovy Československa v českém politickém spektru v letech 1939–1945." *Moderní dějiny* 2 (1994): 163–70.

Komunistická strana Československa. *Poučení z krizového vývoje straně a společnosti po XIII. sjezdu KSČ. Rezoluce k aktuálním otázkám jednoty strany: schváleno na plenárním zasedání ÚV KSČ v prosinci 1970*. Prague: Svoboda, 1988.

Konrád, George. *Anti-Politics*. New York: Harcourt Brace Jovanovich, 1984.

Kopecek, Herman. "*Zusammenarbeit* and *spoluprace*: Sudeten German-Czech cooperation in interwar Czechoslovakia." *Nationalities Papers* 24, no. 1 (1996): 63–78.

Kopecký, Petr. "From 'Velvet Revolution' to 'Velvet Split': Consociational Institutions and the Disintegration of Czechoslovakia." In *Irreconcilable Differences? Explaining Czechoslovakia's Dissolution*, edited and translated by Michael Kraus and Allison Stanger, with a foreword by Václav Havel, pp. 69–86. Lanham and Oxford: Rowman & Littlefield, 2000.

Kořalka, Jiří. *Pozvání do Frankfurtu*. Prague: Melantrich, 1990.

———. *Tschechen im Habsburgerreich und in Europa, 1815–1914: Sozialgeschichtliche Zusammenhänge der neuzeitlichen Nationsbildung und der Nationalitätenfrage in den böhmischen Ländern*. Vienna: Verlag für Geschichte und Politik and R. Oldenbourg, 1991.

Korbel, Josef. *Twentieth-Century Czechoslovakia: The Meanings of Its History*. New York: Columbia University Press, 1977.

Kosmova kronika česká. 6th ed. Edited by Karel Hrdina and Marie Bláhová. Translated by Zdeněk Fiala and Marie Bláhová. Prague: Svoboda, 1975.

Kostlán, Antonín. "Kralovská česká společnost nauk a počátky nové tolerance." In *Mezi časy . . . Kultura a umění v českých zemích kolem roku 1800*, edited by Zdeněk Hojda and Roman Prahl, pp. 98–105. Prague: KLP-Koniasch Latin Press, 2000.

Kovtun, Jiří. *Slovo má poslanec Masaryk*. Prague: Československý spisovatel, 1991.

Kramer, John M. "The Environmental Crisis in Eastern Europe: The Price for Progress." *Slavic Review* 42, no. 2 (Summer 1983): 204–20.

————. "Chernobyl' and Eastern Europe." *Problems of Communism* 35 (November–December 1986): 39–58.

Kraus, Michael, and Allison Stanger, eds. *Irreconcilable Differences? Explaining Czechoslovakia's Dissolution*. Foreword by Václav Havel. Lanham and Oxford: Rowman & Littlefield, 2000.

Krejčí, Jaroslav. *Czechoslovakia at the Crossroads of European History*. London: I. B. Tauris, 1990.

Krejčí, Jaroslav, and Pavel Machonin. *Czechoslovakia, 1918–1992: A Laboratory for Social Change*. New York: St. Martin's Press, 1996.

Křen, Jan. *Konfliktní společenství: Češi a Němci*. Prague: Academia, 1990.

————. "Die Vergangenheit bei Tschechen und Sudetendeutschen." *Bohemia* 34, no. 2 (1993): 381–89.

Kubů, Eduard, and Jana Šetřilová. "Hrad a Alois Rašín v letech 1922–1923: zápas o deflaci a omluvu legionářům." *Český časopis historický* 93, no. 3 (1995): 451–69.

Kun, Miklós. *Prague Spring–Prague Fall: Blank Spots of 1968*. Budapest: Akadémiai Kiadó, 1999.

Kundera, Milan. *The Book of Laughter and Forgetting*. Translated by Michael Henry Heim. New York: Knopf, 1980.

Kusin, Vladimir V. *From Dubček to Charter 77: A Study of "Normalization" in Czechoslovakia, 1968–1978*. New York: St. Martin's Press, 1978.

————. "Husák's Czechoslovakia and Economic Stagnation." *Problems of Communism* 31 (May-June 1982): 24–37.

————. "Dissent in Czechoslovakia After 1968." In *Dissent in Eastern Europe*, edited by Jane Leftwich Curry, pp. 48–59. New York: Praeger, 1983.

Kysel, Peter. "Czech Market Takes Pride of Place in European Emerging Markets." *Central European* Emerging Securities Market Supplement (October 1994): 10.

Lacina, Vlastislav. *Hospodářství českých zemí, 1880–1914*. Prague: Historický ústav ČSAV, 1990.

————. "Měnová politika v prvním desetiletí Československé republiky." *Český časopis historický* 91, no. 1 (1993): 1–17.

————. *Zlatá léta československého hospodářství 1918–1929*. Prague: Historický ústav AV ČR, 2000.

Lansbury, Melanie, Nigel Pain, and Kateřina Šmidková. "Foreign Direct Investment in Central Europe Since 1990: An Econometric Study." *National Institute Economic Review*, no. 156 (May 1996): 104–14.

Laun, Rudolf. *Les prétentions des Tchécoslovaques á des territoires allemands*. The Hague: Martin Nijhoff, 1919.

Lederer, Jiří. *Jan Palach. Zpráva o životě, činu, a smrti českého studenta.* Prague: Novinář, 1990.

Leff, Carol Skalnik. *National Conflict in Czechoslovakia: The Making and Remaking of a State, 1918–1987.* Princeton, N.J.: Princeton University Press, 1988.

———. *The Czech and Slovak Republics: Nation Versus State.* Boulder, Colo.: Westview Press, 1997.

Lemberg, Hans. "Masaryk and the Russian Question Against the Background of German and Czech Attitudes to Russia." In *Thinker and Politician.* Vol. 1 of *T. G. Masaryk (1850–1937),* edited by Stanley B. Winters, pp. 283–301. New York: St. Martin's Press, 1990.

———. "Die Tschechoslowakei im Jahr 1. Der Staatsaufbau, die Liquidierung der Revolution und die Alternativen 1919." In *Das Jahr 1919 in der Tschechoslowakei und in Ostmitteleuropa,* edited by Hans Lemberg and Peter Heumos, pp. 225–48. Munich: R. Oldenbourg, 1993.

Liehm, Antonin J. "The New Social Contract and the Parallel Polity." In *Dissent in Eastern Europe,* edited by Jane Leftwich Curry, pp. 173–81. New York: Praeger, 1983.

Lipscher, Ladislav. "Beschwerden der Sudetendeutschen im wirschaftlichen Bereich während der ersten tschechoslowakischen Republik." *Jahrbuch für Zeitgeschichte* (1982–83), pp. 33–57.

Lipták, L'ubomír. "Príprava a priebeh salzburských rokovaní roku 1940 medzi prestavitel'mi Nemecka a slovenského štátu." *Historický časopis* 13 (1965): 329–65.

———. "Mad'arsko v politike slovenského štátu v rokoch 1939–1943." *Historický časopis* 15, no. 1967 (1967): 1–35.

———. *Politické strany na Slovensku, 1869–1989.* Bratislava: Archa, 1992.

Litsch, Karel. "K výročí 17. listopadu 1939." *Acta Universitatis Carolinae. Historia Universitatis Carolinae Pragensis* 29 (1989): 9–13.

London, Artur Gerard. *The Confession.* Translated by Alastair Hamilton. New York: William Morrow, 1970.

Lorenzová, Helena. "Pražská léta Augusta Gottlieba Meissnera. Časopis *Apollo.*" In *Mezi časy . . . Kultura a umění v českých zemích kolem roku 1800,* edited by Zdeněk Hojda and Roman Prahl, pp. 88–97. Prague: KLP-Koniasch Latin Press, 2000.

Lukes, Igor. "Did Stalin Desire War in 1938? A New Look at Soviet Behaviour During the May and September Crises." *Diplomacy and Statecraft* 2, no. 1 (1991): 3–53.

———. "Stalin and Beneš at the End of September 1938: New Evidence from the Prague Archives." *Slavic Review* 52, no. 1 (1993): 28–48.

————. "Czechoslovak-Soviet Relations from the End of World War I to Adolf Hitler's Machtergreifung." *Diplomacy and Statecraft* 5, no. 2 (1994): 248–86.

————. "The Birth of a Police State: The Czechoslovak Ministry of the Interior, 1945–48." *Intelligence and National Security* 11, no. 1 (1996): 78–88.

————. "The Czechoslovak Partial Mobilization in May 1938: A Mystery (Almost) Solved." *Journal of Contemporary History* 31, no. 4 (1996): 699–720.

————. *Czechoslovakia Between Stalin and Hitler: The Diplomacy of Edvard Beneš in the 1930s.* New York: Oxford University Press, 1996.

————. "Stalin and Czechoslovakia in 1938–39: An Autopsy of a Myth." *Diplomacy and Statecraft* 10, no. 2-3 (1999): 13–47.

Lutovský, Michal, and Naďa Profantová. *Sámova Říše.* Prague: Academia, 1995.

Macartney, C. A. *The Habsburg Empire, 1790–1918.* New York: Macmillan, 1969.

Macek, Josef. *Hospodářská základná a královská moc.* Vol. 1 of *Jagellonský věk v českých zemích.* Prague: Academia, 1992.

————. *Šlechta.* Vol. 2 of *Jagellonský věk v českých zemích.* Prague: Academia, 1994.

————. "The Monarchy of the Estates." In *Bohemia in History*, edited by Mikuláš Teich, pp. 98–116. Cambridge: Cambridge University Press, 1998.

Macura, Vladimír. *Znamení zrodu: České obrození jako kulturní typ.* 2d ed. Jinočany: H&H, 1995.

————. *Český sen.* Prague: Nakladatelství Lidové noviny, 1999.

Magna Moravia: Sborník k 1100. výročí příchodu byzantské mise na Moravu. Prague: Státní pedagogické nakladatelství, 1965.

Magocsi, Paul Robert. *The Shaping of a National Identity: Subcarpathian Rus, 1848–1948.* Cambridge, Mass.: Harvard University Press, 1978.

Mamatey, Victor S. "The Slovaks and Carpatho-Ruthenians." In *The Immigrants' Influence on Wilson's Peace Policies*, edited by Joseph P. O'Grady, pp. 239–49. Lexington: University of Kentucky Press, 1967.

————. "The Battle of the White Mountain as Myth in Czech History." *East European Quarterly* 15 (1981): 335–45.

————. "The Czecho-Slovak Agreement of Pittsburgh (May 30, 1918) Revisited." *Kosmas* 2, no. 2 (1983): 41–48.

Mamatey, Victor S., and Radomír Luža, eds. *A History of the Czechoslovak Republic, 1918–1948.* Princeton, N.J.: Princeton University Press, 1973.

Mareš, Miroslav. "Pravicový extremismus a romská menšina v České republice." In *Národnostní politika v postkomunistických zemích*, edited by Břetislav Dančák and Petr Fiala, pp. 94–123. Brno: Masarykova univerzita, Mezinárodní politologický ústav, 2000.

Masaryk, T. G. *Cesta democracie I: Soubor projevů za republiky, 1918–1920*. Spisy T. G. Masaryka, 3. Prague: Čin, 1933.

———. *Cesta demokracie III: projevy, články, rozhovory, 1924–1928*. Spisy T. G. Masaryka, 35. Prague: Ústav T. G. Masaryka, 1994.

———. *Cesta demokracie IV: projevy, články, rozhovory, 1929–1937*. Spisy T. G. Masaryka, 36. Prague: Ústav T. G. Masaryka, 1997.

———. René Wellek, ed. *The Meaning of Czech History*. Translated by Peter Kussi. Chapel Hill: University of North Carolina Press, 1974.

Mastný, Vojtěch. *The Czechs Under Nazi Rule: The Failure of National Resistance, 1939–1942*. New York: Columbia University Press, 1971.

———. "Stalin and the Militarization of the Cold War." *International Security* 9, no. 3 (1984–85): 109–29.

Mathesius, Vilém, ed. *Co daly naše země Evropě a lidstvu*. Vol. 1, *Od slovanských věrozvěstů k národnímu obrození*. Vol. 2, *Obrozený národ a jeho země na fóru evropském a světovém*. Prague: Evropský literární klub, 1940.

Matthews, John P. C. *Majales: The Abortive Student Revolt in Czechoslovakia in 1956*. Cold War International History Project Working Papers, 24. Washington, D.C., 1999 <http://cwihp.si.edu/publications.htm>.

Maur, Eduard. *Kozina a Lomikar*. Prague: Melantrich, 1989.

McCagg, William O. *A History of the Habsburg Jews, 1670–1918*. Bloomington: Indiana University Press, 1989.

McGrath, William J. "Student Radicalism in Vienna." *Journal of Contemporary History* 2 (1967): 183–95.

Menclová, Dobroslava. *České hrady*. Prague: Odeon, 1972.

Mendelsohn, Ezra. *The Jews of East Central Europe Between the World Wars*. Bloomington: Indiana University Press, 1983.

Metternich, Clemens Wenzel Lothar Fürst von. *Memoirs of Prince Metternich, 1815–1829*. Vol. 1. Edited by Prince Richard Metternich. Papers classified and arranged by M. A. de Klinkowstrom, translated by Mrs. Alexander Napier. New York: Harper & Brothers, 1881.

Mezník, Jaroslav. *Čechy a Morava v 14. století*. Prague: Státní pedagogické nakladatelství, 1991.

Mikulec, Jiří. *Pobělohorská rekatolizace v českých zemích*. Prague: Státní pedagogické nakladatelství, 1992.

Miller, Daniel E. *Forging Political Compromise: Antonín Švehla and the Czechoslovak Republican Party, 1918–1933.* Pittsburgh: University of Pittsburgh Press, 1999.

Minulost našeho státu v dokumentech. Compiled and edited by Státní ústřední archiv v Praze. Prague: Svoboda, 1971.

Mlčoch, Lubomír. "Czech Privatization: A Criticism of Misunderstood Liberalism (Keynote Address)." *Journal of Business Ethics* 17, no. 9–10 (July 1998): 951–59.

Musilová, Dana. "Zásobování a vyživa českého obyvatelstva v podmínkách válečného řízení hospodářství (1939–1945)." *Slezský Sborník* 89 (1991): 255–66.

Myant, Martin. *The Czechoslovak Economy, 1948–1988.* Cambridge: Cambridge University Press, 1989.

Naegele, Jolyon. "End Note: Postwar Decrees Haunt Czech Relations with Berlin, Vienna." *RFE/RL (Un)Civil Societies* 3, no. 8 (February 20, 2002) <http://www.rferl.org>.

Navrátil, Jaromír, comp. and ed. *The Prague Spring 1968: A National Security Archive Documents Reader.* Edited by Antonín Benčík, Václav Kural, Marie Michálková, and Jitka Vondrová. Translated by Mark Kramer et al. Budapest: Central European University Press, 1998.

"Nedotknutel'né piliere padli: Slovenský a český historik hodnotia význam 28. októbra 1918." *Pravda,* October 27, 1992. Bratislava.

Nejedlý, Jan. "O lásce k vlasti." *Hlasatel Český* 1, no. 1 (1806): 3–5.

Nejedlý, Zdeněk. *Komunisté dědici velkých tradic českého národa.* 3d ed. 1946. Prague: Československý spisovatel, 1950.

Němec, Petr. "Die Lage der deutschen Nationalität im Protektorat Böhmen und Mähren unter dem Aspekt der 'Eindeutschung' dieses Gebiets." *Bohemia* 32 (1991): 39–59.

———. "Das tschechische Volk und die nationalsozialistische Germanisierung des Raumes." *Bohemia* 32 (1991): 424–55.

Němeček, Jan. "Armadní general Lev Prchala a československý odboj v Polsku." *Historie a vojenství* 43 (1994): 107–32.

———. "Milan Hodža v USA a spory o řešení slovenské otázky 1941–1944." *Moderní dějiny* 7 (1999): 103–21.

Novák, Arne, and Jan V. Novák. *Přehledné dějiny literatury české od nejstarších dob až po naše dny.* 4th ed. 1936–39. Brno: Atlantis, 1995.

Novotný, Václav. *Od nejstarších dob do smrti knížete Oldřicha.* Vol. 1, part 1 of *České dějiny.* Prague: Jan Laichter, 1912.

———. *Od Břetislava I. do Přemysla I.* Vol. 1, part 2 of *České dějiny.* Prague: Jan Laichter, 1913.

————. *Čechy královské za Přemysla I. a Václava I., 1197–1253.* Vol. 1, part 3 of *České dějiny.* Prague: Jan Laichter, 1928.

————. *Rozmach české moci za Přemysla II. Otakara, 1253–1271.* Vol. 1, part 4 of *České dějiny.* Prague: Jan Laichter, 1937.

Obrazová, Pavla, and Jan Vlk. *Maior Gloria svatý kníže Václav.* Prague: Paseka, 1994.

Okáč, Antonín. *Český sněm a vláda před březněm 1848: kapitoly o jejich ústavních sporech.* Prague: Nákladem Zemského Národního výboru, 1947.

Orton, Lawrence D. *The Prague Slav Congress of 1848.* Boulder, Colo.: East European Quarterly, 1978.

Paces, Cynthia. "Religious Heroes for a Secular State: Commemorating Jan Hus and Saint Wenceslas in 1920s Czechoslovakia." In *Staging the Past: The Politics of Commemoration in Habsburg Central Europe, 1848 to the Present,* edited by Nancy M. Wingfield and Maria Bucur, pp. 209–35. West Lafayette, Ind.: Purdue University Press.

Palacký, František. "Idea státu rakouského." *Národ* II, no. 132 (May 16, 1865).

————. *Dějiny národu českého v Čechách a na Moravě.* 1848. Prague: B. Kočí, 1908.

Palacký, Franz. "Eine Stimme über Österreichs Anschluss an Deutschland." In *Gedenkblätter: Auswahl von Denkschriften, Aufsätzen und Briefen aus den letzten fünfzig Jahren,* pp. 150–52. Prague: Tempsky, 1874.

Pasák, Tomáš. *17. listopad 1939 a Univerzita Karlova.* Prague: Karolinum, 1997.

————. *Pod ochranou Říše.* Prague: Práh, 1998.

————. *Český fašismus, 1922–1945, a kolaborace, 1939–1945.* Prague: Práh, 1999.

Pasák, Tomáš, and Robert Kvaček. *JUDr. Emil Hácha.* Prague: Horizont, 1997.

Pastor, Peter. *Hungary Between Wilson and Lenin: The Hungarian Revolution of 1918–1919 and the Big Three.* Boulder, Colo.: East European Quarterly, 1976.

Patschovsky, Alexander. *Die Anfänge einer ständigen Inquisition in Böhmen. Ein Prager Inquisitoren-Handbuch aus der ersten Hälfte des 14. Jahrhunderts.* Berlin: W. de Gruyter, 1975.

————. *Quellen zur böhmischen Inquisition im 14. Jahrhundert.* Weimar: Böhlau, 1979.

————. "Ketzer und Ketzerverfolgung in Böhmen im Jahrhundert vor Hus." *Geschichte in Wissenschaft und Unterricht* 32 (1981): 261–72.

Paulová, Milada. *Dějiny Maffie: Odboj Čechů a Jihoslovanů za světové války, 1914–1918*. Prague: Československá grafická unie, 1937.

———. *Tajný výbor Maffie a spolupráce s Jihoslovany v letech 1916–1918*. Prague: Academia, 1968.

Pánek, Jaroslav. *Poslední Rožmberkové: velmoži české renesance*. Prague: Panorama, 1989.

———. *Zápas o Českou konfesi*. Prague: Melantrich, 1991.

Pech, Stanley Z. *The Czech Revolution of 1848*. Chapel Hill: University of North Carolina Press, 1969.

Pekař, Josef. *Postavy a problemy českých dějin*. Prague: Vyšehrad, 1990.

Pěkný, Tomáš. *Historie Židů v Čechách a na Moravě*. Prague: Sefer, 1993.

Pelcl, František Martin. *Paměti*. Translated and edited by Jan Pan. With a foreword by Jiří Černý. Prague: Státní nakladatelství krásné literatury, hudby a umění, 1956.

Pelikán, Jiří, ed. *The Czechoslovak Political Trials, 1950–1954: The Suppressed Report of the Dubček Government's Commission of Inquiry, 1968*. Stanford: Stanford University Press, 1971.

———. *The Secret Vysočany Congress: Proceedings and Documents of the Extraordinary Fourteenth Congress of the Communist Party of Czechoslovakia, 22 August 1968*. Translated by George Theiner and Deryck Viney. New York: St. Martin's Press, 1971.

———. *Socialist Opposition in Eastern Europe: The Czechoslovak Example*. Translated by Marian Sling, V. Tosek, and R. Tosek. New York: St. Martin's Press, 1976.

Perman, Dagmar. *The Shaping of the Czechoslovak State: Diplomatic History of the Boundaries of Czechoslovakia, 1914–1920*. Leiden: E. J. Brill, 1962.

Pernes, Jiří. *Spiklenci proti Jeho Veličenstvu: historie tzv. spiknutí Omladiny v Čechách*. Prague: Mladá fronta, 1988.

———. *Pod moravskou orlici aneb dějiny moravanství*. Brno: Barrister & Principal, 1996.

Peroutka, Ferdinand. *Rok 1918*. Vol. 1 of *Budování státu: Československá politika v letech popřevratových*. 2d ed. Prague: František Borový, 1933.

Pešek, Jiří. *Jiří Melantrich z Aventýna: příběh pražského arcitiskaře*. Prague: Melantrich, 1991.

Petráň, Josef. *Staroměstská exekuce*. 3d revised and expanded ed. Prague: Brána, 1996.

Petráň, Josef, and Lydia Petráňová. "The White Mountain as a Symbol in Modern Czech History." In *Bohemia in History*, edited by Mikuláš Teich, pp. 143–63. Cambridge: Cambridge University Press, 1998.

Piekalkiewicz, Jaroslaw A. *Public Opinion Polling in Czechoslovakia.* New York: Praeger, 1972.

Pierson, Jeffrey D. "Changing Czech Energy Policy." *The OECD Observer,* no. 191 (December–January 1994–95): 35.

Pithart, Petr. "Paradoxy rozchodu: Filozofické a mravné hlediska a evropské paralely." In *Rozloučení s Československem: Příčiny a důsledky česko-slovenského rozchodu,* edited by Rüdiger Kipke and Karel Vodička. Prague: Československý spisovatel, 1993.

Plaggenborg, Stefan. "Maria Theresia und die böhmischen Juden." *Bohemia* 39, no. 1 (1998): 1–16.

Pleiner, Radomír, and Alena Rybová, eds. *Pravěké dějiny Čech.* Prague: Academia, 1978.

Pokračovatelé Kosmovi. 1st ed. Translated by Karel Hrdina et al. Prague: Svoboda, 1974.

Polišenský, J. V. *The Thirty Years War.* Translated by Robert Evans. Berkeley: University of California Press, 1971.

Poulík, Josef, and Bohuslav Chropovský. *Velká Morava a počátky československé státnosti.* Prague and Bratislava: Academia and Obzor, 1985.

Program československé vlády Národní fronty Čechů a Slováků přijatý na první schůzi vlády dne 5. dubna 1945 v Košicích. Prague: Ministerstvo informací, 1945.

Prokš, Peter, ed. *Politické programy Českoslovanské a Československé sociálně demokratické strany dělnické, 1878–1948.* Prague: Historický ústav AV ČR, 1999.

Purš, Jaroslav. "Tábory v českých zemích v letech 1868–1871 (Příspěvek k problematice národního hnutí)." *Československý časopis historický* 6 (1958): 234–66, 416–70, 661–90.

Purš, Jaroslav, and Miroslav Kropilák, gen. eds. *Přehled dějin Československa do r. 1526.* Vol. 1, part 1 of *Přehled dějin Československa.* Prague: Academia, 1980.

———, gen. eds. *Přehled dějin Československa, 1526–1848.* Vol. 1, part 2 of *Přehled dějin Československa.* Prague: Academia, 1982.

Pustejovsky, Otfrid. *Schlesiens Übergang an die böhmische Krone: Machtpolitik Böhmens im Zeichen von Herrschaft und Frieden.* Cologne: Böhlau Verlag, 1975.

Pynsent, Robert B. *Questions of Identity: Czech and Slovak Ideas of Nationality and Personality.* Budapest: Central European University Press, 1994.

Rada, Ivan, et al. *Dějiny zemí koruny české, I: od příchodu slovanů do roku 1740.* Prague: Paseka, 1992.

Rak, Jiří. *Bývali Čechové: české historické mýty a stereotypy.* Jinončany: H&H, 1994.

———. "Tylova píseň v dobovém politickém kontextu." In *Locus amoenus—Místo líbezné: Symposium o české hymně, 27. X. 1993,* edited by Jiří K. Kroupa, compiled by Jiří Šubrt, pp. 37–40. Prague: KLP-Koniasch Latin Press, 1994.

Rak, Jiří, and Jan P. Kučera. *Bohuslav Balbín a jeho místo v české kultuře.* Prague: Vyšehrad, 1983.

Rambousek, Otakar, and Ladislav Gruber, comps. and eds. *Zpráva dokumentační komise K 231.* Louvain: Členové dokumentační komise K 231 v exilu, 1973.

Rašín, Alois. *Paměti dr. Aloise Rašína.* 2d ed. Compiled by Ladislav Rašín. Memorabilia. Brno: Bonus A, 1994.

Rataj, Jan. "O rasový národ: k proměnám nacionalismu v druhé republice." *Historie a vojenství* 42 (1993): 80–94.

———. *O autoritativní národní stát: ideologické proměny české politiky v druhé republice, 1938–1939.* Prague: Karolinum, 1997.

Renner, Hans. *A History of Czechoslovakia Since 1945.* Translated by Evelien Hurst-Buist. London: Routledge, 1989.

Řepa, Milan. *Moravané nebo Češí? Výjoj českého národního vědomí na Moravě v 19. století.* Brno: Doplněk, 2001.

Reynolds, Michael. "Central and Eastern Europe Moving Closer to the EU." *International Financial Law Review* 13, no. 9 (September 1994): 31–33.

Riegger, Johann Anton von. *Skizze einer statistischen Landeskunde Böhmens.* Leipzig: Widtmann, 1795.

Rose, Richard, and Christian Hearpfer. "Fears and Hopes—New Democracies Barometer Surveys." *Transitions Newsletter* (1996).

Rothschild, Joseph, and Nancy M. Wingfield. *Return to Diversity: A Political History of East Central Europe Since World War II.* 3d ed. New York: Oxford University Press, 2000.

Roubík, František, ed. *Petice venkovského lidu z Čech k Národnímu výboru z roku 1848.* Prague: Československá akademie věd, 1954.

"Rukopisy Královédvorský a Zelenohorský. Dnešní stav poznání." *Sborník Národního muzea* Řada C, no. 13–14 (1969).

Ryback, Timothy W. *Rock Around the Bloc: A History of Rock Music in Eastern Europe and the Soviet Union.* New York: Oxford University Press, 1990.

———. "Dateline Sudetenland: Hostages to History." *Foreign Policy* 105 (Winter 1996–97): 162–78.

Rychlík, Jan. "České obyvatelstvo na Slovensku v letech 1938–1945 (Postavení zaměstnanců v soukromém sektoru)." *Slovanské historické studie* 17 (1990): 174–85.

Sabina, Karel. *Vzpomínky*. Prague: František Borový, 1937.

Šafaříková, Vlasta, ed. *Transformace české společnosti, 1989–1995*. Brno: Doplněk, 1996.

Sak, Robert. *Rieger: Příběh Čecha devatenáctého věku*. Semily: Město Semily, 1993.

Saxonberg, Steven. "A New Phase in Czech Politics." *Journal of Democracy* 10, no. 1 (1999): 96–111.

———. "Women in East European Parliaments." *Journal of Democracy* 11, no. 2 (April 2000): 145–58.

Sayer, Derek. *The Coasts of Bohemia: A Czech History*. Princeton, N. J.: Princeton University Press, 1998.

Schiller, Charles A. "Closing a Chapter of History: Germany's Right to Compensation for the Sudetenland." *Case Western Reserve Journal of International Law* 26, no. 2–3 (Spring–Summer 1995): 401–35.

Schmidt-Hartmann, Eva. "Tschechen und Sudetendeutsche: Ein Muhsamer Abschied von der Vergangenheit." *Bohemia* 34, no. 2 (1993): 421–33.

Schorske, Carl E. *Fin-de-Siècle Vienna: Politics and Culture*. New York: Knopf, 1980.

Schramm, Gottfried. "Tschechen und Deutsche in der ersten Republik." *Bohemia* 29, no. 2 (1988): 383–90.

Schuselka, Franz. *Deutsche Worte eines Österreichers*. Hamburg: Hoffman & Campe, 1843.

———. *Das Revolutionsjahr, März 1848–März 1849*. Vienna: Jasper, Hügel & Manz, 1850.

Schwan, Alexander. "German Liberalism and the National Question in the Nineteenth Century." In *Nation-Building in Central Europe*, edited by Hagen Schulze. Leamington Spa: Berg, 1987.

Secrétairerie d'État de sa Sainteté. *Le Saint Siège et les Victimes de la Guerre, Janvier 1944–Juillet 1945*. Actes et Documents Du Saint Siège Relatifs á la Seconde Guerre Mondiale, 10. Città del Vaticano: Libreria Editrice Vaticana, 1980.

Seton-Watson, Robert W. *A History of the Czechs and Slovaks*. 1943. Hamden, Conn.: Archon Books, 1965.

———. *The Southern Slav Question and the Habsburg Monarchy*. 1911. New York: H. Fertig, 1969.

Shanafelt, Gary W. *The Secret Enemy: Austria-Hungary and the German Alliance, 1914–1918*. Boulder, Colo.: East European Monographs, 1985.

Shawcross, William. *Dubček.* Revised and updated ed. 1970. New York: Simon & Schuster, 1990.

Shepherd, Robin H. E. *Czechoslovakia: The Velvet Revolution and Beyond.* London and New York: Macmillan and St. Martin's Press, 2000.

Šik, Ota. *Plán a trh za socialismu.* 3d ed. Prague: Academia, 1967.

————. *The Third Way: Marxist-Leninist Theory and Modern Industrial Society.* Translated by Marian Sling. London and New York: Wildwood House and International Arts and Sciences Press, 1976.

————. *Jarní probuzení: iluze a skutečnost.* 2d ed. Prague: Mladá fronta, 1990.

Šimák, Josef Vítězslav. *Středověká kolonisace v zemích českých.* Vol. 1, part 5 of *České dějiny.* Prague: Jan Laichter, 1938.

Šimečka, Milan. *The Restoration of Order: The Normalization of Czechoslovakia, 1969–1976.* Translated by A. G. Bain, with a preface by Zdeněk Mlynář. London: Verso, 1984.

Simes, Dimitri K. "The Soviet Invasion of Czechoslovakia and the Limits of Kremlinology." *Studies in Comparative Communism* 8 (1975): 174–80.

Sked, Alan. *The Decline and Fall of the Habsburg Empire, 1815–1918.* New York and London: Longman, 1989.

Skilling, H. Gordon. *Czechoslovakia's Interrupted Revolution.* Princeton, N.J.: Princeton University Press, 1976.

————. *Charter 77 and Human Rights in Czechoslovakia.* London: Allen & Unwin, 1981.

————. "Independent Currents in Czechoslovakia." *Problems of Communism* 34 (January–February 1985): 32–49.

————. "Masaryk: Permanent Dissenter: The Hilsner Case and Anti-Semitism." *Cross Currents* 8 (1989): 243–60.

————. *Samizdat and an Independent Society in Central and Eastern Europe.* Columbus: Ohio State University Press, 1989.

Sklenář, Karel. *Památky pravěku na území ČSSR: Od lovců mamutů ke státu Přemyslovců.* Prague: Orbis, 1974.

————. *Obraz vlasti: Příběh Národního muzeum.* Prague: Paseka, 2001.

Škvorecký, Josef. "Hipness at Dusk." *Cross Currents* 6 (1987): 53–62.

Sláma, Jiří. "Boiohaemum-Čechy." In *Bohemia in History,* edited by Mikuláš Teich, pp. 23–38. Cambridge: Cambridge University Press, 1998.

Slejška, Dragoslav, and Jan Herzmann. *Sondy do veřejného mínění (Jaro 1968, Podzim 1989).* Prague: Svoboda, 1990.

Slezák, Lubomír. "Sudetští Němci a hospodářství první republiky." *Moderní dějiny* 2 (1994): 123–41.

Šmahel, František. *Husův proces v Kostnici*. Prague: Melantrich, 1988.

————. *Doba vymknutá z kloubu*. Vol. 1 of *Husitská revoluce*. Prague: Historický ústav Akademie věd České Republiky, 1993.

————. *Epilog bouřlivého věku*. Vol. 4 of *Husitská Revoluce*. Prague: Historický ústav Akademie věd České Republiky, 1993.

————. *Kořeny české reformace*. Vol. 2 of *Husitská revoluce*. Prague: Historický ústav Akademie věd České Republiky, 1993.

————. *Kronika válečných let*. Vol. 3 of *Husitská revoluce*. Prague: Historický ústav Akademie věd České Republiky, 1993.

————. "Středověké 'obrození' českého národa." In *VII. sjezd českých historiků, Praha 24.-26 září 1993*. Prague: Historický ústav, 1994.

————. "The Hussite Movement: An Anomaly of European History?" In *Bohemia in History*, edited by Mikuláš Teich, pp. 79–97. Cambridge: Cambridge University Press, 1998.

Smelser, Ronald M. *The Sudeten Problem, 1933–1938: Volkstumspolitik and the Formulation of Nazi Foreign Policy*. Folkestone: Dawson, 1975.

————. "At the Limits of a Mass Movement: The Case of the Sudeten German Party, 1933–1938." *Bohemia* 17 (1976): 240–66.

————. "Nazis Without Hitler: The DNSAP and the First Czechoslovak Republic." *East Central Europe/L'Europe du Centre-Est* 4, no. 1 (1977): 1–19.

————. "The Expulsion of the Sudeten Germans, 1945–1952." *Nationalities Papers* 24, no. 1 (1996): 79–92.

Sokol, Martin. "Ako došlo k vyhlašeniu Slovenského Štátu? Moje poznámky k marcovým udalostiam 1939." *Historický časopis* 39 (1991): 323–29.

Sommer, Karel. "Zatčení a internace Andreje Hlinky." *Slezský sborník* 96, no. 2 (1988): 106–18.

"Soubor opatření ke zdokonalení soustavy plánovitého řizení národního hospodářství po roce 1980." In *Příloha hospodářských novin*, 1980.

Spector, Scott. "Německá, židovská a česká identita v Praze. Felix Weltsch a Egon Erwin Kisch." *Slovanský přehled* 84, no. 1 (1998): 39–46.

————. *Prague Territories: National Conflict and Cultural Innovation in Kafka's Fin de Siècle*. Berkeley: University of California Press, 2000.

"Speech by the Prime Minister of the Czech Republic, Milos Zeman, Brussels, 16 March 1999." Online document, 1999 <http://www.nato.int/docu/speech.htm>.

Sperber, Jonathan. *The European Revolution, 1848–1851*. Cambridge: Cambridge University Press.

Spěváček, Jiří. *Karel IV. Život a dílo, 1316–1378*. Prague: Svoboda, 1979.

————. *Král diplomat (Jan Lucemburský, 1296–1346)*. Prague: Panorama, 1982.

————. *Jan Lucemburský a jeho doba, 1296–1346: K prvnímu vstupu českých zemí do svazku se západní evropou*. Prague: Svoboda, 1994.

Spinka, Matthew. *John Hus at the Council of Constance*. New York: Columbia University Press, 1965.

————. *John Hus' Concept of the Church*. Princeton, N.J.: Princeton University Press, 1966.

Šrobár, Vavro Ján. *Osvobodené Slovensko: pamäti z rokov 1918–1920*. Prague: Čin, 1928.

Staněk, Tomáš. *Odsun Němců z Československa 1945–1947*. Prague: Naše vojsko, 1991.

Statistická ročenka Československé socialistické republiky 1973. Prague: Státní nakladatelství technické literatury, 1973.

Statistická ročenka Československé socialistické republiky, 1980. Prague: Státní nakladatelství technické literatury, 1980.

Statistická ročenka Československé socialistické republiky 1982. Prague: Státní nakladatelství technické literatury, 1982.

Štěpánek, Zdeněk. "Péče o utečence z okupovaného pohraničí Moravy a Slezska v letech 1938–1939." *Časopis Matice moravské* 112 (1993): 43–54.

Stern, J. P. "Language Consciousness and Nationalism in the Age of Bernard Bolzano." *Journal of European Studies* 19 (1989): 169–89.

Stoianovich, Traian. *Balkan Worlds: The First and Last Europe*. Armonk, N.Y., and London: M. E. Sharpe, 1994.

Stokes, Gale. *The Walls Came Tumbling Down: The Collapse of Communism in Eastern Europe*. New York: Oxford University Press, 1993.

————, ed. *From Stalinism to Pluralism: A Documentary History of Eastern Europe Since 1945*. New York: Oxford University Press, 1996.

Stone, Norman, and Eduard Strouhal. *Czechoslovakia: Crossroads and Crises, 1918–1988*. New York: St. Martin's Press, 1989.

Stroehlein, Andrew. *The Failure of a New History: Czechs and the Czech-German Declaration*. Telford, Shropshire: Central Europe Review, 2000 <http://www.ce-review.org>.

Stryjan, Yohanan, and Eva Maskova. "The Reshaping of the Czechoslovak Economy." *Economic and Industrial Democracy* 13, no. 4 (November 1992): 561–82.

Suda, Zdeněk L. *Zealots and Rebels: A History of the Communist Party of Czechoslovakia*. Stanford: Hoover Institution Press, 1980.

Suk, Jiří, comp. and ed. *Občanské fórum, listopad-prosinec, 1989. 1. díl-události*. Prague and Brno: Ústav pro soudobé dějiny AV ČR and Doplněk, 1997.

———, comp. and ed. *Občanské fórum, listopad-prosinec, 1989. 2. díl-dokumenty*. Prague and Brno: Ústav pro soudobé dějiny AV ČR and Doplněk, 1998.

Suppan, Arnold. "Masaryk and the Trials for High Treason Against the South Slavs in 1909." In *Thinker and Politician*. Vol. 1 of *T. G. Masaryk (1850–1937)*, edited by Stanley B. Winters, pp. 210–24. New York: St. Martin's Press, 1990.

Šulc, Zdislav. "Systemové základy ekonomické transformace." In *Transformace české společnosti, 1989–1995*, edited by Vlasta Šafaříková, pp. 114–94. Brno: Doplněk, 1996.

Šusta, Josef. *Poslední Přemyslovci a jejich dědictví, 1300–1308*. Vol. 1 of *Dvě knihy českých dějin: kus středověké historie našeho kraje*. 2d ed. Prague: České akademie věd a umění, 1926.

———. *Počátky lucemburské, 1308–1320*. Vol. 2 of *Dvě knihy českých dějin: kus středověké historie našeho kraje*. 2d ed. Prague: České akademie věd a umění, 1935.

———. *Soumrak Přemyslovců a jejich dědictví*. Vol. 2, part 1 of *České dějiny*. Prague: Jan Laichter, 1935.

———. *Král cizinec*. Vol. 2, part 2 of *České dějiny*. Prague: Jan Laichter, 1939.

———. *Karel IV. Otec a syn, 1333–1346*. Vol. 2, part 3 of *České dějiny*. Prague: Jan Laichter, 1946.

———. *Karel IV. Za císařskou korunou, 1347–1378*. Vol. 2, part 4 of *České dějiny*. Prague: Jan Laichter, 1948.

Taborsky, Edward. "Czechoslovakia's 'University of November 17th'." *East Europe* 21, no. 4 (1972): 7–11.

———. "Tragedy, Triumph, and Tragedy: Czechoslovakia, 1938–1948." In *Czechoslovakia: The Heritage of Ages Past*, edited by Hans Brisch and Ivan Volgyes, pp. 113–34. New York: Columbia University Press, 1979.

Taylor, A. J. P. *The Habsburg Monarchy, 1809–1918: A History of the Austrian Empire and Austria-Hungary*. 1948. Harmondsworth: Penguin Books, 1985.

Tejchman, Miroslav. "Slovensko-Rumunsko-Chorvatská spolupráce v letech druhé světové války a Mad'arsko." *Slovanský přehled* 78 (1992): 158–70.

"That Lingering Question of Sudetenland." *The Economist* 339, no. 7968 (June 1, 1996): 47.

Thám, Karel Hynek. *Obrana jazyka českého proti zlobivým jeho utrháčům, též mnoha vlastencům v cvíčení se v něm liknavým a nedbalým.* Prague: Schönfeld, 1783.

Thun-Hohenstein, Joseph Matthias Graf von. *Der Slawismus in Böhmen.* Prague: J. G. Calve, 1845.

Thun-Hohenstein, Leo Graf von. *Die Stellung der Slowaken in Ungarn.* Prague, 1843.

Tierney, Brian. *Foundations of Conciliar Theory.* Cambridge: Cambridge University Press, 1955.

Tigrid, Pavel. *Kapesní průvodce inteligentí ženy po vlastním osudu.* 2d ed. Prague: Odeon, 1990.

Tobolka, Zdeněk. *Slovanský sjezd v Praze roku 1848.* Prague: Šimáček, 1901.

———. *Politické dějiny československého národa od r. 1848 až do dnešní doby.* Vol. 1. Prague: Československý kompas, n.d.

Toma, Peter A. "The Slovak Soviet Republic of 1919." *American Slavic and East European Review* 17, no. 2 (1958): 203–15.

Toma, Peter A., and Dušan Kováč. *Slovakia: From Samo to Dzurinda.* Stanford: Hoover Institution Press, 2001.

Tökés, Rudolf L. *Bela Kun and the Hungarian Soviet Republic: The Origins and Role of the Communist Party of Hungary in the Revolutions of 1918–1919.* New York: Published for the Hoover Institution on War, Revolution and Peace by F. A. Praeger, 1967.

Transparency International. "New Index Highlights Worldwide Corruption Crisis, Says Transparency International." Press release, 2001 <http://www.transparency.org/cpi/2001/cpi2001.html>.

Trapl, Miloš. "Začlenění římskokatolické církve do české společnosti po roce 1918." In *Československo 1918–1938: Osudy demokracie ve střední Evropě,* edited by Jaroslav Valenta, Emil Voráček, and Josef Harna, pp. 141–47. Prague: Historický ústav AV ČR, 1999.

Třeštík, Dušan. *Počátky Přemyslovců: vstup Čechů do dějin (530–935).* Prague: Lidové noviny, 1997.

———. *Češi: Jejich národ, stát, dějiny a pravdy v transformaci. Texty z let 1991–1998.* Brno: Doplněk, 1999.

Turek, Rudolf. *Čechy na úsvitě dějin.* Prague: Orbis, 1963.

———. *Čechy v raném středověku.* Prague: Vyšehrad, 1982.

———. *Slavníkovci a jejich panství.* Hradec Králové: Kruh, 1982.

———. *Počátky české vzdělanosti: od příchodu Slovanů do doby románské.* Prague: Vyšehrad, 1988.

Tvarůžek, Břetislav. "Okupace Čech a Moravy a vojenská správa (15. březen až 15. duben 1939)." *Historie a vojenství* 41 (1992): 30–65.

———. "Wehrmacht proti českému lidu a za upevnění němectví v Protektorátě." *Historie a vojenství* 43 (1994): 87–131.

United States Department of State. *Foreign Relations of the United States, 1948. Volume IV. Eastern Europe and the Soviet Union.* Washington, D.C.: United States Government Printing Office, 1974.

Unterberger, Betty Miller. *The United States, Revolutionary Russia, and the Rise of Czechoslovakia.* Chapel Hill: University of North Carolina Press, 1989.

Urban, Otto. *Česká společnost, 1848–1918.* Prague: Svoboda, 1982.

———. *České a slovenské dějiny do roku 1918.* Prague: Svoboda, 1991.

———. *České a slovenské dějiny do roku 1918.* 2d ed. Prague: Aleš Skřivan ml., 2000.

Valenta, Jaroslav. "Legenda o 'rebelech, s nimíž se nevyjednává'." *Moderní dějiny* 2 (1994): 197–214.

———. "Nezdařený pokus o jednání mezi Čechy a Němci na přelomu let 1918–1919." *Moderní dějiny* 3 (1995): 229–40.

Valenta, Jiří. *Soviet Intervention in Czechoslovakia, 1968: Anatomy of a Decision.* Rev. ed. 1979. Baltimore: Johns Hopkins University Press, 1991.

Vaněk, Miroslav. "Porobení přírody." In *Proč jsme v listopadu vyšli do ulic,* compiled by Jiří Vančura, pp. 133–54. Brno: Doplněk, 1999.

Vaňous, Jan. "East European Economic Slowdown." *Problems of Communism* 31 (July–August 1982): 1–19.

Vaško, Václav. "Kardinál Beran a jeho zápas s totalitou: Portrét osobnosti." *Soudobé dějiny* 8, no. 2–3 (2001): 384–408.

Válka, Josef. "Rudolfine Culture." In *Bohemia in History,* edited by Mikuláš Teich, pp. 117–42. Cambridge: Cambridge University Press, 1998.

Váňa, Zdeněk. *The World of the Ancient Slavs.* Translated by Till Gottheiner. London: Orbis, 1983.

The Vita of Constantine and the Vita of Methodius. Translated by Marvin Kantor and Richard S. White, with an introduction by Antonín Dostál. Ann Arbor: University of Michigan Press, 1976.

Vladislav, Jan, ed. *Václav Havel: Living in Truth.* London: Faber & Faber, 1986.

Vlnas, Vít. *Jan Nepomucký: česká legenda.* Prague: Mladá fronta, 1993.

Vošahlíková, Pavla. "Czech Culture in the Struggle Against Fascism in World War II." *East Central Europe/L'Europe Du Centre-Est* 17 (1990): 131–53.

———. "Vliv Národních listů na utváření českého veřejného mínění ve 2.

polovině 19. století." In *Bratří Grégrové â česká společnost v druhé polovině 19. století*, edited by Pavla Vošahlíková and Milan Řepa, pp. 39–48. Prague: Dr. Eduard Grégr a syn, 1997.

Vyšný, Paul. *Neo-Slavism and the Czechs, 1898–1914*. Cambridge: Cambridge University Press, 1977.

Wandycz, Piotr S. *Czechoslovak-Polish Confederation and the Great Powers, 1940–43*. Indiana University Publications, Slavic and East European Series, 3. Bloomington: Indiana University Press, 1956.

———. *France and Her Eastern Allies, 1919–1925*. Minneapolis: University of Minnesota Press, 1962.

———. "The Little Entente: Sixty Years Later." *Slavonic and East European Review* 59, no. 4 (1981): 548–64.

———. *The Twilight of French Eastern Alliances, 1926–1936: French-Czechoslovak-Polish Relations from Locarno to the Remilitarization of the Rhineland*. Princeton, N.J.: Princeton University Press, 1988.

———, ed. "List Jana Masaryka do Stalina." *Zeszyty Historyczne* 100 (1992): 83–87.

Wangermann, Ernst. *From Joseph II to the Jacobin Trials: Government Policy and Public Opinion in the Habsburg Dominions in the Period of the French Revolution*. Oxford and London: Oxford University Press, 1969.

Wargelin, Clifford F. "The Economic Collapse of Austro-Hungarian Dualism, 1914–1918." *East European Quarterly* 34, no. 3 (2000): 261–88.

Wheaton, Bernard, and Zdeněk Kavan. *The Velvet Revolution: Czechoslovakia, 1988–1991*. Boulder, Colo.: Westview Press, 1992.

Whiteside, Andrew G. *The Socialism of Fools: Georg Ritter von Schönerer and Austrian Pan-Germanism*. Berkeley: University of California Press, 1975.

Wiarda, Howard J. *The Politics of European Enlargement: NATO, the EU, and the New U.S.–European Relationship*. East European Studies Occasional Papers, 67. Washington, D.C.: Woodrow Wilson International Center for Scholars, 2002.

Williams, Kieran. *The Prague Spring and Its Aftermath: Czechoslovak Politics, 1968–1970*. Cambridge: Cambridge University Press, 1997.

Wilson, Paul. "Religious Movement in Czechoslovakia: Faith or Fashion?" *Cross Currents: A Yearbook of Central European Culture* 7 (1988): 109–19.

Windsor, Philip, and Adam Roberts. *Czechoslovakia 1968: Reform, Repression, and Resistance*. New York: Columbia University Press, 1969.

Wingfield, Nancy Meriwether. "Czech-Sudeten German Relations in Light of the 'Velvet Revolution': Post-Communist Interpretations." *Nationalities Papers* 24, no. 1 (1996): 93–106.

———. "Conflicting Constructions of Memory: Attacks on Statues of Joseph II in the Bohemian Lands After the Great War." *Austrian History Yearbook* 28 (1998): 147–71.

———. "When Film Became National: 'Talkies' and the Anti-German Demonstrations of 1930 in Prague." *Austrian History Yearbook* 29, no. 1 (1998): 113–38.

Winters, Stanley B. "Jan Otto, T. G. Masaryk, and the Czech National Encyclopedia." *Jahrbücher für Geschichte Osteuropas* 31, no. 4 (1983): 516–42.

———. "T. G. Masaryk and Karel Kramář: Long Years of Friendship and Rivalry." In *Thinker and Politician*. Vol. 1 of *T. G. Masaryk (1850–1937)*, edited by Stanley B. Winters, pp. 153–90. New York: St. Martin's Press, 1990.

———. "Passionate Patriots: Czechoslovak National Democracy in the 1920s." *East Central Europe/L'Europe Du Centre-Est* 18, no. 1 (1991): 55–68.

———. "The Period of Transition from the ČAVU to the ČSAV (1945–1952)." *Historická Olomouc* 9 (1998): 293–308.

Wolchik, Sharon L. "The Scientific-Technological Revolution and the Role of Specialist Elites in Policy-Making in Czechoslovakia." In *Domestic Policy in Eastern Europe in the 1980s: Trends and Prospects*, pp. 111–32, edited by Sharon L. Wolchik and Michael J. Sodaro. New York: St. Martin's Press, 1983.

———. "Economic Performance and Political Change in Czechoslovakia." In *Prospects for Change in Socialist Systems: Challenges and Responses*, edited by Charles J. Bukowski and Mark A. Cichock, pp. 35–60. New York: Praeger, 1987.

———. *Czechoslovakia in Transition: Politics, Economics and Society*. London: Pinter, 1991.

Wood, Barry D. "Czech Republic: Country at the Heart of Europe Looks to Join EU." *Europe*, no. 372 (December–January 1997–98): 28–29.

Wright, William E. *Serf, Seigneur, and Sovereign: Agrarian Reform in Eighteenth-Century Bohemia*. Minneapolis: University of Minnesota Press, 1966.

Zacek, Joseph Frederick. *Palacký: The Historian as Scholar and Nationalist*. The Hague: Mouton, 1970.

Žák, Václav. "The Velvet Divorce—Institutional Foundations." In *The End of Czechoslovakia*, edited by Jiří Musil, pp. 245–68. Budapest: Central European University Press, 1995.

"Zákon ze dne 29. února 1920, kterým se uvozuje Ústavní listina Československé republiky." Electronic Library of the Chamber of Deputies, Czech Republic <http://www.psp.cz/docs/texts/constitution.1920.html>.

Zapletál, Vladislav. "K událostem roku 1919." *Acta Universitatis Palackianae Olomucensis: Historica*, no. 21 (1981): 25–43.

Zatkuliak, Jozef, ed. *Federalizácia československého štátu 1968–1970: vznik česko-slovenskej federácie roku 1968*. Prague: Ústav pro soudobé dějiny AV ČR, 1996.

z Březové, Vavřinec. *Husitská kronika, Píseň o vítězství u Domažlic*. Edited by Marie Bláhová. Translated by František Heřmanský and Jan Blahoslav Čapek. Prague: Svoboda, 1979.

Ze starých letopisů českých. Translated and edited by Jaroslav Porák and Jaroslav Kašpar. Prague: Svoboda, 1980.

Zeman, Zbyněk. *The Masaryks: The Making of Czechoslovakia*. London: Weidenfeld & Nicolson, 1976.

———. *The Life of Edvard Beneš, 1884–1948: Czechoslovakia in War and Peace*. In collaboration with Antonín Klimek. Oxford: Clarendon Press, 1997.

Žemlička, Josef. *Čechy v době knížecí (1034–1198)*. Prague: Lidové noviny, 1997.

Zinner, Paul E. "Czechoslovakia: The Diplomacy of Edvard Benes." In *The Diplomats, 1919–1939*, edited by Gordon A. Craig and Felix Gilbert, pp. 100–122. Princeton, N.J.: Princeton University Press, 1953.

z Mladoňovic, Peter. *Zpráva o mistru Janu Husovi v Kostnici*. Translated by František Heřmanský. Prague: Universita Karlova, 1965.

Zorach, Jonathan. "The Enigma of the Gajda Affair in Czechoslovak Politics in 1926." *Slavic Review* 35, no. 4 (1976): 683–98.

Zudel, Juraj. "Zmeny československo-maďarských hranic v dôsledku viedenskej arbitráže." *Slovenská archivistika* 26 (1991): 34–43.

Zudová-Lešková, Zlatica. "Obrana národa na Slovensku (Češi v čs. demokratickom odboji na Slovensku v rokoch 1939–1941." *Historie a vojenství* 42 (1993): 77–131.

z Weitmile, Beneš Krabic. "Kronika pražského kostela." In *Kroniky doby Karla IV*, translated and edited by Marie Bláhová, 1987.

NEWSPAPERS AND NEWS DIGESTS

Associated Press Wire Reports: International News. Daily.
British Broadcasting Corporation, BBC Monitoring. Daily.

————. *BBC Summary of World Broadcasts*. Daily.

Český deník. Prague, daily.

ČTK Czechoslovak (Czech) News Agency, ČTK *National News Wire*. Daily.

Foreign Broadcast Information Service. *Daily Reports, Eastern Europe*. Daily.

The Guardian. London, daily.

The Independent. London, daily.

The Jerusalem Post. Jerusalem, Israel, daily.

Lidové noviny. Prague, daily.

Manchester Guardian Weekly. Weekly.

Mladá fronta dnes. Prague, daily.

The New York Times. New York, daily.

The Prague Post. Prague, weekly.

Radio Free Europe/Radio Liberty Newsline: Central and Eastern Europe. Daily.

Respekt. Prague, weekly.

The Wall Street Journal Europe. Daily.

The Warsaw Voice. Warsaw, weekly.

Index

Národní noviny (National News), 119, 125
Naše Slovensko (Our Slovakia, 1907–1910)
    (revue), 163
Nástup (Step Forward) (journal), 192
Nástupists, 192
nation-state
    Czech national renascence for, 98, 110,
        111–12
    homogeneity of, xvii
    idea of, xvii
National Assembly, 267. *See also* Federal As-
    sembly
National Committee, 118, 182, 210, 212,
    357n21
National Community, 210, 212, 357n21
National Democratic Party, 181, 194, 204
National Endowment for the Humanities, xx
National Front (NF), xxv, 194, 220, 221,
    223, 225–27, 290
National Land Fund, 224–25
National League, 194
National Liberal Party, 136. *See also* Young
    Czechs
National Library of the Czech Republic, xxi
National Museum Library, xxi, 104, 159
National Oath (Jirásek), 170
National Party of Labor, 207
National Socialists, 157, 182, 223
National Theater, 135, 143, 159
National Union, 194
nationalism
    impact of, xvii, 103, 110, 146, 156–57
    neoabsolutism *v.*, 126
nationalization of industry, 223–24, 227,
    240–41
NATO. *See* North Atlantic Treaty Organiza-
    tion
navigation, ocean
    Turkish threat to, 55, 57
Nazi Germany
    Czech peril from, 195
Nazi-Soviet Non-Aggression Pact of August
    1939, 211
Nejedlý, Zdeněk, 238
Němci, 8, 334n10
neo-Nazi ideology, 322
Neo-Slavism, 163
Neo-Utraquists, 59–61, 62–63, 91
neoabsolutism
    Czech movement under, 125–26

nationalism *v.*, 126
    reform of, 128
    state bureaucracy for, 126
    support of, 126
Neolithic Age (New Stone Age), 7
Nepomucene, John, 76
Netherlands
    Bohemian Estates appeal to, 66
    gain of Belgian provinces by, 97
    navigators from, 55
    recognition of, 71
Neue freie Presse (newspaper), 149
Neurath, Konstantin von, 208, 210–12
New Course, 243–44
NF. *See* National Front
Nicholas I of Russia, 103
    Austrian military assistance by, 125
    Austrian ultimatum to, 127–28
    Hungarian surrender to, 125
    reign of, 103, 125
Niebelungenlied, 113
nobility
    in Bohemia, 17–18, 30–31, 42, 58–59,
        116, 129
    church *v.*, 35, 37, 42
    clergy unity with, 22
    as cultural patrons, 109
    Czech national renascence influence on,
        98, 110, 111–12
    income of, 58
    influence/power of, 17–18, 58–59, 72–73
    opposition to Leopold II by, 97
    religious exile for, 71
    Renaissance architecture for, 64
    structural reform of, 87
    support of king by, 31–32
    taxation of, 121
    territorial patriotism for, 99–100
    towns *v.*, 58
    uprising of, 22
normalization, 262–69, 270, 275, 308
North Atlantic Treaty Organization, 324,
    326
Nostitz, Albert, 119
Nostitz-Rieneck, Franz Anton, 98
nostrification law, 183
Notabene Lingua Workstation, xxi
Novomeský, Ladislav, 217, 239–40
Novotný, Antonín, 242, 246, 251, 258, 266

October Diploma, 128
octroi (imperial decree), 123

About the Author

Hugh LeCaine Agnew is an associate professor of history and international affairs and associate dean of Academic Programs at the Elliott School of International Affairs, George Washington University. He teaches graduate and undergraduate courses on Eastern Europe and a European history survey. He focuses on nationalism in the region, especially Czech nationalism. Among his publications are *Origins of the Czech National Renascence* (1993), and numerous articles and chapters on aspects of Czech nationalism and national identity. Recognized as an expert in Eastern European history, he has appeared on C-SPAN, Voice of America's Czech service, and Radio Prague.